Beyond Sex and Gender

First published 2002

SAGE Publications Ltd
6 Bonhill Street
London EC2A 4PU

SAGE Publications Inc.
2455 Teller Road
Thousand Oaks, California 91320

SAGE Publications India Pvt Ltd
32, M-Block Market
Greater Kailash - I
New Delhi 110 048

British Library Cataloguing in Publication data

A catalogue record for this book is available from the British Library

ISBN 0 7619 5599 2
ISBN 0 7619 5600 X (pbk)

Library of Congress Control Number 2001 131873

Printed in Great Britain by The Cromwell Press Ltd, Trowbridge, Wiltshire

Contents

Preface

Even though my co-author, John Hood-Williams, was tragically killed when we were only a very short distance into the work of writing it, the book that follows remains a work on which both of our names appear. In fact, John only ever saw the final version of the first substantive chapter (Chapter 2: 'The Old Configuration'), which we had worked up collaboratively. However, he had written a first draft of portions of what are now Chapters 3, 7 and 9, and there was already work in print, both single- and joint-authored, which was to have constituted some of the foundation for other chapters, as indeed it has. Versions of some of the material on genetics appeared in a series of articles by John over the last few years, notably in 'Is the Genetic Sexing of Humans Tautological?' (1995), 'Sexing the Athletes' (1995) and 'Goodbye to Sex and Gender' (1996). An early formulation of a portion of Chapter 10, originally written by John and subsequently significantly reworked, has also appeared under both our names in *New Formations* as 'Gendered Melancholy or General Melancholy?' Effectively, however, those portions of text written by John before he died, (including that portion of Chapter 10) have been comprehensively revised and, in many cases, all but rewritten, which was inevitable in view of the need to produce a work that was coherent.

The more forceful reason for thinking of this as a shared work, however, has to do with the unique intellectual and pedagogic partnership that we had formed over the preceding ten years. We had differing intellectual formations and our own individual take on things, but on this project we genuinely thought our thoughts together and had managed, I believe, to construct what is probably a fairly rare thing: a joint voice. Although we undoubtedly had quite different writing styles, in the articles we published together we didn't intend readers to be able to see the joins. All of our discussions were aimed at working out what *we* thought, as a unit. At the time of John's death, we still had intellectual work to do in two fairly substantial areas, and the completion of that investigation has undoubtedly affected the configuration of the whole. Writing out of a fractured dialogue, in the ensuing silence, inevitably made me wonder how the resulting book would differ from what would otherwise have been produced. Inevitably, it is neither the book that we would have written together, nor the book that I would have written had I embarked on the project by myself from the outset. However, we had decided essentially where we were going and I think I have been reasonably faithful to that trajectory.

Beyond Sex and Gender is the outgrowth of what was initially an undergraduate (then also postgraduate) course that John and I devised as far back as 1989 and team taught until 1999, originally called 'Explorations in the Study of Gender' and subsequently 'The Problem of Sexual Difference'. As the change of title might indicate, we had difficulty in devising a name for work that was intended to take us beyond the sex/gender distinction. The first title indicated ours and our students' exploratory forays into new terrain but, because it retained the term 'gender', inadvertently produced the problem of attracting those who thought of such courses primarily in terms of issues of inequality and who found our rather different agenda somewhat bewildering. The second more confident title was nevertheless a compromise because it tended to evoke a psychoanalytic problematic to which we were sympathetic – one might even say fairly committed – but whose universalism we were also throwing into question. In that sense, though, the very problem posed by the sexual difference framework (as we chose to understand the term) refers in an indexical way to that whole complex of difficulties which surround the issue of the allegedly foundational and transhistorical character of 'sex', and this makes it peculiarly appropriate as a characterization. In spite of these small local difficulties of nomenclature, however, it was a consistently enjoyable course to teach and I should like to thank all of its students, past and present, for the many stimulating and engaging discussions that we shared over so many years.

Annette Devine also provided invaluable support to both John and myself in the early stages of the project, and, since then, has been a source of innumerable and invaluable practical and emotional moments of sustenance. She also undertook small pieces of research when I was unable to find the time to do so. I should like to thank her, above all else, for her unstinting guidance and help, and for having that very rare quality, which is wisdom. I should also like to thank my sister, Michèle Harrison, for the many stimulating discussions we shared over the months of the book's composition, and, especially for her sage words about Foucault, to which I am indebted for some of the discussion in Chapter 11, and about many other things. My parents, Marion and Reginald Harrison were, as always, indefatigably encouraging. Mike Kelly provided the conditions in which work on the book was both valued and possible, transforming the culture of a department in which research had been a matter of 'sink or swim' into somewhere where intellectual work was treated in the way that it deserves. Chris Rojek was as understanding an editor as any author could hope for and helped me to make the transition to carrying on with the project alone after John was killed. Elizabeth Wells grappled gamely with the complexities of my author-formatted text, which nearly defeated both of us when the files became corrupted. Finally, but by no means least, Richard Oels provided invaluable support and, crucially, cooked me innumerable meals when I had no time to stop, and patiently transcribed my corrupted files almost byte by byte. Inevitably, one has to say that, in spite of use of the word 'we', and notwithstanding all of this wonderful support, responsibility for the text, with all of its possible deficits, rests finally with me. The book is dedicated to John's memory, since it was he who pushed me, finally and not so many years ago, to get into print.

1 The Texture of the World

'Sex' and 'gender' have by now acquired the comforting ring of familiarity – at least in the Anglo-Saxon world. So much so that questioning them seems like questioning the very texture of the world. It is not only that a wide range of politico-social discourses have come to depend upon the distinction, it is that what it describes has become veritably commonsensical. Going against the grain, as we will in this book, therefore runs the risk of appearing perverse and counter-intuitive. For what we shall be arguing is that what we have called elsewhere 'the sex/gender problematic' (Cealey Harrison and Hood-Williams 1997, Hood-Williams and Cealey Harrison 1998), although enormously productive for over a quarter of a century, now needs to be seen to have run its course. We will by no means be the first to have queried the usefulness of the distinction,[1] but perhaps we shall have been the first to seek to reconfigure the field *comprehensively* without leaving the distinction in place.

In describing something as a 'problematic', Althusser sought to indicate that it had a constraining and regulatory character. Certain forms of problematization were typical products of a problematic and, indeed, only certain kinds of questions could be posed. Within a problematic, concepts did a job of work and had what we might now describe as particular discursive effects. A problematic in Althusser's acceptation preserved something of the formal determinative logic of the structuralism from which it derived. Like Foucault's notion of an *episteme* – although without the same historical ambition – it indicated a limitation on the scope of what it was possible to think. Because a problematic constituted a rational and cohesive network of concepts, however, conceptual frameworks came to be seen as incommensurable entities between which transitions were only possible by means of an epistemological break. Like the early Foucault, Althusser was a philosopher of discontinuity.

Whilst not subscribing to the rationalism of Althusser's original notion of a 'problematic', it seems to us to describe very well the way in which the presence of certain concepts acts as a limitation on thought. Because of the network of other concepts in which it is implicated, use of a distinction like sex/gender can generate often unintended and sometimes unwanted consequences. Together these concepts act as regulatory forces on how other things may be conceptualized. In this book we shall explore some of the deleterious consequences of the sex/gender distinction and suggest ways to avoid them.

It is undoubtedly true, however, that some readers will not see the necessity of doing away with the problematic: indeed, they will see it as theoretically and politically undesirable to do so. Although we shall be focusing predominantly on the question of sex/gender as an analytical tool, we should certainly want to argue that there are political as well as other advantages to reorganizing the field. Our primary concerns, however, are with forms of conceptualization and investigation: the sex/gender problematic seems to us not only to hamstring the construction of sophisticated forms of understanding but also to do an injustice to the empirical material it addresses. We shall elaborate on both of these claims in the course of the chapters that follow.

Some initial indications are worth providing though. Our primary objection is to 'gender' understood primarily in terms of a transhistorical label for a category of social agent, unproblematically identified, in this case by biological characteristics. As a term, it combines reference to a social position, with discriminatory, oppressive or inegalitarian content, to a category of social agent to whom this is applied and to the psychic contents and behavioural repertoire classically referred to as 'masculinity' and 'femininity' pertaining to that agent. There is a mode of empiricist and humanist sociology entirely peopled with such categories, variously identified and labelled, and constituting naturalistic reference points: bikers, disabled people, women, housewives, single mothers…and combinations thereof. Such a sociology has commonsensical appeal, but inevitably tends to turn matters of empirical detail into inflections of the general case. In the case of 'gender', the association with matters of 'sex' universalizes the social category by means of a transhistorical reference point, or, more precisely, a transcendental referent.

We have argued elsewhere that use of a concept of gender as a descriptor for more or less unitary categories of people with sexed characteristics – what Connell (1987) has called 'categoricalism' – leads to a particular set of problems (Cealey Harrison and Hood-Williams, 1998). Allied to dominant conceptions of power, it generates the presumption of gender's continuous and undifferentiated presence as a 'social division' and to ahistorical and ethnocentric conflations of very diverse practices and behaviours. The continuous salience of sets of social divisions, gender amongst them, is now a hegemonic tenet of conventional sociology: for positivist research programmes it now constitutes one of a number of 'variables': age, class, 'racial'/ethnic distinctions, disability, and so on. In short, it constitutes one of the dimensions along which human beings can be presumed to vary. Most – although not all – of these variations are conceived of as discontinuous but the presumption is that the characteristics so defined entail either systematically differential treatment or consistently differential constitution – most often both – as a consequence of structural forces.

Two presumptions follow from this. The first is that groupings designated by these characteristics are seen in principle as homogeneous – as 'women' or 'men' – and the second is that, insofar as they are not homogeneous, this is believed to be because of the inflection produced by other 'variables' or 'social divisions' which are fundamental organizing principles of the social order. Thus empirical complexity surrounding gender is to be treated as a matter of increasing particularity and addressed by means of an understanding of the 'interplay' between these organizing principles (Mac an Ghaill, 1994: 4). The metaphors used to describe this pursuit of particularity are various and we have discussed the difficulties they pose in 'More Varieties than Heinz' (1998). Not least of these is the fact that the potential combination of variables one might need to account for *a priori* is so large as to place an unwieldy and ultimately impossible burden on the researcher. There are those, like Rosi Braidotti, for example, who seek to generate a more sophisticated account, defining the particularity of the 'subjects' of feminism in terms of 'axes of subjectification'. 'The question,' she says, 'is how to resituate subjectivity in a network of inter-related variables of which sexuality is only one, set alongside powerful axes of subjectification such as race, culture, nationality, class, life-choices, and sexual orientation' (Braidotti with Butler, 1994: 42). Regardless of the complexity one introduces, however, the fundamentals of the explanatory structure – which could be described broadly as sociologistic and structuralist – remain. Something conceived of as the social simply has a logical and explanatory priority – because it has ontological priority – over that which is defined as 'non-social' (the human being who thereby becomes 'the subject'). More important politically, perhaps, is whether or not the particularity produced in this way is capable of explaining the frequent lack of homogeneity within the designated groupings. We would argue that it is not. We would also query whether or not the particularity of interplay between variables such as gender, ethnicity, class, disability, and so on, successfully accounts for, and is exhaustive of, the behaviours of those who are alleged to belong to groups such as 'women' or 'men'.

Like Denise Riley, we shall argue instead that the attribution of gender to human beings is discursively and historically specific and that, as she puts it, '"women" is a volatile collectivity...so that the apparent continuity of the subject of "women" isn't to be relied upon' (1988: 1). But importantly, Denise Riley is not querying the category 'women' on the basis of some general philosophical anti-foundationalism, but on the basis of historical accuracy. Feminism itself is constitutively intertwined with the variable invocations and non-invocations of the category – with diverse and problematical feminizations and invisibilities – with their political implications and their social and human consequences. This is not merely to say that feminism's object is unstable, but also to say that that feminism is itself formed in the midst of that instability, and that its very substance lies in engagement with it: these instabilities of the category of 'women' are the *sine qua non* of feminism, 'which would otherwise be lost for an object, despoiled of a fight, and, in short, without any life' (1987: 35).

It is the appurtenance to 'sex' that both coheres and naturalizes the idea of 'gender' understood as a *social category*. Although 'gender' as a concept also exists as the generic descriptor for a field of investigation, that field is tacitly grounded in the presupposition of the existence of what are believed to be at least *relatively* homogeneous social groupings, which are mapped onto an apparently straightforward biological distinction. Because of their assumed biological homogeneity, 'women' and 'men' can in a stable way be assumed to be those creatures who are both the object and subject of social action. 'Gender', as a field, is thus understood to be about the vicissitudes that befall such 'women' and 'men' (and perhaps in a primary sense 'women').

'Sex' is conceptualized in this context as an unproblematic referent which defines that which is spoken about and acted upon. It is thus perceived as extra-discursive in at least two conflated senses: it is extra-discursive by reference to the social sciences – insofar as it is not an object of their concern, but belongs to biological discourses – and it is extra-discursive in belonging to a realm which is tacitly seen as external to and independent of human purposes. By contrast, much has recently been made of the idea that 'sex' too is a discursive construct. But what precisely is such a claim to mean? If 'sex' is also discursive, it indicates, initially, the banal fact that 'sex' is also a human concept. The question is what precisely does an assertion of this kind entail? As we shall see during the course of this book, the answer to this question is inevitably complex and can lead one equally well into the counter-intuitively productive or into apparent absurdity. Whatever one makes of it, however, such a claim does open out the possibility of no longer taking 'sex' – as object or concept – for granted. Quite apart from anything else, there is evidence to suggest that 'sex' as a concept is historically specific, which must of necessity imply that the process of differentiating human beings in relation to procreative processes has taken variable forms, with potentially diverse consequences.

This might seem to suggest that, even if one does not retain the term 'gender' to designate categories of people identified by 'sex', it would be possible to retain the notion of 'gender' as a field of investigation. Such a field would explore the construction of configurations of human life which have a putative relation to procreative processes – howsoever these may be understood – and the impact of such configurations on the human beings whose lives are shaped by them. Yet 'gender' as a concept, of course, was also born of feminism, so that it is intrinsically related to the sense that such configurations carry with them deleterious consequences for the human beings who have to live them. Nevertheless, reframing the concept in this way might at least entail exploring a variety of discursive designations, which are discontinuous in their appearance and diverse in their social significance.

But how far does this really take us, and, more importantly, what dangers does it present? It has certain distinct advantages. It allows recognition of what Denise Riley calls the 'stubborn harshness' of gender (1987: 36), the fact that 'gendering', however variable and discontinuous, does have an especially marked obduracy. Indeed, it is this, and the political implications that seem to follow from it, that marks the resistance of commentators to doing away with the idea of 'gender' as a transhistorical social division. Riley's phrase, however, does not indicate where that stubborn harshness resides. A number of writers would link this obduracy to a persistent relation of oppression or inequality, which prompts the question of why that oppression or inequality has come about and seems ubiquitous. The apparent ubiquity of something still often described as patriarchy coincides with the alleged universality of sex and prompts the thought that the one might bear some relation to the other, a thought which many of us no doubt find troubling. What is it about procreation that seems to call up such damaging consequences?

But this is not the only possible way of thinking about it: although the pervasive existence of inequalities between women and men was the initial motivating force for studies of gender and, indeed, for the very development of the concept, the presumption of the universality of such inequality is just that, a presumption. In no sense can one say that there is sufficient historical and cross-cultural evidence to warrant a declaration of universality. In what sense could we realistically say that relations between women and men have been *comprehensively* investigated in *all* societies and cultures? Such presumptions or declarations have had to rely upon theoretical argumentation, which is one of the reasons why the troubling difficulty of the origins of inequality arises.

The obduracy of 'gendering' does *need* to be recognized but perhaps we reach for universalistic explanations rather too rapidly and we should suspend the assumption that what seems so incontrovertible in *our* world is of necessity everywhere the same. It is of course also worth considering the fact that although the process of attributing 'gender' to human beings, and the resulting social and political effects, may shift and, may in itself be discontinuous, it does not mean that discourses and practices do not deal in common currencies, both conceptual and practical – so that obduracy might be read as consistency.

Equally, if, as Riley herself pointed out, feminism itself is bound up with the simultaneous assertion and refusal of the categories 'woman', 'women' and 'Woman', in the various forms in which they appear, it means that the perception of their constancy, through the very insistence of the term(s), is not without its effects. It is constitutive of the terrain of contestation, and that means of the field of social relations. Post-structuralism may have indulged in some false etymologies in drawing attention to the links between 'text' and 'texture', the woven and substantive fabric, the stuff of the world, but it is a useful idea nonetheless. We cannot simply indict the idea of 'women' as an error and move on. The very existence of feminism in the field of contestation tends to bring into being the very thing that it also seeks to dismantle, women as a social category, defined by their oppression.

However, there is more to the obduracy of 'gendering' than the common currency used by different discourses, at least in *our* world, by which one could mean the culture of the West over, at the most, the last couple of centuries. There is plenty of evidence to suggest, most especially from Thomas Laqueur's brilliant book, that the concept of 'sex' as we understand it today – hegemonic, foundational, unquestionable – is of fairly recent constitution. And it is the unquestionable, foundational character of 'sex' that most probably gives 'gender' a large part of its obduracy in our minds and our social lives, because it grounds the insistence of the various invocations of 'women' that we mentioned earlier. Being aware of 'sex' as recently constituted also entails that there must have been other ways of understanding 'woman' and 'man' that did not depend upon it. And there were. They might have been no less insistent than our current configurations, but they were undoubtedly different. Laqueur has a delightful account of what his historical investigations indicate about the nature of human experience in a world in which the visions of bodies were so different from ours:

> A colleague pointed out to me that he heard Mozart's *Così fan tutte* with new ears after reading my chapters about the Renaissance. I have felt a new poignancy in the tragicomedy of eighteenth-century disguise – the last act of *Le Nozze di Figaro*, for example – with its questioning of what it is in a person that one loves. Bodies do and do not seem to matter. I watch Shakespeare's comedies of sexual inversion with new queries, and I try to think my way back into a distant world where the attraction of deep friendship was reserved for one's like. (1990: 23-4)

The hope he expresses is that his work will be liberating, 'breaking old shackles of necessity' and 'opening up new worlds of vision, politics and eros', which indeed he has. If we can do nothing else in response, we ought to pay some attention to the role of the concept of 'sex' at the heart of contemporary processes of 'gendering'. It will not have the glorious elegance of his work, but it will be vital if we are to begin to glimpse those new worlds. We have to retain the sense that not only is the past another country, and that they do indeed do things differently there, but that the present itself, the here *and* the now, needs to be rendered (as it used to be described in the heyday of phenomenology) anthropologically strange.

Allowing for discursive and historical specificity therefore does not mean that sociality dissolves entirely into the episodic – on the contrary. However, it does mean that the *particularity* of references to 'women' or 'men' and the nature *of the absence of such references* have to be attended to, rather than taking for granted a universality of reference which can be assumed to constitute the field. As Hilary Allen (1990) has argued in relation to the use of menstruation as the basis for a defence in a criminal trial, not only are there areas of social life in which reference is *not* made to the gender of human beings, or it is, at any rate, not considered material, but the absence of any specific reference to the 'femaleness' of a defendant might actually represent a preferable state of affairs than its alleged 'acknowledgement'.

Attending to that specificity, then, is a matter of analytical protocol. Where does one begin? With generality, to which one adds complexity, or with specificity? We prefer to begin with specificity and *discover* linkages and forms of coherence, rather than begin with generality and seek to inflect it with complexity. In this book, we are concerned with the *making* of difference, the diversity of ways in which social and discursive demarcations come to be constituted. The problem with retaining the term 'gender' to designate the field covered by these processes is how easily we can slip into old habits of thought, how rapidly we can collapse the reformulation we have given the term above ('*attributing* 'gender' to human beings...') back into what happens to men and women. The very use of the term 'gender', because of its associations with 'sex' gives it a constancy which is, if not unwarranted, then empirically hazardous. If we are to rethink this area, we will find that we have – perhaps temporarily, perhaps permanently – to place the term 'gender' in brackets, in a similar way to the way in which phenomenologists urged us to 'bracket the natural attitude'.

The task here, then, is not one of adding in complexity to the concepts of 'sex' and 'gender' but of disaggregation. Under each of their respective headings lie complex and multifarious sets of processes, which are not well encompassed, nor even usefully gathered together, by those headings. These need to be given empirical space to breathe. Our intention is therefore to explore a number of writers who, we feel, begin to take us towards the reconfiguration of the field currently designated by the sex/gender problematic. Not all of them necessarily had the intention to replace that problematic, but we regard their writing as corrosive or subversive of its assumptions. Little of this work is new, but it seems to us to be foundational, since the problems we are exploring have yet to be satisfactorily resolved. Each of these theorists in their turn moves us a little further forward in that direction, but each, also, takes us only part of the way there.[2]

The heuristic role in this endeavour will be played by the concept whose exploration we have given such prominence to in this book: discourse. 'Discourse', we feel, has suffered greatly from its recent assimilation to conventional epistemologically framed forms of theorizing from which it was explicitly designed to depart. In the current sociological lexicon, the term has come to mean very little more than 'language', or 'a set of ideas', and much effort is then devoted to endeavouring to rescue what is described as the 'extra-discursive' before it slides into an idealist oblivion. In some measure, the gestural force of using 'discourse' in orthodox sociology – rather than, say, 'theory' or 'ideology' – remains, but only in seriously attenuated form: the concept is a pale shadow of its former self. In many settings, it has in fact become almost interchangeable with a concept of ideology, and it performs roughly the same theoretical role, in spite of its intentional departure from the epistemological parameters that inform 'ideology'.

We talked in earlier writings of a 'radical discursivity'. What this gestures towards is a methodological commitment, a commitment to using the concept of discourse in order to make certain things *appear*, rather than an ontological commitment that dictates that, henceforth, the objects in the world are to be divided into the discursive and the extra-discursive. Michel Foucault (with whom the concept is nowadays most strongly associated) carried out, it must be remembered, historical research to do philosophical *work*. He used concepts because, and as long as, they were serviceable, and saw it as his task to show people that it was possible to *think differently* and make something evident which had hitherto not been perceived. He had no intention of supplying a re-description of the world in terms of an alternative *general* theory, characterized by a new set of 'master concepts'. Similarly, in deliberately eschewing the sex/gender distinction, and putting the material that we have side by side, we are endeavouring to make certain things appear, and appear in concert. Most of us already knew that these things were there, for there have been over twenty years of rich and complex work using the concept of discourse, which effectively broke open the field by attempting to dispel some of the presuppositions we are arguing against here. As early as 1978, for instance, the journal *m/f* was arguing against the idea that 'women' were a pre-given unity. But these arguments have not been successful, for then, just as others are now, they were accused of cutting the ground from underneath feminism. As they said in an editorial, '*m/f* has been accused of denying the existence of concrete men and women, or worse, of claiming they are made not of concrete but of words' (Adams and Cowie, 1990: 35).

The persistence of such accusations relates directly to the fact that the theoretical problems that led to them have remained unresolved. Since the heyday of *m/f* what has happened is that they have effectively been side-stepped. Arguments that are in tenor fundamentally unsympathetic to the principles that *m/f* enunciated then and that we have enunciated here have nevertheless absorbed the vocabulary and some of the forms of conceptualization of those whose work they had opposed. Put in a rather over-simplified fashion, what is described as post-structuralism has been rewritten to be more user-friendly, but it is still, really, 'business as usual'. The sex/gender problematic continues to be the overarching sign under which much of the work in this area is carried out, while all the while what sits underneath it becomes more complex.[3] The latter, we would suggest, is perfectly understandable in the light of the former. What we propose to do in this book, then, is to deal with what we regard as some of the unresolved theoretical problems. We do this predominantly through a series of close readings of texts which we see – to use the unfortunate and singularly and ironically inappropriate metaphor – as 'seminal'. The thread that runs through this is the concept of 'discourse', because it is in its current uses that one finds symptomatic difficulties appearing and it is in the construction of alternative uses that one can resolve these.

What the concept of discourse allows one to do is to draw attention to the close interaction between forms of thought and forms of action. It breaks with the epistemological presumption of a divorce between thought and world, in which thought has forever to be adequate to world, and it gestures towards a research programme in which the relation of forms of thought and forms of action is a central *topic* of investigation. There is no *general* realm of 'discourse' that meets another general realm of the non-discursive, between which relations can be specified for all time, on the model of an idealist or materialist philosophy. Hence the fact that we have preferred to use the term 'discursivity', rather than 'discourse', to signal what we described earlier as this *methodological* impetus.

This book was originally to have had a different title, *Making the Difference: Sex, Gender and Discursivity* and it would not have escaped the notice of some readers that that subtitle, *Sex, Gender and Discursivity*, also echoed the title of Ann Oakley's book, *Sex, Gender and Society*, so many years ago. 'Discursivity', however, carried a different conceptual status from 'society', whose position it occupied. And, clearly, as a partial substitute, the idea of 'the discursive' does do something to the ontological weight of a totality like 'society'. What 'the discursive' indicates is that the presumption of a *primary and fundamental* coherence to sociality is perhaps not especially helpful. This observation is of a piece with the remarks we made earlier about 'gender'. The idea of 'society' tends – although this is not inevitable – to presuppose a hierarchy of forms of coherence to the social realm, starting at the broadest level, which constitutes a primary level of determination with the idea of 'system' or 'structure' and moving up or down (according to one's metaphorical preference) through the gradations of 'sub-systems' or portions of a structure. Thus, 'society' can be metaphorically arranged in broadly layered form, through levels of specification and determination. 'Discursivity', by contrast, indicates that forms of coherence are matters for empirical investigation rather than theoretical *fiat*, and that there are no *necessary* forms of coherence given by the organization of an overall structure or system.

However, all three concepts in the sub-title carried a different status from the one Ann Oakley's did in the original title. All three of them were there, precisely, as concepts for investigation rather than as entities, two of them marking the problematic which is the object of our concern, and one of them the heuristic tool we propose to use to reconfigure the field. 'Discursivity' was thus never intended to have the same status as a term like 'society'.

The book therefore begins with an exploration of Ann Oakley's pioneering work, since it was she who played a central role in advancing the use of the distinction between 'sex' and 'gender'. Notwithstanding our critique, it has to be remembered how truly liberatory her work was at the time and has been since. Although reference might legitimately be made to the work of Maccoby and Jacklin (1975) as near contemporaries, or to Hampson and Hampson (1961) Money (1965) or Stoller (1968) as precursors, it was Oakley who was responsible for opening up the study of a new realm designated by the term 'gender'. Defining that realm proved invaluable in countering the assumption that differences and divisions between 'women' and 'men' were both biologically given and unalterable. In that sense, her work effected a revolution in thought. However, the time has now come to examine systematically whether or not the distinction offers the best way of thinking about 'women' and 'men'. We feel, on the contrary, that it does not and, indeed, that, because we are now all of us moving on, it has come to constitute an impediment to that thought. We are certainly not the first to make such an observation, nor, indeed, to bring together a variety of work in the service of the construction of an alternative approach, but what we hope is different here is that no single all-encompassing account of something called 'gender' is being proposed. It can no more be a question of a 'gender order' (Connell, 1987) or of 'performativity' (Butler, 1990), than it is of 'sex-class', 'patriarchy', 'sexual stratification' or a 'sex-gender system', however appealing these solutions may be and however much internal complexity one gives them. We cannot keep excavating the content of 'gender' in a bid to sustain the empirical and theoretical complexities of which all of us now speak. The concept of 'gender' belongs inextricably to the distinction from 'sex' and it seems to us to perform a unifying function that is inappropriate. In the first chapter of our book, then, we identify some of the problems that ensue from using that distinction, whether in its original form or inverted, as it is by Christine Delphy.

Our objective in the chapters that follow is gradually to elaborate a new framework and some new possibilities for analysis, and we do this through consideration of a series of issues. Chapter 3, 'Unpicking the Knot' explores the ways in which the facticity of the sexed body comes to be established. In other words, although the body and the sex that belongs to it now *seem* to us to be obvious, that obviousness is actually the constructed result of a complex series of processes. In this chapter, we concentrate on the neglected but important ethnomethodological account of gender attribution offered by Suzanne Kessler and Wendy McKenna, who sought to uncover the existence of such processes. The difficulties posed by the philosophical anthropology and epistemology deployed by ethnomethodology cannot negate what is effectively the opening up of a completely new empirical terrain, whose implications have to be taken into consideration.

The fourth chapter, 'The Mystery of the Visible' begins with Michel Foucault's *Herculine Barbin*, looks briefly at the way in which Renaissance doctors dealt with sexual ambiguity via the work of Thomas Laqueur, and explores Suzanne Kessler's more recent work on the management of intersex. Whereas Kessler and McKenna's ethnomethodology provides us with the means of 'unhinging' the obviousness of sex, Michel Foucault offers us the mythic moment when that obviousness was born, when an individual's having a *true* sex replaced a world in which bodily morphology provided a badge of social entitlement rather than the indexical signs of a truth. In turn, Laqueur describes the point at which the bodily began to carry the cultural burden of securing what would now tend to be described as the social relations of gender, of literally *embodying* that truth. Once that truth is established historically, a number of things follow, in the construction of the domain of the biological sciences as elsewhere. Suzanne Kessler's more recent work demonstrates the odd confluence between traditional biological accounts of the determinacy of gender in the body and quasi-sociological ideas of its plasticity, deployed by the medical profession across the bodies of intersexed people.

As Thomas Laqueur, whose work we consider in detail in Chapter 5, 'Timely Bodies', demonstrates, there is no *necessary* way, given by the 'facts' of human biology, for somatic and morphological features to be construed. For Laqueur, however, the historical contingency of conceptualizations of the body comes up against what we now 'know' to be its truths and this presents *epistemological* dilemmas, in short, dilemmas that belong to a particular way of conceptualizing knowledge. Laqueur expresses this in terms of his anxieties about what he sees as 'the fraught chasm between representation and reality, seeing-as and seeing' (1990: 14) and we address this as part of our initial foray into the issue of discursivity.

Because Laqueur construes the discursive in terms of a problematic of representation, he reinforces the sense of the closed and autarchic nature of the body whose birth he traced so well in *Making Sex*. In 'Looming Outside the Space Station', Chapter 6, we take up this issue through Bob Connell's contention that at different historical moments and in different social settings, not only do somatic and morphological features carry different meanings, but they have a variety of forms of what he has described as 'practical relevance'. With that concept of the 'practical relevance' of somatic to social, Connell seeks to replace the doctrine of natural difference that he detects in current formulations of the nature of 'gender', in which body and sociality, 'sex' and 'gender', are arrayed in one of two configurations of determinacy, the one to the other. In some senses, the concept of 'practical relevance' still leaves us within the orbit of those two poles, but it does have the virtue of giving a sense of how the body is altered in that encounter with the discursive, which can encompass anything from the scientific to the poetic or the political. In some very suggestive remarks, Connell also raises the issue of the experience of a gendered embodiment, a theme to which we return briefly when we come to consider psychoanalysis.

In Chapter 7, 'Truth is Slippery Stuff', we extend discussion of 'sex' and the discursive by confronting biological discourses head-on, expanding on some of the remarks made by Kessler and McKenna about the genetic sexing of human beings and exploring the work of the biologist Anne Fausto-Sterling who criticizes the construal of what are considered to be the body's genetic markers. In doing so, she gives us a clear sense of what she believes to be at stake in the intra-disciplinary tussles that surround and partially determine them. As such, Fausto-Sterling's work makes no bones about the status – what we might traditionally have called the 'truth-value' – of its own critique. However, in this chapter, we also take forward Laqueur's anxieties about the status of knowledges of the bodily in the light of their discursive and historical contingency, through the Foucauldian-inspired work of the biologist Nelly Oudshoorn. Oudshoorn gives us an account of the formation of specific biological objects associated with 'sex', the so-called 'sex hormones', and of the discourses and practices associated with them. In doing so, she, like Laqueur, has to tangle with the implicit veracity and efficacy of those objects whilst giving us their complexly chequered history. Looking much more precisely at the manner in which sciences are constituted does not give us an automatic means of indicting them, as if for their very historicity. On the contrary, the task of constructing a critique still remains to be done, but, as Foucault taught us, genealogies can be instructive for that purpose.

We examine the issue of 'truth' and critique more directly in Chapter 8, 'Stories for Sexual Difference'. Through the work of Valerie Walkerdine and the Girls and Mathematics Unit at the Institute of Education, we are able to explore what kinds of 'truths' it is that we can consider ourselves to be producing once we engage with the notion of the discursive, for the concept of 'discourse' applies both to what we are examining and to our own intellectual activity. Walkerdine and the Girls and Mathematics Unit provide an account of how the construction of a particular set of truths about girls and mathematics take place, but also a method of critique which does not set itself up as somehow *automatically* 'truer' because it is seen through the epistemological lens of feminism. Instead, they show how 'truths' become operative in the world and the ways in which 'facts, fictions and fantasies' are all interwoven with one another in their construction and deployment. Valerie Walkerdine has also given much more explicit consideration to the role of phantasy in her discussion of how little girls read comics, 'Some Day My Prince Will Come', which we look at in the second half of the chapter. There she discusses the psychic production of feminine desire through the insertion of the child into specific cultural forms and practices, which offer a solution to the dilemmas that that child faces. Walkerdine's analysis of the child's attempt to resolve these dilemmas indicates how identificatory processes can knit human beings into particular 'gendered' portrayals of themselves. What results, however, is not so much 'femininity' – understood as a cohesive and stable psychological structure and a corresponding behavioural repertoire – as a struggle to inhabit positions made available as resolutions to conflicts.

The question of the existence, or otherwise, of gender identity is taken up in Chapter 9, 'The Choreography of Sex', in which we unearth an almost forgotten dramaturgical and ethnomethodological sociology of gender, in the form of Erving Goffman's concept of 'gender display' and Harold Garfinkel's case history of Agnes. In this chapter, we also examine the ways in which the body can be seen to provide the scene for the staging of its foundational role as 'sexed'. Goffman's central point is that 'gender identity' is the effect of a portrayal, of no more than the staging of a set of performances, part of whose content is to 'give off' the impression of their fundamental character. His work suggests that the dichotomization of the population is constituted and sustained through a stylization of behaviours. This is premised on a doctrine of natural expression that treats that stylization as an indexical sign of an underlying reality. Garfinkel's work, which tacitly suggests that the issue of the potential psychical content of identity is more complex, draws attention, like Foucault's, to the fact that the dichotomization of the population is a moral issue, whose existence is decided as a matter of motivated compliance with a legitimate order, rather than 'as a matter of biological, medical, urological, sociological, psychiatric or psychological fact' (Garfinkel, 1990 [1967]: 122). In relation to those such as transsexuals, whose compliance is more obvious to us, Garfinkel coined the notion of 'passing', the process through which they sought to be attributed the sex to which they desired to belong. Both Goffman and Garfinkel allow us to extend the idea found in Laqueur, that the historical appearance of the concept of 'sex' constituted a means of attempting to *secure* the dichotomization of the population. A clear ontological basis, in the form of biology, provided the means for the thoroughgoing feminization of women. An ontology, however, is insufficient to secure a social grouping. In order to do so, it is necessary to have a moral order which ensures the *realization* of the truths to which it appeals. Garfinkel, in particular, gives a picture of the way in which that moral order is constructed and sustained in the life of a specific individual with a problematic biography.

Goffman and Garfinkel, of course, also take us towards the more recent and more fashionable notions of 'performativity' developed by Judith Butler, and in Chapter 10, 'A Melancholy Gender', we look at one aspect of her work. All three of them, Goffman, Garfinkel and Butler, in different ways, move us away from any notion of 'gender *identity*' towards 're-presentational' accounts of gendered behaviours, which suggests that notions of 'identity' have more to do with portrayal than with deep psychological structures. Yet it also appears to be the case that what Butler wishes to do is to use psychoanalysis to provide an account of gender identity. The problem with this endeavour, we shall suggest, does not lie so much with the desire to explore deep psychological structures as with the concept of 'gender identity' itself and with what its use does to the psychoanalysis which is deployed under its heading. In short, the fact that there may be no such thing as 'gender identity' does not of itself mean that there is no psychic adhesion on the part of human beings to particular forms of portrayal or display, but this is, in itself, a complex and contradictory process, which the concept of 'gender' tends to homogenize, over-generalize and sociologize. Butler calls her account a 'hyperbolic' construction but hyperbole implies merely exaggeration. We argue, however, that her account does not accord with what is known from psychoanalysis about the complexity of what it prefers to refer to in terms of 'masculinity' and 'femininity'.

Chapter 11, 'The Vagaries of Language', takes us full circle back to the concern Ann Oakley had had with the continual oscillation between versions of 'woman' and the implications these were supposed to have for behaviour and morality. Denise Riley's solution to avoiding re-treading these paths is to refuse to countenance what she describes as the 'powerful naturalism' of the idea of 'women' in favour of an attempt to analyse some of the myriad ways in which they are constituted in history. Her discussion of these discursive constructions, however, focuses predominantly on the *accounts* given of what women *are*, since her book *Am I That Name?* was an historical sketch which was designed to make the case for a different kind of research agenda for feminism. In that respect, however, it did not undertake the task of exploring precisely what was meant by 'discourse' or precisely how 'characterizations' generated that which they characterized. In this chapter, we therefore undertake to explore some of the difficulties that the concept – in its current form – embodies. In particular, we look at the difficulties of conceptualizing the relationship between discourse and language and the problematic character of the Saussurean account of language that 'discourse' has inherited. This represents, then, the beginnings of a programme for further work.

Over the course of the book, we seek to establish that there are productive ways of working that do not depend upon the analytical distinction between 'sex' and 'gender'. Abandoning that distinction does not make it any less possible to address the oppression of women, although it may well rewrite the political shorthand supplied by the notion of 'gender' as a rather more complex set of processes. More to the point, however, we hope to show that retaining the distinction is in itself problematical. Although it is undoubtedly the case that what the term 'gender' refers to now covers a complex range of conceptualization, its founding moments and the presuppositions these put in place remain tacitly present in the dominant and spontaneous uses of the term. Even where attempts are made to rethink some of these founding assumptions, the constraints that use of the term places upon that theorizing are problematical and hamper the possibility of developing such attempts further.

Social theory is sometimes accused of theoretical ambitions which represent something like the smuggling in of bad philosophy through the back door. There is some truth in this insofar as the desire for grand theorizing (which goes way beyond Talcott Parsons' very explicit architectural constructions) often seems like a desire to generalize which is somewhat premature. Broad conceptual distinctions, such as that between sex and gender, are necessary at a given stage of development, and just *how* necessary is demonstrated by the plethora of work that then ensues. But one has to know when to leave them behind and to recognize what it is that was valuable about them that one wishes to retain. Ideally, in time, they will be replaced by concepts of an equivalent level of generality but concepts whose use is not so much didactic as synthetic. 'Gender' may seem usefully to unify the field for feminism, but it does in fact do so much more, and the consequences of this are rather less happy.

When we started work on it, it was the forlorn hope of this book to banish the paired terms 'sex' and 'gender' from popular and social scientific discourse. All of the contemporary and historical uses of the distinction seemed to us to lead to a series of irresolvable traps that cast their dark shadows over much contemporary social science. Since then, however, our ambitions have become rather more modest with the growing understanding that its roots in our culture go deeper than feminism. What we hope to prompt instead is the necessary scrutiny of the terms, wherever they arise, since a process of being routinely attentive to, and conscious of, the nature of one's conceptual framework seems to us to be vital although all of us tend, after a while, to exempt certain concepts from such scrutiny. We need not only to query the necessity for the presence of a particular concept or set of concepts but to raise questions about what role they are playing, and why. The dream that lies behind the concept of 'gender' is perhaps that of arriving at an account that would explain women's oppression once and for all, in a single comprehensive account. Perhaps *Beyond Sex and Gender* is not entirely innocent of that dream. And yet the sense that we have, and that animates its pages, is that the picture is far too complicated for that to be possible and, that, furthermore, no such account would be viable. It is a snare and a delusion.

There is a lesson in the work of Foucault, but, this time, an unintended one. If Foucault fell foul of a number of historians, the problem was perhaps not a deficit in scholarship – as is sometimes suggested – but the fact that he still remained too much of a philosopher. The grand gesture of marking historical discontinuity (whether one gives it a name like *episteme* or not) is far more seductive than what it was that he said his work was about, a grey and patiently documentary history, a *wirkliche Historie*. The sex/gender distinction has been the grand gesture of feminism, which marked the cleavage with what had gone before, but we must be wary of remaining seduced by that gesture.

Notes

[1]The sex/gender distinction has notably been criticized by Gatens (1983 and 1996), Scott (1986), Connell (1987), Butler (1990 and 1993) Scott and Morgan (1993), amongst others, some of whom then undertake to reformulate the concepts in a different way whilst fundamentally maintaining them. We discuss some of these endeavours here.

[2] In so doing, we revisit some of the same materials explored by Judith Butler in *Gender Trouble* – whether uncannily or inevitably is unclear since they were assembled and selected as teaching materials before she published *Gender Trouble*. Perhaps it is merely that, like us, she regarded these texts as especially important.

[3] As we have argued elsewhere in relation to the work of Judith Butler (Hood-Williams and Cealey Harrison, 1998), working within that problematic tends to prompt the unification of things which perhaps cannot and should not be unified in that form, even if the concepts are themselves rewritten in a singular way. For example, in the work of Butler, 'gender' becomes 'an identity tenuously constituted in time, instituted in an exterior space through a *stylized repetition of acts*' (1990: 140, emphasis in original). 'Sex', similarly, becomes 'an ideal construct which is forcibly materialized through time…not a simple fact or static condition of the body, but a process whereby regulatory norms materialize "sex" and achieve this materialization through a forcible reiteration of those norms' (1993: 1-2).

2 The Old Configuration

In coining the concept of 'gender' so many years ago now, anglophone feminism did what it probably least expected to do: it ended up – rather curiously – sharing a genealogy with its opponents. Since the eighteenth century, a separation had been taking shape between the cultural and social characteristics deemed proper to the sexes and the admixture of corporeal features which were assumed to accompany them, a separation whose intent had been to ground the former in the latter. As an attempt to clarify and secure the difference between two social categories, 'women' and 'men' (and, arguably, the relations of superordination and subordination that were enmeshed in it) it sought to make the body the ontological ground of the behavioural and social components of the distinction between the sexes. Without perhaps intending to do so, feminism sharpened that separation and produced two somewhat contradictory effects. In arguing against the basis of the distinction between the sexes in the body, it made of the body a pre-social and extra-social, but fundamentally residuary category – since the better part of the distinction now belonged to 'gender' – whilst, at the same time, leaving it as the ontological basis of 'gender' in the form of 'sex'.

Ann Oakley's pioneering work of 1972, *Sex, Gender and Society*[1] is aware of the historicity of the debate about sex differences but finds itself caught in a contradiction. Her introductory chapter implicitly locates itself within that historic debate, in which the arguments in favour of sex differences as against the equality and similarity of women and men, and the sharpness of separation between male and female roles, interests, activities and personalities, wax and wane. The current period, according to Oakley, is typical of one in which the roles and statuses of men and women are changing but, unprecedentedly, it also offers the possibility of the technological control and manipulation of reproductive processes. The present day existence of a Women's Movement suggests that basic issues to do with the role of women have never been resolved. Arguably, what Oakley sets out to do in *Sex, Gender and Society* is to resolve these issues. So whilst she clearly indicates that concern over the differences between the sexes is symptomatic of historical periods of social upheaval and the reappraisals they engender (and thus could be expected to reappear periodically), she also seems to want to settle the matter once and for all. The questions that she poses are indicative of this:

> The *enduring* questions are these: does the source of the many differences between the sexes lie in biology or culture? If biology determines male and female roles, how does it determine them? How much influence does culture have? (1972: 15, emphasis added)

The questions then are transhistorical, yet Oakley describes the *raison d'être* of the debate about sex differences in terms of the inter-implication of questions about nature with issues of moral and political right. Periods of time when women's rights are in the ascendant are periods when the similarity of women and men is asserted and made possible; periods when differences are insisted upon and enforced in practice are periods when women's claims to equal treatment are in retreat. Why then continue to occupy that ground?

The burdens of philosophy

The key to Oakley's continuing acceptance of a terrain in which the social and political rights of women and men are bound up with their nature is to be found in an assumption made in her opening sentence. 'Everybody knows', she says, 'that men and women are different' (1972: 9). In short, whether or not differences exist is not in question. But, she says,

> Behind that knowledge lies a certain uneasiness: *how* different are they? What is the extent of the difference? What significance does it have for the way in which male and female behave and are treated in society? (ibid.)

The first questions, she suggests, are *factual* ones, the last is a question of *value*, and confusion has arisen in the debate over sex differences because they are not always separated. The questions she describes as enduring make it clear that there are two contenders for the source of this difference, biology and culture, and one would expect each of them to be a candidate for factual status. This set of questions, however, makes the issue of behavioural differences and differences in treatment – in short, what she designates as social or cultural – a matter of *value* . Only one of the sources of difference, the biological, carries ontological weight. This is made even clearer at the end of the chapter, where the sex/gender distinction is introduced:

> However much we *could* change the traditional involvement of women with their biological roles, the direction of change remains a question of choice and of value. It is not enough to point out that the traditionally incontrovertible argument for the sex-differentiated society has had its foundations removed with the advance of pills, loops, rubber devices, synthetic human milk and sterilised feeding bottles. Arguments long believed in have an alarming tendency to remain suspended in thin air by the slender string of passionate, often irrational, conviction. They seem not to need their foundations to survive. (1972: 15-16)

What she refers to as 'women's biological roles', by which is understood their reproductive function, constitutes the *foundation* on which matters of value might properly be decided, assuming a rational assessment of their nature and extent were to be conducted. Conceptions of masculinity and femininity lag behind advances in technology which have altered 'the *necessary impact* of biology on society' (1972: 16, emphasis added). The analytical distinction between 'sex', understood as the biological differences between male and female (genitalia, procreative function), and 'gender', understood as the social classification into 'masculine' and 'feminine' is necessary, according to Oakley, in order to bring clarity into the debate about sex differences. Her aim is to replace dogmatism with insight (1972: 9).

She quotes Webster's dictionary to argue that sex refers to 'the two divisions...of human beings respectively designated as male or female' and to show that gender is something else, '...any of two or more subclasses...that are partly arbitrary, but also partly based on distinguishable characteristics such as...sex (as masculine)' (1972:7). In fact, Oakley was somewhat optimistic in assuming that the English language already made the distinction that she wanted to establish. The Chambers dictionary published at the same time says that 'masculine' is the adjectival form of the noun 'male', describing 'masculine' as 'characteristics...peculiar to a man or the male sex: mannish of that gender'. Even the contemporary definition given in the *OED* allocates the term gender, in Oakley's sense, to a very marginal place. Lest we think that this is merely a matter of the anachronism of the *OED*, it is worth keeping in mind the continuing and close association between 'male' and 'masculine' and 'female' and 'feminine'. The presumption is *still* that the one set of categories – those belonging to 'gender' – is based upon or the *property of* the other, the predicate of a subject. Even Webster's had only said 'partly arbitrary' and had clearly linked 'gender' to 'distinguishable characteristics'.

Oakley's opening paragraph thus maps questions of fact onto biology and questions of value and choice onto sociality. This association of biology with facticity and sociality with evaluation has a further set of consequences, which is marked by her crucial statement that: 'The constancy of sex must be admitted, but so also must the variability of gender' (1972: 16).

Facticity, in other words, implies transhistorical constancy, whereas evaluation and choice imply variability. The social realm, in short, becomes a volitional and, even, an ideational sphere. In sociological terms, this is a surprising characterization, especially for a non-phenomenological sociology. It may well be that, for Oakley, applying such a characterization to gender nevertheless allows the sociology of structures, institutions and patterned social organization to survive intact, although it would make them all evaluative in origin.

We shall have occasion to consider the alleged fixity of the natural and the biological in what follows, but in *Politics and Class Analysis* (1987), Barry Hindess warns against the implied suggestion that we can always do something to change social arrangements that are not naturally given:

> To say that certain features of social arrangements may vary from society to society is not necessarily to say that they are amenable to deliberate political action. (1987: 77)

Possibly, but not *necessarily*. The reasons for this are much more familiar to us now and concern, at the very *least*, the terms of political calculation and the conditions of political intervention. The simple fact of noting historical variation tells us nothing about the conditions needed to effect particular forms of social transformation, which require so very much more specific an analysis.

Ever since Oakley's inaugural work, however, it has seemed as if the body has been unproblematically *there,* constituting the solidities of 'women' and 'men', and the social world has been one in which *representations* of women and men held sway: we were socialized into roles, with all the connotations these have of drama and performance, and we conformed to stereotypes. There is a sense, then, in which 'sex' was somehow seen to refer to a biological *reality* and 'gender' to the way in which that 'reality' was construed.

So although the distinction between 'sex' and 'gender' does not represent the same thing as a difference between reality and representation, the two sets of differences have a tendency to conflate. The distinction between 'sex' and 'gender' carries with it the sense that the body is somehow '*more* real'. The social is the realm of the construct *par excellence*, and constructs carry with them the notion of *falsity*. Social constructs are seen to be less recalcitrant, less inert than biological differences.

The sex/gender distinction thus ends up carrying with it considerable theoretical baggage, theoretical baggage whose effects we shall encounter in due course. It maps onto a further set of philosophical oppositions: between fact and value, between nature and culture, between reality and representation and between true and false. We shall see these reappear in what follows, in both negative and positive guises.

These theoretical encumbrances are not Oakley's, however, and the association of the natural with that which we cannot change and of the social with the politically malleable has a much longer and broader history. In some ways, Oakley simply echoed and exacerbated what we 'knew' already. The very earliest attempts to think the distinction between women and men in a way that opens it up to philosophical speculation or sociological investigation and political action is marked by the same theoretical configuration.

In a time before the advent of feminist sociologies, Talcott Parsons' (1949) attempt to argue that the purpose of sex-role differentiation was to minimize the potential strain produced by the occupation system in a mobile class-divided society – which is a wholly and self-containedly sociological explanation – rests finally upon the allegedly biological 'fact' of the bearing and nurturing of children. Two separate explanatory principles, the one sociological, the other biological, are at work, and the latter constitutes the ultimate basis of the former.

And in what might be deemed to be the first feminist foray of the 'second wave', Simone de Beauvoir (1972 [1949]) tussled with an analogous problem. She confronted the paradox, the contradiction even, between the mysterious and allegedly threatened reality of femininity and the residence of that femininity, literally, *in utero*. She strove hard to disentangle that paradox, but was unwilling to resolve it in the direction of a nominalism that regarded women simply as human beings labelled 'women': 'the anti-feminists have had no trouble in showing that women simply *are not* men' (1972 [1949]: 14). On the contrary, she regarded human biology not merely as constant, but as positively cloying, a sexually differentiated reality that constituted the very peculiarity of the human being. That which was universal, which was fundamentally *human*, and to which woman needed to accede, was the transcendence that made of her a potentially free and autonomous subject whose projects reached out to new liberties. What oppressed woman was her reduction to the immanence of physiological, psychological or economic forces. Defining woman according to the biological realities of her life was a denial of her humanity, producing her construction as object, as Other.

Everywhere, then, attempts to argue the social and the political are haunted by the supposed solidities of biology, like Marley's ghost trailing its chains. In both of these quite distinct pieces of writing, the same assumptions about the variable and contestable social order and the inert and solid realities of biology can be found, a number of years before the terminological distinction between 'sex' and 'gender' was made and justified conceptually.

A doctrine of natural difference

The sex/gender distinction, then, locates itself firmly within what Connell has described as a doctrine of natural difference, in which, as he puts it, 'the notion of natural sex difference forms a limit beyond which thought cannot go' (1987: 66). In that respect, Oakley's work shows a clear continuity with that of its predecessors and opponents. The problem posed is simply that of determining what it is that properly belongs to the natural and what it is that does not. That which is natural can be ceded to the expertise of the biological sciences. That which can be recuperated as social is demonstrably malleable and susceptible to transformation. What she did, however, which was absolutely fundamental, was to re-order the relation between the two domains, from one of determinacy to one of relative autonomy.

In *Sex, Gender and Society,* she investigates in detail the biological claims about sexual difference and the evidence concerning cultural variations in behaviour and characteristics. The initial problem, though, is whether that disentangling of 'nature' from 'culture' can ultimately be performed, and, whether, in fact, apportioning the determination of characteristics and features to one or the other, and thus destining them either to be confirmed as fact or disputed as value, is the appropriate gesture to make. Their distribution between two *general* domains is an ultimately impossible and fruitless endeavour. To take a mundane example, is the morphology of Arnold Schwarzenegger's body nature or culture? Is pumping iron easily or even usefully apportioned between the physiological and the social?

The assumption, which is hardly peculiar to *Sex, Gender and Society,* is that the facticity of biological processes entails an integrity that makes them both independent of, and impervious to, social and psychological forces, which is why the arena of disputation comes to be organized in this way. Both Oakley's 1972 book, *Sex, Gender and Society,* and the later *Subject Women* (1981) set themselves up in terms of an evaluation of what really *can* be established and confirmed and what is malleable and contestable, with the result that the field commanded by biology shrinks in favour of gender. Yet we know from a number of sources how bodily aptitudes, and perhaps even evolutionary developments, may depend upon social relations (Hirst and Woolley, 1982). And, if nothing else, the work of the physiologist W. B. Cannon (1942) and Lévi-Strauss subsequent work on the effectiveness of symbols (1977) both suggest the permeability of biological processes to emotional and psychological states whose origins lie in the social world, an idea which is finding expression now in developing fields such as that of psycho-neuro-immunology. In fact, Oakley's own discussion in *Subject Women* also suggests as much, in relation, for example, to the impact of social situation on testosterone levels in animal studies (1981: 54-5). More prosaically, we now live in a world humming with the implications of genetic engineering, which introduces a qualitative leap into processes of selective breeding practised on flora and fauna for generations. In short, we are well aware, not only of the malleability of biological processes, but of the idea that they are crucially open to environmental forces and to intervention. The sex/gender distinction, however, pushes us in a different direction, towards confirmation of the facticity of the biological but to a restriction in its scope, a status that makes it both residuary and powerful.

Those who insist on attempting to pack the world into the ill-fitting categories of 'nature' or 'culture' face a further set of problems, which the sex/gender problematic inherits. First, having distributed the determination of characteristics and features between 'nature' and 'culture', there seems no obvious way to reconnect them. Oakley, for example, seeks to explain average differences between men and women in relation to a whole series of variables such as mortality rates, accidents in the home, resistance to the effects of smoking, death from infectious disease, suicide, mental disorder and aggressivity. She refers first to biological factors and second to social factors, so, for example, male aggression, 'To some extent...*is* biologically determined' (1972: 42), but it is also said to be socially determined by culturally specific expectations about male and female behaviour:

> One interpretation of this finding might reasonably be that the biological drives responsible for this sex difference account for the remarkable consistency in female-passive and male-aggressive behaviour. But Kagan and Moss show conclusively that the change in the female's aggressiveness and the male's passivity is associated with, and therefore probably *caused by*, specific social factors. (1972: 65, emphasis added)

In other words, there is a split between the two forms of explanation, which comes to be reflected in the presentation of the argument. Having been separated *grosso modo* by the problematic, the two then have to be reconciled.

Interestingly, however, this process of reconciliation implies a relation of interaction between two distinct but connected sets of processes, rather than a relation of 'fact' to 'value', and could remove the self-containment attributed to biological processes by the original distinction. In short, there are different and contradictory gestures being made at different levels of theorizing, but these gestures are also constitutively intertwined. One of them, which consists of arguing, either historically or logically, for a *general* relation between 'sex' and 'gender', is the effect of making the original distinction. The other, which consists of distributing and reconciling determinations, is the effect of trying to carve out the realm called 'gender', and identifying what is variable and socially determined – 'variability', as Christine Delphy points out, 'being the proof that it is socially determined' (1993: 3).

Because Oakley is trying to establish what belongs to 'gender', both *Sex, Gender and Society* and *Subject Women* make strenuous attempts to explore the detail of biological claims against cultural evidence. Since then, however, with some notable exceptions, few have been concerned to address biological discourses as such, and, as Hughes and Witz (1997) have noted, the bodily has gone into recession. The additional and more important problem is that where attempts have been made to recuperate the body, it continues to carry with it the self-evidence of the original distinction. Hughes and Witz, for example, suggest the importance of considering 'the ways in which women may actually "live" their bodies *precisely as such*' (1997: 56, emphasis in original), in which the combination of quotation marks and emphasis indicates something of the tension the recuperation produces.

Prompted in part by post-structuralism, an awareness of the constructedness of the corporeal, and, in particular, of its discursive character, has extended 'gender' to the body. Indeed, Oakley herself wrote recently that: 'ultimately sex is no more natural than gender' (Oakley, 1997: 30) and briefly discusses some of the theorists whose work we shall be considering in this book, for example Thomas Laqueur and Nelly Oudshoorn. But the combination of gendering with the prior self-evidence of the sexed body now produces a paradox: Hughes and Witz, for instance, argue that 'there may be for women *gendered* modes of bodily materiality', a phrase which is ultimately enigmatic (1997: 56). We also now encounter the notion of 'physical gender' (Davis and Delano, 1992). Within the same theoretical object, the body, the material realm of 'sex' meets the immaterial – now frequently understood as 'discursive' – realm of 'gender'.

In short, making the distinction between two general realms, 'sex' and 'gender', automatically produces the problem of their putative relationship. If 'sex' does not play the determinative role in 'gender' and they are relatively autonomous, what precisely is the link between them? More specifically, why and how does a particular set of morphological and physiological differences (those associated with reproduction) prompt a particular set of social (i.e. gendered) relationships to arise – if that is indeed what they do? Since Oakley made the original distinction, attempts to answer this question have not been notoriously successful. According to her own account, there must be something – some intrinsic quality – about these differences that demands evaluation. And if 'gender' is held to be built upon but distinct from 'sex', what role does the concept of sex play? The answer is that, in many respects, it seems as if 'sex' is simply there to provide the naturalistic referent for the concept of gender. It is as if 'gender' were the sign – or perhaps the signifier – for 'sex'.

This has a further set of consequences. What 'sex' does in relation to 'gender' is to establish the *a priori* unity of the *social groupings* 'women' and 'men'. We might argue that the fact that the terms 'women' and 'men' exist already entails the fact that the groupings exist, but that would be to assume a unity of reference for these terms, every time they are used, which is simply not the case. There are crucial differences between being designated a 'woman' in Shi'ite religious belief, with consequent effects upon religious, social and political practice (Modares, 1981), and being designated a 'woman' in nineteenth-century European philanthropy, or in late twentieth-century radical feminism. Indeed the very transformation of the spelling from 'women' to 'wimmin' in the 1970s was an indicator of this.

That unity of reference is evidently being asserted on another basis, that of the (sexual) identity of 'women' and 'men' allegedly given by biology. The designations of 'woman' described earlier are deemed to be applied to a pre-existent object, 'woman' or 'man', of which the social grouping is merely derivative. In short, the groupings that are presumed to exist are *sexed* groupings.

Discussions of 'sex' usually revolve around reproductive capacity. Yet few would want to draw any *definitional* conclusions as to the social groupings designated as 'women' and 'men' from an ability to reproduce. At any one moment in time, and for the majority of their lives, the vast bulk of people that we might want to call 'women' or 'girls' are incapable of reproducing, being too old, too young, too malnourished, at the wrong moment in their menstrual cycle, lacking the appropriate organ(s), etc. Clearly, the social appurtenance of human beings to these groupings is not really established on the basis of *actual* reproductive capacity. Within the concept of 'sex' is embedded a normative ideal about functional reproductive competency, from which some members of the group 'women' and 'men' inevitably depart, but 'sex' in the everyday sense cannot refer directly to such competency.

Oakley's exploration of 'sex' in both 1972 and 1981 nevertheless focuses on chromosomes, internal and external genitalia, secretions of the endocrine system ('hormones'), boys who have lost their penises and menstrual cycles, all of which are generally considered to be tautologically related to reproductive processes. Her discussion of 'gender', which in both books logically occupies far greater space, focuses on heterosexuality, family relationships, socialization, personality and waged work. If *contra* sociobiology, 'sex' is not the motor force in such things as heterosexuality, family relationships, personality, and so on, but nevertheless constitutes its basis, what does it mean to assert that? How does 'sex' come to be *translated* into 'gender' – literally moved to another place? How does 'nature' become 'culture'?

The simple answer to this, of course is that no such general translation takes place; it is a false problem generated by the distinction. Consider, as a comparison, the concept of 'race'. If one suggests that biological differences between human beings constitute the ontological ground for distinctions between social groupings, the way is open for a series of such claims, some of which have only recently been repudiated. Logically it might be asserted that people with black skins are ontologically different from those with white skins. In such a schema, black skin might be granted facticity. Certain sectors of the population do, after all, suffer a higher incidence of sickle cell anaemia than others. Why should these groups not be regarded as ontologically distinct? Racists, those experts in reading the text of the body, have also been able to detect differences between groups, 'racial' or otherwise, whose skin colour is similar: appearances may be deceptive but a good enough 'science' will always decipher the signifiers for the Jew, the homosexual, the gypsy. What this should alert us to is the potential source of a doctrine of natural difference, and the purposes that might be served, albeit unintentionally, by its maintenance.

In a curious way, then, Oakley's distinction makes the opposite gesture to that which has been made with the concept of 'race', which is now permanently in quotation marks even though it continues to constitute the absent presence within the concept of 'ethnicity'. Discussions of 'ethnicity' have moved towards concepts of racial*ization*. Feminism, by contrast, was to find itself sharpening the ontologization of the corporeal which was already in progress, whilst trying to dismantle its traditional implications. 'Sex' anchors 'gender' in a way that 'race' does not anchor 'ethnicity'. Developing a concept of gender out of a concept of sex has meant not only continuing to occupy fundamentally the same conceptual terrain as one's opponents, but leaving in place a residual but key concept of sex that was to act as a lodestone on 'gender'. As Christine Delphy put it, gender had not 'taken wing' (1984: 24).

Trying to take wing

Delphy's work (1984, 1993) provides a powerful critique of the central assumptions in Oakley's inaugural book. Her comments represent an inversion of Oakley's assumptions about natural difference and, as such, an inversion of one of the most widely held of beliefs, which remain central to sociological writings today, that 'sex' constitutes the basis for 'gender'. Her first radical comment, one that we take up in a number of ways elsewhere in this book, is that far from sex preceding gender, gender precedes sex, in other words that the division of 'sex' marks a *social* division. That which is assumed to be given by biology is really the use of biology for social ends (1984).

This indicates the fact that there are no *necessary* consequences that derive from the 'biological facts' of human reproduction, and, hence, that no necessary social divisions arise from them. Gayle Rubin, she points out,

> maintains that in human society sex inevitably gives birth to gender (Rubin, 1975). In other words, the fact that humans reproduce sexually and that males and females look different contains within itself not only the capacity but also the *necessity* of a *social* division, albeit the social form varies greatly. (1984: 24-5)

What Delphy usefully draws attention to here is that the *non-social* is assumed to generate, in and of itself, a *social* division, which, within the ontological distinctions made by the social sciences, appears anomalous. Nature gives rise to culture. But, according to Delphy, this is erroneous and, failing an account of the mechanism by means of which it occurs, the logical answer is to suggest that both the biological differentiation and the social division are made of the same stuff.

In other words, there are many physical traits but this in no way implies what it means to affirm them. Some people have black skins, some have blue eyes, some are tall and some fat, but this no more causes the social division of people into separate groups on these various bases than the fact that some people are designated 'male'. The fact that some of these characterizations are used to justify social distinctions whilst others are not is itself a demonstration of the arbitrary character of the divisions made and indicates the non-necessity of so doing.

Such an argument is simple and elegant though it runs absolutely counter to the vast slew of sociological writings on gender which almost always affirm exactly the opposite. It also runs counter to those feminists who believe in some essentially feminine qualities that are attached to women by virtue of their sex – as earth mothers, nurturers, eco-warriors, peace protesters and so on. The logic of Delphy's argument is that all this is so much tosh. There may be some association between those marked out as belonging to a particular 'sex' and such characteristics under present arrangements, but in some post-feminist revolutionary future – the outlines of which we can hardly be expected to fill in – such qualities will be randomly distributed among the population. As such, characteristics will not be able to be labelled 'masculine' or 'feminine', since gender will not exist, nor will they be deemed to exhaust the range of human possibilities.

Such a world would be one in which there would be no presumption of consequences to the biological category 'sex', or perhaps we should say that there would be no necessary, no systematic, no general significance given to human procreation. The characteristics that men currently have, in a world in which they operate as dominants, would not be the ones they would possess in the new world. The fear that women and men would become the same or that women would become like men is therefore, in Delphy's view, groundless.

In complaining that gender had not 'taken wing', Delphy was arguing that it has not given rise to the theoretical development that it carried in embryo:

> The concept of gender carries in one word both a recognition of the social aspect of the 'sexual' dichotomy and the need to treat it as such. If gender was from the start a social construction, it was not built on just any thing. It was set on anatomical sex like the beret on the head of the legendary Frenchman. And since its creation, gender, far from taking wing, has on the contrary seemed to cling on to its daddy. (1984: 24-5)

Two things are worth noting about this passage. The first, that the term 'sexual' is in quotation marks, actually produces a paradox. Whilst the scare quotes would seem to throw the reality of the sexual dichotomy into doubt, she also talks of the social *aspect* of the 'sexual' dichotomy. Although this is undoubtedly the result of the attempt to inhabit both the traditional sex/gender problematic and her own point of view simultaneously, we will see this ambivalence over the idea of 'sex' reappear in what follows. The second point is that the relationship of 'gender' to 'sex' is, in her memorable image, that of a signifier to a signified – the beret of the legendary Frenchman is the emblem of his 'Frenchness'. What she will seek to argue is the opposite, that 'sex' is the marker or sign for gender. The division of 'sex' is the product of the hierarchy of gender. By contrast, the way in which gender has continued to be thought of is in terms of the logical and chronological priority of sex.

She is therefore dismayed that writers consistently use composites such as 'sex/gender' or 'sex and gender' – in which the forward slash and the 'and' denote the fact that gender has not separated itself from but always resides with sex. Worse still, whilst sex can be spoken of without gender, gender cannot, it seems, be spoken of without sex, and in that context it becomes obvious that the dependent term 'gender' is but a way of paying lip-service to the social aspects. Delphy believes that sex is being treated as if it were the container and gender its (variable) content and what seems to be the limit of radical thinking is little more than an alteration in content. In making sex the basis of gender, the very existence of genders, of different social positions for males and females, is taken for granted, although its consequences may vary – historically and socially. Politically, therefore, she calls for a far more radical conception: an indifference to sex.

To say that gender produces sex, that a social way of discriminating picks out some set of traits, and uses it in an argument to justify and explain and, indeed, found difference, is in Delphy's work, as in Monique Wittig's, determined by the oppression of women. Wittig (1992) argues that just as the category of 'slave' disappears with the disappearance of slavery so the category of 'sex' disappears with the disappearance of the oppression of women. Hierarchy is, of necessity, prior to division (Delphy, 1993: 7). This, then, is the second fundamental criticism that Delphy's work represents for Oakley's concept of gender. As we have seen, for Oakley in *Sex, Gender and Society,* gender is about difference. It is not, centrally, about oppression, power, discrimination and so on. It certainly allows for an analysis that identifies such things but, unlike Delphy, it does not connect them definitionally. Since Oakley published her inaugural work in 1972, many have sought to redefine gender in precisely these terms. To take one of what could have been innumerable examples, Savage and Witz say that 'the whole point of "gendering" sociological discourse itself has been to establish how male dominance and male power is embedded and sustained by *social* practices, not premised on biological imperatives' (1992: 54, emphasis in original). This is straightforwardly to assert a particular kind of feminist character for a concept of 'gender'.[2] By contrast, in Oakley's original definition, gender should also presumably be useful for exploring societies where no such dominance exists. Delphy (1993) argues that the origins of the notion of 'gender' lie in research by Margaret Mead on the prescribed differences between the sexes and subsequent work on 'sex roles' by broadly Parsonian theorists. Covering both Mead's concern with the differential psychology of the sexes and 'sex role' theory's concern with the division of labour by sex, Oakley's work was predominantly concerned with establishing social determination. The 'value' given to sex differences is not automatically *bound* to a concept of power, even if it is set in a political context.

By contrast, Delphy's usage connects gender and patriarchy – as a system organized around the oppression of women – *definitionally.* Just as it is racism that produces race, so sexism produces sex (as the 'foundation' for gender). We must recognize instead that 'hierarchy forms the foundation for differences – for all differences not just gender' (1993: 6). The feminist project will then necessitate the disappearance of difference (of gender), and hence, of sex. Those who find it difficult to imagine the possibility of a world in which sex differences have no social consequences are those who think that difference comes first and hierarchy second, but for Delphy the two are co-terminous and the disappearance of the one is the disappearance of the other.

Delphy's substantive work has analysed marriage as an economic relationship in which the unpaid labour of women-wives is appropriated by husbands (Delphy and Leonard, 1992). Contrary to the characterizations of radical feminism that believe it to be biologically based or biologically reductionist, Delphy has always insisted on the importance of social relationships to an understanding of men's general oppression of women. She rigorously refuses, unlike, say, Firestone (1971), the common suggestion that it is the fact that women have babies that leads to their enslavement. Such enslavement is always analysed in terms of the social relationships (essentially the marital relation) in which babies are conceived and reared. She has been inspired by Marx's analyses and focused upon the marital relationship as a key relationship of production in a domestic mode of production. This relationship is characterized along Marxist lines: it is a relationship of appropriation, a class relationship in which husbands exploit wives. Whilst Delphy's clear-headed observations on sex/gender (not the core focus of her work) open up the possibility of a considerable advance on the original notions proposed by Oakley, they leave us with a number of puzzles.

Inverting sex and gender

The logic of Delphy's position forces us to recognize that in certain circumstances men are women. Since sex is not the basis of gender – rather gender is the basis of sex – the possession of particular morphological or physiological characteristics (say, genitalia) cannot guarantee membership of the class 'women' or the class 'men'. These positions are social positions into which people with, and people without, such genitalia are recruited. Some 'men' are 'women' and some 'women' are 'men'. Examples of the former might include the batmen to army officers or young boys at the wrong end of the fagging system in some English public schools. That 'men' may be 'women' is entirely consistent with Delphy's writing. Her point may be that such examples are rare and that *typically* women are 'women' even if some men are 'women'. For Delphy a key mechanism here is the fact that only people definitionally labelled 'women' (or more accurately 'female') may be able to enter into the social relationship 'marriage' as wives and it is because only 'women' can be wives that sex is tied to gender. In most cases. It would be recognized that there are other wife-like positions, as in the examples given above.

It is also recognized (although this might not be generally understood) that, in Delphy's concept of patriarchy, oppression does not flow from 'men' to 'women' in an all-encompassing fashion. She accepts that, in domestic modes of production and familial relationships, 'men' appropriate the labour of other men as well as the labour of women-wives. This is particularly so in systems of primogeniture where the labour of younger sons and daughters and wives is appropriated by elder sons. The eldest son may be privileged by systems of inheritance that leave the younger sons landless. For similar reasons, women may be 'men': they may be patriarchs running domestic modes of production appropriating the labour of daughters and sisters as well as that of sons and brothers.

We might also note that patriarchy is not here regarded as a system in which men *qua* men oppress women *qua* women. Men are 'men' only insofar as they are members of a social class, which is what 'men' means here. It is not then a question of the personal characteristics of men – whether they be charming or violent – any more than it is a question of the personality of the bourgeoisie in an analysis of the oppressive relations of capitalism. The manners of men are, in a crucial sense, irrelevant. Men who are running around trying to be 'new men' are wasting their time, in this scenario.

A question frequently raised at this juncture is that of origins. If gender produced sex, how might it have done so and how did gender come into being in the first place? Delphy's answer to such a question is that we do not know:

> The search for 'origins' is a caricature of even this falsely historical procedure, and this is one of the reasons I have denounced it, and why I shall continue to denounce it each and every time it surfaces – which is, alas, all too frequently. (1984: 18)

There are numerous speculations about pre-historical origins and about early hunters and gatherers but according to Delphy, they are simply that: speculations. Since such origins are by definition pre-historical we must deal with what is, not with some fantasy concerning how it might have come about.

In one sense this is a proper reply to the speculative pre-histories of writers such as Desmond Morris who have been subjected to such trenchant critique by Bob Connell (1987: 68-9). In another sense it will not do, if only because, even allowing for the possibility of anthropological ethnocentrism, the account she presents automatically invokes evidence concerning the apparent ubiquity of a distinction between 'women' and 'men'. 'Gender' is everywhere because 'sex' is everywhere – or, at least this is what we tend to assume. To make difference – all difference – an effect of power means that wherever differentiation between human beings occurs, we can assume the existence of a relation of oppression. Since we find an absence of sexual differentiation both unthinkable and empirically and historically unverifiable, this means that we are constrained to consider the possibility that sexual difference (which for Delphy always amounts to sexual exploitation) participates in something rather more universal than we might want to admit. Are we to suppose that there is either some innate proclivity – not of course grounded in sex – on the part of 'men' (who, we must remember, at this point do not even exist) to exploit those who are 'not men' and bond together in order to do so? Alternatively, is there some inevitability about such a pattern of social organization, even though Delphy explicitly denies that there is anything about human reproduction *per se* that engenders gender?

The main problem with Delphy's inversion of the sex/gender problematic – which should perhaps be written gender(sex) – is precisely that it does force us towards a question of origins, because the concept of 'sex' makes an implicit claim of universality, whilst 'gender' points towards historical processes. We might remember at this point that Engels also felt it to be necessary to account for origins in *The Origins of the Family, Private Property and the State*. Where a social relationship – that is to say, a relationship of oppression – is arbitrary, rather than based upon some form of necessity, but apparently ubiquitous, the question that always arises is 'how did it come about?' If 'sex' does not inevitably give rise, by whatever mechanism, to 'gender', but 'gender', *qua* social relationship, gives rise to 'sex', the problem it presents us with is *why*? How is it that, at some moment, a group, presumably without a notion of sex, constitutes itself as a 'gender' group, an appropriating class, and in so doing produces 'sex'? What is the basis for that group's coming to be constituted as a group, and is their discovery of the relevant biological distinctions merely coincidental? Why did the group that we now recognize as 'men' band together to exploit that group that became what we now call 'women'?

It is important to note that the question is only generally posed where the relationship is one of oppression and apparently universal scope, and the presumption is that the key to the nature of the relationship is to be found in its origins. The arbitrariness of the relationship is the sign of its susceptibility to social transformation, in other words of its 'political' character, and the key to its transformation is to be sought in the moment of its birth. If, as Engels asserts, it was born with the advent of private property, its death is to be sought in private property's abolition. By contrast, a relationship that is not one of oppression can, *pace* the palaeontologists, happily lose its origins in the mists of time.

Delphy complains that writers from Murdock to Rubin share the naturalist premise that the first division of labour is founded on the different functions accorded to people through biological sex. She objects to the fact that this fails to explain either the 'natural reason for this division of labour' (1993: 4) or why it is extended into all fields of activity (i.e. it fails to explain gender). However, her own account of causation is that 'men' exploit 'women': hierarchy founds division. But why would they? Is this explanation any less 'naturalist'? Does this beg the question any less vividly than Rubin herself? And is it any more plausible?

One of Delphy's objections is also to difference theorists: those who, like some psychoanalysts, believe that sex has an intrinsic salience which founds difference. Although psychoanalysis has been right to recognize the symbolic importance of sex, what it has failed to take account of, in her view, is that this significance is the product of gender – the *end* of a long progression, not an explanation of that progression. However, given the suspicion over the naturalistic assumptions of Gayle Rubin or the equally naturalistic assumptions of Christine Delphy herself – where our choice is between the salience of sex or the apparently innate proclivity for oppression on the part of men (a group which is only constituted in the founding moment of that oppression) – the analysis of *what is,* and of how that state of affairs gets reproduced in the development of the infant, seems a perfectly proper form of investigation. Indeed, given an understandable reluctance to debate myths of origin, Delphy's own work is precisely of this order: an analysis of what is.

Delphy's work, then, both solicits and refuses the idea of origins. It suggests that the traditional sex/gender problematic takes the very existence of genders for granted (in its concept of 'sex') and she seeks, precisely, to account for their existence, yet her explanation drives us back to an unaccountable origin because it provides neither necessity nor motivation for what it discovers: that 'men' and 'women' only exist because 'men' oppress 'women'.

We might also reflect that this approach to 'gender' and 'sex' is the product of a certain kind of feminism which grounds itself in the idea of power deriving from the domestic mode of production and marriage and marriage-like relationships. In so doing, it constitutes a homogeneous group of men as the main enemy (with a few exceptions). However, it is also one that constantly slips between a technical definition of 'men' – in which 'men' can be 'women' and 'women' can be 'men' – and the commensensical definition of 'men' as people with a penis. The technical definition of 'men', where men may not be men at all, collapses into empirical men seen about you every day.   The possibility of such a collapse is evident in the concession made in *Close to Home*:

> One of the axioms, if not the fundamental axiom, of my approach is that women and men are *social* groups. I start from the incontestable fact that they are socially named, socially differentiated, and socially pertinent, and I seek to understand these social practices. How are they realized? What are they for? It may be (and again this remains to be proven) that women are (also) females, and that men are (also) males, but it is women and men that interest me, not females and males. (Delphy, 1984: 24)

Although 'sex' is assumed to be the marker or sign for 'gender', the fact that the two do not rigorously coincide opens up a gap in the definition of gender as a class-like grouping comprised of biologically marked beings, and allows for a conventional definition of the biological marking.   Either the biological marking is a *function* of the relationship of exploitation or it logically pre-exists, and is independent of, that relationship.   In a sense, however, it seems as if Delphy's argument needs *both* of these to be the case.   In a later book, written with Diana Leonard, we read that:

> Male unpaid workers are exploited not because they are men, but because they are young or old; whereas female unpaid workers (daughters, sisters, mothers and wives) are exploited because they are women. (Delphy and Leonard, 1992: 130)

a position which is both empirically satisfying and theoretically impossible, given that women 'as such' (i.e. as females) *do not exist*, or rather they only exist as the product of a relationship of exploitation.   The problem lies in the ambiguity of the term 'women': it is absolutely compelling to read 'women' as 'females' (i.e. as biological entities) but, given the *theoretical* definition of 'women', that option also has to be refused.

As we noted earlier, Delphy has suggested that the fear that, in the future, women and men would become the same, or that women would become like men, is groundless.   This is true, but for an interesting reason: men and women would not be the same because there would be no such people as 'men' and 'women'.   A society in which human reproduction is not associated with difference will be one that consists of people who are not *identifiable* as men and women.   There would be people with a penis and people without, but since this is not implicated in a relation of difference, where are we to find men and women?   If that agglomeration of things we now call 'sex' is not marked as a set of indicators of difference, they will not allow social recognition of genders. In a society in which having black skin had no social consequences, in what sense would one be able to speak about 'black people'?   Only in the same sense as one currently speaks of green-eyed people.   Such people do not have identities or social characteristics ordered around the colour of their eyes. There are no green-eyed people: there are only people with green eyes.   In Delphy's world there would then be no masculine or feminine identity, no masculinity or femininity and no men and no women. This is certainly a defensible position but what needs to be made clear is that the object of feminism, in this argument, is the elimination of women and it is perhaps this that many writers have found unthinkable.

Finally where does this argument leave 'sex' and 'gender'? 'Gender' is best thought of here as a two-class system, which divides people according to their position within a domestic mode of production. It is not 'about' sex. 'Sex' is connected to 'gender' contingently, via the fact that only women may be wives and only men may be husbands. It is both a necessary means of identification of dominant and dominated, and arbitrary. 'Gender' is a category in which the class 'women' may include what ordinary language calls 'men' and where the class 'men' may include what ordinary language calls 'women'. Our view is that this depends upon a sociological analysis of the relationships between men and women that is unsustainable. This is not the place to produce a full-scale critique of the assumptions or results of materialist feminism. However, we have sketched in some of its limitations, such as its ambivalence about 'sex', its collapse of the abstract into the commonsensical and its simultaneous solicitation and refusal of origins. There are also inevitably problems with its attempt to ground in one relationship (marriage) the large measure of male/female relations – which thus constitutes the primary locus for the subordination of women – and its depiction of society as divided into two huge class groupings, into which everyone is recruited (whether actually married or not). It is an account in which sexuality is reduced to a kind of family work and in which the notion of family system and family structure fans out to embrace the entire social scene (Delphy and Leonard, 1992).

What is more important about this is that, in this inversion of the sex/gender topology, the theoretical compass of 'gender' becomes even more restricted than in the original problematic. In Oakley's version, the tethering of 'gender' to 'sex' crucially constrains the scope of the concept of gender by identifying it with the distribution of the population into two broad categories of human being, to whom things may be done and to whom things may happen. Delphy correctly identifies the limitations of this:

> [gender] now seems to be taken at its most minimal. It is accepted that the 'roles' of the sexes vary according to the society, but it is this *variability* which is taken to sum up the social aspect of sex. The content (gender) may vary from society to society, but the basis (sexual division) does not. (Delphy, 1984: 24-5)

To dispute that basis changes nothing if the existence of the two *social* categories goes unquestioned. Even though 'women' can be 'men' and 'men' can be 'women', the continuing presence of 'sex', even as an effect and as a sign, universalizes genders. Attributing a primacy to 'gender', understood as a social division, in effect merely exacerbates the problem originally detected by Delphy herself. To echo her, the very existence of genders continues to be taken as given, not as an inevitable outgrowth of biology perhaps, but as a function of apparently unmotivated but universal 'domestic modes of production'. Where the traditional sex/gender problematic allowed 'gender' to represent the frills and furbelows of a minimalist base, 'sex', Delphy's version produces 'gender' as a very limited if omnivorous feature of social relations and this shuts down the potential of the concept of gender still further.

Whether 'gender' precedes 'sex' or 'sex' precedes 'gender' is in some measure immaterial if 'sex' provides the grounding of gender. For Delphy, that grounding is a political rather than a theoretical question – in other words it is a matter of power rather than ontology – but it is nonetheless ubiquitous for all that. In point of fact, as we have seen, Delphy maintains both positions simultaneously, one, more commonsensical, in which 'sex' refers to what we routinely take it to be and another in which 'sex' dissolves into 'gender', and both are equally necessary. Without the former, the meaning of 'gender' would tend to disappear entirely. In that sense it seems as if gender simply *cannot* take wing. It is inevitable that it be tethered. So is it possible to rethink what has hitherto been described as 'gender' without grounding it in 'sex'? Before we can answer that question, perhaps the time has come to confront the obdurate presence and apparent consistency of 'sex'. It is to this that we now turn.

Notes

[1] *Sex, Gender and Society* was re-issued in 1985 with a new foreword in which Oakley wrote: 'It is consoling to note that nothing has happened since 1972 to alter the basic themes.' This edition does not therefore seem to us to mark a significant departure in thinking. Be that as it may, our concerns are with what the original 1972 edition sought to establish and succeeded in bringing into being. And Oakley was correct: writing in the intervening years had not displaced her basic assumptions.

[2] By the time Oakley writes 'A Brief History of Gender' in *Who's Afraid of Feminism*, however, she makes it clear that the relation of gender to power is absolutely central but also 'one of the most problematic aspects of its history' (Oakley, 1997: 53).

3 Unpicking the Knot[1]

As the previous chapter indicated, the importance of Christine Delphy's endeavour lies in her querying the naturalistic basis of 'gender' in 'sex'. 'Sex', which, these days, appears to be both ubiquitous and obvious, is, for Delphy, the product of a set of social relationships. The existence of a biological marker is the product of the 'recognition' induced by the presence of sex-classes. Everybody 'knows' that men are men and women are women. The power of this obviousness is to be seen in the expert analyses of sociology no less than in the folk knowledge of the person in the street. Both sociology and folk knowledge begin with, and take for granted, a reality whose facticity neither cares to consider – with a few remarkable exceptions. In this chapter we explore attempts to analyse just how this 'obviousness' is produced.

We remarked on the fact that 'sex' in the everyday sense cannot coincide with *actual* reproductive capacity. We know that the people we routinely call 'women' and 'men' are simply not being defined in these terms; nevertheless we *also* know that functional reproductive capacity operates as a normative ideal within what we ordinarily call 'sex', and thus within the definition of the groupings. That normative ideal will even mark stereotypical images of 'women' and 'men' with characteristics that are socially 'recognized' to indicate reproductive potency; within the explanatory framework of sociobiology these will be the presentational signs, be they morphological or vestimentary, that are assumed to signal fertility to potential mates. By the same token, however, a large number of 'women' and 'men' will depart from the norm, and yet they will confidently be identified as 'women' and 'men'. They will be located absolutely unproblematically on the basis of an unquestioned matter of fact: that there are two, and *only* two, sexes. How then does this overwhelming confidence in the reality of 'two sexes' get produced? How does the sense of the facticity of sex itself, in all its solidity and obduracy, come into being?

If one were to ask most people in our society how the sex of a person could be determined, they would most likely reply 'by their genitals'. However, we rarely see the genitalia of many of the people whom we meet every day; we might have friends whom we have known for years whose genitalia we will never see and we interact with, read about, see on television and in films literally thousands of people whose sex seems to us obvious and unremarkable. Furthermore, although we assume that we are using biological criteria when we classify human beings into one of two sexes, biological definitions of 'sex' do not refer *primarily* to the presence of particular genitalia, but to something that cannot be seen: the role of a person in the business of sexual reproduction, for which the genitalia act as an index. Genital morphology certainly *is* used in the process of determining sex, but only at birth, as part of a process of initial assignment. Add to that the fact that, as we have indicated, for a whole variety of reasons, the majority of people that we might want to call 'women' or 'men' might not be in a position to reproduce and we have a situation in which the everyday obviousness of 'sex' and our confidence in its clear and unambiguous presence requires explanation.

It seems, then, that in allocating another to what we have hitherto thought of as a sex, we are referring neither to functional capacity, nor to genital morphology. It is only when that deceptively easy process of allocation is interrupted – either because of a process of reflection or because of a potential ambiguity in what we are assessing – that we become conscious of the *process* of making a judgement, our confidence may momentarily slip, and we find ourselves casting around for cues. If the process can be interrupted and thrown into doubt, how then is this sense of certainty normally generated? One answer is that the 'reality' of two sexes is created and sustained, essentially, by a complex process of *attribution* – an interactive process identified and explored by Suzanne Kessler and Wendy McKenna in their all too neglected ethnomethodological study of gender, published in 1978. There is, of course, also a history to 'sex' and hence a history to these processes, which we shall consider in due course. First, though, we focus upon one important analysis of contemporary (i.e. post 1860), and specifically Western processes and, in particular, upon the deployment of biological knowledge. By using a range of bodily 'facticities', these processes produce – out of potential uncertainty – quite definite conclusions as to the reality of human sex.

An ethnomethodology of sex/gender

Kessler and McKenna's key argument is simple. It is that what they refer to as 'gender attribution' is *primary* in all other components of gender, in which they include *even* 'those aspects of being a woman (girl) or a man (boy) that have traditionally been viewed as biological' (1978: 7). They use 'gender', rather than 'sex' to emphasize their view that, as they put it, 'the element of social construction is primary in *all* aspects of being female or male' (ibid., emphasis added). Thus 'gender' encompasses everything that we would normally divide, sociologically, between 'sex' and 'gender'. By attribution they mean the active process of 'deciding whether someone is male or female, every time we see a new person' (1978: 2). In keeping with the tenets of ethnomethodology, their interest is in the daily production of the reality known in sociology, and increasingly in the folk world (in a way which is interchangeable with 'sex') as 'gender'. For them, therefore, gender *is that* process and nothing more: 'Gender, as we have described it, consists of members' methods for attributing and constructing gender' (1978: 162). Gender is to be regarded as a 'practical accomplishment' achieved through particular social practices that create it routinely, and such practices are necessarily reiterative. They are continuously in play and gender is governed by present participles in which one is always doing gender, accomplishing it, making it. Gender is process, not product and gender *attribution* forms the foundation for understanding all of its other components, amongst which they list such things as assignment, identity, role, and gender-based categories, such as heterosexual/homosexual.

Every day gender attribution goes on smoothly despite the fact that there are no characteristics that are always, and without exception, the property of one gender. This is to say that there are no psychic or behavioural characteristics (like crying, aggressivity, or passivity), no visible features (whether physical, like beards – the bearded lady is still a lady – or cultural, like skirts) no non-visible characteristics (like genitals) and no – to the lay person – unexaminable characteristics (like gonads or chromosomes) that unambiguously inform us of a person's gender. A biology textbook might define males for us as 'sperm producers' but this is of little assistance in gender attribution. Despite these difficulties, we nevertheless make such attributions without effort, for one hundred per cent of the people that we meet, and, ordinarily, without hesitation. And although, having made it, we might qualify it by noticing a gesture or a way of walking and remarking that 'He is a rather effeminate man', or observing some facial hair or a deep voice and thinking 'She is a rather masculine woman', such qualifications nevertheless rarely extend to the thought that '*Maybe* he is a man' (1978: 2). In other words, the categories are apparently clear, mutually exclusive and, for us, entirely exhaustive. They admit of no ambiguity or uncertainty, and ambiguity or uncertainty about attribution merely prompts the search for sufficient cues for the decision to become *un*ambiguous. Neither are we able to resist making such a classification in the first place. All human beings, alive or dead, are believed by us to belong to one or other category.

This business of gender attribution is more than mere inspection but it involves a process so taken for granted, so everyday, that even to draw attention to it opens the writer to the charge of triviality. However, the claim that this process is central to the whole issue of gender has very radical implications. Such a conception is diametrically opposed to that of Oakley where, as we have seen, gender is both the outgrowth of, and something that has been differentiated from, sex. Here there is no virtue in differentiating 'sex' from 'gender': the distinction 'is a technical one, applicable to scientists in the laboratory and some textbooks, but little else' (1978: 7). Like Delphy – but for rather different reasons – sex itself is seen as the product of gendering processes, in this case, of gender attribution. It cannot therefore be regarded as its *raison d'être*.

Gender attribution is thus the continuous interactive process whereby one both presents oneself as gendered and is allocated a gender by everyone with whom one interacts. This process results in the obvious 'fact' that the other person is either 'male' or 'female'. The knowledge used to establish that fact is part of what Schutz once termed 'cook book knowledge', the practical knowledge that people within a society possess in order to operate successfully – their *methods* for operating. People who present ambiguous or contradictory signs, amongst those routinely deployed in the process of presenting oneself as male or female, produce unease. They trouble what is normally a smooth business but, by so doing, they may bring those processes to light. It is for this reason that transsexuals, in the process of transition from one gender to another, have been of such interest. Such people have an especially conscious relationship to what is typically taken for granted knowledge: particularly in the early stages of their transition, they are in the position of having to learn what must be done in order to be attributed the gender they desire. To their surprise, Kessler and McKenna discovered that there was actually no prohibition on asking people, albeit sometimes in a joking manner, what gender they were, although those asked reported unease and embarrassment 'indicating that something had gone wrong with the interaction' (Kessler and McKenna, 1978: 3).

Kessler and McKenna assert that 'what it means to *be* a male or a female is merely another way of asking how one *decides* whether another is male or female' (ibid.). Hence an apparently ontological question is said to be answerable in terms of social processes. The study of gender is then, first and foremost, the study of the methods of assigning it, and the method for investigating those methods is essentially to devise ways of asking people to make attributions and examining how they do so.

One typically ethnomethodological investigation was to play a version of 'Twenty Questions' with people and observe the rule-guided behaviours they used to infer the gender of an individual from a random set of yes/no answers to questions about their characteristics. Interestingly, only 25 per cent asked about genitalia, with most concentrating on behaviour or 'secondary gender characteristics'. When questioned as to why they had not asked about genitalia, they equated this with a form of cheating, tantamount to asking directly 'Is this person male [or female]?' Some of those who did pose such questions refused to ask any more, on the basis that none were necessary, in spite of inconsistencies in the other answers they had received. A few respondents, however, strove hard to make sense of inconsistencies in the answers to the questions and were led to postulate bearded women, men who were transvestites and a hermaphrodite or a transsexual. Of those who did ask directly about genitalia, most asked about the presence of a penis.

Kessler and McKenna came to a number of conclusions as a result of this experiment, the most interesting of which, confirmed by the experience of transsexuals, is that, once an attribution is made, almost any piece of information can be filtered through it and made sense of. Following Garfinkel (1967), they describe the existence of 'cultural genitals':

> The cultural genital is the one which is assumed to exist and which, it is believed, should be there. As evidence of 'natural sexuality,' the cultural genital is a legitimate possession. Even if the genital is not present in a physical sense, it exists in a cultural sense if the person feels entitled to it and/or is assumed to have it. (1978: 154)

This is the way in which they explain a child who sees a picture of a person in a suit and who says: 'It's a man because he has a pee-pee' (ibid.). They discuss this in relation to research by Birdwhistell which denies the importance of genitalia and so-called 'secondary sexual characteristics' as gender markers for human beings, suggesting instead that non-verbal behaviours such as facial expression, movement and body posture are predominant (1978: 155-7). This is so marked that post-operative transsexuals can find the attributions made of them to be all *too* successful:

> Janet, a male-to-female transsexual, described a visit to a gynecologist who, not knowing that Janet was a transsexual, told her that there was a cyst on one of her ovaries. Janet protested that this was impossible. The doctor explained that he ought to know since he was a gynecologist, whereupon she countered with, 'Well, I ought to know; I'm a transsexual.' This example not only attests to the excellence of male-to-female genital surgery, but it also provides a good illustration of the construction of gender. The doctor, having decided by visual inspection (undoubtedly prior to Janet's undressing) that she was female, would interpret anything else he saw or felt in the light of that attribution. The swelling beneath her abdominal walls must be a cyst; there was no reason to expect it to be a prostate gland. As a nurse who heard this story so aptly phrased it: 'If you hear hoofbeats, you don't look for elephants.' (1978: 130-1)

One may wonder, of course, at why a transsexual is visiting a gynaecologist in the first place, but what it does illustrate so beautifully is the power of attribution processes. What they put in place is the dichotomization of the genders, with subsequent evidence being fitted into the presumed allocation. Given that everything would have conspired for the gynaecologist to think Janet a woman, other possible cues that negate that fact will not be noticed. As another transsexual quoted by Kessler and McKenna said, 'Gender is an anchor, and once people decide what you are they interpret everything you do in the light of that' (1978: 6).

A second study carried out by Kessler and McKenna, which they called the 'overlay study', was aimed at establishing which cues were picked up and how, using bodily outlines and the manipulation of combinations of morphological characteristics and clothing. Predictably, cues were found not to work additively – that is to say on the basis of a process of ratiocination – but in a gestalt-like fashion. Amongst the numerous findings of this study, however, was one that will perhaps seem a little more surprising:

> The predisposition to think and guess 'male' irrespective of external stimuli is reflected in other cultural phenomena such as the use of the generic 'he.' Had our participants been asked to attribute gender to an inkblot, they might have responded 'male' more often than 'female.' However, the participants were not just 'thinking male' (making judgements irrespective of stimuli) but actually 'seeing male,' filtering the external stimuli through 'androcentric' gender attributions. In other words, not only is there a tendency to respond with a 'male' answer, but on practical occasions people's perceptions are that such stimuli look 'male.' (1978: 149-50)

As they point out, although one might be able to attribute this to poor draughtsmanship on the drawings used in the experiment, overall 57 per cent of the figures with breasts were seen as 'male'. What is striking about this study is the relative difficulty Kessler and McKenna had in securing 'female' attributions, as compared with the decisive weight carried by 'male' characteristics, particularly the penis. This leads them to suggest that there is in effect only one cultural genital, which is the penis, with women tending to be attributed the lack of a penis, a conclusion that will not come as news to Freudians.[2]

Young children also proved to be 'better' at attributing gender to clothed than to unclothed figures, presumably because genitalia do not yet feature largely in the methods they use for attributing gender. In fact children supply some of the most interesting insights into the ways in which we learn to make attributions:

> Jesse (six years old) was asked to draw a picture of a boy and a picture of a girl. When questioned by an interviewer: 'What makes her a girl?', he answered, 'Because there is a sun and girls go out on sunny days.' 'What makes this other drawing a picture of a boy?' 'Because I colored it and the man is out tonight. He has to work at night. The moon and he is outside.'

Loren (4½ years old) explained that his drawing of a boy differed from his drawing of a girl 'because it (the boy) has no long hair; cause the eyes are different; they are rounder; because he is bigger than a girl. She (the girl) has long hair; and she has little curlies in her hair; and she has ears; and because she is smaller' (1978: 81). The answers the children gave also did not correspond to the pictures that they drew: 'Jesse's picture of a boy also has a sun in it; Loren's girl has round eyes and his boy has ears too' (ibid.). What is clear is that there are learning and sense-making activities in play here, as well as processes of accounting and rationalization, which are distinct from the processes involved in the production of the drawings. What this suggests to Kessler and McKenna is that the social construction of the reality of gender is a developmental process through which children acquire, in much the same way as they acquire language, knowledge of the rules required to attribute gender successfully. Initially the 'reasons' they give for an attribution can be as idiosyncratic as a long tongue or webbed feet; adults by contrast 'know' what the appropriate signs are and that the signs are invariant. This knowledge builds up and solidifies into a set of certainties about gender which Kessler and McKenna calls 'incorrigible propositions'.

According to Kessler and McKenna, there are three such 'incorrigible propositions' that are central to the methods used in gender attribution and which, as we shall show in more detail later on, are historically specific. The first is that gender is a dichotomous category and every human being must be a member of one or other gender. They have to belong to one or other grouping and, even in the grave, they remain members of a gender category. Second is the rule of gender invariance: ordinarily one does not, and may not, switch from one gender to another. In the last twenty years or so, there has been considerable media attention focused upon male to female transsexuals and some attention paid to female to male. One might then say that in our own time the rule of gender invariance has weakened, but what transsexuals illustrate more clearly is the continued existence of the first of the incorrigible propositions, namely that the existence of a sharp dichotomy characterizes the gender order. One has to belong on one or other side of the divide. There is no gender continuum and no room for ambiguity. Transsexuals are not so much threats to this proposition as the victims of it.

The existence of the rule of gender invariance means that, when a gender attribution has been made, it is difficult to shift it. As in the case of the first of the propositions, however, a challenge to it has recently emerged in the form of 'transgender' or 'third gender' persons, but these can be regarded rather more as refusals to belong to either of the available gender categories than as challenges to the principle of gender invariance, because of the third 'incorrigible proposition'. This is that members' methods for attributing gender are grounded in an assumedly biological reality. It is in that 'reality' that the ultimate truth of gender is assumed to be located and biology acts as a final arbiter for any given allocation (and not, for example, a deity, or some other criterion). What is interesting about the emergence of 'transgender' persons, though, is that they implicitly draw attention – because theirs is a form of resistance to classification – to the fact that an allocation is being made, and that that allocation is decisive and obdurate.

The primacy of gender attribution

We have noted that the argument that gender is fundamentally tied to gender attribution and presentation has been coupled to the assertion that attribution is *primary* in understanding all the other components of gender. Indeed some of these components make no sense without the presence of gender attribution. If we were to consider gender identity or gender role or the gender-based categories available to our society for describing people – transsexuals/non-transsexuals; transvestites/non-transvestites; homosexuals/heterosexuals; feminine/masculine – all of these are dependent upon gender attribution. Consider the categories of homosexual and heterosexual. These refer to people who have been classified on the basis of their gender and the gender of their partners. But attaching this designation – homosexual/heterosexual – depends upon the *prior* attribution of a gender to those so designated. Knowing someone is homosexual does not tell you if they are male or female (the designation 'lesbian' itself depends upon the attribution of female gender to a person and to that person's partner(s)). Gender attribution is a necessary condition for the application of the label 'homosexual': it 'determines the label' as Kessler and McKenna put it (1978: 15) and the label depends upon at least two attributions. In that sense, the primacy of gender attribution is about the *logical* priority it has in making sense of the category.

The primacy of attribution can also be seen in all of the other components referred to above. When a child is born it is assigned a gender and this is merely a particular case of gender attribution, typically involving nothing more than a visual inspection of external genital morphology.[3] Such an attribution may now be made from the inspection of an ultrasound scan of the foetus. The process may have been technologized but it is essentially the same. Gender role, for example, is assumed to be related to a prior gender assignment and understanding of its appropriateness or otherwise is premised upon that process of assignment, which produces the *fact* of 'maleness' or 'femaleness'. Gender identity, as defined by Kessler and McKenna, is essentially the self-attribution of gender, which may or may not use the same rules as those used for attributing gender to others. For example, a person wanting to make the transition from the male to the female gender may typically ascribe the male gender to other people using cues and beliefs that rest, ultimately, on the view that males possess a penis. However, in attributing gender identity to himself, he may disregard the importance of the possession of a penis and attribute a female gender identity to himself on other grounds. Garfinkel's case history of Agnes, which we discuss in Chapter 9, represents just such an instance.

The primacy of gender attribution thus refers primarily to the ways in which it can be seen to play a foundational role for social interaction and for the understanding of various facets of gender which are logically dependent upon it. In order meaningfully to interpret aspects of another's identity or behaviour, or, for that matter, our own, we have first to make a gender attribution. Kessler and McKenna refer to the unease people experience in attempting to interact with those who seem to them to be ambiguous, those for whom a classification has not been able to be made. This they take as evidence for the way in which gender pervades everyday life.

However, primacy clearly also refers to the dominance in *our* culture of assumptions about dichotomy, invariance and a physical basis for gender, and it is this that predisposes us to the sense of there being an objective reality to the two biological 'sexes': 'In the process of attributing "male" or "female," dichotomous physical differences are constructed, and once a physical dichotomy has been constructed it is almost impossible to eliminate sociological and psychological dichotomies' (1978: 164). By contrast, they say that they will argue 'that the fact of seeing two physical genders is as much of a socially constructed dichotomy as everything else' (1978: 6). And although they argue that the ways in which biologists distinguish between the 'sexes' is very different from everyday gender attribution processes, the criteria that biologists *do* use are rooted in those everyday processes. This means that science 'justifies (and appears to give grounds for) the already existing knowledge that a person is either a woman or a man and that there is no problem differentiating between the two' (1978: 163).

As with Delphy's account, this is precisely to invert the expected ontological order between biological and social, 'sex' and 'gender', and it implies that the empirical construction of difference is pre-emptive and presumptive. This leads Kessler and McKenna to query, for example, the value of 'sex difference' research in favour of a non-dichotomized investigation of biological factors in behavioural differences (1978: 72).

Much of the effort of their book, and the impact of their use of ethnomethodology as a theoretical framework, is therefore directed towards unhinging some of the most powerful assumptions in our culture. Consequently, they also devote a whole chapter of their work to the phenomenon of the berdache – a gendered category, largely found in Native American culture, which goes beyond the dichotomous model we take for granted – in an attempt to demonstrate that what we take to be inevitable and necessary features of gender construction are not necessarily to be found elsewhere. What is contingent or correlative in relation to gender for us might be taken by others to be its defining characteristic, or might indeed not even feature in their construction of the world.

But Kessler and McKenna face difficulties in the endeavour to explore the phenomenon of the berdache. They try strenuously, and with some difficulty, to extricate the anthropological data they are examining from what they describe as the positivist framework which takes it for granted that there are two genders in the dichotomous form in which we understand them, always, and in every culture. They are therefore appropriately critical of the ethnocentric assumptions made by some ethnographers in the field. But precisely because of this ethnocentrism, the answers to the queries they raise in relation to the berdache are necessarily inconclusive. Without an understanding of how gender was construed in another culture that is sufficiently distanced from our own incorrigible propositions, it is difficult to know what to make of the ethnographic findings, '[s]ince anthropologists used their own culture's gender dichotomy as criteria for evaluating the berdache' (1978: 28). Even where anthropologists have sought to get around the problem by a literal translation of the labels applied to the berdache (which come in a multiplicity of forms from culture to culture), it is not clear what we should make of these and of such things as the variable application of pronouns (1978: 35). For example, how are we to interpret a label like 'human-it', which seems to bear no reference to anything we might recognize as a 'gendered' appellation?

> To further complicate the analysis, there is not always a correspondence between the pronouns used to address individuals and the pronouns used to refer to them. A particular hermaphrodite, whom Edgerton (1964) observed, was usually referred to as a woman but was addressed as 'serrer' which means 'male and female yet neither male nor female.' This is analogous, according to Edgerton , to our concept of neuter and was a pejorative when addressed to a 'normal' person. His analogy is, we think, a forced one, since the translation clearly goes beyond our sense of neuter. 'Neuter' means no gender and we assign this only to nonhuman objects. The translation of 'serrer' implies a concept for which we have no term. This introduces the seemingly insurmountable problem of concept translation through language translation. (1978: 34-5)

Beyond this also lie more general methodological problems concerning hearsay evidence, representativeness, the potential prejudices of non-anthropological investigators and the attempt at an intelligible rendition of data to members of one's own culture, to name but a few.

From Kessler and McKenna's own work, then, it is not clear that claiming a primacy for gender attribution is permissible for any more than our own society. By their own account, the rules of clear dichotomy, of invariance and of a biological basis appear to be historically and culturally specific. We might even hazard a guess that the primacy of gender attribution they detect is *itself* linked to these features. This is not to say that gendering may not be a very significant feature of social relations in other cultures, but the primacy identified by Kessler and McKenna seems so strongly tied to the nature of its incorrigible propositions that it would probably be unwise to generalize the claim beyond our own social order.

They nevertheless tentatively assert that assignment of individuals at birth to categories in accordance with some concept of gender seems to be universal, as is the understanding of individuals as to what category they belong to – whether it coincides with their original assignment or not. They assert that there has never been a report of a culture without such categorization (1978: 39). From our vantage point, however, a universal claim of this kind gets referred back to biological exigencies. But Kessler and McKenna explicitly deny that there is any biological imperative that demands such categorization, which imperative they reduce, at most, to a necessity for sperm and egg cell carriers to identify one another, something which would not require extension beyond the years of fertility, never mind beyond death. Indeed, whether or not successful reproduction would require sperm and egg cell carriers to be able to identify one another is a moot point – random promiscuity would probably work just as well.

In short, the universality of gender categories *of one kind or another* is not being asserted on the basis of the saliency of aspects of human morphology or the necessary impact of reproductive processes on human society. Indeed, the biological or morphological rationales provided by people for their attributions are – correctly in our view – regarded by Kessler and McKenna as an index of the rules for giving acceptable *evidence* for the making of attributions within a particular culture, and, as they say: 'Giving a reason is not the same [...] as making the categorization in the first place' (1978: 6). Like Delphy, they argue against Rubin's (1975) claim that it is the existence of the two biological 'sexes' that comes to be transformed into the social categories of gender. Rubin's analysis, they say, still takes for granted the objective reality of two biological 'sexes' (1978: 163).

Yet there nevertheless appears to be a partial answer to the question of universality given by Kessler and McKenna under the auspices of biology, which is not dissimilar to that of Rubin. They cite research by Lewis and Weintraub which suggests that infants under a year in age are capable of making some kind of differentiation between pictures of 'female' and 'male' infants and that these differentiations are more accurate than those of adults (1978: 166-7). 'Is it possible,' they ask, 'that there is some ability which human beings have to differentiate sperm and egg cell carriers which is then overlayed and superceded by learned members' methods for constructing gender? (1978: 167) Hence the difficulty that transsexuals allegedly have in 'passing' in front of small children (ibid.). 'Differentiation' in this instance would mean no more than that another was the same or different from oneself, and there is no necessary coincidence between being an egg carrier and being female and being a sperm carrier and being male. Yet to say this is to come up against the fact that, given the pre-eminence of biological knowledge for us, these are virtually tautologically definitional criteria for the two categories of 'male' and 'female'.

This account also sits uneasily with their demonstration that children *need to learn* how to attribute gender and acquire the repertoire of reasons that constitute acceptable evidence, which is clear from the fact that the accounts map onto one another. The way in which these two forms of explanation – the one about members' methods and the other about biologically based capabilities – are held apart is by referring to the one as gender attribution and to the other (distinguishing between 'sperm and egg cell carriers') as 'gender' differentiation, [4] with the term gender being used because no other appropriate term exists. Their rationale for this is that it cannot be assumed that infants are making gender attributions before they have acquired that culture's methods for 'seeing and doing' gender (1978: 187). Their argument is that 'male' and 'female' are not the same thing as 'sperm and egg cell carriers', for 'male' and 'female' are clearly *social* constructions, which are not co-terminous with the capacity for reproduction. From a biological standpoint, of course, this lack of coincidence is dealt with by means of the ideal *telos* of reproduction. 'Males' and 'females', whatever their individual reproductive capabilities or status, only exist *as such*, as far as the biological sciences are concerned, because of the requirement of the species to reproduce.

The fact that we can read this question of 'sperm and egg cell carriers' ambiguously here, in terms both of the post-hoc construction of biological criteria by which members' method for attributing gender are justified *and* as the reflection of a biological 'reality', is crucial. On the one hand, 'sperm and egg cell carriers' might itself be the retrospective interpretation *we* make of what babies are doing, in the light of our categorizations of human beings into two genders. On the other hand, the suggestion seems to be that we are referring to some innate biological form of recognition related to reproduction. But of course the very fact of making that distinction between 'gender' differentiation and gender attribution means that, precisely, the question of why gender is universal is not answered.

As in the case of Delphy, it is the extension of sociality *qua* construction to what would normally be construed as unproblematically universal, namely everything that surrounds reproduction, that automatically prompts the question 'why?' Why, if gender is a construct, is it universal? 'Gender' differentiation seems like a partial, if tangential answer to that question. In a sense, 'gender' differentiation is the residuary 'biological' category once sex has been rewritten as 'sex'. What we shall find, however, is that the dilemma of how to reconcile (or not) 'male' and 'female' with 'sperm and egg cell carrier' bespeaks a broader one, for it is specifically in relation to biology that the difficulties attendant upon their position become more evident.

Biology and gender

Kessler and McKenna argue that, in our society, biological knowledge holds a special place in members' methods for attributing gender. Within biology – a term they use inclusively to refer to genetics and the study of chromosomes, anatomy, endocrinology, and so on – 'sex' is a term used generally to refer to people's roles in reproductive processes. Nevertheless their concern is that we should understand that 'sex' is the product of particular practices by particular members (biologists) who, like all other members, *socially* construct the fact of seeing two distinct 'sexes' as a result of these practices. Even the biologist Lillie, who, writing in 1932, denies there is any such entity as 'sex', insists that 'in nature is a dimorphism within species into male and female individuals, which differ with respect to contrasting characters' and that sex 'is merely a name for our total impression of the differences' (Lillie cited in Kessler and McKenna, 1978: 74). There is a prior belief in differentiation, which then prompts the search for its basis. Hence Kessler and McKenna's expansion of the term 'gender' because of their emphasis on the primacy of social construction in *all* aspects of being female or male, including the biological. Since 'gender' is a term designed to refer to social aspects of men and women such an expanded usage is logical. In short, they argued (in 1978), what Ann Oakley herself finally came to argue (in 1997), that 'cultural construction applies also to sex' (Oakley, 1997: 48).

The expansion of the scope of 'gender' (and sometimes the term) to cover aspects previously regarded as the province of sex is one that recurs again and again in recent writings on sex/gender and we will revisit it in variant forms in the work of Goffman, Laqueur and Butler. For Kessler and McKenna it means that they *almost* seem to view the 'cultural/biological distinction traditionally associated with the usage of gender versus sex' as no more than a matter of the nomenclature used to distinguish what is investigated in a laboratory setting (1978: 7). But not quite. Although the distinction is technical from an ethnomethodological viewpoint, it is nevertheless argued to have an important influence on members' methods for attributing gender and, precisely because it does so, they devote a whole chapter to discussing that which falls under that heading (what is conventionally described as sex) and to debating the interrelationships between biology and other aspects of gender. In short they simultaneously deny and maintain the distinction.

If we view science as a way of constructing the world, then the question of whether gender is totally biological or totally environmental can be seen, according to Kessler and McKenna, in a new way: it is like asking if a coin is 'really' heads or tails. Gender is at once totally environmental and totally biological. This is a rather difficult statement to get to grips with: is it intended to indicate that it is impossible to divorce a biological organism from the environment that it inhabits, that gender is *simultaneously* environmental and biological? It seems not. As ethnomethodologists, Kessler and McKenna present the issue somewhat differently. In other words, depending on the methods and assumptions that are applied to what is being observed, gender is whatever we make of it. In seeing the biological sciences as supplying information on the foundation for all behaviours, we tend to overlook the fact that they represent only one of an infinite number of ways of seeing the world. This does not mean that reality should or should not be constructed in this way; it only means that it is important to be aware that it is constructed. (Kessler and McKenna, 1978: 42)

This is potentially confusing: in keeping with ethnomethodological assumptions, they appear to maintain an epistemological agnosticism about the knowledge claims of biology as a whole ('gender is whatever we make of it') but the chapter itself proceeds to engage with these knowledge claims, both 'by presenting the biological facts about gender and what they suggest about the biological foundations of gender identity, role and attribution, within a biological framework' and by mounting 'a critical analysis of biologists' views of gender as they reflect the process of a socially constructed gender dichotomy' (1978: 44). For example, Table 3.1 (1978: 69) summarizes their view of the 'Relationship between Biological Factors in the Development of Gender and the Components of Gender'. They find, for instance, that there is 'no' relationship between chromosomes and gender identity and that there is a 'possible' relationship between prenatal hormones and gender role. Nevertheless, they make a distinction between discussing the relationship between (biological) sex and gender from within a 'positivist perspective' (as here) and from a perspective that regards both as 'a social construction' (1978: 68). This distinction enables them to argue from the premises of biological assumptions concerning, for example, the influence of prenatal hormones on gender identity and role (1978: 70-1). To say, as they do, that biological knowledge is 'socially constructed' is not then apparently to say that what it describes does not have effects or even that it is 'untrue'. On the face of it, though, they do not commit themselves as to the truth of biologists' claims, which is what one would expect: phenomenological (and, hence, ethnomethodological) approaches, precisely, *suspend belief.* They 'bracket the natural attitude' in order to investigate how that natural attitude is constituted. Kessler and McKenna therefore attend to the fact that the biologists' reality is real for biologists and indeed has a wider currency in our own culture. Yet debating the potential contributions of prenatal hormones to gender role would seem to presuppose an acceptance of the premises of biology, not merely its 'positivism' – its epistemological premises – but its ontology.

Their interest, of course, is not primarily in asking questions about knowledge claims but in examining the methodical, interactional work which constructs the reality that is lived, whether that be the reality of Western biologists or of a Yaqui shaman. In practice, however, this results in the two strategies we have identified, both of which challenge biological claims. The first finds them engaging with biological debates *within* what they term a positivist framework, as we have noted. This has them debating the logic of such arguments and assessing the evidence that is put forward. For example, they point out that, if biologists believe that male and female human biology causes behavioural differences, we must first establish that there really are marked differences in such behaviour. They refer to the fact that even writers well known for sex difference research, such as Maccoby and Jacklin, conclude that such research ends up discovering that few reliable differences exist (1978: 72). Or, again, they suggest that, if one really wanted to know about the effects of gender hormones on gender role, the best research strategy would be to look for intragender differences. This would enable one to control for any other gender differences, which is not possible in intergender comparisons. Research, they suggest, should match persons on all the relevant biological characteristics except for the level of a particular hormone and one could then investigate differences in gender role and look for correlations (1978: 72).

But, if their first strategy is to inhabit the logic of the arguments, the second is to question the 'incorrigible propositions' that biologists hold by virtue of being members of the culture. (Note that both of the examples above *also* involve the querying of gender dichotomy, as one of the incorrigible propositions). They also point out that biological facts have a history and give the example of developments in the methods used to determine death (1978: 42). Like gender, one of the incorrigible propositions relating to scientific (but not religious) views on death is its dichotomous character: one either is or is not dead. However, recent medical developments have disturbed the straightforward scientific attribution of death. Is someone whose heart beats only because they are attached to a respirator alive or dead? How may a person have 'live' organs (necessary for transplants) but be 'dead'? Can EEGs which measure brain activity determine the moment of death when even jelly produces appropriate signs when hooked up to EEG machines (Kessler and McKenna, 1978: 43-4)?

These medical developments have not resulted in any alteration in the basic proposition: one either is or is not dead. They have not led doctors to embrace the category of the zombie or of the undead. The incorrigible propositions regarding gender also hold that it is dichotomous and, here too, new discoveries are interpreted in the context of this proposition rather than as challenges to it: '[t]his fact is not to be challenged by any data, but all data is to be fitted into this framework' (1978: 74). This means that gender attribution, as both presumption and practice, forms one of the fundamental premises informing biological research.

Using death as an example demonstrates just how problematical this issue is. Presumably the reason that doctors have not modified their basic presumption that life and death are dichotomous is for the simple reason that an inevitable set of consequences – barring mistaken allocations – usually attend the declaration that someone is dead, in other words putrefaction and decay. It is not a consequence of the *declaration* but the declaration represents no less of a judgement for all that. The fact that the attribution has become considerably more problematical and that this renders the dichotomy far from simple and, even, that technological developments have introduced grey areas between the two states, so that there is both a conceptual and a practical failure of the dichotomy, has not meant its abandonment; it has simply turned it into a shorthand to describe a sum total of features that together produce a qualitative discrepancy between two states, which is *tied to a set of consequences*. But gender is not of this order: no inevitable set of consequences follows upon the classification of someone by sex: reproduction is not putrefaction – and it has a rather more optional quality to it.

But looking at death also prompts the question of why there should be a problem here at all. Why should the fact that the declaration of death involves a socially constructed definition and a process of judgement or attribution be in conflict with the physiological process defined by this means? If, as the review of a recent book by Geoffrey Bowker and Susan Leigh Star (Ritvo, 2000: 39) suggests, all classification, although it has benefits, affects what it classifies and the conventions it puts in place shape the world, it should come as no surprise to us that classification should be both social construction and a useful means of grasping the empirical material it purports to analyse. As Harriet Ritvo points out in her review (ibid.), classification is best understood as a sustained negotiation between the material to be classified and human need. Why then does the idea of the social origins of the classification seem to present a difficulty for the status of the phenomenon it seeks to explain?

Phenomenology, epistemology and ontological commitment

The short answer to this lies in the metatheoretical status given to the ethnomethodological account. In some parts of their text, as we mentioned earlier, Kessler and McKenna take up a relatively agnostic position as to the contribution that biological processes might make to gender differences or similarities. In that sense, as they saw it, their own account was neither more nor less 'real' or 'true' than any other. In describing the beliefs of a Yaqui shaman that people might turn into birds, they argue against the case that the shaman is 'incorrect', has 'primitive' beliefs or is 'misinformed':

> Ethnomethodologists challenge this interpretation of the shaman's behavior, not
> by asserting that we are wrong in seeing his actions in this way, but rather by

contending that the shaman's interpretation is as real for him as ours is for us. Indeed, both realities are created in the same way – through methodical (i.e., orderly, systematic and thus recoverable) interactional work which creates and sustains whatever reality one is living, be it that of the shaman, the 'man in the street,' the biologist, or any other reality one could name. (1978: 5)

The shaman's belief, the biologist's research findings or indeed, the ethnomethodologist's account, are just so many alternate 'worlds', constructed through interactional processes, and about whose contentions it is not possible to adjudicate. Kessler and McKenna thus essentially stand aside from the nature/nurture debate and confine themselves to a focus upon the way in which a reality of two, and only two genders is constructed. Yet that debate does also come back to haunt them and, in some senses, force an engagement from them. Why does this happen?

The key lies in the implicit knowledge claim they make, which is sustained by the theoretical provisions of ethnomethodology. As a theoretical tool, the power of phenomenological sociology and, by extension, ethnomethodology lies in what amounts to a relativizing force: the leverage it provides for opening out facticities. Because of its focus on knowledge as processual and interactional, it undermines the sense that there are such things as 'irreducible facts'. Instead 'facts' are complex constructions, which acquire their facticity and solidity intersubjectively (Kessler and McKenna would say interactively), via something that resembles a conspiratorial agreement to define social situation, world, relationship, and so on, in a given way. This includes the definition of supposedly 'natural' phenomena. This means that Kessler and McKenna resolutely refuse to take for granted the existence of two 'biological' sexes (1978: 163). They provide a good brief summary of their theoretical assumptions at the beginning of the book. In describing the concept of 'incorrigible propositions' or the 'natural attitude', they say:

> The most basic incorrigible proposition is the belief that the world exists independently of our presence, and that objects have an independent reality and a constant identity. For example, suppose you look out your window and see a rose in the garden, but when you go out to pick it, you cannot find it. You do not assume that the rose turned into something else. You keep looking until you either find the rose or figure out what conditions existed to make you think there was a rose. Perhaps it was the configuration of shadows, or you might notice a butterfly that you mistook for a rose. By interpreting the results of your search in this way, you thereby verify the reality and constancy of objects like roses and butterflies, and validate that they exist independently of your interaction with them. (1978: 4)

There is a philosophical anthropology here which implies that the way in which human beings orient themselves in the world is to construct a sense of reality for themselves out of a set of phenomenal appearances. It is therefore not legitimate simply to take for granted the reality and constancy of objects such as roses or butterflies, and it becomes necessary to see all such objects as *constructs*. In short a potential conflict is set up between the 'reality' of rose or butterfly and the 'reality' of the processes of human cognition. The inevitable problem this poses, however, is the self-referential one of applying such an insight to the very knowledge that declares it so; and a set of paradoxes can then ensue.

However, this problem does not arise because of the nature of this insight: it would be a perfectly plausible account of the psychological processes involved in human cognition. It is because the philosophical claim stands upon an epistemological ground. A psychological claim would have no necessary implications for the reality of the objects of human cognition *qua* objects. But the derivation of this claim from the epistemological terrain of phenomenological philosophy extends the range of its application to cast doubt upon the objects themselves when it is translated into the empirical domain of a sociology.

Phenomenological philosophy had set out to establish the grounds of human knowledge, bracketing the reality or otherwise of the contents of consciousness and discovering its intentionality, in other words that consciousness was always consciousness *of* something. Intentionality is a fundamental feature of consciousness, comprising the object as perceived (the *noema*) and the act of perception (the *noesis*), and this is isolated by the phenomenological reduction which establishes what is given in consciousness once the object has ceased to be treated as real. It is a matter of identifying the phenomenon, the object as it appears in the mind. In that sense, phenomena are pre-theoretical. In other words, none of this applies to the world of empirical objects.

In its transformation into a sociology, two things happen: first, the whole discussion of phenomena, of reduction and of intentionality is *transferred* to an empirical realm and, second, phenomenology acquires more than a suspension of belief, the epistemological agnosticism about the solidity and constancy of objects, all objects, any object, required for the purposes of the philosophical investigation.[5] For it acquires an ontology concerning *social reality*, which the philosophical framework did not necessitate or concern itself with. In one sense, the agnosticism of the philosophical framework is more radical. What the sociology represents is the selective application of agnosticism to some objects rather than to others. In short, it turns agnosticism into scepticism.

Whatever the claims made in its name, it is inconceivable that Kessler and McKenna would not want their work to be taken as a contribution to knowledge, and, as such, as describing the 'reality' of the processes they analyse. Indeed they say that their 'perspective is that the reality of gender is a social construction' (1978: 6). Thus it is the apparent *denial* of the traditional status accorded to gender – as grounded in the objective reality of two biological 'sexes' – which is the most powerful, but also the most problematical part of their work.

Two quite contradictory contentions that point in different directions but are also absolutely integral to one another come together in their writing. Their agnosticism as to *all* knowledge claims and investigation into their cognitive conditions of existence – the heritage of phenomenology – opens up the theoretical *s*pace in which the constructedness of gender attribution can be identified, by identifying all objects of knowledge as constructs. The formal principle is to cast into doubt the 'reality' of all such objects. However, Kessler and McKenna's commitment to the nature of gender attribution as a set of social and interactive processes grants 'reality' to one set of objects. Hence the fact that the conflict between the 'reality' of biological sex and that of these social processes is a *partial* one, and a commitment to biology's own terms of reference is both retained, and negated in principle.

This is why, amidst the agnostic claims, they suggest that attention to the process of gender attribution would itself have the potential to alter the nature of the research programmes in the biological sciences. Since 'sex difference' research is premised upon the presumption that male/female is an *unproblematic* dichotomy, i.e. on the same gender attribution process used by the rest of us, the conclusion that the biological sciences would alter if the reality of gender attribution were taken on board is inescapable. Agnosticism has to collapse into scepticism for the very simple reason that there is ontological competition between the idea of 'sex' as premised upon gender attribution processes by biologists, (which is a *social and interactive* process) and sex as a biological entity. If sex as a biological entity is premised upon the idea of 'sex' as a product of gender attribution processes, then doubt is automatically cast upon that biological entity, since it is dependent upon unexamined and commonsensical constructions. The radicalism – but also the problem – of Kessler and McKenna's position is the apparent undermining of the notion of 'sex' *in toto* as an entity and with it of the totality of biological research associated with the notion, because of the declared primacy of gender attribution.

The problems Kessler and McKenna face over the status of biological knowledges in relation to 'gender' are not peculiar to them. There are post-structuralist and other versions of the same dilemma, which is produced by the extension of the domain of the social and historical into what had hitherto been taken for granted as biological. But it is the extension of a particular version of the social and historical that in tying it to the bases of human knowledge – be it conceived of in linguistic terms or not – turns it into an *epistemology* and makes it seek to adjudicate the claims of other disciplines in their totality.

It is therefore not entirely clear from Kessler and McKenna's work just what status the 'findings' of orthodox biologists should have. Phenomenological sociologies deny the reality of the 'objects' detected by positivist sociology, the most fundamental of which is 'social structure', which they regard as an hypostatized fiction invented by sociologists. It belongs to the same natural attitude that decrees that 'there is reality and constancy to qualities like race, age, social class, and, of course, gender, which exist independently of any particular example of the quality' (1978: 4). From the vantage point of phenomenology, positivist sociology starts to look like some sort of Platonic world of essences, hence the substitution effected, of these 'objects' of research, for intersubjective processes that construct a *sense* of 'reality' for these qualities and objects. It is these intersubjective processes that constitute the 'realities' of phenomenological sociologists and ethnomethodologists, something they would be the first to admit. Nevertheless, because they apply the same criteria to their own work in defining it as a construction like any other, these claims also have no status other than the metatheoretical: they are 'second order constructs', constructs of constructs.

Of course the problems of relativism and infinite regress in relation to phenomenological sociologies are well known. It is interesting that, in discussing the idea of the 'differentiation' between 'sperm and egg carriers, Kessler and McKenna raise just this problem, saying:

> If we assert that reality is a social construction, why stop at gender as a social construction? Why not assert that 'sperm carriers' and 'egg carriers' are as much of a construction as 'male' or 'female'?

Quite so. But their answer to this question is not very satisfying:

> We all have to make a decision to take something for granted, to stop somewhere; otherwise it would be impossible to get out of bed in the morning. Our decision has been to stop here; others may wish to go on. (1978: 169, n. 8)

What this looks like is acceptance of a minimalist base compatible with an acknowledgement of human reproduction. The attempt to bring the infinite regress to a halt at *this* point, however, signals that there is much more work to be done on the problem of the dual status of biology as 'construct' and as 'fact', which is one of the things we shall seek to elaborate in the chapters that follow.

Apparently paradoxically, then, the work of Kessler and McKenna couples what is at the broadest level a theoretical failure, evidenced in the ambiguous status of biology, to a number of empirical successes. Not only was their work on the social processes of gender attribution ground-breaking but their capacity to rethink the assumptions underlying biological research and open it out to a consideration of its social constitution is invaluable. The attempt to treat all aspects of being a 'woman' or a 'man', including the biological, as being all of a piece by placing them under the single heading of gender attribution, although unduly homogenizing, also has the virtue – in a way which runs counter to the metatheoretical status provided by ethnomethodology – of beginning to breach the divorce between the cultural and the natural. It does not successfully reformulate the problem but it does at least pose the issues in a way that demands a resolution.

The natural attitude

In translating the idea of the 'natural attitude' to the social realm, however, phenomenological sociologies open out the possibility of a reconsideration of the basis of that 'natural attitude', and this is their tremendous legacy. Rather than to construe it in terms of a philosophical anthropology, as something which is proper to the way in which human beings 'forget' how it is that they constituted for themselves a sense of the reality of the world they inhabit – on the model of learning to ride a bicycle and then forgetting how it is that one stays aloft – it is open to them to consider the very process of 'forgetting' itself. What seems like a necessary feature of human functioning – the taking for granted of the processes of sense-making and the 'glossing' and other practices required for smooth social functioning – could be opened out further by phenomenological sociologies. It is open to ethnomethodology in particular to move consideration of these processes away from the purely linguistic, from the universalities of conferring meaning to examination of the construction of those meanings themselves. Considered purely in terms of signification, we already have the work of Roland Barthes in *Mythologies* (1973) to demonstrate the skilful way in which contemporary myths generate the sense of the 'naturalness' of their propositions by appearing to hijack that which is regarded as merely denotative of a 'reality'. There is therefore already the sense that the 'naturalness' behind the 'natural attitude' – the experience of that which is unproblematically given – is itself culturally specific and constructed through specific significatory practices. More interesting, however, is the sense that 'naturalness' is not just an *idea*. Kessler and McKenna themselves have an interesting discussion of the manner in which transsexuals can secure the attribution of 'naturalness' for their elected gender. It is this, they suggest, rather than a particular gender itself, that needs to be sustained for successful passing: 'discrediting gender attributions is matter of discrediting naturalness' (1978: 160). That naturalness is constituted by what they term the 'historicity' of gender, which is sustained by a particular, concrete instance of gender attribution that puts in place the sense of its permanence and 'reality'. Almost nothing can discredit such an attribution, not even the disappearance of all of the signs originally used to make it. Once an attribution has been discredited, however, any feature can be produced as a 'good reason' for the discrediting. It is an all or nothing situation, in which the attribution either holds or collapses entirely. Before we consider that crafting of the sense of 'naturalness' as it applies to sexual differentiation, we need to look a little more closely at how our own sense of the way in why biology supplies the unambiguous foundation for gender – in the form of 'sex' – has been constructed. To begin with, we look at one grouping who appear to defy what we now take to be 'nature' – hermaphrodites – and at the attempts of people not so very far distant from ourselves to recuperate them into the fold of what Kessler and McKenna would call two 'genders'. We turn our attention to Foucault's *Herculine Barbin*.

Notes

[1] The phrase 'the knot of natural difference' belongs to Connell and is taken from the first heading of his chapter on 'The Body and Social Practice' in *Gender and Power*.

[2] In her later book, *Lessons from the Intersexed*, Suzanne Kessler argues that in the intervening period since *Gender: An Ethnomethodological Approach* was published, it looks as if a cultural vagina may have emerged but that certainly a cultural clitoris has not (1998: 157, n. 15)

[3] Kessler and McKenna point out that the relationship between this biological factor and gender attribution is unequivocal in at least this one instance of attribution which is assignment at birth. However, in keeping with the cultural role ascribed to the penis, they say: 'There is some question as to whether the formula is really labia and vagina = female, or whether it is instead no penis = female, since at birth there is no search (i.e. an internal examination) for a vagina or clitoris' (1978: 58).

[4] They talk of further research being needed into children's 'gender' differentiation processes (1978: 167). What is not entirely clear here is the status of the scare quotes around this reference to 'gender': does it indicate some doubt over whether or not the empirical evidence demonstrates that these infants make distinctions on the basis of what we would routinely call 'sex', or does it imply a distinction between social and psycho-biological processes? 'Gender' differentiation is described in terms of sameness and difference, of knowing whether or not someone is similar or different from oneself, but

the rider that is added is 'perhaps in terms of some basic reproductive criteria' (1978: 166).

[5] In 1973, James Heap and Phillip Roth established very clearly what kinds of transformations take place when phenomenological philosophy is appropriated to serve sociological purposes and which of these appropriations are fundamentally distorting of the philosophical concepts. They believed that phenomenology, properly understood, could indeed make a contribution to sociology, properly understood. A 'systematic and disciplined inquiry into Husserlian phenomenology and its derivatives (transcendental, psychological, hermeneutical and existential phenomenologies)' was necessary in order for us to 'save ourselves from the problems of what is called phenomenological sociology' (Heap and Roth, 1973: 365). Zygmunt Bauman, writing on the philosophical status of ethnomethodology, is much less sanguine about the relation between phenomenological philosophy and sociological appropriations of it. For him, ethnomethodology reproduced, on the cognitive plane, 'the same insoluble dilemma which crucified early existentialism on the moral one' (Bauman, 1973: 17).

4 The Mystery of the Visible

In 'The World of Wrestling', Roland Barthes describes the hyperbolic signs proffered to the public by wrestling as 'a pure and full signification, rounded like Nature' (Barthes, 1983: 29). Although we may now seem to be a world away from the doctrine of signatures in which the conformation of the world revealed its nature and God's purpose, at least one perception of nature is that of an asignificatory plenitude, sufficient unto itself, whose very facticity dispenses with the need for a hermeneutics. Nature doesn't present us with *signs*: its meaning shines forth clearly, fully, unproblematically. As we shall see later on when we come to look at Goffman's work, what we can refer to for the moment as 'gender(sex)' partakes of this plenitude through what he calls 'the doctrine of natural expression', by means of which bodies and behaviours are recruited into the staging of their 'natural' characteristics (1979: 6-7). Hermaphrodite bodies, however, either resist meaning or have it in excess, *contra Naturam.*[1]

Michel Foucault gives us to understand, however, that there was once a world, not so long ago, 'where all that counted was the reality of the body and the intensity of its pleasures' (Foucault, 1980: vii) and, in that world, hermaphroditism presented the clarity of a *choice*. Hermaphrodites were simply those in whom a mixture of characters coexisted; in our terms, they embodied a juxtaposition of the two sexes. When the time came to name the child, the father or godfather was advised to choose the more vigorous of the two sexes, and hermaphrodites were free to make a different choice on reaching adulthood, on the strict proviso that they then stuck to this choice thereafter. We have to remember that this takes place in a world in which morphology acts primarily as qualification for a social status, with attendant rights and privileges, and not as a key to some underlying reality. As Laqueur points out, what mattered was whether or not one was deemed to be appropriately qualified to behave in a particular way, say, to play the man's part in intercourse, and thus to accede to the privileges and obligations of that status (Laqueur, 1990: 134-6). Juridical concern was with behavioural transgressions, with those who assumed what they were not *legitimately* entitled to assume.

The birth of 'sex' as an ontological category

What develops subsequently, and changes this political landscape, is the notion of each individual having 'his or her primary, profound, determined and determining sexual identity': the notion of 'sex' as an ontological category is born. And with it, behaviour becomes irrelevant, or is at most adduced as supporting evidence. Hence the tragedy of Alexina – *aka* Herculine Barbin, whose history is recuperated by Foucault in the book of the same name – the hermaphrodite whose social and legal status is altered in defiance of the whole of the life she has previously lived. By the middle of the nineteenth century, hermaphrodites like Herculine presented the doctors with the task of deciphering 'the true sex that was hidden beneath ambiguous appearances' (Foucault, 1980: viii). The ontological status given to 'sex' turns the admixture of the hermaphrodite into a number of veritable deceptions or disguises of nature, making of the individual in most cases a 'pseudo-hermaphrodite'. Sexual irregularity belongs, more or less, to the realm of the chimeras, of those fictions 'which, whether involuntary or self-indulgent, are useless, and which it would be better to dispel' (Foucault, 1980: x).

Foucault links this ontologization of 'sex' to the perception 'that there exist complex, obscure and essential relationships between sex and truth [which] is to be found – at least in a diffused state – not only in psychiatry, psychoanalysis and psychology, but also in current opinion' (Foucault, 1980: x). Practices or behaviours which deviate from what we take to be the 'truth' of sex constitute, he says, errors in the most traditionally philosophical sense, in other words, 'a manner of acting which is not *adequate to reality*' (ibid., emphasis added). And it was this that Herculine came up against, in a medico-legal investigation that resulted in the official redefinition of her status as a man, and her subsequent suicide.

Sex is thus seen to constitute one of the most profound truths about the individual, the key to that individual's identity and the determination of his or her character. It is both profound in its location, in the depths of the soul, and profound in its veracity: it provides a true picture. It constitutes what is *real*. Herculine had the misfortune to live on the cusp of a new world, at the precise historical moment when investigations of sexual identity were at their most intense. The environment of the religious boarding schools in which she grew up, and subsequently taught, was privileged in its insulation from the developing processes of identification, characterization and classification of the perversions taking place between 1860 and 1870, of which she is to become both exemplar and victim. It was this insulation that made the shock of going from what Foucault describes as 'the happy limbo of a non-identity' (Foucault, 1980: xiii) to becoming one of these sexual anomalies all the more intense.

Grins without a cat

Herculine, or – according to her own appellation – Alexina, leaves behind a memoir which records the life that she had before a meaning was imposed by the doctors on her indeterminate anatomy. But that memoir is not written from the vantage point of the 'man' she has now become: as Foucault puts it, 'the narrative baffles every possible attempt to make an identification' (Foucault, 1980, xii). Written in a style which 'was not only a way of writing but a manner of living' (ibid.), it does not record the experiences of someone who tries to recall what life was like before he became 'himself'. Instead, Alexina has been deprived of the world of sensation and feeling she used to inhabit, in which the unspoken enigma of what she was tinged with desire the confidences, caresses and kisses of the boarding school. 'One has the impression', says Foucault, '...that everything took place in a world of feelings – enthusiasm, pleasure, sorrow, warmth, sweetness, bitterness...' (Foucault, 1980: xiii).

In the text itself, there is a play of masculine and feminine adjectives which Alexina applies to herself and, although they are predominantly feminine before she possesses her lover Sara and masculine afterwards, Foucault points out that this systematization does not seem to describe the consciousness of being a woman becoming the consciousness of being a man; rather 'it is an ironic reminder of grammatical, medical and juridical categories that language must utilize but that the content of the narrative contradicts' (Foucault, 1980: xiii-xiv). Those who now describe a change of sex live in a world categorically divided into two sexes and any unease about their identity usually finds expression in a desire to be the 'other' sex. Alexina lives in an intensely monosexual world in which her indeterminacy and ambiguity troubles with desire and enhances the tender pleasures that already belong to that world, rather than prompting a search for identity. In that world, because identity was not problematized, such things could remain enigmatic; it was a world in which 'grins hung about without the cat' (Foucault, 1980: xiii). Its monosexuality is virtually that of an absence of distinctions, in which the small measure of difference supplied by Alexina provides the basis for adding an enigmatic thrill to the relations between the girls, precisely *because* they are all girls in a presumedly heterosexual world, and there is no prospect of anything else.

Of course, Foucault's point is not that there was once a pre-lapsarian world innocent of distinctions but that there came a point when the manner of making a distinction changed. In other words, the attribution processes described by Kessler and McKenna belong to a particular *kind* of world in which 'sex' (or – in their terms – the biological factors in gender) has ontological status. That is to say that, in Stephen Gaukroger's words, 'sex' belongs to 'the structured set of kinds of entity *in terms of which* explanations can be given in a discourse' (Gaukroger, 1978: 39, emphasis added). What Foucault would describe as a new 'regime of truth' comes into being, in which the attribution of 'sex' to a human being necessarily entails certain types of consequence, both in discursive and practical terms.

Redefining Alexina

In Alexina's case, the attribution processes are themselves interesting. In Kessler and McKenna's terms, they really constitute reassignment processes, which, because they result from an uncertainty about the original assignment, are processes of detection which bring into relief the bases of judgements about 'sex'. The investigations undertaken in relation to Herculine are notable for a number of features. First, they are construed as investigations of *identity*. Determining Alexina's sex means determining who or what she is. Second, some of the evidence adduced demonstrates how sex and identity are conjoined through the medium of sexuality: Dr Chesnet, who reports on the case, says of Alexina, '[h]er tastes, her inclinations draw her towards women', in order to demonstrate that she is *really* a man. Sex is a matter of organs, certainly, but only in the light of their purpose. It is a reversible proposition: a man is naturally drawn to women, so someone whose inclinations draw her towards women is likely to be a man. Sexuality is entirely reproduction. The organs that are regarded as determining are also those most closely associated with procreation: Alexina lacks a womb but does have testicles.

> What shall we conclude from the above facts? Is Alexina a woman? She has a vulva, labia majora, and a feminine urethra, independent of a sort of imperforate penis, which might be a monstrously developed clitoris. She has a vagina. True, it is very short, very narrow; but after all, what is it if it is not a vagina? These are completely feminine attributes. Yes, but Alexina never menstruated; the whole outer part of her body is that of a man, and my explorations did not enable me to find a womb. Her tastes, her inclinations, draw her towards women. At night she has voluptuous sensations that are followed by a discharge of sperm; her linen is stained and starched with it. Finally, to sum up the matter, ovoid bodies and spermatic chords are found by touch in a divided scrotum. *These are the real proofs of sex.* (Chesnet in Foucault, 1980: 127-8, emphasis added)

The decisive organs are those that would allow Alexina to play the male role in reproduction, i.e. to *fertilize* by means of sperm (regardless of whether or not she was capable of playing the male role in intercourse). The structured way in which the judgement is arrived at is based upon the ontological *weight* to be assigned to different organs. In short, as Gaukroger indicates, an ontology constitutes an ordered *set* of entities, amongst which some are more dominant in the provision of an explanation. In Alexina's case, organs, inclinations and bodily morphology are all explored and identified, but the clinching factors are those that relate to reproductive potential.

Third, there can only be *one* true sex, and adherence to it is a *moral* question. In Kessler and McKenna's terms, it has become a world in which there are two, and only two genders, and they are mutually exclusive. By the 1860s, there was no longer the possibility of Alexina having *two* sexes juxtaposed, as both canon and civil law in the Middle Ages would have indicated (Foucault, 1980: vii), hence the disappearance of free choice. Nevertheless, although sex is to be regarded as the key to identity, behaviour can deviate from its true path. Alexina was to be asked to adhere to the sex identified for her by those who were expert in its determination. The fear was that if the *true* sexual constitution were not properly recognized, individuals might profit from their anatomical anomalies in the pursuit of licentious behaviour. Both human beings and nature might be dissembling. The medical diagnosis could thus serve the function of re-establishing the moral legitimacy of the true sex through the good offices of the law, hence the fact that Auguste Tardieu's 1874 book on Herculine was entitled *Question médico-légale de l'identité*. Indeed the first part of Tardieu's book had originally appeared in *Annales d'hygiène publique et de médecine légale* in 1872, a title which makes the nature of the preoccupations surrounding Herculine abundantly clear.

That confused combination of facticity and determinacy with morality is one that we still find in discussions of what is nowadays called 'sexual orientation', a term which neatly combines a notion of geographical co-ordinates with volition. Dr Goujon who publishes an article on Alexina's anatomy in 1869 suggests that the case raises several physiological and medico-legal questions, principally because the formation of the external genital organs permitted Alexina to play either the masculine or the feminine role in coitus, without distinction (Goujon in Foucault, 1980: 131). But Goujon nevertheless goes on to identify the imperforate penis as really a clitoris, in spite of having said of Alexina earlier that 'he was manifestly a man' (ibid.). All the effort of the text (and, one might say, the discourse) is devoted to endeavouring to make a clear set of distinctions, to allocate organs decisively in the face of evidence which is recalcitrant. There is no room in this account for truly hybrid organs, or for organs that might pre-exist a differentiating process, such as those familiar to us and to the medicine of the 1860s from embryology. Alexina represents a medical mistake, which careful examination can put right. Such medical mistakes, of which Goujon cites several, usually come to light through some sexual (reproductive) irregularity. He mentions a monk who revealed his sex by having a baby, an individual registered as a girl who asked to marry a girl made pregnant by him, a midwife alleged to have violated a pregnant woman, stating that 'it would be easy to multiply examples of this kind' and suggesting that, if they were brought together, they 'would become a precious guide for doctors who are called on...to pronounce a judgement' (Goujon in Foucault, 1980: 137-8). Just as there would be now, there is talk of the benefits of surgery.

The purpose, then, is to arrive at an exact diagnosis to assign Alexina 'to his true place in society' (Goujon in Foucault, 1980: 131). Nevertheless, the subsequent discussion of the facts of the case engages Dr Goujon in an exploration of embryogeny, which describes how the same basic embryological ground plan forms the basis for subsequent conformations, both normal and abnormal, and in a consideration of the organic analogies between male and female. More than once, he makes reference to the way in which the same anatomical features give rise to differential components, 'new proof of the differences of structure or purpose that nature is able to impart to organs that are fundamentally identical' (Goujon in Foucault, 1980: 142). So, although the intention is that the organ establish Alexina's 'true place in society', that is, guarantee the social polarity, it is not, intrinsically, ideally suited to that purpose. That 'true place' is predominantly determined in relation to fitness for marriage and reproduction: 'Procreation is the natural goal of marriage, and Alexina possessed the organs that are characteristic of his sex and whose functions he exercised' (Goujon in Foucault, 1980: 143). The biological order (testicles) guarantees the social order (procreation in marriage). Alexina, however, produced no spermatozoa.

Candidate organs and immoral lusts

The same concerns with morality lie at the heart of the involvement of Renaissance doctors in the law. Thomas Laqueur (1990) records the way in which, prior to the change which sees Alexina suffer for her indeterminate organs, possession of a penis was construed as if it were 'a certificate of sorts, like the diploma of a doctor or lawyer today, which entitled the bearer to certain rights and privileges' (1990: 134-5). What mattered were the social categories which were based upon a set of distinctions – hot/cold, active/passive, and so on – for which the penis was no more than a sign, and although doctors were called upon to adjudicate as regards indeterminate organs, organs might constitute no more than one amongst a number of considerations. Behaviour, such as the capacity to act the passive or the active role in intercourse, might, for example, be the means of determining which category a hermaphrodite ought to belong to, whereas by the time Alexina comes along, behaviour is subordinate at best and, mostly, plays little part in the determination. Certainly Alexina's being drawn to women provides an additional indication of her maleness, but the *predominant* evidence is biological, and, indeed, the attraction itself is read as biological. This used not to be the case. As an illustration of this, Laqueur tells the story of two women, Marie de Marcis and Henrika Shuria, between whom the courts chose to make a distinction. Marie de Marcis, for whom medical and other testimony confirmed that she was female and had menstruated, was tried for sodomy for claiming to be a man and sleeping with another woman whom she wanted to marry. The emphasis of the court was not on her possession of a uterus that bled, but on whether or not the organ with which she penetrated her partner was entitled to be considered a penis. Proof of ejaculation demonstrated that it was and so the court declared that Marie was entitled to become a man once she had reached the age of twenty-five. Henrika Shuria, by contrast, declared herself 'weary of her sex', dressed as a man, enlisted in the army and was described as engaging in 'licentious sport with other women', one of whom 'burned with immoderate lusts' for her. Her clitoris, which was described as 'not unlike a boy's member', she chose to expose outside her vulva, but in the court's opinion this did not make it a penis. She escaped being burned at the stake as a tribade (one who illicitly assumed the man's role in intercourse) but her sentence was paradoxical:

> ...a merciful judge recommended that she be 'nipped in the bud, and sent into exile.' She was, in other words, relieved of the organ that she supposed would allow her to leave the sex of which she had grown weary; but she was punished with exile, a man's sentence (1990: 137).

As with the burning of the false Martin Guerre, the concern is with the 'flouting [of] the conventions that make civilisation possible' (1990: 138), akin to the flouting of something akin to the sumptuary laws of gender. There is no sense in which the doctors' interventions are there to determine the 'real' and *final* proofs of sex, as they were for Herculine. Henrika Shuria is seen as playing for advantage, whilst not having the appropriate credentials. Cases of hermaphroditic 'men' using the ambiguities of their bodies to 'have it both ways' attract the same opprobrium and fatal consequences. What is crucial is that the social categories be respected.

No distinction is made here between what we would nowadays call 'gender' and 'sex' and, in spite of the concern with organs as badges of entitlement, 'sex' has no logical and ontological priority over something we would now refer to as 'gender'; instead they are one and the same, in a way in which they are not for Alexina's doctors. For Goujon et al., the only matters to be decided are strictly biological; all else follows from that. By the time we reach Alexina, the concept of 'gender' has yet to be coined, but the now limited specification given to 'sex' has already carved out the appropriate conceptual space and pattern of determination for it to be able to appear. By contrast, although Renaissance doctors are still called upon to determine who belongs to which category, consideration of the bodily is intimately bound up with social status and lacks the hard facticity with which we have come to associate it in the wake of the nineteenth century. Laqueur cites the pre-eminent medical-jurisprudential text on the subject, Paolo Zacchia's *Questionum medico-legalium*, in which organs not only have what is to us a surprising contingency but the language used to describe them is political and legal:

> The clinical and professional tone of the *Questionum* – case histories, taxonomies, learned reviews of the literature on various points – would lead one to assume that organs will be treated as the sign of something solidly corporeal, something that thoroughly informs its subject and determines its identity. But Zacchia, like Montaigne, treats organs as if they were contingent certificates of status: 'members conforming to sex are not the causes that constitute male or female or distinguish between them...Because it is so, the members of one sex could appear in someone of the opposite sex.' (Laqueur, 1990: 140)

Zacchia's language, most blatantly in his discussion of clitoral hypertrophy, reveals his fundamentally cultural concerns. 'It should be enough now to observe,' he argues, 'that, in regard to women who have turned into males, in the most, this has followed a promotion (*beneficium*) of the clitoris, as several anatomists think'. He does not use the obvious noun for what might have happened, *incrementum* or *amplification*, an enlargement, and writes instead of *beneficium*, a kindness or favour, especially in the political sense of an advancement or a grant that endows ecclesiastical property or a feudal right.

What has changed by the nineteenth century, in short, is the disposition of the language. A discrete scientific language with definable objects of concern distinct from issues of political and legal order and moral propriety has come into being. The fact that it is seen as holding the key to such political, legal and moral issues does not prevent it from being defined as ontologically distinct. Zacchia, for example, maintains that men cannot turn into women, but he does so not on the grounds of biological impossibility, but on metaphysical grounds, that nature tends towards perfection: why therefore would men become women, thus becoming more imperfect?

A language struggling to be born

Laqueur illustrates the moment when a scientific language of the sexed body is struggling to be born by examining how generation is imagined in the work of William Harvey, the man credited with the discovery of the circulation of the blood and with the idea that all life originates in the egg. Harvey's work is poised at the join between two discursive regimes, 'its claims to epistemological authority, its experimental strategies, and its ontology of reproduction...cast overtly in the language of the new biology' but also still deeply embedded in accounts of Nature which clearly exhibit to him old and fundamental truths about the hierarchy of creation (1990: 142). Unlike his work on the circulation of the blood, in which no such difficulties arise, his *Disputations Touching the Generation of Animals* tell story after story, Laqueur points out, without ever achieving closure: 'stories multiply but go nowhere' (1990: 143). His insistently empiricist epistemology, which advocates going directly to the book of Nature because it is so clearly legible, is ultimately bound back into an account of generation in which an idea – the *primordium* or egg – is ignited by the male in the body of the female:

> Harvey's new epistemology and substantive discoveries led right back to new versions of old stories. Generation, the body's most social function, remained beyond the reach of a nonexistent neutral language of organs and functions. Desperate to understand how it all worked, Harvey spun story after poignant story about sexual difference, always pretending that it was Nature herself who spoke. (1990: 148)

In Harvey's world, unlike that of Alexina's doctors, it was not the body that bore the brunt of carrying sexual differentiation. That body was a part of a much larger story of resemblances and hierarchies, of microcosm and macrocosm, of similitude and signs. According to Laqueur, two fundamental transformations have yet to take place, which will allow for the invention of the idea of sex as we know it. The first of these has to do with epistemological concerns and comprises two elements. One of these is the spread of an idea of reason, facticity and science, which will divide the possible from the impossible:

> Lactating monks, women who never ate and exuded sweet fragrance, sex changes at the whim of the imagination, bodies in paradise without sexual difference, monstrous births, women who bore rabbits, and so on, were the stuff of fanaticism and superstition even if they were not so far beyond the bounds of reason to be unimaginable. Skepticism was not created in the eighteenth century, but the divide between the possible and the impossible, between body and spirit, between truth and falsehood, and thus between biological sex and theatrical gender, was greatly sharpened. (1990: 151)

Having a true sex thus also means the truth of having a sex. But since the truth of having a sex does not entirely sever its links with the matter of the social status of being a 'man' or a 'woman', the dream of reason dissembles: 'sex' as we understand it today continues to serve functions other than those of scientific enlightenment.

The other epistemological element concerns the end some time in the late seventeenth century of 'the episteme "in which signs and similitudes were wrapped around each other in an endless spiral" in which "the relation of microcosm to macrocosm should be conceived as both the guarantee of that knowledge and the limit of its expansion"', which is recorded by Foucault in *The Order of Things*. All of the complex circularities of this world were, Laqueur says, 'reduced to a single plane: nature'. In this context an idea of sex emerges as 'the flat, horizontal, immovable foundation of physical fact' (ibid.).

However, the second transformation is that which takes place in the political sphere. The eighteenth century in particular will be the era of the contestation of the old order – it is, after all, the century that culminates in the French Revolution – and relations between women and men and the proper status of each will be one of the things in contention. Once either a transcendental order or time-immemorial custom ceased to be an appropriate justification for the regulation of human affairs, the body, Laqueur says, became decisive (1990: 152). Laqueur puts this in a way which is both helpful, and, as we shall see later, profoundly problematical: he says that the cultural work that had previously been done by *gender* devolved onto *sex* (1990: 151). In other words, the corporeal comes to be simultaneously the domain of facticity and the true *and* the ground on which claims about social relations may be entertained and adjudicated. The body is made to provide the foundation for sexual differentiation in all its aspects.

The management of the intersexed

For us, at the turn of the millennium, the body can even be made to bear difference to the extent of having that difference carved upon it, of being forbidden to speak ambiguity or resemblance. Genital organs now have to be fundamentally decisive, to the point where they are seen to 'demand' to be reshaped by surgery in order to restore the natural order of things, as Suzanne Kessler notes in her recent book, *Lessons from the Intersexed* (Kessler, 1998: 37). Perhaps fortunately for her, Alexina was subjected to no more than diagnosis and reclassification, which was no less tragic in its consequences for all that. But the medical management of intersexuality now tends to involve surgery, surgery of dubious physiological value and questionable psychological and social benefit. Kessler supplies a veritable catalogue of horrors of such surgical endeavours, carried out with what are, undoubtedly, the best of intentions, but, on the face of it, little critical evaluation. They are carried out predominantly with a view to the social and psychological adjustment of parents and children, but without evidence of the problems that are said to ensue if no surgical 'correction' is undertaken.

Basing most of her research on the United States, Kessler argues that intersexuality has come to be considered a treatable condition of the *genitals*, to be resolved expeditiously before the age of eighteen months, when, according to the theories of gender endorsed for this purpose, such as in the work of John Money (1965), a child will have developed a gender identity. Based upon premises about the malleability of children and gender, psychological and medical intervention is used to decide and reconcile assignment and genitalia (Kessler, 1998: 14-15). With the aim of sustaining the general impression that a child's 'true' sex has been discovered and maintaining the credibility of the medical profession, it is seen as important to assign a gender decisively, unambiguously and irreversibly and as rapidly as is compatible with proper clinical assessment. Where corrective surgery is deemed 'necessary', it is to be started in early infancy, in the case of clitoral reduction sometimes by three months of age (1998: 16).

Physicians find themselves caught between a rock and a hard place: they feel an urgent necessity to provide an immediate assignment but doing so may mean making an assignment that has to retracted, something which is seen as particularly problematic. Parents, having been given a specific assignment, will need to be convinced to accept a particular clinical course of action based upon a different one. This can mean an awkward period in limbo, during which the medical specialists will endeavour to 'normalize' the child's condition for the parents, which entails focusing on the failure of the genitals clearly to signal their relation to the baby's 'real' membership of one or other category. Assignment also works retroactively, thus creating what Kessler and McKenna (1978) had earlier described as the historicity of gender. 'Re-assignment' becomes 're-announcement' so that '[t]he gender always was what it is now seen to be' (Kessler, 1998: 23).

Although an attempt is made to perpetuate the notion that good medical decisions are being based upon the child's real sex, it is evident that judgements are being made about cultural functioning and the psychological adaptation of parents and children, leading, for example, to the reassignment of some children with an XY chromosome pattern to the female gender because of the lack of an 'appropriately-sized' penis (1998: 19). There is a curious paradox whereby medical teams are looking for biological causes whilst effectively deciding upon courses of action on the basis of, and convincing parents of the importance of, judgements about social factors. At the heart of this contradiction lies the production of a 'real' or 'natural' sex by artificial means. In defiance of the belief amongst sociologists that they make precious little impact upon the world, the basis of this is curiously sociological: what the doctors are doing is supplying genitals which accord with the gender the child will be socialized into: 'The physician/parent discussions make it clear to family members that gender is not a biological given (even though, of course, the physicians' own procedures for diagnosis assume that it is) and that gender is fluid' (1998: 24). By contrast, in 'normal' births, nothing is done to disturb the presumption that gender is biologically given.

Since Herculine's day, factors such as gonads have receded entirely from view in favour of the social and sexual appropriateness of the genitals, but heterosexuality remains a dominant consideration. According to Kessler, doctors now view decisions based primarily upon chromosomes and gonads as wrong, and proper to ill-informed lay opinion (1998: 27). A 'female' without a vaginal opening is considered unacceptable, since she would have no means of 'receiving' the penis. This phallocentrism is mirrored by the aesthetic basis of the judgements used to determine whether or not a child's phallic tissue is adequate enough in size and shape to make it into a male (1998: 25-6). Conversely, a perfect penis is too good to overlook:

> These guidelines are clear, but they focus on only one physical feature, one that is distinctly imbued with cultural meaning. This becomes especially apparent in the case of an XX infant with normal female reproductive gonads and a 'perfect' penis. Would the size and the shape of the penis, in this case, be the deciding factor in assigning the infant as a 'male,' or would the 'perfect' penis be surgically destroyed and female genitals created? Money notes that this dilemma would be complicated by the anticipated reactions of the parents to seeing 'their apparent son lose his penis.' Other researchers concur that parents are likely to want to raise a child with a normal-shaped penis (regardless of size) as 'male,' particularly if the scrotal area looks normal and if the parents have had no experience with intersexuality. Elsewhere, Money argues in favour of not

neonatally amputating the penis of XX infants since fetal masculinization of brain structures would predispose them 'almost invariably [to] develop behaviorally as tomboys, even when reared as girls.' This reasoning implies first that tomboyish behavior in girls is bad and should be avoided and second that it is preferable to remove the internal female organs, implant prosthetic testes, and regulate the 'boy's' hormones for his entire life than to overlook or disregard the penis. (1998: 25-6)

Of course what is never at issue is simply to let these children be. Life-threatening issues aside (such as the risk of severe electrolyte imbalance in those with congenital adrenal hyperplasia, a condition that masculinizes an XX foetus), there is no sense in which whatever adjustment may be necessary should be made by those with whom the child interacts, rather than by the child's body. Kessler quotes one intersexual as saying: 'It is difficult to be Black in this culture, too, but we don't bleach the skin of Black babies' (1998: 35).

What this amounts to is the maintenance not merely of the belief, but of the *reality*, of gender as dimorphic, of human beings consisting of two exclusive types, 'male' and 'female', 'in the face of incontrovertible physical evidence that this is not mandated by biology' (1978: 31). Although doctors are aware that concordance amongst the recognized markers of gender, such as chromosomes, gonads, genitals and hormones, may not be there, and that dimorphism may fail, they, like those in Herculine's day, regard it in just the same way – in the truest sense as a philosophical 'error') – and they adjust what they find to conform to 'reality' or what is 'natural'. They adjudge nature to have failed in her proper task and make the correction for her. This can extend to telling lies to a patient in order to naturalize her gender assignment, such as telling someone with androgen insensitivity that her ovaries were diseased and had to be removed, when neither ovaries nor uterus would ever have been present (1998: 29). More importantly, perhaps, and sometimes more painfully from the patient's point of view, is the way in which the functionality, sensitivity and integrity of variant genitals may be sacrificed to a normative ideal.

Defining and producing genitals

Among the most alarming elements in Kessler's research evidence are the attitudes to variant genitals embedded (not too deeply, she says) in the medical literature and the surgical consequences that follow. Larger-than-average clitorises are repeatedly described as 'embarrassing' or 'offensive', or 'obtrusive', 'ungainly' or 'disfiguring'. As Kessler points out:

> If the clitoris is troubling, offending, and embarrassing, who exactly is troubled, offended, and embarrassed and why? Not only are these questions not answered by intersex specialists, they are not even asked. A comment from an intersexed adult woman about her childhood is a relevant counterpoint: 'I experienced the behaviour of almost everyone towards me as absolutely dishonest, embarrassing.' Her comments remind us that objects in the world (even non-normative organs) are not embarrassing; rather, people's reactions to them are. Another intersexual woman's 'uncorrected' clitoris was described by her sexual partner as 'easy to find.' Whether a clitoris is easy to find is arguably of some

importance in sexual interactions, but it is not a criterion that physicians use for determining the suitable size for a clitoris. (1998: 36)

On the contrary, sexual pleasure may even be subordinate to cosmetic considerations. Kessler quotes a not untypical comment by a physician that the clitoris is 'not essential for *adequate* sexual function and gratification' but that its presence is desirable for the purposes of sexual stimulation *providing* that presence 'does not interfere with *cosmetic, psychological, social and sexual* adjustment' (1998: 37, emphases Kessler's). The penis fares quite as badly, since below a certain size it is treated as if it does not actually exist. In this instance, however, the emotionality of the language is reserved for child rather than organ: a boy with an 'insignificant' organ is described as '*doomed* to life as a male without a penis' which means that he *must* be raised as a girl (ibid.). The language here is pitying, whereas in the former it was pejorative. Equally, as we mentioned earlier, it is the organs themselves that speak to us and '*demand*' alteration.

Beyond this language lies the construction of a set of standards which create for the organs a series of norms which are sometimes narrower than the range of 'normal' variation. For example, the location of the urinary outlet in the penis (the meatus) is decreed as needing to be in the centre of the glans, but, as Kessler observes, a study of men admitted to hospital for the treatment of prostate and bladder conditions found only 55 per cent of them had the meatus in this position. Equally, there are published guidelines for clitoral and penile size which are devised so as to leave a 1.5 cm gap between the two sets of measurements, a clear no man's land, an empty space which no child should occupy (1998: 43). In the context of the fact that, in one study, clitoral lengths that were reduced ranged from 1.5 to 3.5 cm, a small size by any stretch of the imagination (but obviously not for surgeons contemplating clitorises!), the concerns of one urologist that a girl not spend her life with '*a big huge phallus in the lower end of the abdomen*' seems all the more peculiar. The insistence that clitorises not be conspicuous also extends to a desire to make sure that they are concealed behind the labia, which is sustained by a surgical technique that recesses them behind the labia, which, when they swell during arousal, produces painful erections (1998: 45). Some surgeons even go so far as to suggest the complete excision of the clitoris, sometimes for no other reason than that it produces a more acceptable appearance. More recently those who oppose such practices have developed what are described as 'resections', in which portions of erectile[2] tissue are removed and the glans is grafted back onto what remains (1998: 47). But, in spite of attempts to measure the conductivity of clitoral nerves at the time of the surgery, intersexed people themselves report results in terms of sexual pleasure which are far from satisfactory (1998: 56).

There is quite a marked discrepancy between the plentiful anecdotal evidence from those who have undergone genital surgery that they have suffered sexual impairment, sometimes to the point of losing genital sensation altogether, and the failure systematically to assess sexual responsiveness through follow-up studies. The results of some forms of surgery, such as vaginal surgery, however, are acknowledged to be relatively unsatisfactory, in terms of both post-operative complications and ensuing sexual activity. Scarring, swelling and pain, subsequent stenosis, or narrowing, requiring additional surgery and a high percentage of urinary-tract complications are all mentioned (1998: 61-3). Yet surgeons persist with it, presumably in the vain hope of making heterosexual intercourse possible. Of course such surgery will apply to all those with a female gender assignment, including those defined as having a phallus which is too small to sustain a male assignment. However, the corrective surgery performed on those who are seen as having potentially adequate penile size can be little better. The most common type of surgery, the correction of hypospadias, in other words of urinary openings that are in the 'wrong' place, has led some doctors to coin the term 'hypospadia cripples' for those whose penises do not function or look any better after surgery (1998: 69). Furthermore, those undergoing these surgeries may be paying the price of urinary tract infections, fistulae (holes), hair growth inside their new tubes and scar tissue, not for the sake of being able to urinate *per se*, but in order to be capable of urinating in an approved manner – standing up and able to demonstrate their prowess in urinating against that of other boys. As Kessler points out, this is also to ignore the historicity of urinary postures (1998: 70-1).

The descriptions surgeons give of the corrective surgery they practise on intersexed people gives the impression that they do not think they are doing any more than simulating the 'real thing', although some of them speak almost like sculptors for whom the end-product was always inherent in the stone and needed merely to be helped to appear. The acknowledged difficulty of phalloplasty, however, does tend to be taken to mean that a penis is believed to be something which one has to be born with; it cannot be made. This makes it even more evident that such surgery as is practised is predominantly about maintaining dichotomous gender rather than producing sex – as this is understood by those in the medical profession (1998: 50-1). Surgeons practising vaginoplasty, whether it is on the intersexed, on transsexuals or on those who have suffered genital cancer, give every impression of endeavouring to create a *plausible* vagina, a mock-up, rather than a real one. Kessler puts it quite nicely: 'according to the professional literature, a woman needs an approximate vagina for a hypothetical penis' (1998: 109).

According to Kessler it is commitment to the gender dichotomy and to surgical advancement that provides the momentum behind the pursuit of surgery. Although surgeons may admit to the problems attendant upon current surgical techniques, they do not, by and large, do so in print and the general medical consensus about surgery is that it is considered to be worthwhile:

> Parenting a female with clitoral insensitivity and vaginal complications is seen as preferable to parenting a female with a larger-than-typical clitoris and a smaller-than-typical vagina. Parenting a male with a scarred and insensitive penis is seen as preferable to parenting a male with a normally functional (but small) one or one that does not permit a direct urinary stream. Nowhere in the medical literature is there an acknowledgement that these are value judgements. (1998: 75-6)

Retrieving intersexuality

Kessler poses an important question in relation to this unhappy and frankly bizarre state of affairs:

> If genitals are not completely dimorphic, if genital surgery to create dimorphism is problematic, and if people under certain conditions are capable of accepting genital variability, then why is intersexuality managed in the way that it is? Why are unusually sized and shaped genitals not accepted as reasonable markers of gender – gender either as we know it in the two-option scheme or as we could know it in a new gender system? Why does the 'solution' to variant genitals lie in knives and not in words?

She answers this by exploring two different subjects: the criterion of heterosexuality and the history of cosmetic surgery. The criterion of heterosexuality, as it is deployed in the clinical literature, presents something of a curious picture and is differentially presented for each gender. She quotes one group of surgeons for whom – judging by the order in which these considerations appear – the phallic requirement for men comprises, first of all, a successful urinary conduit, second, the validation of one's masculinity amongst one's peers (the so-called 'locker room factor') and, last of all, satisfactory sexual functioning. For women, it is unclear whether or not possession of a vagina is a necessary condition for heterosexual activity understood in terms of the provision of satisfaction for a male penis, or whether the relationship of activity to anatomy should be reversed, in other words that being a woman is *prima facie* about having a vagina (and thus being capable of heterosexual intercourse, whether this occurs or not). In fact, this discrepancy also relates to distinct categories of patient: for the intersexed, the vagina does not seem to be optional; the sense is that there is a *need* to create it. For those suffering from genital cancers, there is evidence that some surgeons see reconstructive vaginoplasty as optional because the genital is not fundamental to the identification of their patients as *women*, and that for others success is measured by the restoration of the *capacity* for intercourse, regardless of whether or not that capacity is ever invoked. To Kessler, this suggests that the vagina is primarily playing the role of a marker for gender differentiation Those who have already been identified and lived as women do not find themselves unmarked by the loss of the vagina, any more than Bobbit ceased to be a man the minute he lost his penis (although it was subsequently restored to him, and the sequence of events seems to have enhanced his potency sufficiently to supply him with a successful career in pornographic films). In that sense, it is the belief in two genders that grounds both heterosexuality and decisions about genital surgery (1998: 108).

The matter of cosmetic surgery suggests that it is not merely an outgrowth of assumptions about gender but also one of their progenitors. Plastic surgery, be it cosmetic or corrective, serves to shape, literally as well as metaphorically, the nature of sexual differentiation. From breast augmentation and liposuction, it now looks as if cosmetic surgery is moving inexorably to labial trimming and penile enhancement, with implants of fat and the 'release' of ligaments to make penises bigger, longer and allegedly better functioning (thus presenting a marked contrast to the world of Ancient Greece, where small penises were considered endearing and large penises comic).

However, the potential implications of such elective genital surgery may not be univocal. Whilst it undoubtedly appears to be setting tighter norms for what is acceptable or desirable by reducing variability, it has the potential, precisely because it is cosmetic and elective, to trivialize, to denaturalize and, according to Kessler, to destabilize the significance and importance given to genitalia – and hence to gender. It all depends, however, on the types of genital formation that are requested. Recently Western societies have seen the emergence of 'third gender', 'transgender' or 'non gender persons', some of whom demand the removal of all signs of differentiation on which a gender attribution might be able to be made and some of whom demand the construction, from a perfectly 'normal' accoutrement, of ambiguous genitalia. Alongside this, however, is the instructive example of rhinoplasty which, as Kessler points out, usually results in those who elect to change their noses selecting the small upturned ones: 'Promoting elective genital surgery could lead to less tolerance for variability, rather than more' (1998: 119).

Both surgery on the intersexed and elective genital surgery, from the point of view of their practitioners, look to be responding to the constraints of real world demands. The surgeons, endocrinologists, paediatricians and other medical professionals do not in any way see themselves as shaping that world, nor do they assume the possibility that what *is* is open to redefinition and re-negotiation. However, in the last ten years or so, and as a direct outgrowth of the widespread practice of surgery on intersexed infants, an intersexual movement has developed on whose agenda is the decrease if not the cessation of such surgery. Making links with female genital mutilation in parts of Africa and the Middle East and showing a number of similarities with the movement to halt and indeed reverse male circumcision, the intersexual movement has also led to the attempt to construct 'intersexuality' as a public identity – to replace the diagnostic category of the 'intersexed' (deemed a 'problem') with recognition of their distinctiveness, as a physiological, political and social grouping. Psychologically and socially, they seek the restoration of their integrity and, on a model similar to that of the disability or the gay movement, assert the validity and legitimacy of a differential biology against the social intolerance that demands that they adapt themselves (or *be* adapted) to the world of two dichotomous and mutually exclusive genders. Individual responses to their experiences and the manner of their politicization of intersexuality are very variable. Some are using 'intersexual' as a modifier for the existing gender categories, while others are promoting the idea of a third gender category:

> This validation of intersexuality is revealed in the way some intersexuals experience their genitals not as a clitoris, a penis, or even as microphallic tissue. 'I wish there was a way of talking…without intrinsically distorting things by misinterpreting them as either male or female.' Another objects to applying the term 'phallic clitoris' to a larger-than-typical clitoris because that assumes that the appropriate place for the phallus is on the male. Intersexuals' clitorises 'are

not phallic, they are phalluses in themselves, however decidedly different from the male penis.' (1998: 85)

The biologist Anne Fausto-Sterling (1993) has suggested that biological variation implies the possibility of five sexes (the two usual ones and three intersexed ones: female pseudo-hermaphrodites, male pseudo-hermaphrodites and true hermaphrodites), which she argues would help to dissolve gender oppositions. Kessler (1993, 1998), however, insists that this continues to give overwhelming significance to the genitals and ignores the fact that in everyday life there is no sex, only gender, because attributions are made without reference to genitalia. What has primacy here, she says, is the gender that is performed (1998: 90).

The development of what we might describe as sexual technologies, the ability to intervene surgically, hormonally, and so on, brings into being the possibility of dislocating what Kessler has described as the gender/genitals matching system, or at least of disrupting the coalescence of the markers that allow a gender attribution to be made. Alongside those who now identify themselves as 'she-males', 'chicks with dicks', 'testosterone women' and so on, for whom having a surfeit of sexual equipment is eminently desirable, is the following case history:

> A happily married heterosexual man requested estrogen treatment to enlarge his breasts because, as he told physicians, stimulation of his nipples was erotic and he wanted to increase his pleasure. His wife was supportive of the request. The clinicians, who prescribed the hormone treatment in spite of the fact that they did not think he evidenced any gender dysphoria, concluded that 'the sexual significance of his breasts was more important [for him] than their morphological aspects.' The man received the treatment, grew breasts, and at the one-year follow-up interview reported being satisfied with his body and his life. What is astonishing about this case is that the Dutch physicians were able to treat the breasts as not necessarily a gender cue. (1998: 123)

Only in Holland. Perhaps, however, by Kessler's own account, the reaction of the Dutch physicians is not so surprising after all. A clear gender attribution had been made and the request has, furthermore, taken place in the context of a conventional heterosexual arrangement. The very thing that makes the case history astonishing is perhaps also the very thing that made it possible and relatively unproblematic from the point of view of the doctors.

Kessler makes a very important point in relation to the 'mismatch' or 'contradiction' between morphological cues and eroticism, which relates equally to intersexuality: what is the place of organs in sexual attraction? For example, quite apart from sexual attraction to intersexed forms by those who are ordinarily gendered, what are we to make of the popularity in countries like Italy or Brazil of transsexual prostitutes? How should we envision the sexual orientation of men who define themselves as heterosexual but declare a preference for male-to-female transsexuals – many of them pre-operative and with fully functioning penises – because they make better women? (As one interviewee pointed out on an edition of *Eurotrash*, not only do they lavish more care upon themselves, and not 'let themselves go', but they are better able to understand 'a man's needs'.) As Kessler says: 'In what sense could a woman with a vagina who is sexually gratified by being penetrated by a "woman" with a large clitoris (that looks and functions like a penis) be said to be a lesbian?' (1998: 124). Whether such conformations are 'natural' or surgically or hormonally crafted, they still scramble our comfortable definitions of sexual orientation in terms of attraction to people with like or different genitalia: 'If gendered bodies fall into disarray, sexual orientation will follow' (ibid.). We shall also see such definitions undermined further when we come to consider the psychic content of such behaviours – or, indeed, of 'normal' ones.

Sex and gender as social construction [1]

These three historical examples, Foucault's, Laqueur's and Kessler's, give us three very variable pictures of the interweaving of moral and political concerns with the understanding of bodily features. What Foucault so very clearly makes evident for us is the manner in which the medico-legal discourse functions to secure a particular set of social arrangements. Unlike Kessler and McKenna, Foucault is not in any way concerned with something that one might call 'gender', and with the generality or otherwise of some kind of differentiation between human beings related to reproductive processes; his work in any case tends to steer away from generalities in favour of ruptures and discontinuities. Precisely because of that, he is able to give an account of the 'moment of birth' of a very particular, culturally specific form of differentiation, that of the European post-Enlightenment period. It gives us an account of a close and empirically very specific association between knowledge of the bodily and moral and political concerns. That very small snapshot, however, represents the putting in place of a new discursive order, which gives a new status to the bodily in its capacity to determine the proper social arrangements and moral order between 'women' and 'men' and it will be crucial for what is to follow. The body has become the basis and guarantor of those arrangements.

The Renaissance doctors described by Laqueur, by contrast, had no need of such a basis; they had available to them a metaphysical order whose features could be read in the book of Nature. Harvey's troubles with the matter of generation are born of the all-enveloping character of that order which does not allow an empirical science of difference to come into being because there is as yet no necessity for it. The place of women and men is still secure. Just as Foucault would have hoped to do, Laqueur's work has the virtue, through its presentation to us of a proximate past, of making the present 'anthropologically strange'.

By our own day, through the very oddity of the way in which anomaly is handled, we can see the collision of several contradictory discursive strands: those that implicitly take for granted the foundation of gender in the bodily, in the 'naturalness' of sex as an entity; those that assert the social and psychological malleability and constructibility of gender, and those portions of the biological sciences in which there is recognition of the potential lack of confluence between the range of biological components which are deemed to constitute sex.

In spite of its empirical specificity, however, Kessler's later work still asserts that she takes a 'social constructionist' approach, defined rather sweepingly as follows:

'By "social construction," we mean that beliefs about the world create the reality of that world, as opposed to the position that the world reveals what is really there' (1998: 133, n.1).   In relation to her earlier work with McKenna, her all-encompassing use of the term 'gender' seems all the more credible now. It is quite evident from the material she proffers here that, even where we might believe irreducible issues about biology to be being addressed, we are witness to an intimate interconnection between a number of rather heterogeneous things: social and moral imperatives as regards the proper adjustments of parents and children and the clarity of social categories; the enhancement of surgical technologies; investigative processes designed to establish an aetiological history and diagnostic judgement within a medical framework; the management of clinical decision-making and patient–doctor interaction; the deployment of biological knowledges in a practical setting, and so on. In short, it is not reasonable to seek to pare away the understanding of the bodily from the precise context in which it is enmeshed, and there is quite obviously a sense in which this is all 'socially constructed'.

Nevertheless, the terms in which she defines 'social constructionism' are far too broad, for there is a general claim about the relation between beliefs and the world in which they are to be found. To many people, her definition might seem to be the burden of the concept of 'discourse' as it is currently understood.   Yet in Foucault's work, where that use predominantly originated (although, incidentally, it does not appear in *Herculine Barbin*), it means something rather more circumspect than this. Certainly the term 'discourse' does entail a re-evaluation of the role of ideas, from a representational account of what they are, to a sense that they are of the world, that they are solidary with other features of that world and have effects within it. But there is an important difference between this and a statement that decrees that beliefs create reality, which is much closer to an idealist ontology because of the distinction made between 'beliefs' and 'reality'. This distinction, which is proper to epistemologies of one kind or another, makes us take one step forward and two steps back. First, it allows for the conflation of 'social construction' with the realm of 'beliefs'; second, it reproduces the problems we noted earlier in relation to Kessler and McKenna's use of an ethnomethodological framework, although it does have the virtue of dismantling 'sex' and 'gender' as two general realms, the biological and the social, confronting one another across the body. In this sense, the overarching role performed in her work by the concept 'gender' does make it possible genuinely to encompass *everything* concerned with the making of this kind of a difference.

What Kessler allows us to see, as does Foucault, is how the ontological status accorded to 'sex' functions in a variety of settings. Just because the concept of 'sex' has now acquired ontological status – the ontological status that made it into the relatively unquestioned basis for the concept of 'gender' – does not mean to say that we should assume that its role is henceforth everywhere the same. What this work starts to suggest is that we should cease to think of the relation between what we have hitherto called 'sex' and 'gender', and of the forms of explanation that pertain to them, as a confrontation between two incommensurable 'realities'. If we go by Kessler's account of the management of the intersexed, it might make more sense to think of 'sex' as a sub-heading of 'gender'.

However, if we retain these terms in the dominant ways in which they have been understood so far within feminism, the one denoting the realities of biological reproduction and the other the social interpretation and management of these realities, the one solid and the other interpretative, the one material and the other ideational, we shall be no further forward, as we shall see in the next chapter. An inadequate theoretical framework will bind our ankles and stymie our progress, returning us always to the same dilemmas. In order to consider this, we must examine what our reading of the past needs to do to our reading of the present for us to be able to move forward and, as Foucault wished us to do, 'to think differently'.

Notes

[1] Describing the particular view of 'natural' held by physicians responsible for the management of the intersexed, Suzanne Kessler writes: 'Although the "deformity" of intersexed genitals would be immutable were it not for medical interference, physicians do not consider it natural. Instead, they think of, and speak of, the surgical/hormonal alteration of such "deformities" as natural because such intervention returns the body to what it ought to have been if events had taken their typical course. The non-normative is converted into the normative and the normative state is considered natural' (Kessler, 1998: 31). Indeed, the idea of a *statistical* norm, in which normal values cluster around a mean or mode, is applied to questions of genital size and results in the ablation of a part, and sometimes *the whole,* of clitorises deemed 'over-large' or the reassignment of children with 'inadequate' penises to the category 'female'. These are seen as correctable 'birth defects'. For an extended discussion of different ways of conceptualizing what is 'natural', Kessler also refers us to Smith (1979).

[2] Medical preference is no longer for referring to clitoral tissue as 'erectile', on the basis that whilst it becomes engorged with blood, it does not, properly speaking, become erect. Specialists in histology would be better able than we to ascertain the ideological content of a claim of this kind. Certainly, there is recent evidence that would suggest that the clitoris should no longer be regarded as a miniature homologue of the penis, but as an organ with its own distinctive physiological characteristics, including, allegedly, double the number of nerve endings found in the penis and a much larger, if concealed, structure than that which is normally assumed to constitute it.

5 Timely Bodies

Foucault's work traces a mythic historic moment when 'sex' as an ontological category comes into being, or is, at any rate, symbolically consolidated, in Western societies. In keeping with Foucault's other writings, the moment is more figurative, the events more emblematic than historically foundational. Thomas Laqueur's work, on the other hand, has both a longer historical scope and broader empirical purchase. He too, however, begins his book *Making Sex* with an emblematic moment.

That moment is about two interpretations of the same tale, fifty years apart (1990: 1).[1] The interpretations concern the place of the female orgasm in the act of generation. The tale concerns the daughter of innkeepers, apparently dead and laid out, but made pregnant by the monk entrusted with holding vigil over her body. The girl, subsequently discovered to be alive, denies all knowledge of the origins of her pregnancy. The first interpretation reads the tale as a tale of fraud, for it is well known that conception could not have taken place without the girl's pleasure, for 'apart from pleasure nothing of a mortal kind comes into existence'.[2] The second was given as one of many proofs that orgasm was irrelevant to conception. As Laqueur puts it, an interpretive chasm separates the two interpretations. Pleasure went from being something as integral to conception and as unquestioned as the warm glow is to the good meal that supplies it, to a peripheral, contingent and expendable adjunct to the sexual act. This applied in principle to both sexes, but it was in the newly established independence of generation from pleasure that women's sexual nature could be redefined, that they could come to be seen as passive and passionless, and, eventually, as 'not much troubled with sexual feelings' (1990: 3-4).

It is difficult to realize today just how radical a transformation this apparently small shift entailed. As Laqueur points out, the commonplace of much contemporary psychology and popular culture, that men want sex while women want relationships – now used, incidentally, as one of the premises of the new and allegedly ground-breaking evolutionary psychology – is the precise inversion of pre-Enlightenment beliefs about men and women. Contrary to this apparently hoary old truth, notions extending back into antiquity equated men with friendship and women with fleshliness. It was women whose desires knew no bounds, whose reason had so little resistance to passion. Now they were to become, as Laqueur so delicately describes it, 'creatures whose whole reproductive life might be spent anesthetized to the pleasures of the flesh' (1990: 4).

But what is the more profound significance of this 'contingency of delight' (1990: 3)? It marks, Laqueur says, the advent of a *biological* signpost of incommensurable sexual difference. And that is new. Prior to the Enlightenment, the feebleness of women's reason in the face of passion, the unboundedness of their desires, had had to do with their place on the ladder of creation, but this was not given by any notion of their 'biology'. They were fundamentally a lesser, imperfect version of man, who himself, in medieval theology, would have been placed below the diverse orders of the angels, but above the whole of the animal kingdom. This was indicated by, but not the result of, the way in which women's bodies demonstrated a lack of 'vital heat'. This caused them to retain inside their bodies structures that in men would have been on the outside: 'women are but men turned outside in', as early nineteenth-century doggerel would have it (1990: 4). Laqueur refers to this in shorthand as 'the one-sex model'. What moves in to replace this view is a notion of a fundamental polarity between the sexes based upon discoverable biological distinctions: '[n]o longer would those who think about such matters regard woman as a lesser version of man along a vertical axis of infinite gradations, but rather as an altogether different creature along a horizontal axis whose middle ground was largely empty' (1990: 148).

From the one-sex to the two-sex model

It is important to understand that we are not comparing like with like here, for herein lies the subtlety of Laqueur's argument. This is not the simple reorientation of an axis of difference from hierarchy to opposition, premised on fundamentally the same grounds. On the contrary, it looks like an inversion of the ontological order of priorities. Women's and men's bodies in pre-Enlightenment accounts are indices of a *metaphysical* reality, more profound and more fundamental than the disposition of organs. Indeed, the disposition of organs shows a mutability which, for the modern mind, would simply provoke incredulity: a girl chasing her swine suddenly springs an external penis and scrotum, men associating too much with women lose the more perfect hardness of their bodies and regress towards effeminacy (1990: 7). As Caroline Walker Bynum (1989) has pointed out in another context, bodies do strange and remarkable things – male ones lactate, the bodies of female saints are miraculously preserved after death – but this is related to a completely different understanding of what bodies *are*. It is not merely that bodies are seen as in some way *permeable* to what we would now describe as cultural understandings. It is that the entire order of things bears a different complexion. Bodily morphology, far from providing *evidence* for the truth of the world order, instead merely 'makes vivid and more palpable a hierarchy of heat and perfection that is in itself not available to the senses' (1990: 27). Laqueur summarizes the issue like this:

> I want to propose instead that in these pre-Enlightenment texts, and even some later ones, *sex,* or the body, must be understood as the epiphenomenon, while *gender,* what we would take to be a cultural category, was primary or 'real.'

Gender – man and woman – mattered a great deal and was part of the order of things: sex was conventional, though modern terminology makes such a reordering nonsensical. At the very least, what we call sex and gender were in the 'one-sex model' explicitly bound up in a circle of meanings from which escape to a supposed biological substrate – the strategy of the Enlightenment – was impossible. In the world of one sex, it was precisely when talk seemed to be most directly about the biology of two sexes that it was most embedded in the politics of gender, in culture. (1990: 8, emphasis in original)

What looks from our point of view like an inversion of the ontological order of things persists across the best part of two millennia and more. Laqueur finds it, differently, in Galen and Aristotle and notices its persistence into a nineteenth-century science that was open to both models, the one-sex or the two-sex model. That is not to say that a *single* account of what bodies are and do persists over more than two thousand years, a period in which, as Laqueur himself stresses, social, political and cultural life changes dramatically:

I want to lay claim to a different historical domain, to the broad discursive fields that underlie competing ideologies, that define the terms of conflict, and that give meaning to various debates. I am not committed to demonstrating, for example, that there is a single, dominant 'idea of woman' in the Renaissance and that all others are less important. I have no interest in proving that Galen is more important than Aristotle at any one time or that a given theory of menstruation was hegemonic between 1840 and 1920. (1990: 23)

This is analogous to what Foucault would have described as an episteme,[3] but what is different here is that there is no question of one discursive field decisively and once and for all replacing another (1990: 21). Not only is the history of the difference of woman from man over the two millennia of the 'one-sex' model complex, but the modern polarity of two incommensurable sexes is less secure and unambiguously dominant than it first appears. However, as Foucault suggests, to the question of whether or not we *truly* need a *true* sex, we, in the modern world, have tended to answer yes '[w]ith a persistence that borders on stubbornness' (1980: vii). What Laqueur is interested in, then, is that which consistently frames the way in which bodies are thought about from the period of classical antiquity until approximately the end of the eighteenth century, and which is so very different from our own frame of reference. Then, around 1800, as he puts it, 'to use Virginia Woolf's device, human sexual nature changed':

By around 1800, writers of all sorts were determined to base what they insisted were fundamental differences between the male and female sexes, and thus between man and woman, on discoverable biological distinctions and to express these in a radically different rhetoric. In 1803, for example, Jacques-Louis Moreau, one of the founders of 'moral anthropology,' argued passionately against the nonsense written by Aristotle, Galen and their modern followers on the subject of women in relation to men. Not only are the sexes different, but they are different in every conceivable aspect of body and soul, in every physical and moral aspect. To the physician or the naturalist, the relation of woman to man is 'a series of oppositions and contrasts.' In place of what, in certain situations, strikes the modern imagination as an almost perverse insistence on understanding sexual difference as a matter of degree, gradations of one basic male type, there arose a shrill call to articulate sharp corporeal distinctions. (1990: 5)

What is crucially different post-1800 is the attempt to ground social roles, what we would now call 'gender', in nature, in what we would now call 'sex'. As we indicated earlier, the biological is seen as the foundation and guarantor of particular sets of social arrangements (1990: 29). What is interesting about this is that before the end of the eighteenth century, no one had felt the need to do so. Woman's place in the world order was not the problem that it seemed to become at the end of the Enlightenment. Laqueur does not account for what caused this change in very much detail but he does make two kinds of claim. The first of these is that, whatever else might have had an effect, the change did not come about because of advances in medical science. Thus, it is not the case that the ancients were quite simply wrong and that the march of modern science rectified our understanding. Indeed there is a discrepancy in time which means that the re-evaluation of woman's sexual pleasure, and of her nature as a sexual being, occurs approximately one hundred years before the relevant discoveries could command sufficient authority to support the new point of view (1990: 9). Moreover, some scientific advances, such as those in developmental anatomy (germ-layer theory) pointed in the opposite direction, for example towards a morphologically androgynous embryological ground plan. Instead there is a general epistemic shift in the way in which the body is regarded: instead of constituting a microcosm of a much larger order of signification, it becomes a much more limited object in an increasingly regionalized science: 'Science no longer generated the hierarchies of analogies, the resemblances that bring the whole world into every scientific endeavor but thereby create a body of knowledge that is, as Foucault argues, at once endless and poverty–stricken' (1990: 10).

The second claim that Laqueur makes is that 'no one was much interested in looking for evidence of two distinct sexes, at the anatomical and concrete physiological differences between men and women, until such differences became politically important' (ibid.). In other words, the ontological inversion was in some sense *motivated*. It is worth remembering here that changes in the epistemic landscape were also linked to religious and, consequently, political changes. The demotion of the metaphysical order was, at the same time, a disassembling of the old social order. Laqueur insists, however, that transformations in the social and political landscape were not in themselves sufficient to produce the re-interpretation of bodies:

The rise of evangelical religion, Enlightenment political theory, the development of new sorts of public spaces in the eighteenth century, Lockean ideas of marriage as a contract, the cataclysmic possibilities for social change wrought by the French revolution, postrevolutionary conservatism, postrevolutionary feminism, the factory system with its restructuring of the sexual division of labor, the rise of a free market economy in services or commodities, the birth of classes, singly or in combination – none of these things *caused* the making of a new sexed body. Instead, the remaking of the body is itself intrinsic to each of these developments. (1990: 11)

This looks like a broadly Foucauldian point, insofar as what we are seeing is a new *disposition* of things, of which the relevant changes are an integral part – rather than a pattern of historical causation. Laqueur does however talk of the *dependence* of the construal of bodies on prior and shifting epistemological and political grounds (1990: 17). These remain rather generally specified but the important point is that at the heart of the change was the disaggregation of the link between 'the intimate, experiential qualities of sexual delight' and the metaphysical order of things (1990: 11). One thing that the pre-Enlightenment world did seem to show – unlike our own – was a coherency all the way from the experiential to the cosmological.

Mutable morphologies and fungible fluids

To call the modern polarity an ontological *inversion* of what went before is therefore satisfyingly tidy but not entirely accurate. The pre-Enlightenment world is rather more of a piece than that. As Laqueur, and indeed as Caroline Walker Bynum (1989) pointed out, it is a world marked by a psychosomatic unity unimaginable to us and a cosmic order in which what we would now think of as the physical is at once and fundamentally *meta*physical. The ways in which the body is imagined are various, inconsistent and mutable, but they all share this in common: the argument is made that woman is but a version of man. Instead of a heterosexual complementarity of organs, in which the vagina is the 'sheath' intended for the reception of the penis, no such a term as 'vagina' exists until around 1700 and it is conceptualized instead as an interior penis. Ovary and testis share the same name and the scrotum is seen to have its counterpart in the uterus. The distinctive use of that organ for the bearing of a child is explained by Aristotle, for example, in terms of a critical difference between bearing and begetting. In the act of generation it is the male who supplies the effective cause, the artisanal and informing principle, while the female supplies the material cause, the passive matter that is shaped by the ideational principle provided by the male. In this 'one-seed' account of generation, however, (as distinct from the 'two-seed account' of Galen or Hippocrates) the *sperma* produced by the male – for which the ejaculate acts as the vehicle – is an immaterial substance, which fashions the *catamenia* produced by the female much as the swordsmith's *art* fashions a sword. The male's part in generation is produced by *pneuma* or breath, which accounts for the foamy character of the ejaculate, and this is, precisely, not substantial. The matter all lies with the female. But even here, the nature of the *catamenia* as a substance remains obscure. Aristotle insists that, although it is a menstrual residue, it is not to be confused with the *visible* blood, since 'the greater part of the menstrual flow is useless, being fluid' (Aristotle's *Generation of Animals*, cited in Laqueur, 1990: 42). Sperm, menstrual blood, milk – both reproductive and non-reproductive fluids – belong, in these pre-Enlightenment accounts, to an economy of fungible fluids. What unifies male and female in this apparently most dichotomous of pre-Enlightenment accounts (Aristotle's is different in this regard from, say, Galen's), is a hierarchy of blood in which the male is able to animate matter – but only under ideal conditions. Semen from boys, old men and those who have intercourse too frequently may lack or lose this ability. So neither 'maleness' nor that which characterizes it has any 'material' stability. In texts such as these, the apparent substantiality of observable biological features fades into and out of existence like the smile of the Cheshire cat.

For the Galenic account, the comparison between male and female is like the comparison between the eyes of the mole and the eyes of other animals. The relevant structures are present but they are imperfect because the mole is more or less blind. The female generative parts remain inside the body, a stunted version of the male. For each body part found in the male, Galen, as a professional anatomist, can describe its counterpart in the female, but, as such, these parts are *illustrative* of the higher order of things, not their cause or basis. Sexual hierarchy is instantiated by the body not produced by it. But what also sometimes happens in accounts like that of Galen, and between different accounts, is that complementarity or opposition between male and female can be argued for, and, in the next moment, denied. Furthermore, these ambiguities or potential contradictions do not seem unduly disturbing. There are undoubtedly ratiocinative efforts enlisted in arguing for the respective meanings of these apparently contradictory states of affairs, but there is nothing invested – as there would be now – in the coherency of 'biological' accounts. A good example is provided by Isidore of Seville's three different accounts of the nature of seed. Writing the first major medieval summary of ancient scientific learning in the sixth and seventh centuries, Isidore of Seville is, as Laqueur points out, working in a very different social context, as a Christian encyclopaedist, from that of an Athenian philosopher or an imperial Roman doctor such as Soranus, whom he also discusses. But the structure of Isidore's argument is paradigmatic for this very long-standing tradition of understanding sexual difference:

> Isidore simultaneously holds three propositions to be true: that only men have sperma, that only women have sperma, and that both have sperma. It takes no great genius to see that these would be mutually contradictory claims if they are understood as literal truths about the body. But they would be perfectly compatible if they are seen as corporeal illustrations of cultural truths purer and more fundamental than biological fact. Indeed, Isidore's entire work is predicated on the belief that the origins of words informs one about the pristine, uncorrupted, essential nature of their referants, about a reality beyond the corrupt senses. (Laqueur, 1990: 55)

The first of these propositions – that only men have *sperma* – is an explanation of consanguinity in which inheritance and legitimacy pass through the father's blood, whilst the second – that only women have *sperma* – defines illegitimacy. While the legitimate child issues from the father's seed, the illegitimate child belongs to the mother alone, issuing from her seed. In the third case, Isidore is trying to explain the resemblance between parents and children, and, in that instance, the child resembles the father if the father's seed is more potent and the mother if the mother's seed is more potent. In this explanation, each conception involves a battle for domination between mother's and father's *sperma*. As Laqueur makes clear, these different accounts are not really about bodies at all or, rather, what we would recognize as the bodily is subordinate to issues surrounding power, legitimacy and fatherhood, which would in any case not be resolvable by reference to the body at all (1990: 57).

Safeguarding the father

Laqueur goes on to give a very interesting explanation – deriving from Freud – about the way in which paternity was conceptualized before the discovery of distinctive germ cells in the mid-nineteenth century. Prior to that, believing in fatherhood is analogous to the belief in the Hebrew God:

> The Judaic insistence that God cannot be seen – the graven image proscription – 'means that a sensory perception was given second place to what may be called an abstract idea.' This God represents 'a triumph of intellectuality over sensuality (*Triumph der Geistigkeit über die Sinnlichkeit*), or strictly speaking, an instinctual renunciation.' (ibid.)

Because belief in fatherhood is a supposition, an inference, whereas motherhood 'is evident from the lowly senses alone', fatherhood 'represents a victory of the more elevated, the more refined over the less refined, the sensory, the material. It is a world-historical *Kulturfortschritt*, a cultural stride forward' (1990: 57-8).

Laqueur wants to suggest that the one-sex model can be interpreted as an exercise in safeguarding the Father, as he who stands for order and civilization. Were it not to be so, were the male not more self-evidently potent than the female, there might be no need for him at all. Woman cannot provide both the site for conception *and* an active principle of generation: according to Aristotle, that would make it possible for them to inseminate themselves and 'dispense with men', a manifest absurdity. Similarly, according to Galen, if the female seed were as potent as the male's, 'there would be two principles of motion in conflict with one another' (Galen's *On the Usefulness of the Parts of the Body*, cited in Laqueur, 1990: 58). Laqueur notes that 'an immense amount of effort and anxiety' had to be deployed in the demonstration that the male's is the more potent contribution. 'Perhaps,' he says, 'the confident assertions that "there needs to be a female," that the creator would not "make half the human race imperfect and, as it were, mutilated, unless there was some great advantage to such a mutilation," hides the more pressing but unaskable question of whether there needs to be a male. After all, the work of generation available to the senses is wholly the work of the female' (1990: 58-9).

The demonstrations of the proper order of things are ingenious and, in many cases, represent triumphs of what would appear to us to be contorted ratiocination, and new forms of cultural and religious order – such as the advent of Christianity – present new sets of intellectual dilemmas in the ordering of social and sexual worlds. Such things as Christianity's opposition to infanticide

– which diminished the power of fathers – or its advocacy of virginity – which the ancients would have thought injurious to health – had the effect of shifting and problematizing a whole series of other relations between human beings, their bodies and the social order. However, a variety of accounts of the body and what is now deemed to belong to it – generation, sexual passion, organs, and so on – are still to be found side by side: 'It is a sign of modernity to ask for a single consistent biology as the *source* and *foundation* of masculinity and femininity' (1990: 61, emphasis added).

The closed and autarchic body

One of the primary reasons for the longevity of the one-sex model, according to Laqueur, is precisely its polyvalency, the fact that it could 'register and absorb any number of shifts in the axes and valuations of difference' (1990: 62), which is the direct result of the fact that it is not the body that carries ontological status. The transformation wrought after the Enlightenment is that the body is to become what Laqueur describes as the *epistemic foundation* for prescriptive claims about the social order. Insofar as knowledge of the bodily becomes the means of legitimating moral and political imperatives, however, the body becomes both less polyvalent and more crucial. Laqueur cites the endless stream of books, and chapters of books, whose titles indicate their intent. Like those identified by Foucault in relation to Alexina, their concern is with what the physical can reveal about the moral, and their specific preoccupation is with *women* – examples include Roussel's *Système physique et moral de la femme* and Brachet's chapter 'Etudes du physique et du moral de la femme'. If the physical logically pre-exists, and is independent of, but offers a key to the moral, it is all the more powerful for all that. It is important that the body appear to be, as Laqueur puts it, closed and autarchic, apparently outside the realm of meaning. Of course, we know from the preceding chapter that this is not what actually happens: the autarchy of the body, and its alleged 'independence from meaning' is more a matter of declaration than of anything else. Laqueur points out that the general shift in the way in which bodies were interpreted could not have been due, even *in principle*, to new scientific discoveries:

> In the first place, 'oppositions and contrasts' between the female and the male, if one wishes to construe them as such, have been clear since the beginning of time: the one gives birth and the other does not. Set against such momentous truths, the discovery that the ovarian artery is not, as Galen would have it, the female version of the *vas deferens* is of relatively minor significance. The same can be said about the 'discoveries' of more recent research on the biochemical, neurological, and other natural determinants or insignia of sexual difference. As Anne Fausto-Sterling has documented, a vast amount of negative data that shows no regular differences between the sexes is simply not reported. Moreover, what evidence there does exist for biological difference with a gendered behavioral result is either highly suspect for a variety of methodological reasons, or ambiguous, or proof of Dorothy Sayers' notion that men and women are very close neighbors indeed if it is proof of anything at all. (1990: 9-10)

Although recent research presents itself as disinterested, understanding of the body is clearly not innocent of other concerns, as we shall demonstrate in due course. What it *is* and what it gives us to understand about how our world should be ordered has instead become fundamental. Indeed, after a period in which social scientific accounts of human life were popular, the current ascendancy of biology, and of genetics in particular, means that the stakes are once again high: there is a significant investment in what bodies are and the nature of the body has come to be seen as rather more decisive than it once was – and not merely in the realm of sexual differentiation.

It would perhaps be possible to argue that the body's apparent cultural innocence is there all the better to secure the 'nature' of women and men and the social arrangements between them – although it is clearly not this imperative alone that drives biological research into the difference between the sexes. Indeed, it is an interesting paradox that, in the one-sex world, in which male dominance appears less disturbed by emancipatory claims, a thinker like Aristotle insists that an animal is not 'male or female in virtue of the whole of itself but only in virtue of a certain faculty and a certain part', that is uterus and penis and testes (Aristotle's *Generation of Animals*, cited in Laqueur, 1990: 31). By contrast, in the two-sex world, in the late nineteenth-century writings of Patrick Geddes for instance, we meet with the familiar argument that the destinies of men and women were decided in the dim and distant evolutionary past:

> Differences may be exaggerated or lessened, but to obliterate them 'it would be necessary to have all the evolution over again on a new basis. What was decided among the pre-historic Protozoa cannot be annulled by an act of Parliament.' Microscopic organisms wallowing in the primordial ooze determined the irreducible distinctions between the sexes and the place of each in society. (Geddes cited in Laqueur, 1990: 6)

In fact, Geddes actually descends to the level of cellular physiology to argue that female *cells* are fundamentally distinct from the male, being anabolic – i.e. conserving of energy – rather than catabolic – putting out energy. Female is hence different from male in every fibre of her body. What is striking about his evolutionary argument, of course, is its very familiarity, not least in the newly popular 'Darwinian' psychology. The resurrection of such contentions, at a distance of more than a century, ought, unfortunately, to be more surprising than it is.

Of language and the flesh

Laqueur makes the point, however, that the body does not give itself to be 'read' in one way rather than another. Difference and sameness are everywhere but the decision to render them significant and the reason why this is done is decided in a space other than that of empirical investigation. Difference and sameness are inherently unstable. In this context, he mentions Freud's fundamental insight that the body does not *per se* generate two sexes, nor is there, underneath it all, any 'correct' representation of difference. It is all a matter of what one is looking for. In this sense, Laqueur's insights are similar to Kessler and McKenna's: to frame it in ethnomethodological terms, it all depends upon the universe of meaning within which one exists.

Laqueur concludes from this that, for ourselves as much as for the pre-Enlightenment world, in other words regardless of how difference is understood, whatever one might wish to say about (what we would now call) sex is already intimately bound up with gender. Sex, he says – and it is significant that he uses this term straightforwardly and apparently unproblematically here – is only explicable in the context of battles over gender and power (1990: 11). Yet, however historically specific the understanding of the body, he wishes to insist upon that body's substantiality because, he says, under the impact of Foucault, various forms of deconstruction, Lacanian psychoanalysis, and post-structuralism generally, it threatens to disappear entirely. In spite of this, however, 'the flesh...will not long allow itself to remain in silence' (1990: 13).

Although his work is itself implicated in such developments, he wishes to maintain an 'Archimedean point', a point of leverage, which is 'not in the real transcultural body but rather in the *space* between it and its representations' (1990: 16). Laqueur seems to eschew the idea of a self-evident, enclosed and stable body, the 'real transcultural body', and yet, if that is the case, how can a space be maintained between it and its representations? What might such a space consist of? It is also unclear whether the space is merely between the body (however it may be understood) and its representations, or whether the 'real transcultural body' *is* in play, and the potential ambiguity renders the statement enigmatic.

What he is anxious to retain, through keeping open this space, are two things. The first is the capacity to fulfil an ethical obligation, which is to take account of human suffering and of the fact that such suffering, and the injustice to which it is related, are often gendered. It is the correspondence of such suffering to the corporeal signs of sex which requires that a concept of sex be retained (1990: 16). The second is the acknowledgement of the advances represented by current scientific knowledges of the body. This why he stresses that our becoming human in culture 'does not give us license to ignore the body' (1990: 13). Whether either of these requires a concept of sex in order to be intelligible is debatable. We shall tackle the latter of his two concerns a little later. The first would be perfectly explicable in the way in which he describes it, as a gendered form of suffering, providing the account of gender deployed includes some reference to how gender appropriates corporealities. Perhaps the implication here is broader, however, and that is that insofar as reference to 'sex' is required, gender is of necessity non-corporeal.

In short, then, Laqueur wishes to salvage the body from what he sees as its linguistic demise, yet he also regards the body as something that makes its presence felt. In a different set of metaphors, he talks of the body becoming so veiled that it threatens to disappear entirely, of nature 'folding into' culture, and of the 'body's *priority* over language' being eroded. Quoting Maurice Godelier, he observes that 'Society *haunts* the body's sexuality' (1990: 11-12, emphases added). These images of collapse and erosion, or veiling, evanescence and haunting, counterbalanced with assertions of priority and of a refusal to be *silenced*, evince something like a sense or a fear of loss. The flesh speaks, yet is silenced by language – in spite of its refusal to be so. Between the lines one detects something like regret, as if what the investigations of *Making Sex* had banished for ever, were a simpler, pre-lapsarian world in which one could have confidence in what the body *was*.

This is understandable given the way in which the dilemma of the body has been formulated here:

> To a great extent my book and feminist scholarship in general are inextricably caught in the tensions of this formulation: between language on the one hand and extralinguistic reality on the other; between nature and culture; between 'biological sex' and the endless social and political markers of difference. We remain poised between the body as that extraordinarily fragile, feeling and transient mass of flesh with which we are all familiar – too familiar – and the body that is so hopelessly bound to its cultural meanings as to elude unmediated access.
>
> The analytical distinction between sex and gender gives voice to these alternatives and has always been precarious. In addition to those who would eliminate gender by arguing that cultural differences are really natural, there has been a powerful tendency amongst feminists to empty sex of its content by arguing, conversely, that natural differences are really cultural. (1990: 11-12)

What is evident in this passage is the powerful persistence of the presuppositions put in place by the sex/gender problematic. We find again the same series of homologous dichotomies superimposed on one another as we identified in the work of Ann Oakley, the dichotomies that have been the ghostly rejoinder to the distinction between sex and gender since its inception – meaning/reality, nature/culture, biological/sociopolitical. It is a set of oppositions he calls – significantly, as we shall see – 'precarious' and he describes sex and gender as giving voice to alternatives which are in tension. However, what is more important here is the way in which Laqueur's account of feminist scholarship – and of his own work – maps onto the sex/gender distinction one between language and world. It is not by chance, then, that Laqueur's opening chapter is entitled 'Of Language and the Flesh'.

He tells two stories to illustrate this dilemma, one related to his father, the pathologist Werner Laqueur, and the other the poignant story of the death of a middle-aged dentist from oesophageal varices ('I know when one is dead, and when one lives/She's dead as earth,' howled Lear).[4] As a child, he spent many Sunday mornings watching his father do the delicate job of dissection and preparation of specimens for microscopic examination, and subsequently 'reading' what he saw on the mounted slides. Bodies, he says, or at any rate body parts, seemed 'unimpeachably real' and his father had always seemed to be an expert in 'what was *really* there' (1990: 14-15). However, amidst his father's papers, after his death, were to be found offprints of a paper on the influence of various hormones on the masculine uterus, published by him in 1936. Coming well after much of the research for *Making Sex* had been completed, this was genuinely uncanny – *unheimlich* in the classic sense:

> I had read Sarah Kofman on the power of anatomy to 'confuse those who think
> of the sexes as two opposing species.' But my father's contribution to the
> confusion was a complete revelation, genuinely uncanny. It was hidden and yet
> so much of the home – *heimlich* but also *unheimlich* – the veiled and secret made
> visible, an eerie, ghostly reminder that somehow this book and I go back a long
> way. (1990: 15)

The second story he tells concerns the disjuncture he feels between the body as cultural construct and what he defines as the 'real' body, the body on the dissecting or operating table for example. He describes going to hear *Don Giovanni* and hearing the following morning of the death of the patient, 'a fact that seemed of an entirely different order from Mozart's play on the body or the history of representation that constitutes this book' (1990: 14). Both as a medical student attempting to reconcile the anatomical illustrations with what he found on the dissecting table, and as the witness to the desperate struggle to save a life, he is aware of what he describes as 'the fraught chasm between representation and reality, seeing-as and seeing'.[5]

This recapitulation, or gloss, of representation and reality by two versions of 'seeing', precisely because it doesn't quite work, expresses very well the dilemma in which he finds himself. He is caught between two accounts, one of which describes what we think of as two different ontological states and the other two fundamentally similar processes. He talks of the body being 'so *hopelessly* bound to its cultural *meanings* as to elude unmediated access' (1990: 12, emphases added). For that reason, he feels the need to continue to maintain the distinction – fraught chasm though it is – between the body and its representations, and to resist what he sees as the 'emptying out' of sex, the collapse of the bodily into the discursive.

Such a collapse is unnecessary, however, for it is the product of the conceptual distinction between two *general* realms, the linguistic and the extra-linguistic. Laqueur identifies discourse with the linguistic and the body or sex with the extra-linguistic. Thus, all knowledge of the body becomes a form of language, which confronts the 'real', non-linguistic, fleshly body. Because of this, 'sex' as an object seems to have been replaced by, and hence absorbed into, 'sex' as a concept as a result of the very discoveries Laqueur has made. Sociality (at least where it concerns gender) is also quintessentially related to this form of language via the notion of discourse, which comes to be about the meaning we give to the real.

The making of sex

Yet Laqueur has also devoted his book to the *making* of sex, to the construction of that discursive object by means of which we now comprehend the body as an object whose precise characteristics are its enclosure and isolation from matters of sociality, culture and language. It is only for us, *at the end of this long historical development*, that the body seems autarchic and entirely *without* any relation to sociality, obedient only to its own, biological, imperatives.

In this context, Laqueur's description of *Making Sex* as a history of representation is significant.   To construe knowledges of the body as representations suggests that the relation of knowledge to its object is deemed to be mimetic or delegative, since a representation is that which *stands in* for the object in the realm of ideas. Knowledge is there merely to reflect or re-present it – either successfully or unsuccessfully.

What is interesting, then, is that, having traced the origins of 'sex', and marked its intimate association with an agenda designed to secure a social and political difference between the sexes through the apparently decisive autarchy of the body, 'outside the realm of meaning' (1990:7), Laqueur remains caught up in the delineation of the world it has established. He is, in fact, a victim of the very framework whose origins he identifies. When it comes to thinking about the present, in making a clear, one might say an ontological, disjunction between the body and its discursive constitution, it appears as if – paradoxically – he has himself lost the sense that science, as he puts it, 'does not simply investigate, but itself constitutes, the difference' that his book explores, the difference of woman from man (1990: 17).

This might seem an odd remark to make, since the distinction between that object of physiological investigation, the body, and the object of linguistic science, language, seems so commonsensically self-evident. But let us ponder this just for a moment: if we think of language in the terms in which Chomsky understands it, it becomes evident that it represents a biologically given capacity, presumably something which is a product of human physiology – in more senses than one. Just shifting the disciplinary, or, more properly, the discursive focus slightly makes the commonsensical divorce between the two things less obvious.

The science of difference

The cost Laqueur pays for this conflation of the linguistic with the discursive is that he is led to occupy an agnostic position similar to the one espoused by Kessler and McKenna:

> More important, though, I hope this book will persuade the reader that there is no 'correct' representation of women in relation to men and that the whole science of difference is thus misconceived. It is true that there is and was considerable and often overtly misogynist bias in much biological research on women; clearly science has historically worked to 'rationalize and legitimize' distinctions not only of sex but also of race and class, to the disadvantage of the powerless. But it does not follow that a more objective, richer, progressive, or even more feminist science would produce a truer picture of sexual difference in any culturally meaningful sense. (This is why I do not attempt to offer a history of more or less correct, or more or less misogynistic, representations.) In other words, the claim that woman is what she is because of her uterus is no more, or less, true than the subsequent claim that she is what she is because of her ovaries. Further evidence will neither refute nor affirm these patently absurd pronouncements because at stake are not biological questions about the effects of

organs or hormones but cultural, political questions regarding the nature of woman. (1990: 21-2)

This is too pessimistic and all-embracing a conclusion. The sense Laqueur gives us here is that the science of difference is entirely contaminated by cultural, political questions. The final statement in this passage seems to imply that allegedly empirical questions are really nothing of the sort. But not all claims are of the same order. The claim that woman is what she is because of her ovaries is not the same kind of claim as the claim that the ovary releases the egg,[6] or Laqueur would not feel moved to describe the first of these claims as 'patently absurd'. The point is that it is just not reasonable to suggest that the relationship between cultural concerns (what in this context would nowadays be termed 'gender') and knowledge of the bodily (what would nowadays be termed 'sex') is a general one. In the context of sex – but perhaps beyond it as well, for Laqueur also mentions race and class – it is to condemn knowledge of the bodily to be forever bound to inequality and oppression, the political and social imperatives of gender as we understand them.

He seems to be arguing, in a way which is not dissimilar to what one might say about the scientific investigations into 'race', that the whole of the research endeavour marked by the term 'sex' represents, in a veiled way, nothing *other* than a social and political agenda: 'the whole science of difference is thus misconceived'. In other words, 'sex' is as bankrupt as 'race'. And yet, not only does he not abandon the term, but he does not deny the findings arrived at under its rubric ('It is obvious that sex is something more than what society designates, or that naming makes it', he says, quoting Weeks), and he also wishes to mark the empirical success of the biological sciences in that domain:

> Moreover, there has clearly been progress in understanding the human body in general and reproductive anatomy and physiology in particular. Modern science and modern women are much better able to predict the cyclical likelihood of pregnancy than were their ancestors; menstruation turns out to be a different physiological process from hemorrhoidal bleeding, contrary to the prevailing wisdom well into the eighteenth century, and the testes *are* histologically different from the ovaries. Any history of a science, however much it might emphasise the role of social, political, ideological, or aesthetic factors, must recognize these undeniable successes and the commitments that made them possible. (1990: 16)

Laqueur's adoption of the concept of sex and his use of the sex/gender distinction – albeit one that he sees as precarious and as giving voice to a series of tensions – is pertinent here, then, because it leaves him inhabiting the very opposition that his work dismantles. *Making Sex* dismantles it not so much by demonstrating that the origins of 'sex' as a concept are ignoble, if, indeed, that were an appropriate way to think of them, but by the *nature* of what Laqueur discovers, the very fact that he has shown that the construction of the distinctive conceptual space it occupies was interwoven with a social and political agenda. This implies, *at least potentially*, that the divorce between the two was not only *then* but is even now more apparent than real, hence, presumably, the tensions of the formulation:

Sex, like being human, is contextual. Attempts to isolate it from its discursive, socially determined milieu are as doomed to failure as the *philosophe*'s search for a truly wild child or the modern anthropologist's efforts to filter out the cultural so as to leave a residue of essential humanity. And I would go further and add that the private, enclosed, stable body that seems to lie at the basis of modern notions of sexual difference is also the product of particular, historical, cultural moments. It too, like opposite sexes, comes into and out of focus. (1990: 16)

In spite of this, the terrain defined by the formulation of the distinction, however precarious, remains that which he chooses to occupy. We shall explore why in due course.

The compulsions of epistemology

In insisting upon the distinction between the bodily and the discursive, but also undermining it, Laqueur is in fact occupying some classically philosophical positions, which belong most properly to epistemological doctrines. The construction of an opposition between human knowledge or language and the real relates to the problem of the conditions under which one *can* successfully know. And it is indeed an epistemological dilemma that faces him. How is one to have confidence in *any* knowledge of the bodily where it concerns the difference between the sexes when one also knows its ignoble origins? It a classically Foucauldian-inspired dilemma, which makes clear its Nietzschean origins.

The problem with epistemological conceptions, which was identified by Barry Hindess and Paul Hirst many years ago now (1977), is that they are fundamentally self-contradictory and incoherent, hence the problems of infinite regress and the paradoxes that they are inclined to produce. Epistemologies conceive of knowledge in terms of a distinction and a correlation between two self-enclosed realms, a realm of knowledge, and a realm of objects existing outside that knowledge, to which that knowledge may refer. This postulate of a distinction and a correlation has several consequences, the most important of which for our purposes is that it institutes a radical ontological disjunction between knowledge and its objects, which then requires to be, but can never adequately be bridged without the invocation of a privileged method which assures us that knowledge of an object is genuine knowledge. The concept of the 'object of knowledge' thus remains poised uneasily between being internal or external to that knowledge, with the two 'objects' becoming identified with one another when knowledge is successful and divorced from one another when they are not, when methodology fails. Yet, if methodology could guarantee knowledge there would be no errors – barring those caused by its incorrect application. This is of course the dream of empirical science: make sure the methodology is appropriately scientific and knowledge will follow. Without such methodological guarantees, the problem becomes more difficult. One may be left with an agnosticism of the kind that one can find *in potentia* in Kant's transcendental idealism, and in some of those who inherit his philosophical legacy, in which objects *themselves* are radically unattainable and all one has are the objects of human cognition.[7] This is fundamentally the position in which Laqueur finds himself, but which he also seeks to repudiate.

The flesh in its simplicity

Laqueur's understanding of sex as contextual therefore in large part contradicts what one might almost call the nostalgia for that enclosed and stable body which he detects in Foucault's longing for bodies and pleasures – pristine, inherently subversive and free of discursivity – and whose presence he also marks in his own work when he talks of that fraught chasm and insists: 'For all my awareness of how deeply our understanding of what we saw was historically contingent – the product of institutional, political and epistemological contingencies – the flesh in its simplicity seemed always to shine through' (1990: 14). Although he shies away from cleaving to 'the real transcultural body', he also seems to want to endorse it. Oddly, then, it is the contemporary 'realities' of 'sex', whose construction he has revealed, that come to dictate his terms of reference: 'I have no interest,' he says, 'in denying the reality of sex or of sexual dimorphism as an evolutionary process' (1990: 11).

What 'sex' represents here, whether it is the discursive object or the 'realities of the body', is – of necessity – ambiguous, something which, as we noted earlier, is characteristic of epistemological formulations. Sex is both something that science *constitutes* and the autonomous reference point of that science, an ambiguity that is, incidentally, perfectly captured by the linguistic concept of the referent, which is simultaneously internal and external to language. There is the combination of an insistence upon a sharp, ontological distinction between the body (sex) and discourse ('sex') and a constitutive ambiguity ('Sex, like being human, is contextual'), and Laqueur captures this when he talks of the way in which 'the private enclosed and stable body...like opposite sexes, comes into and out of focus' (1990: 16). Put simply, the problematic status of the body is symptomatic.

Of course, it is not that Laqueur needs to escape the sense of the body as unimpeachably real, it is that, in the context of discussions about the difference of women from men, *our* sense of the unimpeachable reality of the body is bound up with the production of the conceptual space of 'sex'. One has, then, to decide what to make of this discovery. Clearly, the distinction between the sexes is not the sole basis on which the autarchy of the body has been established. As Laqueur himself indicates, it was part of a broader set of changes related to the constitution of the empirical sciences, which is precisely why it is so compelling. In seeking to keep the body and its representations apart, he is also seeking to sustain the results of that broader movement, which he describes elsewhere as the epistemic shift that allowed a differentiation between the metaphysical and the realm of the possible (and the elaboration of a concept of sex). Culture, as he puts it, used to suffuse the body. One effect of the construction of the new conceptual space of the empirically investigable body was, at least nominally, to make cultural concerns illegitimate *within* that space.

In one sense, then, it might seem logical that Laqueur should locate himself within the very distinction whose origins he has traced, for it is by no means obvious where else he might stand. The point, however, is that challenging the distinction, from this new historical standpoint, is only fully accomplished when a new discursive space has been brought into being. If sex *was* 'made', what are we to make of 'sex' as we now know it? How should we alter our understanding of sex to take cognizance of the fact that that understanding is contextual? Since understanding alters experience, what might the 'more' be that sex *is*, beyond what society decrees? What – after all – *are* we to make of the science of difference?

The difficulty is that while Laqueur maintains the distinction between 'sex' and 'gender', and identifies it with those oppositions that he does – between language and the extra-linguistic, between nature and culture, between (and here the scare quotes mark the difficulty), as he puts it, ' "biological sex" and the endless social and political markers of difference' (1990: 13) – he cannot create that new discursive space. Furthermore, given that he has associated those aspects of the bodily on which he wants to maintain a purchase with a concept of sex, there is no incentive to do so other than the discomfiture of inhabiting a formulation in tension. Because of the apparent generality of the distinction between the linguistic and the extra-linguistic, this also seems unavoidable. Laqueur is simply, as he noted himself (although with a slightly less painful metaphor), caught on the horns of a dilemma. This dilemma also leads him into another paradoxical position which is that of simultaneously placing the social and political imperatives that produce the markers of difference *outside* the terms of empirical investigation and of *denying* that externality. Sex is both contextual, and hence distinct and distinguishable, *and* impossible to isolate from its discursive milieu.

We are not suggesting that the origin of a concept like 'sex' ineluctably dictates its destiny (and that, in this case, it is destined forever to be corrupt), but, *rather*, that what one has discovered does have to be *worked through* into where one currently finds oneself. In this case, the making of the distinction between what we now term 'sex' and 'gender', or rather between the body (and the legitimated 'scientific' knowledge that pertains to it) and the social world in which that body exists, seems to have been one whose aim was, at least partially, that of concealing social and political imperatives from view behind the protocols of empirical science. It was designed, precisely, to make the alleged social and political implications of its findings unimpeachable. Surely, this means that one cannot unproblematically retrieve and sustain the distinction between 'sex' and social world, however precarious?

Does Laqueur fall into this trap because, as an historian, he has disenfranchised himself from consideration of such issues? 'A historian,' he points out, 'can contribute little to the already existing critical analysis of particular experiments purporting to demonstrate the biological basis of gender distinctions or to lay bare the hormones and other chemicals that are meant to serve as a sort of ontological granite for observable sexual differences' (1990: 21). He does look at the implication of the model of two corporeally based sexes in the politics of gender for the eighteenth, nineteenth and, even, twentieth centuries (at least where it touches on Freud). Yet, perhaps understandably, for it would make his task enormous, he says that he has 'not even scratched the surface of a contextual history of reproductive anatomy or physiology'. Even for scientific problems that he explores in some detail, he says, 'the institutional and professional matrix in which they are embedded is only hurriedly sketched' (1990: 23). But this has its disadvantages, for it is perhaps this that allows him to retain, if somewhat uncomfortably, a hold on a conventional concept of sex, with no need to explore a reformulation. Paradoxical though it might seem, it is his assimilation of all *knowledge* of the bodily to language that necessitates his refusal of the assimilation of the body *itself* to language.

Of language, discourse and the world

Laqueur reads discourse and language as one and the same. He talks of the body as being so entangled with social and political imperatives as to exclude 'unmediated access'. Clearly, if we think in terms of language and meaning, *even* if we try and capture what it is that we cannot get access to, and we talk – as he does – of the body as an 'extraordinarily fragile, feeling, and transient mass of flesh', we can see ourselves as spinning words about that body like silk around a cocoon. And in a sense, too, we can also already consider ourselves to be in the realm of discourse, for the imagery of transience and fragility belongs to a particular way of construing the body, a regulated set of concepts and statements.

But there is a crucial difference between these two ways of describing what we are doing, between talking of words and talking of concepts, for the point of the term 'discourse' was precisely to depart from the distinction between language (or thought) and world, that is to cut across epistemological ways of framing human knowledge. Neither bodies, nor any other kind of what would classically be defined as 'material' objects are absent from discourses, whereas they are regarded as intrinsically so from language or representation. On the contrary, within discourses, ways of talking about and acting upon such things as bodies, and the bodies themselves, are intricately and intimately connected to one another. What this means is that for all practical purposes it is simply not viable, or indeed appropriate, to make a distinction between the body as an object delineated and conceptualized by the biological sciences and the transient mass of flesh.[8] After all, the very sense we have of the 'transient mass of flesh' is dependent upon the ways in which it has been construed for us within discourses and practices like medicine, which (unlike the positivities of biology, say) might give us an acute sense of both its fragility and its extraordinary recuperative powers. (We should not, after all, forget Laqueur's medical background.)

There is no way of talking about the body that is not discursive, but to say this is not to say that we do not have direct access to it. Of course we do, all of the time and every day. Although in one sense we are always in the realm of discourse, discourse is also – absolutely crucially – open to, and implicated in, the objects about which it speaks, whether we are talking about the everyday or the experimental practices and procedures of a discipline like neuroscience or pharmacology. Discourses and the practices to which they are linked have complex and specific and constant relations with one another: they are of necessity interconnected. It is only from within the self-enclosure of a *particular* conception of language that we experience this relation as one of mediation, rather than direct linkage.

This is not to say, however, that all discourses come yoked to a little Siamese twin called 'practice'. Indeed, the nature of discourses and the other practices to which they refer or relate, and the forms of connection between them, are quite diverse in character: the relation of literary criticism to poetry is not the same as the relation of astrophysics to the study of the heavens. But discourse and human activity are never far apart, and 'practice' *can* mean everything from poetry to empirical science. Therefore, if what Laqueur is wanting to keep hold of are the advances provided by scientific discourses which are tied to empirical and investigatory practices, associating these with a conception of language as a fundamentally closed and self-referential system brings with it the seeds of a major problem, for it forecloses all reference to practice by confining discourse within 'meaning' and the consequent self-enclosure of language. It is precisely this problem that Laqueur describes himself as wanting not to inhabit when he talks of the evanescence of the body under the impact of post-structuralism, and his description of being inextricably caught up in a formulation in tension shows a recognition of this.

However, although this view of language has most recently been associated with Saussurean linguistics, and the post-structuralism that followed from it, it represents a much older philosophical tradition (Gaukroger, 1983). We shall return to conceptions of language in due course, but for the moment, we should just bear in mind the fact that it is only one possible characterization of language, albeit a dominant one. Laqueur's own use of the concept of 'representation' is consonant with the post-Saussurean and non-reductive development of that concept in line with the idea of signification, something which is evident in his discussion of the fantastical quality of the characterization of plants and animals: 'Darkness deepens when animals enter into the orbit of culture...' (1990: 18).

In some ways, it is surprising that so sophisticated an analyst of discourse as Laqueur should subsume all of its operations under the heading of language. The assimilation of a very wide range of discourses varying, for us, from, say, palaeontology to psycho-physiology or astrophysics to molecular genetics, into a single linguistic category, that of meaning, collapses quite distinctive forms of contention onto one another. The problem with a category like 'meaning', or, for that matter, 'representation', is that like all linguistic terms of this level of generality, it can be assumed to apply in some measure to all forms of knowledge and, indeed, research, even where the tenor of the research is broadly mathematical. Even the attempt to discuss the sub-atomic in terms of particles or waves – however mathematized – involves the use of a natural language, and hence of meaning.

If the science of difference is misconceived, it has to be on more specific grounds than this, as, indeed, Laqueur indicates by referring to the fact that what are at stake are cultural, political questions – a far more specific category than meaning. For it is no less difficult to ascertain the relation of empirical investigation to such questions for contemporary science than it was for the one-sex model. Why should it not be possible to establish precisely where and how and in what manner political and social imperatives or agendas are interwoven with knowledges of the bodily (as Foucault's and Laqueur's own work – and a number of his comments – make clear)?

A fraught chasm

Part of the difficulty that those, such as Laqueur, whose work is associated with a concept of discourse face is that of the resulting shift in metaphors that it prompts: science is described now as 'constructing' rather than 'discovering'. At best, such phrases struggle to mark the necessary reorientation in the description of scientific activity from the rather passive notions of 'discovery' or 'investigation' to the sense of active engagement and the constitutive role that the term 'discourse' expresses. There is some sense, at least, that what the term 'discourse' captures is the idea of, as Foucault puts it, 'practices that systematically form the objects of which they speak' (1972: 49), which, in its most radical interpretation, is conceived of as – for want of a better phrase – 'the objects in the world'. Whether or not, and to what extent, discourses should be regarded as *bringing into being* the objects about which they speak is a moot point, since it will depend upon which object we are talking about. What is now undeniable is that if we think of our ways of understanding and engaging with those objects as discursively constituted, the problem is going to be having to decide what that means. In other words, if we are no longer to operate in accordance with epistemological accounts of what we are doing and how it is to be validated, how are we to rethink our own activity? As an historian, Laqueur is perhaps not directly confronted with this dilemma within the process of research; he only meets with it when he comes to reflect upon its results. (By contrast, Foucault, as a philosopher, tended, perhaps, to foreground it.)

The contrast between, on the one hand, Laqueur's apparent pessimism about the hopeless entanglement between 'sex' and its 'discursive, socially determined milieu' (1990: 16) – the social, political and cultural imperatives that inform and accompany it – and, on the other, his insistence upon 'sex' as something substantive about which we *know* – the advances made in the science that seeks to comprehend it – represents the interweaving of two essentially contradictory gestures, which are nevertheless indispensable to one another. The former is a necessary condition of the latter: without the enclosure of 'sex' within language, 'sex' as 'object' would not be veiled from view. It is this structure that produces the simultaneous distinction between and conflation of 'sex' as discursive and 'sex' as 'real', and demands their ontological conflict.

In one sense, the problem is that the 'body', whether conceived of as a discrete object of knowledge, or as the 'real' body, is seen as suffering the incursion of something which is alien and external to it, a set of cultural and social concerns whose presence is illegitimate. In the case of the former, empirical knowledge is in some sense vitiated by concerns which seem improper; in the case of the latter, these concerns interfere with our perception of, and access to, the 'real thing'. All knowledge of the body is interwoven with social concerns and the 'real' body is veiled by these: the 'science of difference' is fundamentally a product of those concerns. The social, the political and the cultural are thus being given a *general* priority over the putative priority of the 'real' object, which is, of course, what then requires Laqueur to insist upon the priority of the 'real' body. Furthermore, this appears to be an irredeemable state of affairs that makes knowledge forever inadequate to its object, turning the distinction between them into a fraught chasm, neither wholly there and unbridgeable nor ever really susceptible to being bridged. It leaves one – to change the metaphor – in a truly labyrinthine dilemma.

The solution to this might seem simple: abandon this linguistically based way of framing things. However, we should not be in too much of a hurry to dismiss Laqueur's dilemma, merely because it seems to have arisen out of an erroneous identification between language (as understood by some forms of philosophy and linguistics) and the discursive. It would simply be absurd to suggest that so intelligent a commentator as Laqueur should have countenanced what is apparently a major contradiction at the heart of his description of what he was doing. Instead, we should attend to what is the most interesting aspect of this, namely the fact that the two gestures Laqueur makes are indispensable to one another. If they are held together, in spite of their mutual contradiction, it is perhaps because, together, they capture something important. If there is a desire to insist upon both the discursive constitution of the body *and* its accessibility to scientific understanding (in spite of the description of it as *hopelessly* mediated), it may be because Laqueur wishes to hang onto something significant. It is this that we examine in the next chapter, via the work of Bob Connell. If Laqueur appears to let the sense of practice slip from the way in which he describes 'discourse', Connell, by contrast, makes it central to his account.

Notes

[1] There is some small confusion over timing here: although Laqueur mentions fifty years, the actual dates he gives are 1752 and 1836. However, the point being made is unaffected by this uncertainty. The important thing is that '[n]ear the end of the Enlightenment …medical science and those who depended upon it ceased to regard the female orgasm as relevant to generation' (1990: 3).
[2] This quotation, which comes from Philo, *Legum Allegoriae*, 2.7, is originally cited in Peter Brown (1983), 'Sexuality and Society in the Fifth Century A.D.: Augustine and Julian of Eclanum', *Tria Corda: Scritti in Onore di Arnaldo Momigliano*, ed. E. Gabba (Como, New Press), and is reproduced by Laqueur (1990: 246).
[3] In practice an episteme is slightly different because it refers to the underlying framework that dictates the character of knowledges at any given historical period, so that knowledges as diverse as botany and economics can present similar formats.
[4] Laqueur quotes these lines in parenthesis, just as we have here, although he places them after his observations about the gulf between Mozart's *Don Giovanni* and the hopeless struggle 'to stem the flow of blood from the ruptured oesophageal varices of a middle-

aged dentist, who that morning had walked into the emergency room, and to replace it pint by pint into his veins as they pumped it out of his stomach' (1990: 14).

[5] The way in which he recapitulates the distinction between representation and reality – 'seeing-as' and 'seeing' – is telling, for both 'seeing-as' and 'seeing' could be argued to constitute forms of perception, which psychologists long ago told us was an active and dynamic, what one *could* term – if one were minded to do so – a 'representational' process. It was this observation about perception, amongst others, that made problematical positivist accounts of science, in which theory-neutral forms of observation were assumed to be possible, by stressing the role of 'representation', or, more properly, conceptualization in the process of observation. And whilst observational or experimental procedures may not always depend *directly* upon forms of conceptualization, these forms of conceptualization inevitably enter into the presuppositions as to what it is that is being observed or experimented upon, what will count as appropriate evidence for the predicted or hypothesized potential outcome, and so on. In that sense, 'seeing-as' and 'seeing' are fundamentally indistinguishable from one another (as phenomenological philosophers might insist). The example which Laqueur offers of the body as a cultural construct (a set of more or less schematic anatomical illustrations) meeting the body on the dissecting table, in which the anatomical illustration 'rather hopelessly confronted the actual tangles of the human neck' (1990: 14), misses the fact that the body on the dissecting table is being *perceived*. The inadequacy of the illustrations to their task when confronted with the real body is actually a gap between two not dissimilar sets of processes. Rather than reading it as a gap between 'representation' and 'reality', we could read it much more simply as a mismatch between the illustration and the dissection procedures it was meant to inform, a technological rather than a philosophical difficulty. Otherwise, we remain caught up in an epistemological dilemma in which the 'representation' is forever destined to be inadequate' to the 'real' because it is not *identical* to the 'real', because it does not share the same substantive character but is the forever inadequate stand-in for the substance whose delegate it is. Not only does ontological weight lie with what is allegedly the 'real' but the 'representation' is irrevocably destined to be its pale and ghostly shadow. And surely, the illustration is no less of an 'object' in the world?

[6] Having said that, it is not the *nature* of the claim that protects it from what we might call ideological incursions (see Martin, 1991); it is only that some claims, as Laqueur would say, are patently more absurd than others – at least from where we now stand.

[7] Although Kant's 'categories' provide a privileged set of concepts that permit the evaluation of knowledges, for Kant and for a number of successors of his, since objects must appear for us either in terms of the sensible form in which they are experienced or in terms of the pure concepts or categories in terms of which they are thought, human knowledge can only ever be limited either to the phenomenal, to appearances, or to the noumenal, to what can be thought about but not known. 'Things-in-themselves' are radically inaccessible. 'Objects', as Kant put it, 'conform to the mind', rather than the other way round. The *possibility* of knowledge, however, is based upon the fact that objects in the world must conform to the conditions under which they are susceptible to becoming objects of knowledge. In other words, Kant seeks to establish a middle ground between empiricism and idealism.

[8] We are not ignoring the fact, however, that something is undoubtedly captured by the fact that a conceptual distinction is made between the object of knowledge and the 'real' object, but the point is that this is, precisely, a *conceptual* distinction. That this conceptual distinction serves a function is also clear. We shall therefore need to return to this issue in order to reformulate and redefine what is at stake here, for, in one sense, we clearly cannot be talking about the 'real' object, whilst in another we clearly *are*. This enigma will be clarified in the next chapter, and the aporia dispelled.

6 Looming Outside the Space Station

A similar point to Laqueur's about the lack of self-evidence of the body is made by Bob Connell in *Gender and Power* and, indeed, it forms the basis of his critique of the presumption in our culture that the reproductive dichotomy provides the foundation of both gender and sexuality. The body does not, in and of itself, provide us with the means to make sense of it. On the contrary, we confer meaning upon it. However, we automatically presume that our sense of what that body is about, our sense of the differences it displays emerges *ab origine* from what it *is*, and that this is incontrovertible. 'For many people,' he says, 'the notion of natural sex difference forms a limit *beyond which thought cannot go*' (Connell, 1987: 66, emphasis added). By contrast, he argues that these 'doctrines of natural difference' are fundamentally mistaken:

> What I will challenge is the assumption that the biological make-up of our bodies is the 'basis', 'foundation', 'framework', or 'mould' of the social relations of gender. The argument accepts that there is a strong relation between social practice and biology; indeed 'gender' would be inconceivable without it. I will propose that this relation has a very different character from that assumed by theorists of natural difference. (Connell, 1987: 67)

He agrees with Kessler and McKenna that 'our taken-for-granted assumptions about gender dichotomy are not forced upon us by nature' (1987: 75) and points especially to their examination of the biological literature on gender, which shows it re-creating dichotomies anew where old ones fail. As an instance, he mentions the fact that the International Olympic Committee, in excluding people with intermediate chromosomal patterns from women's events, redefines them as men.

This assumption of a clear-cut dichotomy and of the foundational role it plays is so powerful as to be all-pervasive, regardless of the type of explanation propounded, from sociobiology to feminism, from role theory to psychoanalysis. But there are worlds in which this is not the case. Referring to Kessler and McKenna's work on the berdache and to institutionalized transvestism among American Indian societies generally, as well as to Foucault's *Herculine*, he describes cultures in which gender is not necessarily dichotomous and may indeed be elective, and in which biological criteria do not form the basis of membership. He also mentions, *contra* Kessler and McKenna, studies of transsexuals by Roberta Perkins which show that transsexualism itself does not necessarily assume dichotomy and which suggest that a new gender category is being created, much along the model of the old designation of homosexual men as 'the third sex'. This suggests that, even in contemporary

Western culture, 'the cultural construction of gender has repeatedly failed to produce consistent dichotomies' (1987: 76). We sustain an account of two genders 'despite the *failure* of human reality *on almost any count* to be strictly dimorphic' (1987: 75, emphasis added).

This leads Connell to propose an alternative way of conceptualizing the relation of the body to human history. One of the problems with doctrines of natural difference, he suggests, is that they present biological features of human life as 'a passively suffered condition, like being subject to gravity' (1987: 77). On the contrary, he says, what is deemed natural and what natural differences consist of is a cultural construct. If we really were simply subject to our biology rather than constructors of an idea of gender, he argues, human history would be inconceivable, for that history depends upon the transcendence of the natural through social practice. His alternative account is therefore that social practice involves the appropriation and transformation of the natural world – both physically and in terms of meaning – through a variety of practices, be they sexual, or kinds of labour, forms of power, or any number of others. The connection between social and natural structures is therefore not one of causation but one of *practical relevance*: 'My male body does not confer masculinity on me; it receives masculinity (or some fragment thereof) as its social definition' (1987: 83).

Doctrines of natural difference

Doctrines of natural difference, by contrast, have two fundamentally similar ways of proceeding: they supply either an epiphenomenal account of the relation of social to biological or an additive account. The epiphenomenal account is the account typically found in the writings of sociobiologists. In this type of account, biology – or, as Connell points out, ontology as its surrogate – determines gender: '[s]ociety registers what nature decrees – or becomes sick if it doesn't' (1987: 67). At the time he was writing, most of the literature under this heading was difficult, he says, to take seriously as science; arguably it has now been superseded by far more sophisticated forms of argumentation, although they still show many of the same features. The literature analysed by Connell depends upon crude forms of social analysis, which most sociologists, anthropologists and historians would find laughable, but it also frequently fails to rest upon any serious biological investigation either. It often proceeds, instead, by a series of loose analogies, which are transformed by a set of logical slides into taken-for-granted facts (1987: 68). The structure of argumentation is 'exactly the reverse of what it is claimed to be' (ibid.), beginning with an interpretation of contemporary social life and then calling upon 'evolution', or some kind of speculative pre-history to justify it. It is what Connell describes as a 'mirror construction', reflecting back what is familiar as 'science' and justifying what people wish to believe. More sophisticated accounts are often not much better and what they particularly tend to ignore is the collective and interactive structuring of human action, relying instead upon the presumption of context-free individual predispositions: 'A war, for instance, is a social and institutional process within history, not the sum total of several hundred thousand genetic predispositions towards aggressiveness' (1987: 69). By the same token they often neglect the complexity of the phenomenon they allegedly set out to explain: attempts to show that homosexuality has a genetic explanation, for example, will presuppose that homosexuality is a unitary trait and thus revert to concepts abandoned in sexology in the early years of the twentieth century (ibid.). What is particularly absent, for much of the time, is any sense of the *mechanism* which links, say, genetic information, which after all encodes for the production of proteins, to complex human behaviours. Softer versions of this biological reductionism may well dictate that biology 'sets limits' to social relations, necessitating sexual differentiation and the prohibition on homosexuality, for example, to assure the reproduction of the species. Yet this is both vague and factually wrong: there are societies, for example the New Guinea society studied by Gilbert Herdt, in which homosexuality is institutionalized (Connell: 1987: 72) and an enormous range of social arrangements are compatible with the reproduction of the species. Given the variety of human cultures, one might almost say that these limits mean very little at all. In this context, we should consider the possibility that animal sexualities may themselves be more polymorphous than previously suspected, as evidenced by the contention in a recent book of the existence of homosexuality amongst animals, a contention which gives the lie to the idea that the whole of sexuality is merely expressive of a reproductive imperative that would make all non-reproductive acts into aberrations (Bagemihl, 1999).

The second, additive approach to natural difference replaces this notion that biology places constraints upon or determines forms of sociality by an account that makes biology provide a minimal level of distinction which is then *elaborated* socially. For example, modest average differences in bodily morphology between women and men are culturally marked in dress, either by emphasizing individual features such as breasts or by producing categorical distinctions (men are not supposed to wear dresses, for example). This approach is classically that of liberal feminism and much social science, for example, sex-role socialization theory: '[t]he very term "sex/role" sums up the additive approach' (Connell: 1987: 73). What it often does is to accept some allegedly fundamental feature of sexual difference, e.g. male aggression, but suggest that we have a *choice*, as a society, over whether to enhance or negate this. In this sense, the framework of explanation may not be substantially different from the epiphenomenal approach, but what is striking about it is the contrast between biological constraint and society as agent. Biology is determinative, the social is volitional. More typically, however, what the additive approach seeks to do, according to Connell, is to minimize the biological portion of the equation and enhance the social and additive aspect. One of his objections to it, which is similar to Laqueur's concern, is that it then loses a grip on what he says people find central in their experience of sex and gender, in other words the bodily. Secondly, the addition remains an aspiration: its relative weighting is never established and, he says, it cannot be assumed to be equal in all departments of life (1987: 75).

Transcendence and negation

This is a curious aside for somebody committed to arguing against the idea that the biological forms the 'foundation', 'basis' etc. of human social life, and a telling one. Indeed, his alternative account doesn't necessarily escape the problems he identifies in the additive conception. His fundamental framework appears to derive from Jean-Paul Sartre via Marx's Hegelian *Aufhebung*.[1] He speaks instead of 'transcendence and negation' in order to define the relation of the social to the natural. The social, he says, is radically *unnatural* and thus can never be deduced from nature. What it does is radically to trans-form nature. But it does so by a particular form of connection, which is that of *practice*. And practice cannot afford to ignore the nature of that which it sets out to transform:

> We do not offer coffee to a tree, nor try to paint with sawdust. Nor should we expect someone who is chromosomally male to give birth to a child. Where reductionism goes wrong is in taking these qualities as determinants of the practice. This gets things precisely the wrong way round. Practice issues from the human and social side of the transaction; it *deals* with the natural qualities of its objects, including the biological characteristics of bodies. It gives them a social determination. The connection between social and natural structures is one of *practical relevance:*, not of causation. (Connell: 1987: 78, emphasis in original)

'Dealing with', he says, is not a neutral term. Practice alters what it finds: bits of wood become chairs, human beings become lovers, or angry, or better educated. In that sense, it negates what it finds and such negation and supersession is the basis of human historicity. In constructing gender, social practice neither expresses nor ignores what he describes as 'natural patterns'; it transforms them as part of a continuing historical process: '[i]ts materials are the social as well as the biological products of previous practice – new situations and new people' (1987: 79).

But why 'negation'? It seems a peculiarly strong term for what are effectively being described as variable forms of transformation. In order to explain this, we have to return to what we mentioned earlier: Connell's contention that bodies do not give us an unambiguous set of differences between the sexes. In practice, the concept of 'negation' is being used in two senses here, which are made to overlap: on the one hand, it represents the philosophical conception employed by those like Sartre and Hegelian Marxists for whom there is a radical difference between the best of bees and the humblest of architects, and on the other, it is used to denote the *denial* of a fundamental similarity between the sexes in the interests of a gender system. This explains why sexual difference is not merely heavily marked socially (why would it need to be so if it were self-evident?) but social practices construct women and men as distinct social categories on premises that frequently violate what is biologically the case. For example, at just the age when adolescent girls tend to be bigger and physically stronger than adolescent boys, they are enjoined to be fearful and dependent in relation to males. Similarly, although the distributions in characteristics *within* these social groupings are quite variable and the overlap *between* them considerable, small average differences are converted into categorical differences, in other words they are made discontinuous where they are continuous.

The idea of 'negation', then, is serving a particular function within an argument about gender, which opposes what Connell describes as 'categoricalism' (1987: 56), and it makes an important political point:

> Thus to construct the social category of 'man' or 'woman', with a common identity and interest, requires negation of the serial dispersion characteristic of the array of parallel situations constructed by the biological categories. This is done in practices that assert the solidarity of the sex (or group within it). (1987: 81)

Categorical theories in essence make the same gesture as gender itself endeavours – but ultimately fails – to do, but for different reasons. Whether they issue from a structuralism or from a political account that stresses opposed interests for the purposes of mobilization, categorical theories fundamentally organize their accounts around a single line of demarcation, women to men: 'For all the sophistication these authors show in developing social frameworks, the overall map of gender they show is not too different from one based on a simple biological dichotomy' (1987: 56). Biological differentiation itself does not yield such categories, however; it merely represents a set of dull facticities (only women can bear children, infants require suckling etc.). The limited range of practices and consequences to which biological differentiation gives rise corresponds to what Sartre would have called 'the practico-inert', which results in the possibility of placing people who are logically in parallel situations, like people standing in a bus queue, into rather basic categories (what Sartre refers to as 'seriality'). It is thus incapable of sustaining the gender categories. Social practices, which are engaged in a continual effort to *maintain* these categories are transcendent in the sense that they create *new* facts, in which a structure of symbol and interpretation is woven around natural differences, 'often vastly exaggerating or distorting them' (1987: 80) and carrying the body forward, as he puts it, into the next transaction (1987: 82).

Connell faces something of the same dilemma faced by Laqueur and for some of the same reasons. His account of the creation of these new facts is, like Laqueur's, one that stresses meaning and interpretation. In that context, the body comes to represent the *substance* around which this 'structure of symbol and interpretation is woven' and on which it acts. The idea of carrying the body forward is Connell's way of trying to retain a hold on the bodily in an explanation which is also seeking to talk about sociality as the radically un-natural, with that un-naturalness closely bound to meaning and interpretation, symbol and cognition. In the midst of this, the body is both negated and, he says, it remains a presence, 'indeed a ferment' (ibid.). In opposition to the additive account, he seeks to recoup and salvage 'what people find central in their experience of sex and gender: pleasure, pain, body-image, arousal, youth and ageing, bodily contact, childbirth and suckling' (1987: 74-5). But it is not only a matter of what is peculiar to sex and gender, for 'the body is involved in *every* kind of social practice' (1987: 77, emphasis in original).

The need for this emphasis on the bodily arises, as it did for Laqueur, directly out of the fact that sociality is tacitly equated with symbol and interpretation. There are times when the stress is rather more on processes of cognition and the transformation of (certain aspects of) bodies is subsumed under the more general engagement of human beings with the natural world. Referring to Gordon Childe and expanding on his conception of practical transformation, he says:

> This means both the transformations of the natural world by human practice (domestication of plants and animals, smelting of metal ores, invention of steam engines etc.) that have sustained each stage of historical development, and the changes of practice itself that have made great shifts of social structure possible. Practical transformations open up new possibilities, which are the tissue of human life. But they do this by creating new social pressures and risks. (1987: 77)

At others, however, negation becomes more than mere supersession, or *Aufhebung*, and seems to carry a heavier charge. The relation of body to social is then fundamentally one of *contradiction*, in which there is a radical opposition in the respective characters of the body and sociality. By means of this idea, Connell seeks both to stress the degree of transformation *and*, paradoxically it seems, to maintain the sense that the body is intractable and recalcitrant. In the face of a transformative practice in which symbol and interpretation are the major players, and sociality the dominant partner, the body has to be deemed to *resist*, not to be infinitely malleable and plastic, if it is not merely to be swallowed up by meaning. The process must be bi-partite: it must be conceived of as a transformation 'both physically and in terms of meaning' (1987: 78) and out of it must come both social and biological products.

Nevertheless, Connell also wishes to make the body something other than an inert and compelling presence, as he puts it in his memorable image, 'like the monster looming outside the bright lights of the space station' (1987: 83). But how is it not to be such a monster when, even though he goes beyond a simple *opposition* between nature and culture, he seeks to define the body as intractable and recalcitrant, and makes a distinction between this 'presence' and a structure of symbol and interpretation? Here we meet again the familiar distinction between materiality and ideality, between the obdurate presence of the object and meaning. Ideality may well have transformative possibilities and materiality may well be in motion, 'a ferment', but according to Connell, its plasticity is self-limiting, and hence constraining upon what we can do: we are not so foolish as to try to paint with sawdust.

Arguably, what distinguish Connell's approach from the additive approach are predominantly two things: first, it is capable of providing a much more sophisticated account of the *variety* of ways in which the bodily and sociality or the bodily and the discursive are related, and second, the topological disposition of each of those two components is different. The additive account, like the epiphenomenal account, describes the superposition of social to biological. The social is in some senses superstructural, whereas the relation Connell describes is dialectical. Nevertheless, it shares in the same raw materials and it deals in the two general realms of nature and culture. As we have seen before, this opposition is problematical in a variety of ways.

Believing in witches

Let us return to the point about the constraining character of the bodily and the idea of not trying to paint with sawdust or offer coffee to a tree. *We* may not do so – within the terms of reference of our world – but this does not mean that it is inconceivable that one might do so. We may not expect someone who is chromosomally male to give birth to a child, but that is because of the expectations set up for us by our knowledge of chromosomes. The worlds described by Laqueur (or Walker Bynum) show no such certainty: the women who give birth to rabbits, the miraculously preserved saints whose bodies are incorruptible, and the 'men whose heads do grow beneath their shoulders', as Shakespeare put it in *Othello*, are all part of the *plausible* – if not the actual – for the medieval imagination, just as the existence of witchcraft is for the Azande. Beliefs of this kind, even if we regard them as erroneous, do not make life unliveable merely because they violate what we may consider to be empirically possible. On the contrary, the belief in witchcraft among the Azande, as Evans-Pritchard (1937) demonstrated, provides as reasonable a way of regulating one's life as any other. Equally the bodily does not have a *general* intractability and recalcitrance; it rather depends upon what accounts of the bodily of one kind or another seek to do, how they are articulated with particular practices and how they seek to engage with that which they describe. Whether or not we regard it as intractable and recalcitrant depends upon what we wish to do with it, and how we conceptualize that process. In another discursive arena, it might seem fragile and mutable.[2]

Both Mary Douglas and Claude Lévi-Strauss have also explored the manner in which beliefs such as the belief in witchcraft are held and they point out that, as Douglas puts it, '[o]ur view of the world is arrived at piecemeal, in response to particular practical problems' (Douglas, 1995 [1966]: 91). Potentially contradictory beliefs, Lévi-Strauss (1977) argues, are held simultaneously and unproblematically side by side. It is safe to suppose that our own beliefs are held in much the same way: we neither seek empirical confirmation of the validity of the beliefs we hold nor do we expect them to show consistency with any number of other ideas that we adhere to at the same time. What for us is the empirical impossibility of certain beliefs, held by people in societies other than our own traditionally dubbed 'primitive', by no means makes them unusable or, even, ineffective and, as Hirst and Woolley (1982) point out, modern science has by no means eliminated the Zande in us. We are as likely to believe in the efficacy of antibiotics as of Feng Shui. As Laqueur points out, we might of course wish to argue that a girl's suddenly changing sex as she chased her swine over a stile cannot *possibly* have happened, but to do so is also somewhat to miss the point.[3] The paradox, then, is that those whom we deem to have been living all too close to the exigencies of the natural world, and whom we would therefore presume would be perfectly capable of observation, hold views which one would expect, time and time again, to have been disconfirmed by experience.   But the experimental practices of our science, for all that positivist epistemologies might tell us so, are not the same thing as 'experience'.   Indeed, experience itself is not that pristine, nakedly apperceptive innocence which we invoke as an ultimate reference point, the base line against which we tacitly measure all knowledge.

The cassowary and the sagebrush

To represent the body in terms of its practical relevance does have the virtue of indicating that what matters here is how the bodily gets taken up, but this formulation does also tend to make of the body a transhistorical constant, which obscures the very particularities of the ways in which that which is taken up *is* taken up.   Laqueur puts this very well in describing some of the ways in which animals and plants can be conceived of and put to use:

> The cassowary, a large, flightless, ostrich-like, and, to the anthropologist, epicene bird, becomes to the male Sambian tribesman a temperamental, wild, masculinized female who gives birth through the anus and whose feces have procreative powers; the bird becomes powerfully bisexual.   Why, asks the ethnographer Gilbert Herdt, do people as astute as the Sambia 'believe' in anal birth?   Because anything one says, outside of very specific contexts, about the biology of sex, even among the brute beasts, is already informed by a theory of sameness or difference.
>
>   Indeed, if structuralism has taught us anything it is that humans impose their sense of opposition onto a world of continuous shades of difference and similarity.   No oppositional traits readily detected by an outsider explain the fact that in nearly all of North America, to use Lévi-Strauss's example, sagebrush, *Artemisia*, plays 'a major part in the most diverse rituals, either by itself or associated with and at the same time, as the opposite of other plants: *Solidago, Chrysothamnus, Gutierrezia.*'   It stands for the feminine in Navaho ritual whereas *Chrysothamnus* stands for the masculine.   No principle of opposition could be subtler than the tiny differences in leaf serrations that come to carry such enormous symbolic weight. (1990: 19)

Yet in one sense this is precisely what Connell is seeking to capture in stressing the place of symbolism and its material *incorporation* into the natural world.   His inversion of the relationship of social to natural is intended to allow the symbolic weight, practical transformation and engagement with specific aspects of the bodily to come into view.   For instance, he mentions the projection of dramas of power and anxiety onto the hysterical body, because 'depression and dissociation are also experienced in the flesh' (1987: 82) and the ways in which the techniques of arousal and pleasure work *against* immediate bodily demand in sexual intercourse, which, as part of 'the immensely complex edifice of a sexual relationship' is something 'distinct from a rubbing-together of two bodies' (ibid.).   Indeed, in stressing the symbolic and the ideas of transformation and incorporation, he is intending to make of the body – and, incidentally, the *experience* of the body – a fully historical object:

We may say, then, that the practical transformation of the body in the social structure of gender is not only accomplished at the level of symbolism. It has physical effects on the body; the incorporation is a material one. The forms and consequences of this incorporation change in time, and change as a result of social purposes and social struggle. That is to say, they are fully historical. Symbolically, 'nature' may be opposed to 'culture', the body (fixed) opposed to history (moving). But in the reality of practice the body is never outside history and history never free of bodily presence and effects on the body. The traditional dichotomies underlying reductionism now have to be replaced by a more adequate and complex account of the social relations in which this incorporation and interplay occur. (1987: 87)

The varieties of in-corporation

He gives three very varied examples to illustrate the potential complexity of this relation of the bodily to sociality. The first, which draws upon a striking poem by Herrick, Spenser's *Faerie Queen* and Jean Genet's *Our Lady of the Flowers*, explores the centrality of symbolism to sexuality, not merely in literature, but in practices such as the sado-masochistic rituals described by Pat Califia (1983). In that sense there is no difference between the world created by Genet in the pages of *Our Lady of the Flowers* and the scenarios enacted in any number of places – other, perhaps, than their beauty or banality: 'Genet creates here a world of erotic objects in whose ritual dances masculinity and femininity dissolve and coagulate, now taking on sharp edges in the form of the hard youth who combines criminality and desirability, now ambiguous in the shape of Divine' (1987: 84). Fantasy, imagery and enactment cannot be divorced from one another.[4]

The second example concerns the ways in which images of ideal masculinity, constructed and promoted most systematically through sport, enter into the construction of the experience of masculine embodiment. Connell stresses the complexity of the physical sense of maleness, not merely from the vantage point of what it includes kinaesthetically, but in terms of the presence of particular physical skills and the absence of others, the image of one's own body and its presentation to others, and their response to it, the role it plays in different settings and contexts. It develops through, it represents, 'a personal history of social practice, a life-history-in-society' (1987: 84). He talks of the way in which particular combinations of force and skill become strongly cathected aspects of an adolescent boy's life. Together they constitute a model of bodily action, and, one might say, bodily conformation, which are as closely bound in to fantasy as they are to activity – arguably to both simultaneously. There is a lived interiority to the body, which is the compound product of a complex interplay, and whose result is the conformation that we see, as Connell puts it, talking of masculinity, 'a statement embedded in the body' (1987: 85):

> The social definition of men as holders of power is translated not only into
> mental body-images and fantasies, but into muscle tensions, posture, the feel and

texture of the body. This is one of the main ways in which the power of men becomes 'naturalized', i.e. seen as part of the order of nature. (ibid.)

An analogous point can be made about developing the body of a dancer or a boxer. In a way which is rather more systematic than the general notion of the incorporation of masculinity, a dancer learns quite explicitly what the body of a dancer *should* feel like and what are the appropriate mental attitudes that accompany that bodily conformation. It is necessary to recognize *in the body* what form proper posture and movement take: 'Imagine that you have a thread pulling you up through the crown of your head' every aspiring ballet dancer is told. But many a dancer will also have heard of the dedication that drives the dancer right through pain, which Pavlova evinced when she danced on although her feet bled and soaked her shoes with blood. Similarly, as Tony Jefferson (1998) has pointed out in discussing the biography of Mike Tyson, a boxer has to be willing to risk the body in performance, what Feldman (1990) defines as 'hardness', an interiorized quality extracted from undertaking this risk (cited in Jefferson, 1998: 81). Referring to the work of Lois Wacquant on the pugilist's honour, Jefferson describes the way in which a boxer has to develop the mental resolve to fight on regardless of pain, discomfort and possible injury, 'even though the body be broken' (1998: 83).

The unimpeachably macho 'hardness' of the boxer has its feminine and seemingly masochistic (yet heroic) counterpart in the Pavlovan icon presented to the ballet dancer (both male and female). Both represent what Jefferson, following Dutton (1995), has described in terms of a 'metaphor of perfection' (cited in Jefferson, 1998: 80). And in that process too, the body itself is transformed: it becomes a particular kind of object, with a distinctive musculature and capabilities. Body and mind – musculature and skill, fantasy and conceptualization – are also indivisible. This might seem to be no more than Marcel Mauss has already taught us about *habitus*, were it not for the fact that Connell introduces the crucial component of fantasy. Jefferson then takes this one step further by exploring the individual psychical investment involved.

The third example Connell gives refers to something rather different: the political history of the body. Here he ranges from the massively larger rates of trachoma amongst Australian Aborigines (38 times higher than for white Australians), through the struggles for and against contraception (fuelled on the pro-natalist side by fears of imperial and racial decline) to the attempts to cultivate physique through education, which can take us all the way from muscular Christianity and Nazi schooling to current concerns about the practice of sport in schools. This entails making reference not merely to the malnutrition of the children of the poor or the gendered distribution of alcoholism, but to the way in which this gendering or impoverishment is written on the body: Connell refers to Margery Spring Rice's description of the physical effects on working-class wives of back-breaking daily labour, in her words, 'in the small dark unorganized workshop of the home' (Connell, 1987: 86).

Connell's examples, although merely gestural, give glimpses of the richness of what he is endeavouring to capture through inverting the relationship between the body and sociality, but that general formulation does him a disservice.

Framed in this way, the model does little to dispel the dangers we have seen before. Postulating two general realms, the natural and the social, and stipulating the direction and nature of the relation between them (as one of transcendence and negation) is too limiting. It tends to flatten precisely the variety and complexity we have just been describing. When, in addition to that, the distinction between them is made in terms of a distinction between the intractable and the recalcitrant body and the structure of symbol and interpretation that is woven around it, the ontological weight, in spite of the inversion of determinacy between natural and social, invokes the very same ontological order as the epiphenomenal and additive accounts and, at this general level, will tend to rejoin that order. 'Sex' and 'gender' are still fundamentally present, even if gender is seen to be capable of producing something new with those elements of sex which have a degree of malleability.

Of social and other categories

At the same time as Connell proposes a body that is intractable and recalcitrant, he also asserts that it neither sustains dichotomous gender nor does it have meaning in and of itself. This is a claim both about the sources of meaning – in sociality and the non-bodily – and about the body itself. Although the body bears sufficient difference to allow for discussion of 'boys' or 'men' or 'women', and to identify seriality, or for Connell to talk of not contesting the facts of reproductive biology, attempts to secure dichotomy are, he suggests, doomed to failure: '*the biological logic*, and the inert practice that responds to it, *cannot sustain the gender categories*' (1987: 81, emphasis in original). Yet obviously the very notion of seriality embodies a particular kind of meaning and interpretation: it is at least broadly classificatory.

What is hard to distinguish is precisely how Connell sees seriality: on the one hand, he speaks of the lumping together of people into logically primitive categories on the basis of an *external* logic, which is imposed upon them and places them in parallel situations; on the other hand, he talks of the array of parallel situations being constructed by the *biological* categories, by the nature of bodies themselves. He speaks of the biological differentiation of sex in reproduction as a passively suffered condition, a given state of affairs: 'men cannot bear children, infants require suckling, and so on' (1987: 81), although elsewhere he argues against such a view of the body, identifying it as a characteristic formulation of doctrines of natural difference (cf. 1987: 77).

Clearly there is a sense in which an account of this kind, which makes a distinction between levels of practice, and yet simultaneously identifies the difference between those levels of practice in terms of the distinction between *the biological and the social*, the inert and the meaningful, is not theoretically viable, and this *may* come to affect other aspects of the work. Just as we noticed with Kessler and McKenna, doctrines of natural difference have not *quite* been left behind. The 'practico-inert', in the context of discussions about gender, becomes fundamentally reducible to sex. The general distinction made between meaning, and that which is given meaning, logically requires that 'meaning' be extended to cover *all* descriptions including those that determine certain aspects to be non-meaningful and define them as 'practico-inert', which leaves one on a continually oscillating contradiction of the kind we have identified before. The division between levels of practice, as a division between the socio-symbolic and the practical (the 'limited range of practices and consequences' that correspond to the – passively suffered? – condition of sex), by contrast, seems to place the divide between the meaningful and the non-meaningful between the two levels: 'To construct the social category of "man or "woman" requires negation of the serial dispersion characteristic of the array of parallel situations constructed by the biological categories' (1987: 81). What the biological categories construct are, in other words, not categories in the sense in which we saw them identified earlier, for they embody a wide range of variability within them, and they are tacitly being identified as 'natural'. 'Categories', it seems, are both things that are spontaneously given by 'parallel situations' and things imposed by social practice: 'Social practices that construct women and men as distinct categories by converting an average difference into a categorical difference – "men are stronger than women" – negate the major pattern of difference that occurs within sexes rather than between them' (1987: 80). Gender, in short, actually *contradicts* sex: it represents a paradox. What sociality constructs is a *new fact*, 'in no way implied by the biological condition' (1987: 81).

The body as tabula rasa

Connell and Laqueur are not alone in feeling that they must salvage the body, nor in the particular manner in which they conceptualize it, as having a resistant substantiality. Both of these things are interrelated. As we have shown, the necessity for salvaging it is a direct consequence of the extension of the realm of meaning or language to the bodily, which is felt to cause it to evanesce. But this also implies that there is something arbitrary about how difference is construed. The very concepts of 'meaning' and 'interpretation' place the origination of such meaning with the human subject and this automatically entails the sense that the body is not itself the generator of such meanings as are conferred upon it. Dichotomy, then, is only one possible meaning, which negates or misrepresents aspects which could lead to an entirely different interpretation. Thus, for Laqueur, the evidential material supplied by the body is in no way unambiguously dichotomous and indeed can plausibly be turned to the one-sex model. Or, at least, there is enough evidence there to make of the one-sex model a perfectly reasonable inference in a given set of social and political circumstances; hence, also, the fact that elements of the one-sex model persist in diverse forms to this day, existing as a kind of delirium within the world of two sexes. It is found, Laqueur says, in anything from some of rhetoric of evolutionary biology, to the Marquis de Sade, much of Freud, and slasher films: 'The specter of one sex remains: "the womanliness of woman" struggles against "the anarchic assertors of the manliness of woman"' (1990: 21). For Connell as well, categoricalism not only goes beyond whatever difference gets established by biology (by converting the average into the discrete, the continuous into the discontinuous), it also goes *against* the evidence: it negates by distorting.

A paradox immediately presents itself, however: how do we know that there is distortion here? How do we discriminate between meanings if there is no ascertainable relationship between the body and the way in which it is understood (it does not give itself to be understood in this way rather than that)? In itself, the body seems to be conceptualized *both* as something specific, which can be represented in ways which are more or less correct or more or less absurd, *and* as a kind of a blank canvas on which a given society's predilections about difference can be projected. Laqueur and Connell, like Kessler and McKenna before them, denaturalize for us the perception of sexual difference as dichotomy. But if the body does not sustain dichotomy, is it because a partial and distorting use of the evidence is required to do so, or is it because, as we now tend to refer to it, sex is a construct and dichotomy is the content of that construct? Both possibilities seem to be entertained simultaneously by both Connell and Laqueur (and, as we saw earlier, Kessler and McKenna), which at the very least implies a certain commonality to their theoretical architecture.

Sex and gender as social construction [2]

Clearly the problem lies in the question of what it means to be a 'construct'. Although the metaphor belongs to engineering or architecture, the dominance of a conception of language within the way in which 'social construction' has come to be conceptualized takes it a long way away from the implications of such a metaphor. That which is constructed is normally taken to be that which is solid; it may be regarded as the realization of an idea but it is a realization in bricks and mortar, steel, concrete or any other kind of material. Indeed, providing the construct stands up at all, it is the perfect interconnection of the two, of what would traditionally be referred to as the ideal and the material. In many ways, Connell's work, like Kessler's later work, points directly to such an interconnection. But continuing to sustain an idea of interconnection in this way is also to sustain an idea of a distinction between two realms, the ideal and the material, which is what got us into trouble in the first place. It is just not helpful, in fact it is profoundly *un*helpful, to continue to speak in terms of such categories – which is just what Connell's work tries to tell us, although, fundamentally, he remains its prisoner. Insofar as a construct is deemed to be ideational it is also tacitly assimilated to notions of creation, fiction or belief. Belief, for instance, is by its very nature deemed to be ungrounded in any practice, and, specifically, in any practice that puts that belief to any test, that assays whether or not any consequences it declares itself to have are validated. Unless we are to ditch entirely the protocols of empirical investigation that we have established for ourselves and which, in some respects at least, demonstrate a marked success, allowing bridges to stand, the internal combustion engine to function and antibiotics to work, we shall need to think of 'constructs' rather differently, for some of them undoubtedly seek to have, and succeed in having, a purchase upon their object.

The notion of social construction, however, is a particularly powerful one for it allows one to open up the whole question of the body afresh. As Nelly Oudshoorn puts it in her book *Beyond the Natural Body*, exposing what she calls the myth of the natural body as a construction allows one to challenge the facticity and self-evidence of biological 'facts'. However, she too, like Connell and Laqueur, talks of the absence of an *unmediated* knowledge of the body, arguing instead that our perceptions and interpretations of it are *bounded* by the language that we use.[5] We shall return to Oudshoorn's work in the next chapter. The important point, however, is that as long as the idea of a self-enclosed language remains central to the discussion of the constructed character of the natural body, the solidity of the allegedly 'material' side of the equation will tend to melt into air as the 'ideal' side acquires more ontological weight. And what is solid only melts into air because our means of engaging with it are counterposed to it as insubstantial.

Connell's anxiety, like that of Laqueur, and a number of commentators who have either sought to reject or to supplement the notion of 'sex' as a discursive construct, is to continue to maintain his purchase on what matters most to people about the experience of the bodily. Both Connell and Laqueur appeal, *through* the mediation, to the sense of a *directness* of bodily experience, which will cease to be captured if we allow it to be eclipsed by language or meaning. But experiential immediacy by no means suggests the absence of fantasy, ideation or social symbolism – on the contrary, as Connell himself suggests so vividly. Although Laqueur and Connell both recognize this, they are also struggling to reach, and endeavouring to capture, a sense of the body *itself*. We are in a truly labyrinthine place, in which, whichever way we turn, our exit is a lure and we are seemingly blocked by yet another dead end. We therefore have to start to find a path out of it.

Out of the labyrinth

We should go back to that insistence of Laqueur's upon maintaining a space between the body and its representations. For, if we insist that that thing which we define as a biological system and which we call a 'body' is a different kind of object from a medical illustration, we nowadays risk accusations of the banal or the blindingly obvious. Clearly, then, Laqueur cannot be intending something that has connotations of absurdity, just as we cannot seriously suppose that those he was arguing against when he made his declaration of an Archimedean point – Rubin (1975), Ortner and Whitehead (1981), Scott (1986), Bleier (1984) and so on – can have intended the apparently absurd proposition that bodies are made of no more than language and culture. So he must intend something more. The key to this lies in the epistemic shift that constructed modern science: it is precisely because of it that we risk accusations of pointing out the obvious. If Laqueur, Connell and others fear losing their grip upon the body it is obviously not because they would lose their purchase upon the body *in general* but because areas of investigation and concern would be eclipsed. It would be difficult indeed to eclipse our general conception of the body as substantive. In that sense, we already *assume* there to be a 'space' between the body and how that body is understood.

Let us consider the concept of 'discourse' in a little more detail for a moment. It refers very specifically to the fact that knowledges, techniques, the powers they establish and that which is the object of all of these, be it bodies, madmen or fools, or the fossil record, are interconnected within a discursive order. As such, discourses are not identifiable with natural languages or, even, with *arrangements or forms* of language, conceived of within the terms of its traditional, philosophically based acceptation. Nevertheless, the fact that knowledges, powers, and what have traditionally been defined as 'material' objects are interconnected, and that one can assert that the relations between them are variable and complex, does of course imply that they are all conceptualized as substantively distinct from one another. In that sense, then, we have conceptualized a 'space' between them. But it is various forms of *analytical* separation or delineation that have constituted them for us as different objects or domains. Such a separation or delineation might take place, for example, at the point at which the object of a science comes to be constituted and defined at the birth of that science, like Durkheim's delineation of the domain and characteristics of 'social facts'. Or it might be a function of the process of empirical investigation and be most evident at the point at which we need to draw attention to a discrepancy between the predicted behaviour of an object (the way in which it is being 'represented') and the behaviour it appears to exhibit (the evidential material being produced by the experimental procedures). What this means is that our perception of the body as a distinct object, with its own conditions of existence and regulatory mechanisms, is an early product of the repertoire of biological knowledges that we have available to us. The bodies that Laqueur has identified for us, which are expressive of a metaphysical order of things, are neither the same kind of object, nor do they have the same ontological status. Their boundaries are permeable to the universe in a way which we can no longer understand and they have a mutability which is unimaginable to us. In short, the space that we are talking about, between the body and its representations, is a function of the analytical distinctions operated by the modern biological sciences which gave us a sense of what it is that bodies can and cannot do, and what they consist of. We should therefore conceive of that space as analytical rather than ontological.

Of bodies, tables and other solid objects

This will still appear to defy our commonsensical sense that there *are* ontological distinctions between 'objects' of various kinds, so let us turn to something that can also be experienced at a more commonsensical level, and this, in turn, will lead us to rewrite our notions of ontology. To take an example, the blue or red table on which we need to place things disappears in relation to the table as it is understood by the physicist as being colourless and mostly comprised of empty space, in which probabilistically positioned electrons circulate. If we go into more detail, the properties of these electrons become stranger. Although from one vantage point they might be described as substantial, they can also appear to be in two places at once, since they can be thought of as wave-like rather than particulate. Furthermore, the only apparently 'substantial' components, which are to be found in the protons and neutrons of the nuclei of the atoms that comprise our table, are themselves being rethought by contemporary physics. If we go still further, beyond even the weirdness of the quantum universe into cutting-edge mathematics and physics, we find that things become stranger still. Under the impact of Gödel's incompleteness theorem, matter is itself becoming nothing other than interactions of randomness: 'Space and time and all objects around us are no more than the froth on a deep sea of randomness,' and 'Empty space is a swirling chaos of *virtual* particles' (Chown, 2000: 26, emphasis added). Like a Leibnizian monadology, this is a mathematical space in which 'pseudo-objects' that have no *intrinsic existence* (merely a set of more or less strong relations with one another) are capable, with random noise, of giving rise to structures and objects and the properties of our space and known universe: 'So something like our space assembles itself out of randomness' (Chown, 2000: 27). Substantiality assembles itself out of insubstantiality, out of randomness – a property or a predicate without an object. This is clearly the point at which the capacity of natural languages to describe such phenomena breaks down, and without mathematical insight, appears to produce gibberish.

  The significance of this, however, is like the significance of the microscope to its early users: change the frame of reference and what you are explaining takes on a different character. Furthermore, even solidity, substantiality, materiality can resolve itself into something else. In short, ontologies themselves are not what philosophy has classically taken them to be, namely descriptions of that which *is*. Since we now understand that even the 'is-ness' that is depends upon the frame of reference that we use, never mind the fact that the substantiality of matter has ceased to be self-evident, we need to leave behind nineteenth-century philosophical oppositions, such as that between matter and ideality, and the conventional understanding of the ontological. Ontologies are best understood as discursively constructed and as serving particular purposes. Perhaps the most useful description of an ontology is the one given by Stephen Gaukroger (1978), which is that it is 'that primary structured set of entities in terms of which explanations can be given *in that discourse*' (1978: 39, emphasis added).

The ontologies of modernity

We could perhaps regard these forms of analytical, and by extension ontological separation, between, for example, knowledges and their objects, as just so many uses of shorthand were it not for the fact that they are also implicated in forms of thought in which our world is deeply embedded, and which are more than merely conventional. These forms of separation, which belong to the construction of highly specific and regional sciences in which there is a careful delineation of what properly belongs to the empirical domain and what does not, are quintessentially modern – and if they have their advantages, they also have their disadvantages. For example, Norbert Elias (1994) has traced the ways in which the very philosophical separation which lies at the basis of epistemological conceptions, the separation between knower and known, came to be formed, something he attributes, broadly speaking, to the increasing instinctual renunciation demanded by the civilizing process. Elias makes the point that the deferral or renunciation of instinctual satisfaction, what Freud would have referred to by means of the concepts of repression and sublimation, produces an experience of separation from the world which is peculiar to recent European social history.[6] It is an experience which we could call a quintessentially modern one. It forms the basis of the perception of the individual as a closed and independent entity and of the intellectual constructions of *homo philosophicus, homo sociologicus* and *homo oeconomicus*: 'The idea of the "self in a case"... is one of the recurrent *leitmotifs* of modern philosophy, from the thinking subject of Descartes, Leibniz's windowless monads, and the Kantian subject of knowledge (who from his aprioristic shell can never quite break through to the "thing in itself")...' (1994: 207). According to Elias, that experience of separation is itself the basis not only for classical epistemological positions, but also for the sense of self-enclosure that underlies such things as the intellectual dilemma of 'structure' and 'agency' in sociology, for the tendency to make the 'truly real' either the *sui generis* existence of the social world or the individuality and interiority of the human being. The severance of the 'inside' of the human being from the 'outside' thus produces a series of theoretical impasses, which can only be overcome, he says, by a different conceptual starting point, something he finds signs of in very few places, with the possible exception of Leibniz's metaphysical attempts at a solution: '...monadology represents an early advance in the direction of precisely the kind of model that is urgently in need of further development in sociology today' (1994: 205).

Modernity, then, brings into being, or at any rate *sharpens*, a series of forms of distinction, between knower and known, between individual and social, between knowledge and its object. Furthermore, it produces the anatomization and specification of procedure that lie at the heart of empirical science as much as at the core of a social order in which 'discipline' is the dominant paradigm for the regulation of human affairs (Foucault, 1979a).[7]

The space which Laqueur seeks to retain, so that flesh does not fold into language, can therefore be argued to have derived from the break-up of the relative intellectual unity and cohesion of the pre-Enlightenment world that he traces, and the opening up of conceptual spaces between object, procedure and question. The birth of empirical science has not entirely removed the impact of questions deriving from 'elsewhere', but it *has* opened up a set of distinctions between different kinds of question – the religious and the scientific, the moral and the factual, and so on – and made more explicit issues of the legitimacy of premises, inferences and conclusions, in a manner which goes beyond the logical, rhetorical or religious concerns that were the preserve of medieval thought.

The Archimedean point

One of the components of the space that Laqueur wants to retain, then, is already deeply marked in our world, so one has to assume that it is what that space makes possible, its empirical successes, that he wants to keep a hold of. Since an Archimedean point is the point around which a lever turns, the metaphor is clearly designed to signal that Laqueur does not want to see areas of concern and engagement closed off by the conceptual reformulation of the idea of the body. It is, of course, not merely the empirical science of the body that he wants to retain; it is also, as we indicated earlier, 'acknowledging the shameful correspondence between particular forms of suffering and particular forms of the body, however the body is understood' (1990: 15-16). His concerns, then, are both political and empirical, and it is the concept of sex that unifies them.

The problem is that having the concept of sex do duty for both sets of concerns is potentially contradictory. The difficulty with the sex/gender distinction is that it does, precisely, inherit that sense of the neutrality of the knowledge of the body in respect of political and social questions, which originally led social scientists to leave everything encompassed by the term 'sex' – and the knowledges that pertain to it – alone. And yet, Laqueur's own work indicates that it is *not*, and has not *been*, neutral in that regard. Logically, then, we cannot take the concept for granted, or leave the sciences alone to get on with it, and must needs consider the impact of political and social questions upon it. Furthermore, if 'sex' is implicated in human suffering, we need to ask what role the sexing of human beings is playing in that regard. Both in its constitution and in its effects, we have to scrutinize it. In these terms at least, the separation we have inherited in the form of 'sex' and 'gender' makes no sense if the history of the construction and sequestration of 'sex' is intimately bound up with an agenda premised on inequality and oppression.

If, on the other hand, we are aiming to validate the aspect of those knowledges that, under the rubric of 'sex', addresses the 'understanding [of] the human body in general and reproductive anatomy and physiology in particular' (1990: 16), and within which such progress has been made, we cannot afford to leave the sciences alone either, for, in this regard, political and social questions are to be ruled out of court. In this context, however, we might wish to drive an even deeper wedge between what belongs most properly to 'sex', to the body, and what represents the incursion of political and social concerns. But, if sex is always contextual, that separation cannot logically be effected, once and for all. Inevitably, these two things are of a piece. Modern science may not be a primary source for the suffering of bodies, but, as Kessler's work on intersex has shown, how the body is understood scientifically can nevertheless be implicated in human suffering.

Precisely because sex, like being human, is contextual and '[a]ttempts to isolate it from its discursive, socially determined milieu are as doomed to failure as the *philosophe*'s search for a truly wild child', then, there is no obvious virtue in maintaining the distinction between 'sex' and 'gender'. But we do not need to fear losing our grip upon the body if we abandon it – at least not unless, like those feminists Laqueur takes issue with, we seek to subsume everything under 'gender', with all of *its* connotations of ideality and fictionality. When gender is read as discourse, and discourse is understood as language, as Laqueur has pointed out and his struggles in 'Of Language and the Flesh' testify, we *do* face difficulties.

The problem of the relation between the body and discourse can therefore be reformulated. As Connell says, 'in the reality of practice the body is never outside history and history never free of bodily presence and effects on the body' (1987: 87). Indeed, the complexity of the empirical material addressed by Laqueur might be seen to point us in that direction, since the very thing it *does* demonstrate is how particular are the links between knowledge of the bodily and cultural, social and political concerns: knowledge and other forms of social practice are not easily divorced from one another.

Initially, let us just take the question of the place of such concerns within the space of an understanding of the bodily. If, as Laqueur suggests, the science of difference answers to questions ('which ones count and for what ends') that are decided outside the bounds of empirical investigation, then it is important to identify and name them. In a contemporary context, the notion of the 'externality' of a set of concerns to a discourse can be reframed as a decision about the legitimacy of those concerns in relation to what the investigative practices purport to be doing – what evidence is to count, how that evidence is to be adduced, what is to count as proof, what forms of argument are admissible, what protocols of argumentation are deemed permissible, and so on. In short, it is a decision about discursive boundaries and contents. The simplest of these might concern such things as the non-reporting of 'negative' data; the most complex might concern some of the rhetorical ploys or literary figuration deployed in a discourse. Modern science allegedly gives decisive weight to the evidential in determining the legitimacy of its inferences; forms of discursive exploration of this kind would shift attention back towards its more concealed elements, those which it takes for granted, such as its premises and terms of reference. It would also set such items in their institutional and professional contexts. Laqueur does understandably say that there is simply too much to do in the history of biology for any one person to master and that he has given but scant attention to such considerations. But, as we indicated earlier, it may also be in part for this reason that he faces the fraught chasm that he does. Because he is in at the birth of 'sex', which, he says, is only intelligible in the context of battles over gender and power, it is difficult for him not to see the whole science of difference as implicated in these battles and as fundamentally misconceived. But clearly this has to be reconciled with the undeniable advances within that science that he also identifies. The only way to do this is to look in detail at biological discourses.

Evaluating knowledges of the bodily

All of this is by way of saying that we are far more capable of deciding which forms of argumentation within a discourse are legitimate and which are not than Laqueur's discussion would have us believe. Doing so represents a rewriting of

Ann Oakley's endeavour to make a distinction in matters of sexual differentiation between 'fact' and 'value'. It is no longer just a matter of exercising discrimination between the two, of sifting 'fact' from 'value'. Bringing a notion of discourse to bear is a means of transforming the process that she began into a fuller identification and characterization of the elements in a discourse, their allegiances and their potential consequences. Such an approach reinstates the connection between a discourse and its institutional and political contexts. There might seem to be nothing new in this, but the crucial difference is that we cannot suppose that we will be able simply to peel away a set of ideological components from their adhesion to the genuinely scientific contents, and produce a purified, more 'feminist' science, as Laqueur points out. What constitutes a legitimate set of contents for a discourse will depend upon where one is standing discursively, not, we hasten to add, in accordance with the social characteristics and political allegiances of the individual researcher – in the spirit of some kind of cultural relativism – but on the basis of making explicit the origins of discursive elements, their conditions of existence and their potential consequences. For example, Anne Fausto-Sterling's proposal for the recognition of multiple sexes (which the biological evidence would allow) clearly depends upon its own set of political concerns, which would entail replacing the premise about a reproductive *telos* in biological investigations of sexual difference with a social recognition of the right of those with indeterminate anatomies to be genuinely 'intersexed', or, more appropriately perhaps, 'differently sexed'. Whether that would constitute an advance, or open up the possibility of discoveries hitherto foreclosed in reproductive biology, is a moot point, which would have to be argued for. In that sense we share Laqueur's scepticism 'that a more objective, richer, progressive, or even more feminist science would produce a truer picture of sexual difference' (1990: 22), but for a slightly different reason. It is not that a 'truer' picture is nowhere to be found (for why else would he describe pronouncements as 'patently absurd'?), but that we can never be free of the task of scrutinizing research programmes and determining the legitimacy or otherwise of their contents. It is a misconception to think of this in terms of the separation of the wheat of reliable knowledge from the chaff of ideology. On the contrary, it is more like the scrutiny and naming of parts in an otherwise integrated enterprise, and a gesture we shall need to repeat with each advance or discovery.

It is not so much that our access to the world is mediated, then, but that it is conditional upon those processes that have provided us with the knowledges that we have, which are susceptible to scrutiny. Michel Foucault's 'history of the present' did make the conceptions that animate and shape our world appear contingent. But it did not entail the idea that they thereby became just so much thistledown, to be blown away once we have established that they were *invented*. This is in part because they are anchored in a diversity of ways: they are woven into the very fabric of our world, as much through their investigative strategies (into the objects of which they speak) as through the other configurations they help to bring into being. However, it is also because the fact of their being human constructs – even constructs of a particular kind –

cannot *in itself* mean that their contentions are, by that very token, unsustainable.

In that sense Laqueur's contention that questions of sameness and difference are decided outside the bounds of empirical investigative and experimental procedures is not wholly correct. They also live at the very heart of them, closely bound up with other imperatives, such as more general investigative protocols. As we shall see in the next chapter, it is not easy to differentiate what is to count as 'knowledge' from what is to count as 'ideology': they can often be all of a piece. It is understandable, then, that Laqueur should have formed the sense that what *Making Sex* traces is so *inextricably* linked to the cultural politics of what we would now refer to as 'gender'. What it appears to establish is that wherever one looks, at the one-sex or at the two-sex model, what gets said about bodies is apparently deeply implicated in the social and political imperatives to mark difference. It seems almost impossible to divorce the notion of 'sex' and its ontological status from the presumption embedded in it that it defines an incommensurable difference between two categories of being, a polarity that marks every aspect of them, so that 'maleness' and 'masculinity', 'femaleness' and 'femininity' runs through those beings like the writing through a stick of Blackpool rock.

However, the situation will not prove to be as bleak as it seems. Critique has simply become more complicated. In the next chapter, we shall begin to see something of what is entailed when we look at the significance of some of the intra-disciplinary struggles over discursive contents and the definition of the field of investigation, and we shall see precisely what might be meant in this context by 'struggles over gender and power'.

The intelligibility of the body

The body may not spontaneously give itself to be known in a particular way but this does not mean that we cannot adjudicate between forms of argumentation and determine what knowledges about it can reliably be sustained – something of which Laqueur is of course well aware. To say this is therefore not to be agnostic about what the body is, nor is it to treat it as a blank canvas upon which representations flicker in an endless historical kaleidoscope. On the contrary, this is a reference to the nature of human knowledge. The historical inconstancy of the body as an object of human understanding is not peculiar to it – in some respects, with the persistence of the one-sex model, it has shown a *lesser* degree of contingency than many another object of investigation. Rather than dismiss the science of difference as misconceived, then, we should treat it – indeed, it is pressingly important that we should treat it – as perfectly susceptible to evaluation, and in this small measure we must depart from Laqueur and put on the agenda a task that he had decreed was not the historian's.

In that sense, however, the body is no different from any other object of knowledge: it does not contain within it the terms of its own intelligibility. Other areas of investigation will also be bound up, in differential ways, with political and social and cultural concerns. Sexual difference is not privileged in this regard. If knowledges of the body, and of the 'sex' that is deemed to belong to it, are, like other knowledges, always contextual, we can never be free of the task of scrutinizing the manner in which the body is 'represented' precisely because it will not, of itself, tell us of its character. The empirical dream was clearly that investigatory practices, because they engage directly with the object, would be capable of yielding information about that character. But we cannot rely solely on the evidence because the construction of that evidence is, at least in part, a product of the scientific discourse in which it is embedded. We shall need the assistance of other discourses, such as the sociological and the historical, to identify whatever other characteristics the object, as a discursive object, may have. This is not to say, however, that a sociology or a history becomes the means of, as Colin Gordon once put it, slicing through the Gordian knot of epistemology and that it is able to sit in judgement upon the contents of a science.   Neither, as emancipatory epistemologies would have it, is 'being on the right side' sufficient.

Replacing the idea that the medium of human knowledge is *language* with the idea of its being *discourse* was meant to remind us of the fact that knowledge does, in particular and specifiable ways, engage directly with its object. The discursive and the 'real' objects are, at one level, then, one and the same thing, since the *terms* of engagement are always at least partially defined by the discourse. Practices, however, even experimental practices, will always have multiple 'conditions of existence': in short, from the vantage point of the programmatic discourse that sets that practice in place, there are always unintended consequences. Realizing that there is no *necessary* form for an understanding of the body to take and that the knowledges we have elaborated for ourselves are historically specific does also, as Oudshoorn points out, cast a potential doubt upon the 'facts' those knowledges produce. Facticity has become a much more complicated affair.

The very acuity of the problem we have explored over the last two chapters is derived solely from the fact that we have been dealing with an opposition between human language or knowledge and something which appears so resolutely and poignantly substantive, something, in other words, that we ourselves obscured, or veiled from view. Without a sense of the way out of the aporia of the 'discursive' and the 'real' body, Laqueur's nostalgia has been widely shared: numerous articles and books now testify to the dilemma that he identified, but most of them go nowhere useful.[8]   Connell's discussion of the body's relation to the discursive in *Gender and Power* begins to dissolve some of that sense of the unreachability of the body from within discursive accounts, because it opens out the possibility of a consideration of a *relation*, or, indeed, a multiplicity of relations, between the bodily and the discursive.   In the following chapter, we look at the way in which particular biological discourses and investigatory practices come to be constituted and we begin to confront more directly the general question of what kind of 'truth' it is that we lay claim to when we take on the use of a concept of 'discourse'.

Notes

[1] Connell also references K. Kosik's (1976) *Dialectics of the Concrete* (Dordrecht, D. Reidel) and J. Schmidt (1977), who gives an account of Kosik's theory of praxis in 'Praxis and Temporality: Karel Kosik's Political Theory', *Telos*, 33: 71-84.

[2] A good example of this might be the way in which germ cells appear at the point of meiosis when environmental antagonists can wreak such havoc. This might be regarded as being at the boundary between two bodies, but, either way, whether we consider the germ cells to be a part of the parent body, or whether we consider them to be a part of – indeed the foundation of – the body of the child, damage is easily done. For example, the experimental research reported on by Wynn and Wynn (1991) indicates this fragility quite clearly, with a series of periods of susceptibility to damage.

[3] Laqueur stresses the need to avoid reading 'ancient, medieval and Renaissance texts about the body with the epistemological lens of the Enlightenment'. To interpret the description of bizarre occurrences metaphorically or in terms of naturalistic explanations is to use 'an unconscionably external, ahistorical, and impoverished approach to a vast and complex literature about the body and culture' (1990: 7). To read, for instance, the tale of a girl chasing her swine who suddenly springs an external penis and scrotum, reported by Montaigne and the sixteenth-century surgeon Ambroise Paré, in terms of her suffering from androgen-dihydrotestosterone deficiency and of her having been a boy all along, is entirely to fail to *understand* it. It is also no more than speculation. To put it another way, it is not to see the tale at all, but to read *through* it into our own knowledge of the body, on the presumption that we see the body *in its own right*, and that our account is innocent of any knowledge. The body itself sings to us, directly, whereas for our ancestors it was hidden behind a veil of ignorance, superstition and metaphor. This is a very powerful image of what empirical science has vouchsafed to us – direct access to the 'real' – but it is as erroneous as the idea that the ancients experienced the world through a kind of fog or error. Neither is more or less 'direct' than the other, although one of them may be considerably more powerful in practical terms.

[4] Connell uses the spelling 'fantasy', rather than 'phantasy', yet what he describes in terms of cathexis would seem to indicate that what is invoked here is in keeping with a psychoanalytic account. For ourselves, the invocation of a psychoanalytic account is not only fully intended, but vital. However, we have kept to Connell's use of 'fantasy' here since the term seems to be used rather more loosely than in the Freudian account.

[5] The question of the boundedness or otherwise of discourses by the languages, or, more specifically, the forms of conceptualization that they use, is, we believe, a complex matter which requires empirical investigation, rather than something that we can state by fiat by virtue of the fact that all knowledge and investigation takes place within language. For example, although it is clear that the term 'gender' has been used in a variety of ways and that it would be inappropriate to suggest that all of its uses suffered from the same deficits, what we have established through the course of this book suggests that where the sex/gender distinction is tacitly or explicitly invoked, it is very difficult to escape the relatively powerful associations that accompany it. Equally, however, we hope that we have also shown that those associations are about rather more than just language, which explains some of their power. It is not only that the distinction inherited a more profound distinction, which was already in place, it is also that what look like merely *conceptual* distinctions always have much more complex social, and sometimes political, anchorage points. (For a discussion of this see Chapter 8 on Walkerdine et al.)

---

[6] Mary Douglas suggests that what she describes as 'primitive' world views are characterized by a relative lack of differentiation, by which she means a number of things. First, it is a world which is anthropocentric and ego-centred in reference: 'In such a universe the elemental forces are seen as linked so closely to individual human beings that we can hardly speak of an external, physical environment. Each individual carries within himself such close links with the universe that he is like the centre of a magnetic field of force.' Second, 'the self is not clearly separated as an agent. The extent and limits of its autonomy are not defined.' Third, the universe must be interpreted by reference to human beings: 'the cosmos is turned in, as it were, on man. Its transforming energy is threaded on to the lives of individuals so that nothing happens in the way of storms, sickness, blights or droughts except in virtue of these personal links.' Fourth, the universe is personal, not in the sense that it is understood to be a person, but in the sense that 'it is expected to behave as if it was intelligent, responsive to signs, symbols, gestures, gifts, and as if it could discern between social relationships.' The universe is able to make moral judgements about human affairs and respond accordingly. However, Douglas is adamant that these beliefs should not be regarded as the result of so many failures to discriminate appropriately, as if what she calls the 'primitive' represented the child-like. On the contrary, these systems of beliefs relate directly to the patterns of social organization in which they are to be found, to the means through which human beings create a social order and 'commit men and women to its norms', without the specialized social institutions with which to do so, without the 'forms filled out in triplicate, without licences and passports and radio-police cars' (1995 [1966]: 82–93).

[7] Inevitably, this is a gross over-simplification of modernity, but it does allow us to shed a different light upon Laqueur's problem.

[8] Most such articles have evinced a dogmatic insistence on the 'reality' of the body but have failed to solve the theoretical problems because they seem to read what are defined as 'social constructionist' accounts almost as if they wilfully ignored that 'reality'. A game attempt to resolve this dilemma has recently been made by a collection of essays that seeks to bring together the two halves of the equation, the 'discursive' and the 'material', but, as will be evident from the arguments we have mounted here, this doesn't seem to us to represent the answer (see Ussher, 1997). The fact that a 'divide' exists suggests that the manner in which the theorizing is constituted is at fault.

7 Truth is Slippery Stuff [1]

A number of years ago, in the *Independent* newspaper, the understanding of how sex determination works was described as 'the Holy Grail' (Wilkie, 1991). The Grail is a curious object, which Geoffrey Ashe (1974 [1957]) described as a talisman, whose unholy, pre-Christian and magical roots were enhanced rather than diminished by its assimilation into the Christian tales and romances. At times sinister, at times beneficent, but always elusive, '[t]he primitive Unholy Grail may be roughly defined as a miraculous source of well-being, physical and mental, the discovery or rather *achievement* of which unveiled the secret of Life itself' (Ashe, 1974: 187). In the early Grail legends, the hero discovers the Grail and three other talismanic objects – a sword, a spear or a wand, and a flat stone – in a place where everything is bewitched. All four are kept hidden in a castle presided over by a Keeper of the Grail, who is wounded in the thigh and hence immobile, while all around the land is laid waste, a state of affairs which can only be dispelled by the hero asking a key question. If the question asked is the right one, the spell is lifted, the Grail shows itself, the Waste Land is restored and the Grail-keeper healed. With its affinities with fertility myths about cycles of death and rebirth such as those of Osiris or Orpheus and Eurydice, the Grail story seems to embody ancient powers and timeless mysteries. Its very unattainability and fugitiveness is expressed by the fact that as an object the Grail remains enigmatic and mysterious, so that it is never entirely clear what it *is*: sometimes a deep dish, sometimes a bowl, sometimes a goblet, but never categorically specified, in spite of its later association with the cup of the Last Supper.

This sense of the enigma that is sex is perfectly captured by Freud's apparently rather despairing question 'What do women want?' However, the image of the Grail is apposite for a number of much more specific reasons. A general overview of sex determination research reveals two interesting themes, which are interrelated. First, like the search for the Grail, that research often seems to have been intent on the discovery of a final and determining 'key' that would resolve the mystery of sameness and difference once and for all – the key to Life itself. The anxieties raised by feminism, and so well described by Simone de Beauvoir, that women might cease to be what they so ineluctably *are*, trouble the proceedings. The second of the themes, like the elusiveness of the Grail itself, threatens to make these anxieties come true: sex determination research seems to be haunted by the prospect of the dissolution of difference. Just when that key seems to be about to come within reach, it evanesces in the prospect of androgyny, only to glimmer again tantalizingly in the gloom. Its hero-researchers struggle in vain to ask the *right* question perhaps because they misrecognize the fact that there is no *single* question to be asked. Hence the fact that, over the years, the focus of this search has shifted, for example, from organs to the discovery of hormones to genetics. Perhaps, like Arthur's knights, researchers need also to be pure in heart, like truth and science itself.

It is seemingly ironic that some of the most interesting empirical work concerning itself with this search into the basis of the distinction, or with sex difference research in general, has come from investigations that declare themselves agnostic as to truth, or, alternatively, that present an allusive but not very explicit position on the subject. Kessler and McKenna, whom we looked at earlier, represent one such piece of work. Their agnosticism nevertheless allowed studies of gender for the first time to effect a breach in biological studies of sex, because it permitted them to doubt the absolute reality of what lay there and to consider the fictionality of truth, in short that truths, like other discursive effects are in one sense *fabricated*. This is neither to say that truths are 'mis-representations' nor that they are ineffective in the world. We shall therefore seek to confront the question of 'truth' directly in this chapter. Before we do so, however, let us return to the work of Kessler and McKenna briefly in order to expand on some of the areas they opened up for consideration.

The Quest for the Holy Grail

Kessler and McKenna refer to the discovery of 'sex hormones' in the late nineteenth century, which, they report, were at first believed to represent the end of the search for biological criteria that clearly differentiated the sexes. However, they state that it was soon discovered that both males and females produced oestrogen, androgen and progesterone, which cast doubt upon the clarity of a dimorphism between hormones. They describe recent research which indicates that the chemical constituents of these hormones are rather similar, that they are, at times, produced in relatively equal measures, and that progesterone is produced by both sexes in equal measures at all times except around the time of ovulation. It is therefore not easy to see why it should be called a 'female' hormone (1978: 73-4). Furthermore, it has now become a commonplace that women produce testosterone.

We are now in possession of a detailed empirical history of the establishment of 'sexed' hormones, published since these remarks appeared, in which Nelly Oudshoorn (1994) identifies just how precarious a foundation endocrinology provided for the discovery of a basis for sexual difference. Oudshoorn traces the complex of processes by means of which a hormonally constructed concept of the body comes haltingly into existence during the 1920s and 1930s, eventually attaining conceptual dominance for a period of time and producing the corresponding clinical situation in which the hormones oestrogen and progesterone – in what are, incidentally, not nature-identical forms – have become the most widely used drugs in the history of medicine (1994: 9).

We shall explore Oudshoorn's work a little later on. Of the biological sub-disciplines, however, it is now genetics, rather than endocrinology, which is in the ascendant and towards which the search for the basis for all human behaviour has shifted. In the search for the determination of the difference between the sexes, it had already had a part to play before it came to be seen as the encryption of all human behaviours. Kessler and McKenna also have a discussion of the relation between chromosomes and gender, which we can extend in order to explore their contention that a primary facticity is granted to the existence of two genders. Through a discussion of the history of some of the chromosomal and genetic work on sexing human beings and by observing the development of the attempts to sex female athletes for the Olympic Games, in which chromosomes play a privileged role, we can examine the way in which what Kessler and McKenna have described as the social process of attributing gender informs biological research.

Sexing the athletes

The history of modern sex-linked chromosomal theories begins in the early twentieth century with Henking, McClung and others who observed that in certain species of insects the chromosome complement of males and females differed in regard to one specific pair. Males possessed only one of these chromosomes and females possessed two. This chromosome, which occurred singly in males and doubly in females, was named X. Hence, *unequal numbers* of chromosomes were at first thought to be key to sex determination.

However, animal studies showed that having unequal numbers of chromosomes was exceptional and that most had the same number. But male and female did differ in another way. In males a pair of chromosomes was heteromorphic in that a single X was accompanied by a markedly differently sized and shaped chromosome named Y. In females the members of this pair were morphologically identical. In a typical textbook of genetics, Farnsworth writes, 'Since the constitution of this pair of homologues, XX for females and XY for males, was directly correlated with the sex of an individual, these chromosomes were named *sex chromosomes*' (1988: 143, emphasis in original). This was the general understanding established before 1910.

What is not always evident to non-specialists, however, is that the experimental procedures required to identify this morphological difference are themselves complex. Chromosomes are actually very hard to see; as Laura Gould describes it, they 'are hiding in a dense tangle in the center of the cell, defying all but the most powerful microscopes' (1996: 26). In order to produce a karyotype, in other words, an organized picture of the chromosomes in a cell, an elaborate process of staining (chromosomes were named on the basis of this process) and arrangement has to be undertaken in the laboratory. The chromosomes actually have the shape that they do (most of them looking like Xs, including the rather truncated Y) because they are seen in the doubled up form proper to the first stage of cell division. They are therefore really in dyads, joined by what is described as a centromere. These dyads are identified and subsequently arranged according to a series of conventions: for instance, the conventions for cats, known as the Puerto Rico Convention, were decided upon at a conference of mammalian geneticists held in San Juan, Puerto Rico (Gould, 1996: 36). For example, the dyads are lined up in order of their length and according to the position of the centromere along each pair of chromosomes (ibid.). The sex chromosomes are always placed last in the sequence.

Since it became obvious that gametes (e.g. sperm and ova) contained only one set of chromosomes, it also became evident that female ova would always contain Xs whereas sperm could contain either X or Y. This meant that the determination of sex was seen to rest with the male. Not all species, however, carry a Y chromosome. Not only is the lettering and pattern of determination different for different species – birds and snakes will be ZW for females and ZZ for males (Gould, 1996: 156) – but in some species males can be X0 (0 for zero) (Farnsworth, 1988: 144).[2]

By the 1920s, the work of Bridges was suggesting that most phenotypic sex characteristics resulted from the concerted action of many genes. He proposed that a *balanced* set of chromosomes and genes was required for normal development. In other words, 'sex' represents a complex phenotype apparently controlled by numerous genes, some of which are specific to each of the sexes and some autosomal (i.e. shared by both sexes). Bridges' theory, that it was the genic balance, or dosage, that determined sex became widely accepted.

However, work in the late 1950s, notably by Jacobs and Strong, and by Ford, prompted the proposal that the determination of sex in humans has less to do with balance and more to do with the presence of the Y chromosome, which results in maleness, and its absence, which results in femaleness. Jacobs and Strong analysed the chromosomal complement of patients suffering from the condition named after Klinefelter. The literature describes these patients as males with breasts, no spermatogenesis and (very small) external genitalia of the male type. They also show a variable diversity of other characteristics, such as long-leggedness or degrees of mental retardation. Such individuals were found to have an XXY complement. As Farnsworth puts it: 'The chromosome complement in conjunction with the obvious male complement immediately implicated the Y chromosome as the source of maleness' (1988: 160). According to Bridges' theory of genic balance, people with Klinefelter's syndrome should have been female. XXY in *drosophila*, on which Bridges had worked, had resulted in females.

Additionally, in 1959 Ford analysed the chromosomal complement of patients suffering from Turner's syndrome. We are told that 'Such individuals are sterile females with undeveloped secondary sex characteristics, short statures; the reproductive organs are mere streaks of ovarian tissue' (Farnsworth, 1988: 162). Such patients are found to have only one X chromosome present. Again since, in *drosophila*, X0 always results in maleness, the evidence pointed away from Bridges.

The modern sexing of female athletes utilized these developments in chromosome theory. Until 1966 medical certificates signed by a doctor satisfied international athletic bodies as to the true sex of female competitors, but in 1966 a visual inspection was introduced at the European Championships held in Budapest, and by the 1968 Olympic Games in Mexico a chromosomal test was widely used (Dyer, 1982: 65). Having one Y chromosome or part of a Y chromosome present – even if in only some of their tissues – was, and is, enough to disqualify a person from female events, the important point being that it is seen to confer an advantage. Between 1968 and the early 1990s there were at least twelve cases of women withdrawing from Olympic Games having failed sex tests (Hubbard, n.d.).

Despite the confidence of the Olympic Committee in the findings of chromosomal theory, and despite the current literature's satisfaction with the conclusion that the presence of the Y chromosome is determinate of maleness, anomalies remain. For example, the literature recognizes the existence of males who carry two X chromosomes rather than an X and a Y chromosome and a condition called 'androgen insensitivity syndrome' or 'testicular feminization' in which morphological females are born with an XY chromosome complement and internal testes which produce testosterone. In this latter case there is a debate as to whether their bodies are able to respond to this production in a way that would enhance athletic prowess. In North America, there have been successful challenges to sexual attributions (Carlson, 1991). In Britain, Dr Elizabeth Ferris, medical officer to the Modern Pentathlon Association and former Olympic diving medallist, argued that women were not advantaged by the presence of Y chromosomes. She is quoted as saying, 'we must not get hung up on the fact that a woman may have testes' (Hubbard, n.d.) – a remark which would have caused no surprise to Galen but which strikes discord in a culture which has committed itself to a two-sex model for over 200 years.

Advances in molecular biology which enable the precise analysis of genes, coupled with the existence of these abnormal sex types, recently prompted further search for the precise gene located on the Y chromosome that 'causes' sexual division. When David Page, in the USA, identified the specific gene, ZFY, which he had been searching for, it was at first thought by Dr Peter Goodfellow of the Imperial Cancer Research Fund to be the suddenly attainable 'Holy Grail' – the solution to the problem of how sex determination works (Wilkie, 1991). Page et al. (1987) found that this gene was present in the genome of XX males and that it was missing from the XY females. XX males are not that uncommon, with an incidence of about 1 in 20,000 and they have been crucial to Page's work. Unfortunately a puzzling result attended this discovery, namely that this same stretch of DNA is also present in normal X chromosome females (Fausto-Sterling, 1989). Furthermore, Sinclair, working in Australia, found that this gene was not on the Y chromosomes of kangaroos, showing that ZFY was not the sex-determining part of DNA in marsupial and placental mammals. It was therefore not likely to be the sex-determining gene in humans.

Only in 1991, in England at the Imperial Cancer Research Fund, did Goodfellow and his team (which later included Sinclair) isolate a gene called SRY (for sex-determining region of the Y chromosome) and its analogy in mice. By injecting SRY into mice embryos conceived as female they produced mice which at birth were male.

There are a number of remarks one may make about this recent genetic work. It has been construed as an Anglo versus American race, in the same way in which the search to find the structure of DNA itself in the 1950s was construed as a race between Cambridge University and King's College, London. It follows the cultural pattern of collapsing the search for sex determination into a search for *male* determination (the male switch that turns on maleness) with women construed as having an absence of maleness. It has the classic hallmarks of atomistic science: reducing from level to level in the belief that, ultimately, if you get down to a small enough scale, there is *the* sex 'atom' that will confirm for ever what determines our true sex. Page, for example, came to concentrate on only 0.2% of the Y chromosome. After the disappointments of anatomy, hormones and chromosomes, finally, the true sex will have its true sign. In fact, even according to the standards of genetics this is a questionable approach, because, among other things, it would commonly be accepted that *many* genes other than SRY would have to be enlisted in sequence before all of the components of a 'male' mammal were assembled.

However, the principal feature of these studies, to which we wish to draw attention, is the apparent tautology of the work from which the geneticists may never escape. A simple but glaring problem becomes clear when we ask, how did the scientists know that the XX subjects were males? If chromosomal theory provides the marker that determines sex these people must be women. That Page and his co-workers were able to describe them as unusual men shows us that *they must already know what it is to be a man before they can confirm it genetically*. The work appears circular: what in effect occurs is that two separate but equally decisive concepts of 'sex' are in play, one of which provides for unambiguous classification of the phenotype, the other of which acts as the final arbiter of membership. To use Kessler and McKenna's framework, we might say that it seeks to ground in 'sex' what it has already defined through gender attribution. The unusual XX men were deemed unusual because they were all sterile, had small testes, lacked germ cells (the precursor cells for sperm) and so on. They were defined as male, we have to presume (since Page et al. fail to give us such details), because of the appearance of external genitalia and, perhaps, other aspects of bodily morphology. But of course, in some circumstances, *chromosomal* sex carries the day, such as when physicians decide to 'correct' ambiguities in the external genitalia surgically to match the chromosomal pattern (Kessler, 1998: 18). In other words – as we shall show in more detail later on – both the assignment to a sexed category and the definition of unusualness are based on *other* criteria against which the sophisticated genetics work is tested (Fausto-Sterling, 1989).

A glance at any genetics textbook will confirm this. Those familiar with this literature are well aware of a range of 'unusual' cases in addition to those isolated by Klinefelter or Turner. Students of crime and deviance will recall work that found about 2% of males in penal institutions with XYY chromosome complements and thus implicated the Y gene in aggressive or criminal behaviour. Testicular feminization, females with three X chromosomes (as common as 1 per thousand), males with XXYY patterns, reported cases of XXXXYY, XXXX and even XXXXX complements are part of the literature of modern genetics. There are also what are described as 'mosaics' who might, for example, have additional Xs in different cell lines. However, chromosomes have little or no effect on whether or not human beings consider themselves to be 'male' or 'female'. In a person with complete androgen insensitivity – a condition which is genetic but not linked to the 'sex chromosomes' – normal female genitalia develop in an XY foetus, who is consequently assigned to the category 'female' at birth and, with the exception of menstruation, undergoes appropriate pubertal development from the oestrogen produced by the testes (although this may well be assisted medically by additional hormone input).

The gender identities of people with anomalous chromosome patterns are usually in keeping with the gender assignment made at birth (Money and Ehrhardt, 1972, cited in Kessler and McKenna, 1978: 50), and they do not show any behavioural differences from those with typical chromosome patterns. On traditional measures of 'masculinity' or 'femininity', XXY individuals are not 'more feminine', nor are X0 (where 0 represents zero) ones less so (1978: 51). These abnormal sex types are compared against, to switch to another problematic, a set of background expectations summed up, in genetics, by reference to male or female phenotypes. A phenotype refers to the *observable* properties of an organism. It therefore depends upon the perceptions of the geneticist – perceptions which need to be subjected to theoretical enquiry into ways of seeing and interpreting that derive, at least in part, from common-sense knowledge. What Kessler and McKenna would point out here is that, in this respect, biologists are no different to the rest of us.

Kessler and McKenna were among the first writers to open up the question of the importance of the ordinary sense-making activities of biologists and to suggest how central that was to our conception of 'sex'. They enabled sociologists to regard sex as socially produced. Oakley's formulation, as we have seen, made sex both a residual category, but also a lodestone to which gender would always refer, and, in spite of Oakley's own work, had the effect of warning sociologists away from a critical interrogation of the reality of sex – a reality that was the province of other experts from other disciplines. This was in stark contrast to sociological writers on race, who, from the outset, insisted on seeing race as 'race'. In sex/gender Kessler and McKenna offered the possibility for sex to become 'sex', although that did not in fact happen for many years. Whether directly or indirectly, it is Kessler and McKenna's work that enabled the tautologies of the sophisticated geneticists to be observed by investigators such as Anne Fausto-Sterling (1989).

Life in the XY corral

Fausto-Sterling identifies her purpose as that of working out in what manner and to what extent scientific knowledge is rooted in social life (1989: 320). She sets out to demonstrate that experimental results intertwine with social and political factors to constitute the biological canon and that 'the social relations of race, gender, and class have left their imprints on the field of developmental biology' (ibid.). In fact, the details of her argument are more interesting than this description would indicate. She focuses on the development of two central concepts in developmental biology, differential gene expression and the continuity of the germ line. Her initial observations concern the way in which developmental biology, and its predecessor embryology, is being subsumed under the heading of genetics, in spite of its potential to be regarded as a distinctive field in its own right. This results in what she describes as the literal and conceptual decontextualization of both the organism and the egg cell. That subsumption and decontextualization gives primacy to the gene, which in effect *becomes* the organism.

What this entails, in detail, is the demotion of the significance of the cytoplasm of the egg cell, which many embryologists regarded as fundamental to the differentiation into the various cell types during development. The experimental evidence in support of this would make the egg cell the more important of the germ cells, since an egg cell can develop without a sperm, but not vice versa. The reshaping of the fundamental subject matter of the discipline, Fausto-Sterling suggests, is not entirely innocent of the impact of gender. She cites an attempt to discredit groundbreaking work by Ruth Sager on cytoplasmic inheritance by referring to it as 'Ruth's defense of the egg' (Sapp, 1987: 206 quoted in Fausto-Sterling, 1989: 322).

She implies that this is not mere idle gossip but an indicator of a resistance to allowing the female parent to play a more important role in embryological development. This resistance actually leads the research into a conceptual impasse, which effectively ensures that the wrong research questions are posed and that results are inconclusive. As long as the cell nucleus is treated as the key to differentiation, the questions neglect the role of a dynamic nuclear-cytoplasmic interaction, and the issue of how differentiation comes about cannot be decisively resolved.

Fausto-Sterling also explores two other aspects of developmental biology, the more interesting of which for our purposes is her discussion of Page and his co-workers. In that discussion her argument is that 'unconscious assumptions about gender, hidden within the language we use to write about it, have worked to create implausible theories of sexual development' (1989: 326). She deals with three issues, two of which have been referred to before: discoveries described as the keys to sexual development in actuality being only the keys to *male* development, the representation of the male as presence and the female as absence, and the treatment of 'sex' as something clear-cut and unambiguous. The first problem is not dissimilar to the problem about embryological development referred to earlier and entails the collapse of 'sex-determination' into 'testis-determination', with the associated disappearance of 'ovary-determination' in the work of Page et al. This then entails seeing the Y chromosome, or a portion thereof, as a kind of master-switch, 'upon which hinge all sexually dimorphic characteristics' (Page et al., 1987: 1091). Rather than seeing the determination of different tissue types as involving the activation of specific genes or sequences of genes, the implication here is that a female develops when something is lacking (Fausto-Sterling, 1989: 327). There is, of course, a potential justification for this approach that would read it the other way round, namely that the female represents the fundamental embryological ground plan, to which something has to be added to produce the male. Whether either of these is justifiable and represents anything other than a gross over-simplification is of course a moot point. In contrast, Fausto-Sterling describes a model which would suggest that the activation of specific gene sequences to guarantee either a testis-determining or an ovary-determining pathway might be a matter of timing, with the XY activation occurring first and acting to suppress ovary determination. Again, Fausto-Sterling's account of Page and his co-workers is one in which the reduction of sex determination to testis determination distorts the research programme and prevents empirical progress being made, and an investigation into the plausibility of the alternative model becomes unlikely. The same thing also applies to Page et al.'s confident use of the phenotypes of their research subjects to attribute gender, which we mentioned before. Their perception of 'sex' as a clear binary, with no places in between, leads them to be unable to construct satisfactory models of sexual differentiation, which would presumably require them to consider it as a complex *process* rather than looking for the 'master sex-determining locus' (Page et al., 1987: 1091):

> In both XX males and XY females, then, what does the notion of a sex-determining gene mean? Is maleness decided on the basis of external genital structure? Often not, since sometimes physicians decide that an individual with female genitalia is really a male and surgically correct the external structures so that they match the chromosomal and hormonal sex. Is it the presence of an ovary or testis that decides the matter? If so, oughtn't the gonad to have germ cells in it to 'count'? Or is it enough to be in the right place and to have the right superficial histological structure? There are no good answers to these questions because EVEN biologically speaking sex is not such an either/or construct. Page and co-workers chose to leave some of the messy facts out of their account, which makes the story look much cleaner than it actually is. (Fausto-Sterling, 1989: 328-9)

In one sense, of course, Page and his co-workers might see themselves as doing no more than what any scientific researcher does and that is to begin with the phenomenon and seek to account for its causation. In that process, it may well be that the phenomenon is subject to re-interpretation. To an extent, that Page and his co-workers – and indeed, all prior thinkers in the history of genetics – should start with the 'obvious' character of the phenotype is entirely unsurprising. Perhaps, however, as Fausto-Sterling implies, we should expect more from them *as biologists*. What her work suggests is that it is their commitment to the gender dichotomy, and thus to the obviousness of the phenotype, that leads them to 'tidy up' the inconvenient details and prevents them giving due regard to the issues to which she draws attention.

Such an account suggests that 'the direction, subject matter and scope of the field have been affected in particular ways and that scientists operating in other cultures under other belief systems might well have constructed other equally valid accounts of development' (Fausto-Sterling, 1989: 321). Fausto-Sterling's contention is that it is hardly surprising that a field that focuses centrally upon sexual reproduction, the origin of species types, and the transmission from generation to generation of both similarity and difference should be marked by the imprints of racial, class and gender ideology. This is to imply neither individual prejudice nor a set of necessary consequences in terms of truth or falsity (1989: 320). She is being rather more specific than this, which is what we would argue it is necessary to be. For example, she identifies a language of fragmentation and 'striking' cubist imagery in some of the biological literature in the context of the kind of decontextualization that quite precisely makes possible and permissible 'the cloning of domestic livestock by fusing individual cells obtained from fragmented embryos with oocyte fragments' (1989: 322). In the founding editorial of the journal *Gene*, mention is made of 'the elements of physically controlled recombination processes', of 'chemical or enzymatic disassembly', 'recombination processes' and 'reconstructed genes and genomes' (Szybaiski, 1976, cited in Fausto-Sterling, 1989). Certainly there is nothing to say such an approach would not work; indeed it *does*. Similarly, she describes the intellectual move of the 1970s to consolidate the central role of the nucleus in developmental theory by James Watson:

> 'The heart of embryology is the problem of cell differentiation' (Watson, 1976, p. 500). Framing the problem in this fashion accomplishes two tasks. First, it awards priority to the nucleus redefining *the* problem of development as one of the control of gene activity. Second, it removes from the field those problems less well suited to the methods and concepts of molecular genetics, problems such as embryonic regulation, cleavage, gastrulation morphogenesis, cellular determination, regeneration, and multicellular pattern formation, in other words, most of what traditionally trained embryologists would consider to be their subject. (1989: 323)

Clearly, the relations between this and 'racial, class and gender ideology', as Fausto-Sterling puts it, will be complex, and, from the point of view of the non-specialist, inhabit a deep interiority at the heart of the discipline. Identifying its 'imprints' is generally going to require specialist knowledge of the kind Fausto-Sterling has. Alongside this, it will always be fairly easy and entertaining to identify the type of 'romance' that anthropologist Emily Martin has detected in the scientific construal of egg and sperm (Martin, 1991). The subtlety and the critical character of what Fausto-Sterling identifies, however, is far more problematical. For it is not only origins that we may be concerned with, but consequences. The ethical implications of cloning, for example, are not so much bound up with the prospects of producing an endless stream of identical human beings as with those of the type of engineering such a technology might permit one to undertake. Fausto-Sterling points to the implications of the acceptance of German biologist August Weismann's late nineteenth-century germ line theory, originally rejected but subsequently to become central to embryological theory. She argues that its acceptance was related to the profound implications of this theory for contemporary architects of social change, particularly those with a commitment to eugenics:

> The point is not that political philosophies cause bad theory choice, but that there are often several fairly good accounts of existing data available. Which theory predominates depends on much more than just how well the data and the facts fit together. (1989: 324)

In short, there is no rationalist order by means of which truth and ethics line up, or theory and facticity. Even if David Page and his co-workers do face research dilemmas because of conceptual impasses generated by what one might, for the sake of shorthand, refer to as 'ideological' imperatives or assumptions, this in no way implies that they will not make discoveries or that their work is in some sense 'untrue'. One does not write off the whole of the enterprise. In fact, it is precisely this which allows the 'ideological' to be so persuasive, for it can be as rooted in facticity as what we might *prefer* to think of as 'the truth'.

What is significant, however, is that Fausto-Sterling speaks of 'ideology', for the concept of ideology automatically has connotations of truth and falsity, and, for that matter, of distortion. Like Foucault, she is pointing out that ''[w]e must not imagine that the world turns towards us a legible face which we would have only to decipher. The world is not the accomplice of our knowledge; there is no prediscursive providence that predisposes the world in our favour' (Foucault, 1981: 67). Even with the same data, or, more loosely, in relation to the 'same' putative object, a number of accounts are viable. Nevertheless, in referring to the ideological and in indicating that ideological components are related to impasses in theorization, there is the implicit contention that the presence of these components carries a cost in terms of truth: they constitute impediments. In conventional terms, we might say that there *is* such a thing as 'objectivity', and that, as regards Page et al., this is not it.

The sexualization of the world

A similar claim is implicit in Nelly Oudshoorn's *Beyond the Natural Body* when she describes the archaeology of sex hormones in terms of a process of sexualization of the world: 'a world with hormones,' she says, 'looks quite different from a world without them' (1994: 149). At the heart of this process, she argues, is the fact that sex hormones were created as 'material products', and material products constitute 'the strongest tools that scientists have at hand to transform and sexualize the world we live in' (1994: 148). The implication of her fundamentally Foucauldian history is that it might all have been otherwise. The story of hormones is describable as one in which the idea of sexual duality was initially broken apart by scientific discovery and, then, subsequently, reconstituted in a different register by means of the making and marketing of a set of substances, themselves defined as sexed, and the elaboration of an account of the body as hormonally controlled.

Although what is described here is a *transformation* of the world, which might indicate that issues of truth and falsity are not at stake, the historical narrative makes it clear that, at one point, when the sexual specificity of hormones was in doubt, a different kind of panorama could have been constituted, but that there was something of rearguard action on the part of biologists to retain sexual duality:

> Although scientists abandoned the concept of sexual specificity, the terminology was not adjusted to this change in conceptualization. The concept of sex hormones thus showed its robustness under major changes in theory, allowing talk of sex hormones to continue unabated, even though new properties were being ascribed to the hormones. From the 1930s until recently, the names male and female sex hormones have been kept in current use, both inside and outside the scientific community. (1994: 36)

However, this is not described as the result of an ideological impetus on the part of biologists, carried over unchanged into scientific discourse. On the contrary, Oudshoorn talks of 'prescientific ideas' as *cognitive resources* for scientific investigation, which means that they do not survive into the construction of forms of scientific understanding untransformed – and that they might well come to be dispensed with. So, while the *background* to the discovery of sex hormones is undoubtedly the sexualization of the female body described by Riley (1987, 1988) and Laqueur (1990), and the *result*, at the point at which sex hormones come to be marketed for what is predominantly a female population, looks not dissimilar, what happens in between those two moments is something different. Indeed, it means that what emerges at the other end of the process of the birth, isolation, measurement, synthesis, and marketing of sex hormones represents a substantial transformation of the pre-scientific ideas that went into their making.

Oudshoorn argues that one of the ways in which such ideas come to be transformed is via the disciplinary predilections and expectations of scientists, which derive from their background in one or other specialism. She suggests that individual scientists are bound by a 'certain degree of consensus about problem definitions, the acceptability of solutions, and appropriate techniques and instrumentation', which, together, constitute what is termed a 'disciplinary style' (1994: 12). The story of the birth and development of sex hormones illustrates this well, since it is that of a shift from a predominantly biological approach – that of physiologists, gynaecologists, anatomists and zoologists – to a chemical approach – that of laboratory biochemists and the pharmaceutical industry. The eventual characterization of hormones could be regarded as something of a compromise between the conceptualizations developed by the two groups:

> The debate about the terminology and classification of sex hormones makes it clear how the different professional backgrounds of the disciplines involved in hormonal research led to a different conceptualization of sex hormones. Biochemists assigned meanings to their objects of study which were different from those of biologists. The hormone of the biochemist is in many respects quite different from the hormone of the biologist. From the chemical perspective, hormones were conceptualized as catalysts: chemical substances, sexually unspecific in origin and function, exerting manifold activities, instead of being primarily sex agents. From the biological perspective, hormones were conceptualized as sexually specific agents, controlling sexual characteristics. (Oudshoorn, 1994: 36)

Even at their inception, the idea of 'chemical messengers' implied a profound change in physiological paradigms, since it entailed a shift from the notion of the regulation of an organism by nervous stimuli to a notion of its regulation by chemical substances. This meant a transformation from the idea that the essence of 'masculinity' or 'femininity' resided in an organ, a gonad, to an idea that it was a matter of circulating secretions.

Although she does not say as much, one senses that Oudshoorn's sympathies all lie with the biochemists, if for no other reason than that the compromise arrived at between the two positions entails the rather curious allocation of a sex to substances, an idea that makes its way into popular culture. As an instance, she quotes Camille Paglia as saying, in somewhat surreal fashion: 'Lust and aggression are fused in male hormones' (1994: 42). Although this may look like a situation in which oestrogen and testosterone have become synecdoches for female and male, the reality is in fact rather more complicated because hormones are now read as the *means* by which 'femininity' and 'masculinity' are conferred upon human females and males. Our concept of sex has been transformed by biochemistry.

Nevertheless, it might well have been much more comprehensively reshaped. As investigation into sex hormones became more sophisticated, and anomalous discoveries were made, such as the presence of 'female' hormones in the urine of stallions, scientists struggled to reconcile these discoveries with their original conceptions of a duality. The picture that emerges is of a conceptual tussle to make sense of the findings in relation to the idea that there is a self-evident sexual duality, which must be locatable, *somewhere*.

Sex endocrinology – as it came to be called, anomalies notwithstanding – had originally stuck close to the idea that sex resided in an anatomical location, a gonad, and the early technologies focused upon the production of extracts from these organs. It was thus consonant with the commonsense conceptualizations of masculinity and femininity. The isolation of the relevant compounds, however, disconnected masculinity and femininity from anatomy and placed them within mutually exclusive and antagonistic compounds. Hormones represented 'male' and 'female principles'. However, developments in experimental techniques, such as advances in lipid extraction which allowed for the classification of hormones as a new set of substances called 'steroids', and their isolation in the bodies of male and female alike led to a decisive break with the idea of their being sex-specific. Once the techniques became available for biochemists to identify their molecular structure, the idea of duality was problematized further by the discovery of their similarity, since it showed them to be separated from one another by just one hydroxyl group (Oudshoorn, 1994: 25-8). It thus became possible to think of their operation in male and female bodies as synergistic in the creation of male and female characteristics:

> This enabled the Amsterdam School to emphasize a different relationship between female and male sex hormones: instead of an antagonism they reported on the cooperative actions of sex hormones in the development of male secondary sexual organs such as the seminal vesicles, the ductus deferens and the prostate gland. Other scientists reported synergistic actions of male and female sex hormones in female rats, in such processes as stimulation of the growth of the uterus, the first opening of the vagina, and changes in the uterus similar to those seen in pregnancy – processes 'typical of the most female sexual function' (Korenchevsky et al. 1937). (1994: 32)

In both practical and conceptual terms, the chemical messengers thereby broke free from their organic anchorage points. Doubt therefore came to be expressed by the biochemists as to whether or not the appellation 'sex hormones' was even appropriate, on such grounds as the fact that the changes observed in the organism with the administration of these substances relied on rather crude observational techniques (Oudshoorn, 1994: 35). As indicated earlier, their eventual suggestion was that hormones might be better described simply as catalysts. For zoologists and biologists, however, the abandonment of their characterization in sexual terms was inappropriate, because all that the research had done was to complicate the original understanding. So 'sex' was not abandoned within the biomedical sciences, it was reformulated as a compromise between these two positions, a compromise within which 'the biological perspective overruled the chemical perspective' (1994: 36).

What Foucault described as the idea of our having a 'true sex' therefore comes to be transformed into the idea of a non-exclusive continuum of masculinity and femininity which accrue variably and non-exclusively to male and female bodies, an account which 'could now be conceptualized in terms of male/masculine and female/feminine' (1994: 39). Arguably it is this that provides the scientific foundation for the later work of those such as Robert Stoller and Ann Oakley who were able to detach the two halves of each pair from one another and to construct a concept of 'gender'. As Oudshoorn points out, it was in 1935, at around the same time as this scientific re-conceptualization was taking place, that Margaret Mead was able to postulate the idea that masculinity and femininity are randomly distributed in a population but socially ascribed to one or other sex (ibid.).

The sexing of substances

The way in which the hormones came to be sexed, in spite of the potential for the dismantling of sexual dualities that they offered, owed a lot to testing procedures established in the laboratory and subsequently transferred to the clinic. Establishing the sex of certain substances – which in Frank's 1929 account had included, for the 'female principle', an apparently disparate collection comprising 'yeast, the buds of willows, potatoes, sugar beet, rice, ovaries and placenta, the body fluids of males such as blood, urine and bile, and even testes' (quoted in Oudshoorn, 1994: 43) – was largely the product of singling out certain organic changes as indicators. The administration of the relevant substances would produce either the growth of the comb on a castrated rooster or oestrus-like changes in mice or rats deprived of their ovaries (established through vaginal smear tests that were eventually to produce the Pap smear), so much so that quantities were expressed in capon, mouse or rat units. And, since it is more expensive and cumbersome to keep roosters rather than mice, there was an incentive for these eventually to become blood tests. Thus, sex became something whose presence could be measured in the bodies of specific categories of people, including homosexuals, who were deemed to be intermediate between men and women. 'The basic assumption underlying this hypothesis,' says Oudshoorn, 'was that homosexual men were considered more or less "feminine," so that a connection with female hormones as agents of femininity seemed likely' (1994: 56). Earlier postulations of a 'hermaphrodite pubertal gland', of 'deviated cells' which had a 'feminizing or homosexual-making effect' launched this search for hormonal markers of the 'other' sex in the bodies of homosexuals (1994: 57).[3]

Part of this endeavour involved complex processes of classification of characteristics as 'sexed' or not, depending upon their control by specific hormones. This was accompanied by 'an increasing array of technical details', such as the identification of molecular structure or of a melting point or of particular effects, such as the cornification of epithelial cells of the vagina (1994: 59). Because of the difficulty of maintaining a duality in the face of the experimental evidence, however, a series of anomalies occur, such as the redefinition of the plumage of roosters as 'negative feminine characteristics', because they are controlled by 'female' hormones. 'Negative feminine' or 'negative masculine' features were considered to be those whose development was suppressed by sex hormones: ovariectomized hens, for example, produced a male feathering pattern (1994: 61). Since the private joke was that 'there but for one hydroxyl group go I' (Long Hall, 1976 cited in Oudshoorn, 1994: 39), a quantitative model of sex was elaborated in which the degree of masculinity and femininity in a female or male body could be identified, leading to such things as the classification of female pelvises into 'masculine' and 'feminine' types (1994: 39).[4] This provided the means to rescue dichotomy from evanescing entirely. However, out of this was also to emerge another means of differentiating between the sexes: hormonal regulation. Women are henceforth to be associated with cyclicity (and a consequent lability) and men with stability in hormonal regulation.

What is interesting is what this does to our tacit assumption that where 'ideology' is operative, truth goes out of the window. Nowhere does Oudshoorn suggest that hormones are not 'real' or that this knowledge is 'untrue'. Indeed, the scientists' *capacity* to sexualize the world is derived from the material authority that they have as the consequence of the fact that *they bring a reality into being*, a reality that functions in the ways described by the sciences. If hormones acquired a sex, it was because they acquired an independent existence; as Ian Hacking puts it, we called them into existence (1989: 21). Thus, Oudshoorn says, sex endocrinology 'established its material authority by transforming the theoretical concept of sex hormones into material realities with a sex of their own' (1994: 43). In short, they were identified, measured, isolated, given a chemical formulation, synthesized and marketed for therapeutic and prophylactic purposes. In a sense, our doubt about hormones as objects arises not from the problematicity of their sexing but from the fact that Oudshoorn gives us an account of them as a *fabrication* brought into being by social processes. In other words, her challenge is a much broader one.

The materiality of discourse-building

Oudshoorn's work takes off, both chronologically and conceptually, where Laqueur's ends, to the extent of taking up the story through an investigation into the work of Laqueur's great-uncle, Ernst Laqueur, 'about whose isolation of the "female" hormone in the urine of stallions, he said that it raised "the uncomfortable possibility of endocrinological androgyny at the very moment when science seemed to have finally discovered the chemical basis of sexual difference"' (1990: 249). Like Laqueur, she stresses that '[o]ur perceptions and interpretations of the body are mediated through language and, in our society, the biomedical sciences function as a major *provider* of this language' and that, '[i]f understanding the body is *mediated* by language, scientists are bound by language as well' (1994: 3, emphases added). To this extent, her argument repeats the structure of Laqueur's. However, she makes a crucial distinction between her work and that of Laqueur, which concerns what she calls 'the materiality of discourse-building'. In Laqueur's book, she argues, sex and the body are described as if they were merely linguistic constructions, although he comes close to 'the materiality of knowledge production' when he discusses, for example, anatomical practices, and notes their dependence on the greater availability of male corpses – because anatomists relied upon executions and there were more men than women executed (1994: 155, n.18). Feminist debate about sex, science and the body similarly tends to become 'located in the domain of ideas, assumptions, images, meanings and theories' (1994: 12-13):

> Science is not just words. When we enter a biomedical laboratory, we see how scientists use microscopes, test tubes, X-ray apparatus, staining techniques, etc. Once we are aware of this, it seems implausible to reduce science primarily to theoretical interests. The development of scientific knowledge depends not only on ideas, ideologies or theories, but also on complex instruments, research materials, careful preparatory procedures and testing practices. Moreover, as biomedical discourses are the products of material conditions, they have fundamental material effects as well. The biomedical sciences have a material authority that is manifest in the form of diagnostic tools, screening tests, drugs and other regulatory devices. This is a social reality with which millions of people who experience sickness are confronted in their daily lives, a reality that should not be neglected in feminist studies of science. (1994: 13)

To investigate 'scientific facts', then, is 'to set ourselves the task of exposing the concrete, often very mundane, human activities that go into discourse-building in order to explore the processes through which scientific claims achieve the status of universal, natural facts' (1994: 10). Although a scientific fact, she says, 'exists only by virtue of its social embeddedness' (ibid.), she argues that one of the ways in which it achieves that naturalistic status is through its decontextualization, through being made to function in contexts other than that in which it first appeared. This is not merely a matter of the replication of experiments; in the case of hormones, for example, it is a matter of the move of those substances from the laboratory to the clinic, in which they are made to function therapeutically. The 'object', in a sense, becomes 'free-floating'. The idea that chemical substances have a sex is given a concrete embodiment and *secured* by their chemical measurement and their deployment as drugs. Also at stake, however, are the kinds of issues which Thomas Kuhn (1970) drew to our attention, many years ago now, about the establishment of a paradigm within a network of scientists. Oudshoorn stresses that it is through the making of the networks that dominance of a paradigm and the 'facticity' of scientific knowledge claims are constructed and assured: 'scientists have to leave their laboratories and make alliances with other groups' (ibid.).

Scientific facts and artefacts

According to Oudshoorn, the facticity of scientific knowledge claims is achieved by a twofold process, describable in terms of the manipulation of the social contexts in which discoveries take place: a (re)contextualization and a decontextualization strategy. 'Contextualization' refers to the fact that for scientific facts and artefacts to take on universal status, scientists have to establish networks within which their spread can function to universalize them. However, this is not a conspiracy theory. These networks are not established for the purposes of giving scientific findings credibility. On the contrary, practical necessities may well give rise to their formation. For example, the chemical isolation of hormones initially required the acquisition of huge quantities of organic material, which led to the formation of linkages between laboratory scientists and those, such as the manager of a Dutch abattoir, who could supply such materials. Out of this confluence came the foundation of a pharmaceutical company for the manufacture of hormonal products, Organon. These products could then be offered to the gynaecological clinic, with the clinic in its turn, becoming the supplier, not only of consumers for Organon's products, but of additional materials such as urine. In the process, Oudshoorn says, research materials became the carriers of knowledge claims, supplying the links between the three relevant groups: laboratory scientists, the pharmaceutical industry and the clinic (1994: 79). Within this process, women were to come to the forefront as the locus of investigation and intervention, while men faded into the background. The reason for this lies largely in the existence and greater respectability of the gynaecological clinic. Although male hormones will be offered to a small number of urologists for the treatment of their patients, unfortunate associations with sexuality and the so-called 'monkey gland affair' would ensure that it was difficult to construct clinical applications for male patients. Research on female hormones therefore brought in more researchers, there was a greater diversity of groups outside the laboratory who had a stake in the research, and some of these groups made possible the creation and marketing of a set of hormonal products. Some networks, as Oudshoorn says, are easier to create than others: 'With respect to female sex hormones, Organon was quite successful in enrolling the relevant groups to promote new types of drugs to a wide variety of audiences, sponsors and consumers, including general practitioners, psychiatrists, neurologists, medical health institutions, women's clinics, factory boards of directors and insurance companies' (ibid.). Oudshoorn makes the point, however, that it is inadequate to talk of the success story of hormonal pharmacology for women in terms of 'the inadequate but often terminal analysis that men are the problem' (1994: 82), the idea that 'women take the pills, men cash the bills'. On the contrary, interests are not pre-existent; they are produced by the making of links between particular groups, which are necessitated by the technology-in-the-making. Organon, for example, sought to convince medical practitioners of its scientificity and the purity of its products. Thus, hormones were born, literally as well as conceptually, from a sequence of two-way links between institutional and commercial locations: research group and slaughterhouse, slaughterhouse and pharmaceutical company, pharmaceutical company and clinic.

However, according to Oudshoorn, hormones only come to be 'facts' insofar as they become *de*contextualized, and the decontextualization, she says, exists in tension with the contextualizing process, since hormones *function* as facts 'because they become materialized in chemical compounds that could exist independently of the laboratory conditions that shaped them' (1994: 141). These materials, which are initially derived from observations, are then deemed, once they become *sufficiently* context-independent, to enjoy an *a priori* natural existence. Their context-independence is, however, limited: the contraceptive pill, for example, requires for its efficacy a number of social and clinical conditions, which may not exist right across the world. Oudshoorn lists the necessity for a well-developed and accessible health care infrastructure; women who are used to, and accepting of regular medical control; the capacity of those women to negotiate contraception with a partner (and not, for instance, having to conceal contraceptive use), and people for whom the use of prescription drugs is normal (1994: 143). The model we have of the 'discovery' of scientific facts, then, is often belied by the reality of what happens. Although the gynaecological clinic supplied the possibility for clinical trials, in the early stages of their marketing 'female' hormones were 'a product in search of a disease' (1994: 108). Their therapeutic properties were far from established. Their use was initially recommended for menstrual irregularities and the menopause, which promptly took on the medicalized status of the potentially, or actually pathological (the menopause being read as it is now, as a deficiency disease). However, this eventually came to be extended to a startling panoply of conditions – not merely the gynaecological or the psychological, as we might expect, but eczema, diseases of the joints, epilepsy, hair loss, eye disorders, diabetes, haemophilia and even chilblains (1994: 93). Contraception was mooted but not immediately followed up. For men, by contrast, the list of conditions for which 'male' hormones might be deemed useful was very limited, being restricted mostly to prostatic hypertrophy and impotence. In line with the sexed characterization of hormones, this dualism of prescription of 'female' hormones to women and 'male' hormones to men was broken only by the administration of 'paradoxical' hormone therapies (use of the hormones of the 'other' sex) for specific conditions, such as retinitis pigmentosa in men and, in an odd parallelism with the administration of 'female' hormones, menopause and menstrual disorders in women. In spite of the emergence of evidence of potential carcinogenicity for female hormones, they eventually took on the status of universal drugs in terms of both their range of application and those to whom they could be applied, which was potentially all women.

Scientific facticity, then, depends upon artefactual status. In certain respects, this is reasonable. The conventional account of scientific activity would have it that the demonstration of the existence and characteristics of an object would depend upon that science's capacity to isolate it and make evident those characteristics. In a sense, therefore, scientific activity must be about the construction of artefacts, and these requires appropriate technologies, which is why Oudshoorn appeals to the notion of the *materiality* of discourse building.

What get somewhat eclipsed in this account, however, since it stresses the institutional and commercial basis of the decontextualization, are other forms of decontextualization that belong to scientific *protocols* for the establishment of factual status, such as the replication of experiments. If one wants to use the terminology of materiality, these are as material as the commercial manufacture of substances. However, because of the stress on materiality, there is also a relative neglect of the theoretical and experimental bases on which claims to facticity are mounted. Why is this? To answer this question, we need only go back to the title of Oudshoorn's book.

Beyond the natural body

In her opening chapter, Oudshoorn describes the transformation effected in her view of science and the world through finding that it was possible to conceive of scientific knowledge – in this case biological knowledge – other than as a simple provider of objective truth, in which scientific facts 'suddenly leap into existence as the result of observations by clever scientists, who simply read the reality of nature' (1994: 10). Like Laqueur, she suggests that scientists are actively constructing rather than discovering reality, and that what she is questioning is 'the assumption that there exists such a thing as the natural body' (1994: 2). More specifically, she says that 'the *naturalistic reality* of the body as such does not exist' (1994: 4, emphasis added). This particular phrase produces a different inflection from the first, with which it is not strictly speaking co-terminous. Depending upon where one places the stresses within the phrase, on 'naturalistic' or on 'reality', one can read it in one of two ways: either as a reference to naturalism as a philosophical position, which suggests that the body is not as naturalism describes it, or in terms of the non-existence of that which naturalism depicts. Naturalism in the *Oxford English Dictionary* is described as 'a view of the world and of man's relation to it in which *only the operation of natural* (as opposed to supernatural or spiritual) *laws and forces* is assumed'. Thus, the body can be the result of nothing other than the operation of natural laws. If one places the stress on the word 'reality', however, and bearing in mind the challenge to 'the assumption that there exists such a thing as the natural body', one comes closer to the aporetic prospect that the body *per se* does not exist. What we would argue is that this hesitation between the two meanings accurately reflects a tension in Oudshoorn's work.

'Natural' has a particularly long entry in the *Oxford English Dictionary*, exceeding on the same page even the entry for 'nature', and a look at these definitions is enlightening, especially because of the light they shed on the notion that a 'social constructivist' view – such as Oudshoorn defines herself as adopting – entails the eclipse of 'flesh and blood'. One of these defines 'natural' as 'having a real or physical existence, *as opposed to what is spiritual, intellectual or fictitious*' (all emphases added to *OED* entries). This definition, taken together with that of 'naturalism', links an ontology to a realm defined by a set of laws, which are, precisely, laws of nature.

'Nature' itself, apart from its quasi-tautological meanings ('the essential qualities of a thing; the inherent and inseparable combination of properties essentially pertaining to anything and giving it its fundamental character'), is also associated with the idea of the vital and physical powers of the human, which can, incidentally, be inflected with the sexual. More interestingly, it describes 'the *inherent dominating power or impulse* (in men or animals) by which action or character is determined, directed or controlled'. This is contrasted with the human will and, via another meaning, with sociality: 'That no compunctious visitings of Nature Shake my fell purpose' (Shakespeare). Thus, 'nature' ties what is also understood as 'the creative and regulative physical power conceived of as operating in the physical world and as the *immediate cause of all* its phenomena' to a contrast with the human ordering of the world. Nature is the more forceful partner in a contest with human purpose and civilization, and to go against that 'nature', to be contrary to what it prompts, can also be read as 'unnatural, immoral or vicious'.

The 'natural body', then, carries a significant loading, or a loading of significance, and, specifically, one of moral and ontological conflict. Nature, '[t]he material world, or its collective objects and phenomena, the features and products of the earth itself, as *contrasted* with those of human civilization' represents '*the moral state natural to man*, as opposed to a state of grace'. Human nature, unsurprisingly, is the nodal point of a conflict. The 'natural body' will be both that which we cannot defy, which represents our proper condition, *and* that which is inimical to civilization, volition and morality. In that context, the denial of the 'natural body' seems inevitably to be the denial of that which *really* exists.

Seeking to 'go beyond the natural body' thus sets up an ontological competition between the body as defined by a set of 'natural laws' and the body as discursively constructed. But this is not merely a matter of the unfortunate connotations set up by the concepts of 'nature' and 'natural', which afflicts Oudshoorn's description of her endeavour. That ontological competition enters into Oudshoorn's account of the body itself, which is why certain aspects of the scientific endeavour, specifically those involved in the claim to be elucidating the 'natural' laws that govern the body, evanesce in the face of the social relations which are charged, in her account, with the process of *naturalization* of that which is discovered. If what the body *is* is discursively – for which read socially – constructed, rather than naturally given, explanation of that body is provided in terms of different sorts of entities, in this case the processes by means of which scientists construct networks in order to bring a conceptual object, the hormonal body, and a set of substances, hormones, into being. Two accounts of the body, the one which has it subject to a set of natural laws and the one that sees it as discursively constructed, are in conflict.

On the integrity of the object

Resolving this problem, however, is no easy matter. In many respects, Oudshoorn's work seems to provide the answer to the difficulties we identified with Laqueur's account of the discursive construction of the body, because she quite deliberately seeks to get away from an account which is predominantly based on language and representation. Yet it appears to be repeating the same aporias in another key. Paradoxically it seems, it is the fact that, relatively to Laqueur, she instead *neglects* language and theory, and more precisely, the claims internal to the scientific discourses themselves, which constitute the index of a problem.

Part of the answer can be found in the dictionary definitions we examined above and in something Oudshoorn herself points to. Referring to the work of Rosi Braidotti, she describes the way in which the biomedical sciences have led to what she calls 'a fragmentation of the body':

> However contradictory it may seem, the body as a unity, the object of biomedical research *par excellence*, gradually disappeared from biomedical discourse. The practices of eighteenth-century anatomy transformed the body into detachable pieces. Medical men dissected the body into smaller units that were subsequently renamed and classified. These 'organs without bodies,' to use the words of Rosi Braidotti, came to replace the body as a unity... Since the late nineteenth century, medical research has gone well beyond the organs. Research in histology, molecular biology, chemistry, endocrinology and neurobiology focuses on tissues, cells, micro-organisms, hormones and neurotransmitters... Thanks to transplantation science and reproductive technologies parts of our bodies can now be transferred from person to person. (1994: 4)

In short, the 'body' as an object is no longer a concern of the biomedical sciences. They have long since replaced it with a number of other entities. Therefore, is the discursive construct, the 'hormonal body', whose conditions of existence Oudshoorn identifies, a scientific object or an object in popular culture that *derives from* the changes in conceptualization introduced by sex endocrinology? Similarly, who is the prospective or imagined audience for Oudshoorn's work – is it the biomedical sciences, or is it feminism, for whom the concept of a body with a sex has been an anchorage point for the concept of gender?

We might also suggest that it would be possible to make a distinction between the body as an object of medical practice and the objects of biological research, which the term 'biomedical' conflates. The specification of a definable realm within the biological sciences – endocrinology, neuroscience, histology, and so on – allows for the isolation of objects which in another realm might well cease to be of moment: neuroscience, for example, might concern itself with the transmission of impulses from one neurone to the next, but will not *necessarily* have reason to be concerned with the biochemistry of the endocrine system. Each of these regional sciences exists within its own world, for which the 'natural body' such as it is, remains a relatively remote background.

The difficulty with the meta-discourse of the *OED* is, of course, that the discursive origins or operation of a concept like 'natural' is of only tangential concern in the elucidation of meaning: if one had to locate the definitions we described earlier, it would most probably be within philosophical and theological disputation. The difficulty for all of us lies in the fact that, in sedimenting themselves within the language, concepts like 'natural' have become the mechanisms by means of which we begin to think such things as 'the body' when we go beyond the regional specialisms of the biological sciences – whether we be 'lay persons' or specialists in one of those regional sciences.

As such, the 'naturalization' described by Oudshoorn looks like a social process at the *interface* between the sciences and the 'lay' audience for their findings, and between those sciences and the products derived from their activity – which may or may not be a matter for their concern, rather than for the commercial companies who take it upon themselves to produce them. For the sciences themselves, we would argue that the status of the objects of their research is not in doubt to the degree that they would require social processes of naturalization to secure that status. There are undoubtedly processes internal to scientific discourses themselves by means of which their objects come to be established as legitimate, which are concerned with argument, the status of experimental data, the replicability of results, and so on. In the case of hormones, there was a very particular confluence between the discovery of a set of substances and the potential for marketing them for therapeutic purposes, but this is not a history which one could repeat for, say, quarks, whose existence nevertheless has to be established in the laboratory, even if their integrity is fleeting.

However, Oudshoorn's concern with the processes at the interface between scientific and non-scientific (e.g. commercial) activity means that relatively little attention is given to these. She is right, of course, to demonstrate that the resolution of such tussles as the matter of whether or not to define hormones as catalysts or as sexual agents owes something to the ascendancy of one group rather than another, and to their capacity to construct powerful networks for the spread of their definition of the object. The acceptance of an object as scientifically legitimate might indeed owe more to this question of networks at given points in time than to the abstractions of 'pure science', such as how well the empirical data fits the theory. But, in this particular instance, what is interesting is the fact that those who were in the ascendant, the biochemists, did not win the day over the more longstanding incumbents of the field, the biologists. So, while there is something to be said for looking at the institutional anchorage of different groups and the networks and resources available to them, in this case, the likely outcome would seem to point in a different direction. Without an understanding of what went on intra- and inter-discursively, we cannot easily explain this particular result. To do that, we need to go back to the kind of terrain explored by Anne Fausto-Sterling.

Our argument would be, then, that, within the protocols of scientific discourse, scientists have far more powerful tools for establishing the context-independent 'universality' of their objects, with such things as the replicability of experiments. These are by no means always sufficient to assure success, and there is plenty of anecdotal evidence of scientists who lacked the institutional support to make their results stick: in that sense, they may well have been debarred from even entering the terrain of contestation. But these are processes *internal* to scientific discourse-building and what is described as 'the scientific community', rather than processes that establish the acceptance of their objects beyond that community. In some instances, that never happens, nor does it *need* to happen. In that sense, hormones constitute a very particular kind of object, for they had a ready social resonance in the discussion about sex differences and a potential medical and commercial applicability as substances.

It is no accident that Oudshoorn's objective is to demonstrate that the natural body *grosso modo* does not exist, for her political challenge is to the *authority* of the 'biomedical' sciences in respect of feminist claims. Her work allows the area encompassed by 'sex' to be open to contestation. She must, of necessity therefore, issue an ontological challenge of the kind that she does. The virtue of Foucauldian histories such as this one is, after all, that they are pedagogical: they demonstrate to us that things could have been otherwise. What Oudshoorn has to say about the manner in which discourses construct objects, which are simultaneously conceptual and substantive, is undoubtedly very powerful. It is very obvious from her account that, without the concept of the hormonal regulation of bodily processes constructed, via the development of appropriate technologies, by the biochemical sciences, the chemical substances would not have come into being as isolated and manipulable objects; in a certain sense, they would not have *existed* – however much we might postulate *post hoc* that they would always have been operational even without our knowledge. Their advent in the world as configured entities not only revolutionized how we live our bodies in experiential terms today – since we now inhabit a world in which we talk, only partly in levity, of the amount of testosterone or oestrogen in a room – but also insofar as we ingest these substances therapeutically.

However, there are essentially *two* ontologies at work in Oudshoorn's discussion, the one by means of which she sets up the idea of discursivity to compete with the idea of the natural and the ideal/material distinction which she uses in order to stress that discourse entails more than language. These two potentially contradictory forms of conceptualization are solidary with one another because she needs to insist upon the fact that discursive construction is about technological processes and substances and not merely ideas, hence the 'materiality of discourse-building'. This also allows for the efficacy and existence of hormones as *substantive* – if *not* 'natural' – objects to be taken for granted. Discourse thus comes to embody the opposition, material to ideal, that its use was designed to overcome. That opposition, however, is also a necessary one for another and simpler reason, and that is that the emergence of the conceptual object and the 'real' one do not occur by means of the *same* processes: it is quite clear that technologies are not the same thing as forms of conceptualization, even if they are intimately dependent upon one another and so closely interlinked that it makes little sense to talk of them separately. What we might say is that both of these ontologies are necessary for the simultaneity of truths that Oudshoorn wishes to establish, on the one hand that the objects of a science are discursively generated and, on the other that they are, indeed, 'real'. This is extraordinarily compelling as an account, and we are not for a minute decrying it, but it demonstrates in more senses than one that 'truth is slippery stuff', whether we are talking of the complexity of the process by means of which the social reality of hormones is constituted or our own endeavours to 'tell the truth' of that process. In the next chapter, we investigate further what it might mean to 'tell a truth'.

Notes

[1] This phrase belongs to Valerie Walkerdine et al., whose work we explore in the next chapter. In it, they say that they want to explore truth in quite a different way from the way in which it is usually thought about, in a way 'which treats truth not as something easily empirically verifiable but as slippery stuff created out of fantasies and fictions which have been made to operate as fact' (1989: 19). One should not take this to imply that truths are *entirely* created out of 'fantasies and fictions', as against their regulated discursive construction (in accordance with rules of evidence and so on); rather it is intended to draw attention to the presence of fantasies and fictions in the midst of what are supposedly merely empirical claims governed by particular sets of protocols.

Even though we have preferred to leave discussion of what Walkerdine et al. refer to as 'fantasies and fictions' *per se* until the following chapter, 'truth is slippery stuff' seems particularly apposite as a title for this one, because it suggests that the matter of empirical knowledge is not the straightforward matter of evidential proof that many of us have hitherto taken it to be, not only because fantasies, fictions, metaphors and other supposedly unorthodox elements are intimately interwoven with the more orthodox, but because the historicity of 'truth' presents another kind of difficulty, which is bound up, not merely with the particularities of how we conceptualize language, as we indicated when we discussed the work of Laqueur, but with that very language itself. Truths, in other words, are very complex constructions, something we understand well as practitioners but much less well as theoreticians, but they also prove to be, in some senses, *unthinkable* where our very language militates against us.

[2] There seems to be little consistency across species about the size and disposition of these sex chromosomes: in some species the Z and the W constitute a matching pair, but it is the female who bears the marker of difference in the form of the W; in others they are similar but the centromeres are in different positions; in still others the W is tiny, while in some species of rodent there are extra large X chromosomes (Gould, 1996: 154). And so on. A range of puzzles also necessarily arises about the genetic material on these chromosomes: for example, to pose one problem in lay terms, what are we to make of the fact that females have two XXs, which apparently contain more genetic material than the X and Y of the male? The answer to this lies in what is described as 'dosage compensation', by means of which the quantity of product of genetic material is regulated so that it is the same in males and females by, say, the inactivation of certain gene sequences, or compensatory production of gene product. However, this does not happen in all species.

[3] Interestingly, the corresponding treatment was far more popular in the United States than in the Netherlands, which is the predominant focus of Oudshoorn's study.

[4] This was an endeavour that was to remain in place at least until the 1970s with a description of progesterone as the more 'masculine' of the 'female' hormones.

8 Stories for Sexual Difference

The sense that veracity is a complex construct and that truths are operant features of the social world rather than statements conformable with reality *sub specie aeternitas* is perhaps the insight that lies behind Valerie Walkerdine and the Institute of Education's Girls and Mathematics Unit's chapter 'The Truth about Girls' in *Counting Girls Out* (1989). They argue, in a way which is similar to Laqueur's argument about the body, that 'we don't think that finding the truth about girls and mathematics is possible' (1989: 6). They state quite decisively that they 'do not want to argue that current work on girls and mathematics is a false or pseudoscience and that what is needed is a feminist science, which will unproblematically tell the unbiased and undistorted truth' (ibid.). Unsurprisingly, but in a manner which is still counter-intuitive for most of us even to this day, they argue that issues of truth, scientificity and method are more complex than this.

What they undertake to examine in this particular chapter, which is one of three that outlines their approach, is the work on girls and mathematics which is premised upon the assumption of female failure and in particular the work on statistical significance on which many of its claims rest. Anyone with even a modicum of statistical training will remember having a distinction drawn for them between statistical and social significance and struggling to keep to the technical and limited definition of what statistical significance entails. Nevertheless, statistical significance tests remain enormously powerful in social terms, and nowhere is this more evident than in the research on girls and mathematics.

The truth about girls

The Girls and Mathematics Unit make the point that questions about women's minds have been raised for many centuries. At different historical moments, these questions appear in very different forms:

> Let us first examine these, for different concerns at different historical moments have themselves helped to produce different definitions of – and solutions to – the 'problem'. In other words, no single and unbiased research question will locate the absolute truth about girls and women. Rather, it is important to show how different kinds of question lead to different interventions. (Walkerdine et al. 1989: 6-7)

What they are deliberately seeking to oppose is an empiricism in which the current categories, forms of problematization and frameworks of explanation are simply taken for granted. If part of a research endeavour is the reformulation of the research question, or rather the discovery of the right question to ask, this seems only reasonable. But with the use of the term 'empiricism', they are endeavouring to capture something more, namely the idea that one should not simply take for granted the objects that are deemed to exist in the world. This was a crucial insight vouchsafed to us by phenomenology, of which the idea of the discursive has also reminded us, and it was the basis of phenomenology's critique of what it described as 'positivist' sociology. According to phenomenologists, for example, the notion of 'structure' or 'system' was a hypostatized entity invented by sociologists, a notion which, while it might have begun life as a heuristic device, was deemed unproblematically to be a 'thing' by positivism. One such, Walkerdine et al. argue, is the social category 'woman', and, by extension, 'girls':

> Our starting point is that there is no simple category 'woman' which can be revealed by feminist research, but that as feminists we can examine how facts, fictions and fantasies have been constituted and how these have affected the ways in which we have been positioned, understood and led to understand ourselves. (1989: 7)

The perception of girls as a unitary category results, for example, in the perception that any discrepancy between the performance of any girls and any boys must be a categorical difference, in other words, the assumption is that it must be generalizable across all girls in respect of all boys, and such differences prompt an anxiety to discover a reason for the discrepancy. The evidence that Walkerdine et al. reveal here suggests otherwise: not only is the *categorical* character of the difference a fiction; so too is the difference itself.

In this instance, the concern was with the performance of girls in mathematics. More recently, the anxiety has been over the performance of boys on scholastic tasks more generally. What is it about adolescent boys, or about the 'laddish' culture to which they belong, that leads them to fail in school? One might speculate about the complex of political concerns that have led to the identification of either one of these problems. The important question, however, is how the problem comes to be constituted and, one might argue, to take on a life of its own, and it is here that a small amount of political information can reframe what is apparently a purely empirical debate.

The construction of the problem

Walkerdine et al. argue that the way in which the problem of girls and mathematics has been formulated deflects us from the specificity of the issues and the real nature of the debate, and it is this specificity that they seek to uncover and that debate of which they wish to remind us. The concern, first expressed under the government of James Callaghan in Britain in 1976, was about the 'wastage of talent', which was leading young women not to enter careers requiring scientific and mathematical training. Walkerdine et al. point out that concern about education in Britain since the Second World War had focused first on working-class boys, and, then, subsequently, by the 1970s, on girls. Given that this concern was fundamentally meritocratic, the issue was never really about *all* girls, but only about those who might be likely to be doing GCE A Levels and, perhaps, going on to a university degree, a very small percentage of the group overall. Nevertheless, the problem was construed as a generalizable one. Presumably, if the 'best' girls are failing then *all* girls, implicitly, must be failing.

The literature used to understand this presumed wastage varied from American social psychology to a British social democratic interest in aptitude and ability and their discovery and fostering. Needless to say, as Connell's account of doctrines of natural difference would lead us to anticipate, accounts of the reasons for the wastage fell either under the heading of 'nature', e.g. differences in brain lateralization and spatial ability, or that of 'nurture', e.g. experiences of socialization and resulting personality.

Given the specificity of the difficulty – how to get a particular group of girls into high-level careers based on science and mathematics – the formulation of the problem in this way is already quite strange. Clearly, the prevalence of doctrines of natural difference meant that no one felt the need to enquire as to whether or not this particular group of girls was typical of all girls or whether or not what was allegedly happening had anything to do with the 'girl-ness' of the girls. As their most salient and overwhelmingly defining social characteristic in the context of a political concern with the inequalities between women and men, it seemed 'natural' to presume that it was in some way implicated in the cause of the problem. There are already two theoretical and methodological issues here, then: one is whether or not a problem of failure existed; the other is whether or not such a problem as there might have been was girl-specific or related to something else. Where there is a political declaration of concern of this kind, there will inevitably be an incentive for the problem to be demonstrated to exist, or an assumption that such evidence as there is demonstrates the concern to be justified. We shall come to the evidence in due course. First, it is worth looking at the types of explanation provided.

Two sorts of explanation tended to be produced, those that appealed to differences between the sexes and those that appealed to gender-specific experiences or discrimination. Needless to say, the approaches that were most contentious were those that made some appeal to differences between the sexes, such as the arguments about spatial ability, whether this was given an environmental or a genetic formulation (alternative approaches, by contrast, tended to stress the question of whether or not girls were being discouraged from taking courses in science and mathematics):

> The genetic lobby would link the work to differences in verbal and non-verbal intelligence and with research on brain lateralisation. The environmentalists use ideas of sex-role stereotyping to suggest that girls and boys have different play and developmental experiences. There is scant definition, however, of the precise link between performance on visuo-spatial tests and school Mathematics. (1989: 8)

Walkerdine et al.'s analysis of the way in which this problem came to be constructed reveals a series of such lacunae and deficits in reasoning, and this applies as much to the approaches that show an environmental leaning as to those that do not. There is, for example, a literature of 'fear of success', which suggests that it is girls who show an orientation towards traditional femininity who take flight from mathematics, and a literature that talks of maths phobia and anxiety in women. Yet, to espouse the latter is to ignore evidence which suggests that it is not necessarily that men lack anxiety in this regard, but that they are socialized into *not displaying it openly*. For Walkerdine et al., the issue is potentially much more complex than this: 'In our view…anxiety cannot be separated from complex social processes nor from the involvement in Mathematics of fantasies of masculinity and femininity' (1989: 9). What these types of discussion suffer from, then, is not a simple matter of leaving aside evidence to which they should be giving due consideration. It is the same sort of issue as that identified by Zygmunt Bauman (1991) in relation to sociological studies of the Holocaust that seek to establish what produced both its perpetrators and the acquiescence of those who were not its perpetrators. The research can be impeccable in its consideration of the diverse causative factors that might have induced the behaviours, but the difficulty is with the very formulation of the nature of the problem in the first place.

In the case of Holocaust studies, the presumption is that there has been a failure of the civilizing process and that what is needed is more, or better, social engineering. The whole problem is read within a framework of the *failure* of modernity to control sufficiently. Seldom does it cross anyone's mind to suppose – understandably in view of the moral abhorrence that defines the very first approach to the question – that there might be anything 'normal' about what happened, that its components might in any way be *proper* to modernity, intrinsically related to its fundamental characteristics. However, this is not simply a matter of the thought that cannot be thought. In some respects, it has much more to do with the tropes of modernity that govern the whole of sociology than it does with the specificities of this particular moral and intellectual dilemma. Modernity is tacitly construed as the product of the advance of civilization, and the advance of civilization is assumed to be characterized by the increasing regulation of pre- or anti-social human drives, towards aggression for example. Within this framework, the Holocaust has to be assumed to be the unique yet fully determined product of a particular combination of psychological, ideological and structural factors, which it is incumbent upon the research to identify. Of course, what remains fundamentally unchallenged by this framework is the picture of modernity itself and the idea that what is required to prevent a recurrence is effective social regulation. Far more troubling, but potentially far more *challenging* thoughts are not admitted into the frame.

Research on the difference between the sexes takes place within a similarly complacent if somewhat less disturbing context. The presumption is always that such differences exist: what they consist of, what their extent is, and what causes them may be at issue but their existence goes largely unchallenged. Feminism – because it was born out of that terrain – finds itself caught up in tussles over extents and causes. In that sense, 'gender' – at least in its early days – was the answer to 'sex', within fundamentally the same framework. What the detractors of the capabilities of women attributed to 'sex', feminism had attributed to 'gender'. So, just as Bauman argues that Holocaust studies tell us more about the sociology that analyses it than it does about the Holocaust itself, so we might say of research into the differences between the sexes that it tells us more about the social, political and intellectual concerns that animate it than about the difference between boys and girls or women and men.

Both in its more 'progressive' incarnations and in those that are regarded as less so, the research into the 'failure' of girls in respect of mathematics and science, which Walkerdine et al. describe, indicates the way in which that research, because of the very formulation of its research question, is *necessarily* led to neglect disconfirming evidence because its orientation is towards a narrative of female failure. The 'learned helplessness' literature, for example, which suggests that girls develop a feminine passivity, is not borne out by the fact that the very sex differences it is allegedly meant to explain 'are neither as consistent nor as strong as has been postulated' (Parsons, 1983, cited in Walkerdine et al. 1989: 10). The literature that suggests that boys and girls attribute their successes and failures differently, with boys tending to give stable causes such as ability as reasons for their success and external, unstable ones such as lack of effort for their failures, and girls reversing the pattern, shows only slight differences where it affects maths. Girls rate ability as *a little* more significant when accounting for their failures than boys do for theirs.

More to the point, however intuitively and commonsensically plausible such accounts may sound, what cannot be avoided is the fact that '[g]irls' mean scores are roughly equivalent to those of boys, even in secondary school': in short, the very effect the research is allegedly set up to explain is simply not there (1989: 11). Walkerdine et al. mention that their investigation of the six major Assessment of Performance Unit surveys of 1980-2 only show differences in performance in the top 25 and 15 per cent of children in secondary school, certainly those children about whom anxiety is being expressed, but not girls as a whole. Many of these children, but not all, will be middle class. Insofar as not all of them are middle class, however, and working-class girls experience stronger pressures towards sex-typed occupations than do middle-class girls, '[t]here seems to be an important and interesting phenomenon relating to the differential performance, attitudes and experience of middle- and working-class girls' (ibid.). This is a much more specific effect than many of the studies would suggest, which is bound to be overlooked when the predominant concern is with accounting for the alleged failure of girls *per se*.

How girls 'fail'

Walkerdine et al. give a more precise demonstration of this concern by looking in detail at the statistical basis on which many of these arguments are mounted. Many of the British studies on girls and mathematics, they say, centre on interpretations of the findings of major surveys on sex differences. They suggest that, because the surveys are large-scale, there has been a tendency to view their results, and, in particular, any differences described as statistically significant as 'hard fact', where other data are deemed 'soft'. It is in this respect that Walkerdine and the Girls and Mathematics Unit argue that the claims made are unwarranted. Put briefly, the notion of statistical significance is used as a basis for claiming the non-triviality of differences.

Why is this a problem? One issue concerns the application of tests of statistical significance to large-scale social surveys. Statistical significance tests were devised, on the contrary, for small-scale experiments, in order to determine whether or not the results shown could have occurred by chance, or whether further investigation might be warranted. When they are applied to studies that encompass large numbers, a trivially small difference may appear statistically very significant because there is a close link between statistical power and the size of the sample. This can lead to the over-evaluation of what are in effect very small differences (1989: 14). The problem is one that will be familiar to any student on a statistics course: statistical significance is not the same thing as social significance. This is a litany which is invoked repeatedly on such courses, on a par with 'correlation is not causal relationship'.

The problem lies with the word 'significance'. There are at least three things in play. One is that it is very hard, if one is not a statistician, to remember that statistical significance has a precise and technical meaning, which is of course why the litany *is* continually repeated. It is all too easy to think that 'significant' means that the results *matter* in the terms within which one is spontaneously thinking about 'the facts': '[t]his concept of significance is part of the pidgin statistics of social science' (1989: 15). Second, there is the perception of statistical and quantitative data in general as a simple unadorned representation of the nature of the world. The statistical presentation of information conceals the processes by means of which it is produced and reifies this evidence as 'data' – 'given things'. Once evidence is mathematized in this fashion, it is easy to forget that statistical data are quite complex constructions, which, apart from anything else, involve theoretical assumptions and a number of decisions about how to investigate, gather and present data (Irvine et al., 1979). Numbers are seductive. The third point relates to the orientation of the studies that are drawing upon these findings, and that is that the population is being considered along a single line of cleavage, which is assumed to be significant in its own right, that of boy to girl: '[t]he reification of the category "girl" and "boy" produces explanations which favour sex-specific characteristics, so that more complex analyses of masculinity and femininity are impossible' (1989: 13). Put crudely, if you are looking for differences you will tend to find them. Apart from anything else, of course, what this means is that non-differences become non-results: 'similarities are usually treated in terms of their failure to show significant differences' (ibid.).

This is far more important than it appears at first. As Oakley pointed out, claims about the differences between the sexes, especially where they can be validated as 'hard fact', have consistently been used to decree the appropriateness of particular statuses for women. Whatever the good intentions of these particular studies, categorical differences have been politically very important in a history that Walkerdine et al. describe as long and infamous. So it is more than a matter of simply overstating some differences which might be minor ones and, potentially at least, understating others.

The second troubling issue about the status given to what are described as statistically significant differences between boys and girls, then, comes as no surprise. What are crucially being ignored are differences that are much larger in absolute terms, but which either do not have the same political significance or are regarded as politically far *more* troubling. What disappear into the creation of categorical differences between boys and girls are such things as class differences or geographical differences:

> The differences between boys and girls ranged from 1 or 2 per cent to about 8 per cent. They were considerably smaller than the differences between pupils living in metropolitan areas and those in non-metropolitan areas, and were totally swamped by differences between the regions of the United Kingdom or between schools having high or low percentages of free school meals. (1989: 17)

Walkerdine et al. look at two Assessment of Performance Unit (APU) primary mathematics surveys for 1978 and the 1979 Schools Council study in relation to the work that was based upon them (Walkerdine et al., 1989). In fact, the studies themselves tend to be quite circumspect about their results, but their uses have not necessarily been so. The first APU study, for example, states that: '[t]he data on sex differences show a slight, and generally non significant, advantage in boys in most sub-categories, but girls perform significantly better statistically in computation (whole numbers and decimals)' (cited in Walkerdine et al., 1989: 14). All three give little emphasis to an *overall* sex difference (although they *are* comparing the categories of boy to girl on each of a series of sub-categories of tasks) and where statistical significance is mentioned (for sometimes it is not), they stress caution in interpreting it.

The small differences across some of the sub-categories, which Walkerdine et al. estimate to amount to between 1.25 and 3 IQ points, 'a trivially small difference by any reckoning', are then taken by others to indicate that boys perform substantially better (1989: 15). For example, based on these studies, Shuard is quite happy to speak of boys and girls as two distinct groups with markedly different levels of success (Walkerdine et al., 1989: 16). The sub-categories of mathematical performance, however, are also to play a crucial role in the argument about female failure, for even though what is being noted in the studies is *success* on the part of the girls in some of the sub-categories, this will be re-read as female failure. Bound up in the discourse about mathematical ability is a differentiation between skills that are deemed to be a matter of 'rule-following', of which computation is an example, and those which are deemed to indicate 'understanding':

> Mathematics teaching will be approached differently depending upon whether its aims stress one side of the distinction or the other. Which side is stressed may depend upon what the educator thinks Mathematics education is for: what use the pupils will make of it. Those who stress teaching children ultimately to take money and give change in shops, to count components on a production line, to measure up rooms to lay carpets, tend to stress the 'procedural'. Those, on the other hand, teaching budding computer programmers, mathematicians and physicists stress the 'propositional'. However, this distinction is not simply of theoretical value. Ever since the inception of compulsory schooling there has been a debate about what kind of Mathematics was to be taught to different pupils. The distinctions are, of course, class-, gender- and race-specific, and

> naturalistic arguments are brought in easily to show that some pupils are simply
> more naturally suited to the menial rather than the intellectual. (1989: 24)

The assumption, of course, is that it is possible to follow rules without
understanding them, an assumption which demonstrates a degree of contempt
for those who are deemed only to be, or only to be *capable of*, 'rule-following'.
The conceptual distinction within the pedagogical discourse about mathematics
is between someone who can successfully complete a practical task by applying
a procedure without understanding the reasons for doing so, or grasping why
the procedure is effective, and someone who has a deeper comprehension of the
meaning of what they are doing and why the rules work (1989: 23). Whilst it
might be the case that some individuals have acquired a narrative about such
things which they can deploy and others have not, or may indeed not even care
sufficiently about the procedure in question to enquire into its rationale, it is
quite another thing to say that the latter do not *understand* what they are doing.

The anchorage of discourses in the world

What is crucially important about Walkerdine et al.'s study is the way in which
it reveals that discourses are *things of this world*. They are not divorced,
'representational' accounts that more or less successfully hold up a mirror to the
world. On the contrary, they are deeply enmeshed in the construction of that
world. The ways in which they are enmeshed will vary from discourse to
discourse, but they are necessarily related to the variety of practices and other
discourses that they inform and that inform them. And there is *no escaping*
from this. So, although it might seem that Walkerdine et al.'s position is
agnostic with regard to truth, their argument does in fact point to something
rather different, which is that it is simply not possible to produce a
metatheoretical discourse, with an epistemological impetus, in which the
conditions for successful knowledge are given in advance. Such would be the
case, for example, with analyses informed by standpoint epistemologies.
Certainly, if we think of it simply as 'theorizing about theory', metatheory is
continually being deployed (this is one example), but we cannot for all that
consider it to be a higher level and, by that very token, more authoritative form
of theorizing. It must construct its forms of authority differently.

What Walkerdine et al. have done is to reveal something new by altering the
frame of reference surrounding the research results and analysing them within
that. This is not merely a matter of the different theoretical presuppositions
they bring to bear, concerning how 'facts, fictions and fantasies' are
interconnected in the production of positions and understandings, but derives
from what one could characterize as a Foucauldian scepticism about the objects
constructed for investigation. It may be a variation on the traditional theme of
enquiring into whether or not the formulation of the problem begs the question,
but it is a uniquely powerful one. It is the interest in the questions raised and
how they are anchored socially that leads them to look at the ways in which the
discourses are constituted internally. There is a world of difference between
this approach and what we might call a 'diagnostic' type of feminist approach.
In other words, this is not about elucidating the discourse through its context

(the accompanying texts to the central core text that serve either to indict or exonerate it) but about looking at the *relationships* a discourse entertains with other discourses and practices. For example, in the discussion later on in the book of the impact of early socialization on mathematical performance, Walkerdine et al. identify the pivotal role that is alleged to be played by the mother, who is held responsible for providing appropriate early experiences which would allow her daughter to achieve mathematical success. The provision of the right kinds of experiences is believed to foster the propensities for mathematical skill, so that, for example 'helping Mummy cook' will supply her daughter with the valuable means of conceptualizing shape, size and quantity in the production of pastry (1989: 43). This is not a matter of making false claims, in other words, this is not to say that 'helping Mummy cook' will *not* lead to the development of such skills. It may well do that but it is also doing something else, which is much more interesting:

> We want to concentrate here on the way in which routine accounts of intellectual development emphasising a naturally occurring development of logico-mathematical structures do so by sleight of hand. The activities which are supposed to be a part of every small child's day turn out to be produced through a transformation of women's domestic labour into playful learning. We cannot date this shift exactly, but we know that the mother became a pedagogue at about the time when mothering became a naturalised phenomenon. Her role as pedagogue is crucial, for it gives her the task of making the world safe for democracy by ensuring the correct development of her children. In the liberal order it is she who bears the burden of her child's success and failure, and we shall see that non-feminist and feminist arguments alike join forces in holding the mother responsible for her daughter's success or failure. (1989: 38-9)

In short, it is vital to look at discussions about mathematical skill, the differential performance between the sexes and the content of mathematical education in the context of a much broader set of intellectual linkages for the issues that they put on the agenda. Walkerdine et al. therefore refer, at the broadest level, to Foucault's concern with the sciences of population management and the ways in which new forms of power were instituted which were to depend upon the regulation of the population through knowledges such as 'statistics, epidemiology, psychology and developments in medicine, law and social welfare' (1989: 22). At a higher level of detail, they identify the role of the mother as pedagogue in the education – literally the 'leading out' – of naturally occurring propensities associated with the notions of 'reason' and 'reasoning' in the child, and the transformation of her domestic labour into the means by which this is achieved.

The girl in the classroom

More precisely still, one has to look to the role of mathematical education in the production of reason and reasoning and locate within that rather more long-standing assumptions about the female mind. Central to this is a picture of the ideal 'natural' developmental process for the (non-gendered) child which intersects with assumptions about the natural propensities of each sex. One of the most interesting aspects of this is that of the contradictory positions occupied by little girls, in which they have to live both 'girl' (pathological, lacking) and 'child' (susceptible of developing 'reason'). Within the primary school classroom, 'helpful' behaviours, which are tacitly encouraged, and which are often seen as characteristic of girls, are also seen as 'passive' in the context of the ideal intellectual and developmental progression of the child. The naturalized femininity which is appealed to in these discourses is perceived to be ideal as the nurturing basis of the production of knowledge in the child (by the mother) but as representing precisely the *opposite of the capacity* to produce such knowledge in its own right (by the girl) : 'The production of knowledge is thereby separated from its reproduction and split along a sexual divide which renders production and reproduction the natural capacities of the respective sexes' (1989: 31). Femininity is seen as good for nurturing but too passive to produce knowledge. By contrast, the 'child', in the child-centred pedagogy of the classroom, is defined as intrinsically active and enquiring, seeking to discover things for itself. Although this is now changing, at the time Walkerdine et al. were writing, it also meant that where girls *did* discover things for themselves, they tended either to be seen as atypical or their discovery had be re-read in such a way as to accord with their perceived femininity. It would, furthermore, tend to be interpreted as the result of 'work' rather than 'ability' or 'flair'. However, much of the pedagogic framework and at least some of the gendering assumptions described by Walkerdine et al. remain to this day. At the heart of the picture of the active and enquiring child is the trope of 'play':

> What happens when a child produces high attainment as well as behaviour to be read as *work*? If play is the discourse of the school, through what discourse do children read their performance? If *real understanding* is co-terminous with the fantasy of possessing total power and control, how is it distinguished and what is the relation of this to 'getting the right answer', 'being certain'? How does *possession* of *real understanding* provide a fantasy, a chimera, which has constantly and continually to exist out of a terror that lurking around every corner is its other: *rote-learning, work*? Why is there such remorseless and unrelenting pressure to 'prove' that real understanding causes real attainment and that certain children have *it* while others just as surely do not, despite high attainment? (1989: 34

There can therefore be such a thing as 'success' which is not really success because the attainment is not based upon this active and dynamic engagement of the 'child' but on the passivity of 'rule-following': 'it is learning by the wrong means' (1989: 33-4). Overly helpful little girls are not believed to have the characteristics of intellectually successful children: it is difficult to be both the 'ideal child' and the 'ideal girl' at once (and, in a sense the ambiguities around the first of these ideals and what we could identify as the 'gendering assumptions or processes' complicate matters for boys as well as for girls – each fails in a different way). The classroom itself is afflicted by a contradiction between the discourses of a child-centred pedagogy, that stress 'activity, exploration and openness' and a more covert discourse of good behaviour that depends upon co-operation, neatness and rule-following (1989: 32). Qualities that are demanded in terms of behaviour are also overtly disparaged from a pedagogical viewpoint, but differential expectations attend each sex in terms of the demonstration of those qualities.

The regulation of children

Enmeshed in this is a fantasy[1] of autonomy and 'control' over one's own activity, 'an elaborate fantasy of omnipotence, mastery, control', which is offered to the child through practices that seek to mask the power relations that obtain in the classroom and between mother and child (1989: 35). The management of the active, dynamic and enquiring (for which read, potentially unruly) child takes place through the construction and management of this fantasy. The mastery of formal logical reasoning, of the means of making a case, goes beyond the direct transmission of overtly mathematical skills. Rather, logico-mathematical reasoning is at the heart of a more general endeavour, the production of the rational citizen, both reasoning and reasonable, which is in some senses achieved by stealth. Insofar as the inculcation of mathematical understanding is seen as the production of the capacity for reasoning, it is also a party to the production of what is deemed to be the ultimate in rationality – power through the winning mode of argument. An argument, as Walkerdine et al. say, is:

> replete with conflict. The destruction of the other is both feared and desired – necessary, but removed from the form and content of the discourse itself. It is a contest for control, a struggle for power. In these accounts of the production of rational argument relating to home and early education, a central component in the production of the 'capacity' for such argument is how conflict is controlled. In the home, mothers are encouraged to deflect overt conflict so that the child feels it has free will: conflict is channelled into reasoned argument, not fighting. (1989: 35)

The same thing applies to the teacher as to the mother, something which Walkerdine et al. say is the engineering of disciplinary conflicts so that the child believes itself to have 'chosen' that which is really being imposed upon it externally, assuming itself to be the originator of its own actions. This is a powerful illusion of choice and control which 'is…centrally implicated in the concept of "rational argument"' (1989: 36).

Desire, fantasy and fear – and truths

In analysing the positioning of the child in the classroom, Walkerdine et al. look at what they describe as 'the circulation of signifiers' such as *child, teacher, girl*, and, for that matter, *mother* and of dichotomous categories like *active/passive, rote-learning/real understanding*, and at those psychical elements which are implicated in them or engendered by means of them. The discussions of the respective failures of boys or girls, the pedagogical discourses and practices, the developmental psychologies on which they base themselves, can no more be divorced from the sets of fantasies and fears that attend them than they can from the concerns for the management of population that give such a central role to the mother in the developmental nurturing and educational prognosis of her child. The production of the reasoning citizen thus also has to mobilize a set of fantasies about absolute agency which is belied by the realities of the situation in which the child finds itself – hence the fact that Walkerdine et al. also talk about 'fictions'. There are fictions at a number of different levels in their account: there are the fictions of 'control' for the child, but there are also the more general fictions concerning female failure which 'function as fact'. As they point out, a central feature of the production of scientific truths within the apparatuses and technologies of the social is '*proof and practices for the production of evidence*' (1989: 34). Therefore, in spite of the ambiguity of the evidence, the certainty of the existence of *real understanding* is ceaselessly demonstrated. Rather than dwell further on the evidence supplied, they look at the motivation to provide proof: it is not therefore a matter of adjudicating over whether or not girls really *do* achieve real understanding or boys are *only* engaging in rote-learning, since these unitary categories are a part of the very fictions they have been discussing. What they are interested in are the ways in which the signs, as they put it, '"catch up" the subjects, position them and so create a truth':

> Teachers will often go to great lengths to demonstrate that boys have real understanding. By the metaphoric chain created, *activity* is frequently read as a sign of understanding. Understanding, then, is evidenced by the presence of some attributes and the absence of others. Activity – playing, making use of objects (Lego, for example), rule-breaking (rather than rule-following) – may encompass naughtiness, even displays of hostility and conflict towards the teacher. All these and more are taken as evidence. Conversely, good behaviour in girls, working hard, helpfulness, neat and careful work, are all read as danger signals of a lack. The counter-evidence – hard work in boys and understanding in girls – is also produced as evidence, but then other disparaging factors are brought into play... (1989: 34-5)

Truths, then, are by no means simple affairs, and, as we have seen in the preceding chapter, this applies as much to the 'hard' sciences as it does to those endeavours to understand and negotiate the realm generally defined as 'the social'. The modes in which forms of evidence are produced and the ways in which the effects that support them are engineered are going to depend as much upon such issues as how the general field of intervention is construed as on the ways in which the nature of the objects in that field is specified. Whether we are talking about the construction of a problem in developmental biology, for which genetics rather than embryology is deemed to supply the key, or whether we are talking about the construction of a problem in developmental psychology, such as how to identify the causes of the 'failure' of girls in respect of a range of skills, the principle is the same. Discourses can never be said to exist in isolation from other discourses, from a variety of different kinds of practice and from the fantasies and fears that are woven around and into all of these things. As human products, they ceaselessly defy the rational dream that animates them.

For example, at the heart of the child-centred pedagogy and the condemnation of girls for their apparent conformity (which will be demonstrated time and again and helpfully 'confirmed by experience') lies the spectre of its 'other', the spectre of authoritarianism and the old 'talk-and-chalk' pedagogy. Thus, the pathology that is detected is also a threat to the new moral order, which means that the gendering of that pathology – the positioning of little girls – automatically has roots and ramifications beyond the question of the difference between two social categories of child. Into this complicated nexus stray human beings, placed there by their social definitions as 'primary school child', 'teacher' or 'mother'. Other elements that they bring to bear from the rest of their lives will mark them out, say, for failure. Walkerdine et al. have an interesting discussion of the ways in which the discourses used by working-class mothers with their children place them at odds with the discourses that dominate school life, and the ways in which the children experience this 'failure to conform' on the part of their mothers and may seek to resist their own implication in it. Middle-class mothers, for example, 'know' the methods used to teach the alphabet or writing skills. The mother of a child called Sally tries to teach her child to write in the way she regards as 'correct', an endeavour Sally resists. Sally's mother has a sense of the 'proper way' in which children should be taught to write, which the nursery school is not abiding by, and she tries to get Sally to comply with this:

> We could understand this as the child's struggle to be intellectually independent through 'confident challenge', but her rejection must also be bound up with what she perceives as her mother's *lack* of knowledge. Sally must gain control of the lesson, because as far as she is concerned her mother has made it clear that she does not know what is right. (1989: 56)

A child picked out by the school as 'clever' may gain status and power from this, but accompanying this is a widening gap between herself and her mother, which is probably painful for both of them, but which the mother cannot close because she is simply seen as 'lacking': 'Her knowledge is stupid, wrong, pathological, and is therefore no knowledge at all' (ibid.).

Of structure, agency and social categories

Mother and child may both experience pain and discomfort through the ways in which they are positioned by discourses and practices such as the pedagogy of the infant or primary school. As Walkerdine et al. put it, the circulation of meaning for such a signifier as *child* within a range of practices and discourses 'sits uncomfortably upon actual little girls' (1989: 36). Such a description, construed in terms of the *positioning* of human beings, could be susceptible to two different but overlapping interpretations. One of these concerns the fact that particular discourses and practices may place demands upon human beings which it is difficult for them to meet or offer positions which it is difficult for various reasons for them to inhabit (such as, say, the existence of other conflicting accounts of themselves). Alternatively, we could interpret this description as the residue of a rather more general structuralism, in which the dominant part seems to lie with the discourses and practices, because they *locate* individual human beings within them. It is clear from the work of

Walkerdine et al., however, that, if it is such a residue, it does not have much influence. In their account, human beings fully inhabit the practices and the discourses within which they are also located. The location is not *per se* prior to the inhabiting of a position. In some instances, of course, broader social requirements, such as the legal requirement of children of a certain age to attend school, dictate that the children will move into a world within which certain kinds of discourses circulate and certain kinds of practices dominate. But these discourses and practices will also exist in some measure as resources for those children (although to differential degrees for different children), as will other discourses and practices that they encounter, and they will make use of them in just the same way as other human beings do.

Here Valerie Walkerdine's later discussion of the encounter between a female teacher and two nursery school children is instructive (Walkerdine, 1990). In it, two four-year-old boys effectively harass the teacher and that harassment, through which the boys seek to resist her authority as a teacher, has a markedly sexual and sexist content. Their resistance to her 'can be understood in terms both of their assertion of their difference from her and their seizing of power through constituting her as the powerless object of a sexist discourse' (Walkerdine, 1990: 5). The example is both shocking and quotidian. A traditional reading of this encounter would have it that male dominance is learnt early and that it is directly related to the sex of each of the sets of participants. But Walkerdine stresses that this situation does not automatically follow from the fact that the children are boys and that the teacher is female. One of the crucial things that disempowers the teacher is the set of pedagogical beliefs and practices within which she is working, which dictate that explicit sexual references by children are a harmless function of their emotional and psychological immaturity and that such references are best dealt with by ignoring them. Such discourses and practices constitute 'progressive education', whose aim is a pedagogy that produces controlled rather than regimented individuals, with such control being seen as the developmental product of a natural maturational process (Walkerdine, 1990: 6-7). The children, for their part, have detected that sexual references constitute one way in which to rattle teachers about which they can do very little, and have acquired a shrewd understanding of the power conferred by sexist speech over women and girls.

The importance of her argument, says Walkerdine, 'is in the way in which we can assert that relations of power are not invested in unitary individuals in any way which is solely or essentially derived from their material and institutional position' (Walkerdine, 1990: 5). An individual can become powerful or powerless depending, as Walkerdine describes it, on the terms in which their subjectivity is constituted. The teacher has ceased to *signify* as a teacher because of the way in which she is constituted in both the discursive positionings deployed by the boys *and* her own pedagogic principles. A different set of pedagogic principles would have allowed her to react quite differently. Thus 'both female teachers and small girls are not unitary subjects uniquely positioned, but are produced as a nexus of subjectivities, in relations of power which are constantly shifting, rendering them at one moment powerful and at another powerless' (Walkerdine, 1990: 1).

Mothers and daughters

Again, the language here is one of the 'production' of subjectivities by discourses, but it is noteworthy that it is not 'subjects' who are considered to be produced thereby but 'subjectivities' – as the *Oxford English Dictionary* would have it, 'the consciousness of one's perceived states'. Likewise, a 'nexus' represents 'a connected group or series'. In other words, this account draws attention to a connected series of nevertheless diverse *experiences*. Children in a single situation alone – like the children described above – might experience both their power, the power conferred on them by the successful gamble they undertake, and their potential vulnerability in taking that risk (depending upon how calculated it is and how confident they are of success). Across a series of situations, they will be positioned and take up positions in a variety of different ways. The positions are *multiple*, even within a single situation, and discursively generated rather than structurally given.

What is clear from this is just how active a role the children play. In *Counting Girls Out*, there is a very vivid account of the ways in which little girls, at the age of four, seek to avoid some of the difficulties they perceive in growing up by manipulating their mothers into meeting their needs and thus being allowed to remain 'little babies'. Like the little girls confronted with mothers whose 'knowledge' is no knowledge at all, these children not only resist but deliberately seek to *engineer* a situation in which they do not have to confront the unpleasantness of growing up and leaving their mothers to go to school. The boys who harass the teacher, Sally's attempt to wrest control of the lesson and the little girls who seek to remain babies can all be seen to be much more than ciphers for discourses and practices.

We need to look in some detail at the discursive context in which this takes place in order to make sense of the resources that the children use to achieve their objectives. This is a context in which mothers are entrusted with the developmental progression of their children, which they are meant to ensure through the provision of an appropriately stimulating environment. Thus routine domestic tasks can all be turned to account as 'learning opportunities' '[b]ut, warns one school handout, *'don't turn it into a lesson'* (cited in Walkerdine et al., 1990: 39, emphasis added in citation). All domestic labour becomes mothering and mothering becomes the occasion for playful learning. In their research, this was most evident, Walkerdine et al. say, in middle-class homes, in which invisibility is achieved for necessary domestic labour. Cleaning out a fish tank, for example, becomes the means of learning about the size and capacity of different containers, the logic of how to transfer the fish and, even, the principle of refraction of light through glass and water. Working-class mothers, on the other hand, tended to make their domestic chores and the need to perform them explicit.

The 'sensitive' mother (for which read the 'middle-class mother') must be both constantly ready to meet the child's needs and able to achieve the necessary 'house beautiful', clean, well-ordered and undisrupted by the child's demands. Managing these contradictory demands becomes a skill, the ideal performance of which makes it look effortless: 'her work becomes the child's play' (1989: 42). By that token, the working-class mother, who makes a clear distinction between the child's play and her own necessary domestic labour – which she counterposes to one another – must always be reckoned to fail.

Each of these strategies has a corresponding cost. For the middle-class mother, who struggles to achieve the pedagogic ideal demanded by the school and 'good parenting' manuals, the child's demands are endless and cannot easily be refused. For the working-class mother, there is, in terms of the pedagogical discourse, an assumed failure on her part to understand what it is she 'ought' to be doing to ensure her child's educational success, but she is far better able to manage and contain the child's demands:

> It is therefore not difficult to see why middle-class mothers especially allow their time and space to be invaded much more than working-class mothers and how, also, mothers who readily give up their own work to talk, play and rationalise with their daughters are 'read' by the researcher as *sensitive*, constantly attuned to their daughters' needs. We do not see a woman who is, in a very real sense, chained by an awareness of her child's cognitive and developmental 'needs' and of how she fits into fulfilling them, but a relaxed and nurturant facilitator. In short, we see but one facet of the fantasy mother. (1989: 46)

This makes it well nigh impossible for the middle-class mother to resist demands of any kind from her children, being able to regulate them only by combining domestic work and play. In addition to this, the expectations they place upon their children are that they achieve *intellectual*, rather than physical autonomy. Working-class mothers, on the other hand, invert this order of priority and expect their child to become more *physically* self-reliant at an earlier stage:

> Working-class women like Emily's mother tend to regulate and discipline their daughters in a completely different way which makes strong distinctions between domestic work and play and delineates clearly that domestic work has to be accomplished in a specific time, usually before father gets home or she has to go off to work. This means that it is important that the child not interfere, can learn to play by herself, to be self-reliant. Thus if she does interfere she can be told not to be demanding. So the mother makes her power explicit, especially her power to withhold her attention. (1989: 44)

Working-class mothers may use the domestic environment to 'teach' their children but they do so less often and 'do not use such instances as regulative devices' (ibid.). As a result, the apparent contradiction between work and play for the working-class child also becomes the site of resistance between the mother and child, so that the working-class child appears more demanding because the middle-class mother simply gives in more often.

When it comes to negotiating the matter of preparing for school and the ensuing separation, both sets of children would seek to find ways of avoiding growing up, by, say, refusing to perform practical tasks for themselves or presenting themselves as helpless, saying that they cannot fetch something for themselves, do up their own buttons, go to the lavatory, or whatever it may be. There is, as Walkerdine et al. point out, much to be gained for the children from this position of dependency, from re-asserting their capacity to demand that their mother wait on them hand and foot. 'Helplessness' is used as a strategy by the children to attempt to regulate their mothers, getting them to perform tasks they could quite easily carry out for themselves as a means of avoiding the painful prospect of separation:

> This provides a fiction of power and control for them, masking their vulnerability. Regulating the mother who regulates you *is* very powerful. Thus being helpless, attempting to remain a baby, is not simply a learned and reinforced behaviour but can be the site of enormous power and the refusal of the terror and pain of losing mother. Simultaneously, of course, daughters' growing up may be very painful for mothers. When we talk about a 'struggle', it is not only the girls' struggle to grow up which is significant. There is the struggle between mother and daughter, and in addition there is the struggle of the woman herself. For many women who long for the sensations of satisfaction, pleasure, being needed, having an important job to do, that children can provide, it is very hard to let their daughters become 'big girls'. If the modern concept of sensitive mothering sets so much store by mothers as guardians of the future social order, this makes mothering important. (1989: 49-50)

This attempt by the children to avoid growing up is inflected differently for working-class and middle-class children. Although the working-class children in the study more frequently expressed the desire not to be 'big girls', by not being willing to be physically self-reliant, their mothers were less tolerant of this than the middle-class mothers. They need their daughters to be physically independent and be able to 'look after themselves'.

A nexus of subjectivities

The advantage of the idea of the production of a 'nexus of subjectivities' is that it gives a clear sense of the way in which the existence of human beings within a series of discourses and practices answers to trans-individual principles of organization. However, although it is a matter of the circulation of overt and covert meanings about what it is to be 'a child' or 'a mother', these meanings do not circulate outside the context of their utilization by specific children and specific mothers in particular ways. Discourses obey regulatory principles which exceed individual control but only insofar as they are reiterated by human beings. Human beings also always have the capacity (to varying degrees, it has to be said) to inflect, transform and refuse what is said, and how it is said, within a discourse, even where discourses have the potential to render them powerless. Sara Mills (1997) provides a vivid illustration of this in her analysis of the extract from the diary of a seventeenth-century woman, Alice Thornton, in which Alice writes of the death of her newly born son. Contrary to what she describes as a classically Foucauldian analysis, which would see this as a confessional that constructed an ever more compliant subject who accepts all her travails as a sign of her need for an ever greater submission to God, Mills stresses the way in which Alice makes use of the discourse of grace, submission and salvation to turn that discourse to her own account, thus rendering the display of her own worthlessness in the face of God precarious:

> We can see that, in producing accounts of this kind, the writer constructs herself
> as a devout subject, i.e. as a conforming member of a religious group, and this is
> already a position of some strength within the society she lived where only
> 'good' (i.e. obedient and devout) female subjects were revered. However, at the
> same time, we can also see that the amount of work which is required to turn this
> into an account of God's grace is substantial. Alice Thornton's account as a
> whole details at some length the mishaps which befell her: the deaths in the
> family, the loss of her child, her illness. These events could be viewed as signs
> of God's displeasure with her for sin, for example. She gains a certain amount of
> personal power through discourse through being able to force these problems to
> become, despite everything, signs of God's goodness and mercy rather than his
> malevolence. (Mills, 1997: 84)

Referring to Dorothy Smith's recent work on the capacity of human beings to
revise and rewrite discursive procedures in her essay 'K is mentally ill', Mills
argues that one should see discourse less as something to which human beings
are subjected than as a vehicle through which interpersonal relationships are
worked out, complying with certain discursive elements and opposing others
(Mills, 1997: 82) . This approach, then, departs from the anti-humanism which
has hitherto been dominant in the analysis of discourse, without wholly
returning to the humanism which it had so strenuously opposed. In other
words, if human beings are 'positioned' within discourses, it is only in a
metaphorical sense by the discourses themselves, for these provide but do not
dictate places; rather, it is through the deployment of those discourses by *other
human beings*. It is the little boys' desire to wrest power from the teacher and
the availability to them of sexist forms of discourse and their (accurate)
understanding of the forms of reaction available to her (in other words their
familiarity with the terms of the pedagogy she uses) that allow them to take
advantage. Discourses constrain what can be done but they also make possible.

Discourse and psychical investment

It is also important to consider that the circulation of meanings, or 'signifiers' as
Walkerdine et al. describe them, takes place by virtue of the psychical
investments that particular human beings have in them. These investments
may comprise a number of different components, from the desire to see oneself
represented in a particular way to more obscure, and maybe darker, psychical
elements with deep roots in an individual's psychical history. How does such
an investment come about? One answer is through the discourses to which a
child is exposed in growing up, which prove to have a formative significance.
In an earlier (1984) essay entitled 'Some Day My Prince Will Come',
reproduced in *Schoolgirl Fictions*, Walkerdine had sought to understand how
'young girls of primary school age are presented with, and inserted into,
ideological and discursive positions by practices which locate them in meaning
and in regimes of truth' (1990: 87). Using Lacanian psychoanalysis, she
undertakes to explore 'the relation between the psychic production of feminine
desire and cultural forms and practices' (ibid.).

Her account is valuable because it seeks to make a link between cultural and
discursive forms and individual psychical investment and formation. Arguing

against current approaches to sexism in stories for children, Walkerdine sets out to explain what kinds of pleasures it is that are provided by a children's literature of which many parents despair, in other words girls' comics. Hers is a bid to move away from the kind of rationalist account of readership that supposes that little girls might be brought to prefer the story of a princess in dungarees who rides off into the sunset without the prince because she has something better to do, by presenting them with a more 'realistic' alternative to the traditional fairy tale. The evidence, however, is that such alternative tales do not achieve the desired objective. Children persist in wanting those things that seem retrogressive. Little girls insist on wanting to become traditional princesses, just as little boys insist on wanting to run around making machine-gun noises, leading many a self-declared feminist mother to revert to biological explanations.

The literature Walkerdine analyses – British girls' comics of the 1950s to the 1990s like *Bunty* and *Tracy* – is now somewhat dated as a vehicle for the construction of femininity and her account would most probably need to be replaced by analyses of the themed magazines, such as the *Disney* productions or *Barbie*, and magazines such as *Girl Talk*, which now dominate the market for pre-teen girls in the UK. However, these still represent a sharply sexually differentiated literature, which is dramatically 'girlie' in character. As in the remainder of the consumer market, there has been a proliferation of products, as well as a realignment of the age banding for the magazines, with less of a primary/secondary school divide and the creation of a pre-teen/early teen banding, from the ages of around eight to fourteen, for which a typical product might be *Smash Hits*. Magazines also appear and disappear somewhat like mushrooms, and all of this would undoubtedly affect the analysis.

When Walkerdine was writing, however, although these comics were in decline, they had evinced a remarkable consistency in content over the period of their existence.[2] They were marked by particular kinds of narrative in which the heroines had typically experienced a catalogue of frightful events which were frankly incredible. Nearly all the stories were about girls who were the victims of circumstance of a fantastical kind and, over the course of the stories, of other people's malevolence, cruelty and ambition. What marked out the heroines was that they struggled on gamely and without complaint: 'In several ways the stories construct heroines who are the target of wrong-doing and whose fight against private injustice is private endurance, which always triumphs in the end. By contrast, boys' comics deal with public bravery and public fights against injustice which are rewarded openly' (1990: 91). How was the popularity of stories with, on the surface, apparently so little relation to their readers' lives to be explained?

The answer, Walkerdine suggested, lay in the fact that the stories related to the organization of fantasy, and she mentioned in this context Freud's notion of the 'family romance'. The importance of the family romance lies in two elements. One is the way in which children live out their difficulties with family relationships through the construction of fantasied alternatives, a fantastical and, usually a better parentage, which suggests a direct basis for the appeal of stories which in some sense constitute such 'family romances'. The second important aspect of this is more general, and concerns the way in which it suggests that 'reality' is lived by human beings not through the directness of perception but 'mediated' by fantasy. Freud's crucial discovery was that psychical reality not only has its own dynamics, but that, as Laplanche and Pontalis say, it 'presents a consistency and a resistance comparable to those displayed by material reality' (1980: 363). Although Freud makes the point that a human being's life can be dominated by psychical reality to a greater (as it is in neurosis or psychosis) or a lesser degree, to the extent that every human being has a share in unconscious processes, psychical reality can be argued to be in play. In this instance, according to Walkerdine, we are talking about the child's negotiation of the Oedipus complex, to which the stories in the comics provide a fantasied resolution:

> It is my contention that the very 'unreality' of the stories presented in these comics is one basis of their strength rather than weakness. That is, they engage precisely with the kinds of issues mentioned by Freud. They allow engagement with difficult emotions and less than perfect circumstances by devices which permit the young readers to identify with the heroine in the text. Thus they encourage the working out and potential resolution of certain conflicts. (1990: 91)

Thinking of these stories rationalistically, as 'distortions of reality', is missing the point. Readers do not read such stories to see an 'empirical' reality reflected but, as with all narratives, to 'see what happens'. And to *want* to see what happens, they have to be gripped by the stories in some way.

According to Walkerdine, the market for these comics at the time of writing comprised pre-pubescent working-class girls and the stories therefore relate to fantasies[3] about family, sexuality and class. They engage their readers precisely because they allow sufficient distance for these readers to be able to address difficult issues in a way which is not 'too close for comfort' (1990: 93). Removed from the everyday through geographical location, historical period or the use of 'surrogate' families, they offer solutions and ways out of dilemmas, both in fantasy and in practice. Poverty, like being placed into a ghastly surrogate family, is presented as a cruel twist of fate, but one which can be surmounted: 'The stories romanticize poverty and portray a way of dealing with it which is *almost masochistic* – it is desirable precisely because it can be suffered virtuously and moved beyond' (1990: 92, emphasis added). Walkerdine's contention is that it is precisely these distancing devices that make it possible for the readers to identify with elements in the story.

The reader and the tale

The crux of Walkerdine's argument lies in the way in which she defines the text and the process of readership. Unlike a realist account, in which a pre-given subject, 'classed, gendered and "racial"' confronts a text which either reflects or fails to reflect their pre-given 'reality', Walkerdine makes both of these, subject and text, into open processes. A text is an 'ensemble of devices' which makes possible, and we should hasten to add does not dictate, certain forms of engagement and the reader is formed in their engagement with the text:

'Readers are constructed in the text, readers construct readings of the text, a complex interplay which does not recognize a simple split between a pre-given psychological subject who reads and a text in which meaning is produced' (ibid.) The text creates fantasies which can be related, through a complex psychical organization, to the reader's own wishes and desires, in that they provide an imaginary fulfilment for those wishes and desires.

In a way which is almost relentless, the stories Walkerdine analysed show a thematic consistency which is striking: tales of cruelty 'go on and on', pain and humiliation are a constant, misunderstanding and misjudgement are repeatedly visited upon the heroines, whose response to all of these misadventures is a constant and unstinting helpfulness and courage in the service of others. The heroines are repeatedly portrayed as victims, who eventually carry the day because of their devotion to other people's welfare, while what they suffer has the character of a series of *adventures*. The stories supply a consistent value-system to the readers, in which certain emotions are endorsed and celebrated while others are deemed unacceptable:

> What seems to me important about this is that if cruelty is seen as exciting and works at the level of fantasy to romanticize difficult practical and emotional circumstances, this suggests a passive, not an active response to the violence (which in psychoanalysis would relate to the displacement of angry and hostile feelings on to others). It also provides the conditions for resolution: selflessness, even though it brings pain and suffering, brings its own rewards (knowledge of good deeds and righteousness). If the heroines are displayed as passive victims of circumstance, all bad and difficult actions are invested in others. The heroines suffer in silence: they display virtues of patience and forbearance and are rewarded for silence, for selflessness, for helpfulness. Any thought for the self, any wanting, longing, desire or anger is in this way produced within the texts as bad. This provides for the readers a value-system in which certain kinds of emotion are not acceptable, and a set of practices in which their suppression is rewarded by the provision of the longed-for happy family, the perfect bourgeois setting. (1990: 95)

What the comics provide for the readers are models for the regulation of emotions and a reward for doing so, which consists of an idealized family with a desirable house, money and possessions and a happy and untroubled set of relations between family members. Much of what is explored concerns jealousy and sibling rivalry, but always with sisters rather than brothers, and it is always located in characters other than the heroines. The idealized figures they present demonstrate an actively achieved passivity, in which '[t]heir victory is in their very passivity and helpfulness' (1990: 96). Heroines are usually clever, and academically successful, interestingly, in subjects such as mathematics (*contra* the accounts given in the 'stereotyping' literature on children's fiction) and they can 'move mountains (metaphorically of course!) as long as they do it *for others*' (ibid.).

The configuration of femininity would nowadays perhaps be rather different. However, the importance of this analysis concerns the way in which the stories *engage* the reader and offer a particular set of resolutions for an internal struggle with which that reader can identify. A series of what Walkerdine describes as 'signifying chains' link, for example, neatness and helpfulness to academic achievement – particularly in the supposedly 'difficult' 'non-feminine' subjects like mathematics – something which, as we noted earlier, teachers read rather differently. Walkerdine also argues, through reference to the work of Rosalind Coward on sexual violence and Angela McRobbie on romance in a teenage magazine like *Jackie*, that there are other signifying chains that link these stories to traditional forms of romance and to a passive and masochistic construction of feminine sexuality (Walkerdine, 1990: 98-9). The fantasies offered in a magazine like *Jackie* represent 'a fraught and fragile solution, but one that remains attractive precisely because it is the getting and keeping of the man which in a very basic and crucial way establishes that the girl is "good enough" and "can have what she wants"' (1990: 99).

Both sets of fantasies – pre-teen and teenage – represent, Walkerdine argues, fantasies of completion. Referring both to Lacan and to Freud's accounts of desire, she stresses the experience of loss at the heart of mother – child relations, which puts in place a model of 'gratification "which contains the loss within it"' (1990: 101):

> Freud insisted that the pain of separation from the maternal body experienced by the child pushes the infant into a struggle to possess the mother, to be dependent on her and yet to control her. The experience of psychic distress caused through the inevitable failure of the mother to meet the child's insatiable demands sets up a particular dynamic between them. Freud distinguished between need and wish (or desire). He recognised that the fantasy created in the gap between possession and loss was not made good by any 'meeting of needs' because the satisfaction would be only temporary and the object of desire would both constantly shift and be out of reach. (1990: 100)

Into this mix enter rivalries, with siblings and with the father, as well as the struggle involving the transfer of desire from mother to father, within the Oedipal dynamic. Because the dynamic of femininity is about this transfer of desire to the father, and henceforth to heterosexual object choice, the forms of fiction offered first by the comics and subsequently by the teen magazines like *Jackie* can be seen to supply the fantasied means of negotiating and resolving the dilemmas proper to the different stages along this journey. For both Lacan and Freud, however, because demand always exceeds satisfaction, fantasy is deployed to fill the gap between need and wish-fulfilment. For Lacan, this fantasied satisfaction is an illusion, which he described as an imaginary resolution and closure. 'This is why,' says Walkerdine, 'the fantasies of completion and resolution of psychic conflicts offered in children's fiction are so important' (1990: 101). Through such imaginary resolutions, it is not that loss fails to be dealt with (since reactions to it are displaced onto 'bad' characters), it is that it is dealt with in particular ways. The fact that there are 'good' girls and 'bad' girls, 'nice' girls and 'naughty' girls (horrid, angry, jealous) means that 'certain ways of resolving the loss are sanctioned and others prohibited and punished' (1990: 102).

The power of these types of sanction and resolution was evidenced, Walkerdine says, when she interviewed nine- and ten-year-old girls as part of her current research, only to discover that they described anger and selfishness as bad qualities in themselves, some of them to such an extent that they felt that they had no redeeming qualities (1990: 105, n.2). The more general implication of this is that we can regard such forms of fiction as vehicles for the construction through fantasy of what it means to be a 'good girl'. This means understanding cultural products and practices as successful precisely because they are involved in *desire* – in its construction and its fantasied resolution. Thus, 'femininity' is not so much a set of characteristics, identities, norms or images, to which girls conform, as an attempt by those girls to live certain forms of imaginary positioning, attempts which must, of necessity, fail:

> I am not arguing for a position in which psychoanalysis helps us to understand the internalization of norms of femininity through processes of identification. This would be to operate as though girls, in identifying with the texts of comics or with the position of their mother, 'became feminine'. (1990: 102)

Psychically, then, there is no such thing as 'gender identity', at least not as it is characteristically understood in many sociologies (and indeed psychologies) of gender, which assume the existence of behavioural and psychical entities labelled 'femininity' and 'masculinity' as correlates for 'female' and 'male', however produced. They might be deemed to be the products of social learning rather than biological predisposition, but they are assumed relatively unproblematically to exist, even if distributed on a continuum between male and female individuals. Insofar as something called 'gender identity' can be assumed to exist *at all*, we would have to say that it was a fantasy – or probably a multiplicity of fantasies – generated out of the encounter between a desiring and conflictual human being and a set of cultural discourses and practices that offer a (temporary) resolution to both of these, the desire and the conflict.[4] The crucial point here is that the existence of the unconscious shows that these attempts to *be* an identity, what would be described as a 'gender', *do not work* (Mitchell, 1982). Walkerdine quotes Jacqueline Rose as saying: 'What distinguishes psychoanalysis from sociological accounts of gender (hence for me the fundamental impasse of Nancy Chodorow's work) is that whereas for the latter, the internalisation of norms is assumed roughly to work, the basic premise and indeed the starting point of psychoanalysis is that it does not. The unconscious constantly reveals the "failure" of identity' (Rose, 1983: 9). There is, as Walkerdine argues, then, 'a complex and important relationship between theories and practices which produce truth and identities, and the contradictory, multiple positioning of the little girls' (1990: 103).

The question of 'truth', then, is a question that lies at the confluence of a number of different strands, from the discursive production and regulation of knowledges and the realities that these engender to the generation, mobilization and, as Walkerdine puts it, the 'canalization' of desire in human beings. Both of these ideas refuse the notion of 'identity', whether one construes it as a stable social characterization or as a psychical conformation. However, given that the notion of a masculine or a feminine 'identity' has implicitly been at the core of the idea of gender, in the next chapter and the one after, we look into it in greater depth. We do this first by considering the work of Erving Goffman and Harold Garfinkel and an idea of gender as performance which, in one case, explicitly refuses and, in the other, implicitly casts doubt upon the notion of 'gender identity'. Next, we look at what almost seems to be a paradoxical attempt by Judith Butler to lodge an account of the psychical *construction* of 'gender identity' – through the psychoanalytic concept of identification – at the heart of her idea of gender as 'performativity'.

Notes

[1] Like Connell, Walkerdine invokes a Freudian concept but she consistently uses the spelling 'fantasy'. In 'Some Day my Prince will Come', which we discuss later on in this chapter, her first endnote refers to this. In it she appears to indicate that she prefers this spelling because her use of it is different from the Freudian concept, which refers to what Laplanche and Pontalis describe as the 'world of the imagination'. Laplanche and Pontalis note that Freud exploited all of the meanings of the German term *'phantasie'*. Since we ourselves are wishing to deploy a Freudian concept, we have adopted the spelling 'phantasy' elsewhere.

[2] A similar task can also be carried out for boys' comics like the *Dandy* and *Beano*, which John Hood-Williams did in the article 'Stories for Sexual Difference', published in the *British Journal of Sociology of Education* in 1997.

[3] The difficulty one faces over whether or not 'fantasies' described as being about family, sexuality and class are fully characterizable as phantasies in the Freudian sense (i.e. imaginary scenes representing fulfilment of an unconscious wish, in which the subject is located) is paralleled by the variety of ways in which Freud himself characterized the notion of 'phantasy', from day-dreams and waking narratives recounted to oneself, to phantasies which operate as or, at any rate, can be (re)constructed as unconscious scenarios, such as those described in the essay 'A Child is Being Beaten' (Freud, 1919).

[4] Parveen Adams has a very interesting discussion of the way in which culturally given distinctions can offer a temporary resting place and a relatively stable position, a temporary arrest of the drive (which she describes as oscillating – we will examine why in Chapter 10). In discussing Freud's management of the case of Dora, she talks about Freud's own implication in the distinction between written (masculine) and oral (feminine) forms of knowledge, an account she derives from Neil Hertz. She talks about how Freud needs to make a separation between his knowledge and the form of knowledge displayed by Dora in order to place himself in a masculine, scientific and superordinate position. Both their forms of knowledge derive from oral sources, Dora's from Frau K. (although Dora also shows an awareness of masculine, encyclopædia-based knowledge) and Freud's from the speech of the consulting room. Hertz establishes Freud's feminine position – the position from which he wants to extricate himself – by focusing on three anecdotes that place Freud outside a collegial and masculine circle of authority, as the junior colleague to Breuer, Charcot and Brouardel. Hertz, Adams says, describes how Freud manages to assert the authority of his knowledge through taking possession of the field by means of a proper *technique*, the technique of psychoanalysis. But for Freud, as Dora's analyst, 'there remains the constant struggle to transcend the oral sources of knowledge which psychoanalysis necessarily involves, to avoid the feminine position, for there is no general sense in which he can have put himself beyond and outside it' (Adams, 1996: 26).

9 The Choreography of Sex

> All the world's a stage
> And all the men and women merely players.
> They have their exits and their entrances,
> And one man in his time plays many parts,
> His acts being seven ages. At first, the infant,
> Mewling and puking in the nurse's arms.
> And then, the whining school-boy, with his satchel
> And shining morning face, creeping like snail
> Unwillingly to school. And then the lover
> Sighing like furnace, with a woeful ballad
> Made to his mistress' eyebrow. Then a soldier,
> Full of strange oaths, and bearded like the pard,
> Jealous in honour, sudden and quick in quarrel,
> Seeking the bubble reputation
> Even in the cannon's mouth. And then, the justice,
> In fair round belly with good capon lin'd,
> With eyes severe, and beard of formal cut,
> Full of wise saws, and modern instances,
> And so he plays his part.
>
> *As You Like It*, II.vii.139-57

The interesting thing about Shakespeare's, or Jaques his protagonist's speech is that the comedy of the depiction derives from the extent to which, in each of his ages, a man believes in his own performance, even to the point of manifest absurdity or danger. He will seek 'the bubble reputation / Even in the cannon's mouth' or make a woeful ballad 'to his mistress' eyebrow'. And the self-satisfied belly, with its 'eyes severe, and beard of formal cut' bespeaks the pompous combination of embonpoint and moralism that defines a man 'of substance'. Yet, though we recognize the foolishness of taking our own performances seriously, of treating them as if they really *do* have substance, it has taken us rather a long time to take theoretical cognizance of that fact. The problem is that we can always be reminded, by someone, somewhere, that on these performances hinge things that are very 'real' and that comedy can all too easily turn to tragedy. We are therefore enjoined to take them seriously, if for no other reason than that they mean business. The giving of substance to performances such as the judge's may also entail the capacity to pronounce a death sentence. If we persist in refusing to take them seriously, we can always be very effectively reminded of this.

Just because performances can be given effectivity does not, however, make them any the less performances. Phenomenology, ethnomethodology and Goffman's 'dramaturgical' sociology are there to remind us of that fact and of the tacit conspiracy to sustain performances and maintain that this is all 'real'. But it was only really Goffman's dramaturgical sociology that had this rich sense of the absurd. Of course, sociology in the mid-twentieth century had deployed the notion of 'role', but this was somehow set against the background of a philosophical anthropology of a fairly conventional kind, in which one might experience such a distressing thing as 'role conflict'.[1] It took Erving Goffman to take the idea of performance seriously (!) as a thoroughgoing description of the human.

Over twenty years before Judith Butler published *Gender Trouble* (1990), in which she characterized gender partly in terms of performativity, Goffman had written *Gender Advertisements* (1979), in which he talks of 'gender display'. Since such displays are, to borrow metaphors common to Goffman's own writings, performed by actors, we are entitled to talk of them in terms of 'performance'.[2] Indeed, notwithstanding some allusions to 'social structures' and to 'basic social arrangements', he may be read as saying that gender as an identity consists of nothing *other* than display and, more radically, that the social relations of gender are in effect established through such displays: 'If gender be defined as the culturally established correlates of sex (whether in consequence of biology or learning), then gender display refers to conventionalized portrayals of these correlates' (1979: 2). Gender display is, to borrow the title of one of Goffman's other books, the presentation of self as sexed, but the choreographed portrayal it represents is also fundamental to the establishment of those correlates. Displays are, as he puts it, both 'the shadow *and* the substance' (1979: 6).

Gender as display

The origins of the idea of display lie in the work of the ethologists, whose writings have interested a number of influential twentieth-century thinkers, including Jacques Lacan, and whose most famous exponent is Charles Darwin. Darwin's *Expression of Emotion in Man and Animals* is an important text for Goffman as a classic of ethological study. In it, Darwin directly compares a few gestures from a small number of animals with those same gestures found in humans. For example, comparisons are made between what Goffman calls 'displays' – only that term is missing in Darwin – of dominance, appeasement and fear in animals and humans. As Goffman wryly observes, the interest in Darwin's book today is not in what it tells us about our animal natures and the displays that we share with animals but in what it tells us about Victorian notions about the 'character and origins of alignment expressions' (1979: 4, n. 5). Today, Darwin's work supplies a useful cultural history of beliefs about human nature.

Typically, displays are constituted by the formalization – what Goffman describes as the 'ritualization' – of particular sets of emotionally motivated behaviours, which act as stereotypical and hence readily intelligible expressions of an animal's situation and intent. As we might expect, for Darwin, it is the pressure of natural selection that produces displays free from specific contexts, which enable and facilitate efficient communication both between and within species. The communication will be effective if it contributes to survival and this means readily readable behaviours that allow for the negotiation of efficient exchanges. And as Goffman points out, '[I]f Darwin leads here, Mead and Dewey are not far behind' (ibid.). The focus of such a conception of displays as applied to human beings is on their socially situated *enactment*. The premise is not that there is some kind of social structural location within which the performers are embedded and which defines for them what they do. The ethological focus is rather on the practice of the displays themselves and, beyond that, on the unfolding course of events which is based upon them.

Although one may properly characterize displays as at the heart of ethological notions of communication this does not mean that displays are conceived of as language. Displays do not enunciate nor do they articulate something through use of a symbolic language, precisely because they are evidential and conventionalized. In fact, Goffman specifies quite precisely that they do not communicate in the ordinary – he says 'narrow' – sense of the word, although mention *is* made of linguistic elements, such as the use of first names or the connotations of feminine forms in European languages. As he puts it, displays portray an actor's *alignment* – the position the actor appears to be prepared to take up in relation to the prospective unfolding of events in a social gathering. The alignment establishes the terms of the contact, 'the mode, or style or formula for the dealings that are to ensue' (1979: 1). For human beings, displays are indicative of mood, intent, social identity, expectation and relation to others. Human beings give off such indications and to do so is functional in bringing off the interaction in question efficiently. The human version of what the idea of 'display' might mean is a culturally specific and distinctive range of indicative appearances and behaviours, which is specialized and routinized so as to perform this informing role. In that sense, Goffman describes them as 'ritual-like'. People in social situations have to stand up, sit down, move from one room to another, make beginnings and endings. x are functional facilitators of such transitional moments, during which they are especially useful, and of the social situation as a whole.

There are therefore *schedules* of displays to facilitate this social work. For example there are 'brackets' which are concentrated at the beginnings and endings of purposeful undertakings (movements associated with finding a chair and sitting down or getting up to leave) and 'overlays' which sound a single note throughout such an event (standing to attention when addressed by a superior officer). Combinations of these two constitute the schedule of displays 'for any strip of activity'. Displays are therefore specific, occurring selectively, delimitable, even though they may be perceived to colour the whole scene. In addition to their existence in schedules, displays are said to have the following further characteristics. They are frequently of a dialogic and dyadic statement/reply structure, such structures being either symmetrical or asymmetrical (e.g. greetings between guests and hosts or between teachers and pupils) and reversible (i.e. guest can be host at a later date) or non-reversible. Some are particularly geared to the important identificatory function in which actors style themselves so that the social fact of them will be immediately known. Such 'identificatory stylings'' are considered to be the most durable of all displays. Displays may be 'multivocal or polysemic' in that many messages may be conveyed by them simultaneously. Goffman mentions the collegial handshake that follows the official conferment of an award and the father who first raises his hat to his daughter (as a recognition of her as a 'lady') and then bends to kiss her (as kin). The move from one action to the other may be indicatively accompanied by a change in facial expression. Some displays are highly formalized such as military salutes and others much less so. Humans are, distinctively, conscious of displays and may deploy them self-consciously.

Goffman gives many examples of displays – applause, a kiss, raising a hat, salutes, gestures of courtesy, hair, clothing, behavioural style-codes, European court life, military etiquette – and of what ensues when particular displays are not forthcoming – unease, nudging, joking complaint, irony, to which one could add embarrassment and ridicule. Some displays, such as those associated with gender, have the quality of being optional, and even if a certain amount of social control is invested in them, Goffman suggests that, more than anything else, their non-performance provides 'opportunity for a sally' (1979: 3). Displays may become so well established that they can be lifted out of their original context and parenthesized, used quotably and/or as postural resources for mimicry, mockery, irony, teasing – and this quotability is to be observed in the advertisements that are examined in the book. He writes:

> Here stylization itself becomes an object of attention, the actor providing a comment on this process in the very act through which he unseriously realizes it. What was a ritual becomes itself ritualized, a transformation of what is already a transformation, a 'hyper-ritualization'. (ibid.)

Such displays are nevertheless received as if they were natural, but they are no less in need of historical understanding, Goffman says, than a Ford car. Of course, we do indeed think of the biological as central and in addition do frequently draw upon animal life to ground our understanding of such things as gender, but this is itself a cultural matter: animal behaviour operates as a *resource*; it supplies imagery (the dog of fawning, the lion of strength, and so on).

Goffman finds the resource for behavioural imagery in gender displays, however, not amongst animals, but in parent/child relationships. As a resource, this has the advantage, although Goffman does not mention this, of being construed both as human and as 'natural'. Those relations, however, are far from 'natural', although they are widely assumed to be determined by what the child *is*. Goffman's suggestion is that adult interactions, and especially adult gendered interactions, draw extensively on this fund of repertoires that one can observe in (idealized and middle-class) parent/child relationships. He notices many parallels between superordinate, adult male interactions with females and subordinate males. However, they have a more general significance as well, especially as they constitute a 'sex-free resource' because most people of both sexes experience both roles, that of *being* a child and that of caring for one. What is learnt in childhood are modes of handling ourselves in social encounters *'as our means of demonstrating respectful orientation to them and of maintaining guardedness within them'* (1979: 4, emphasis in original). We make that assumption essentially through what a child is privileged to do and must suffer to be done on its behalf by its parents. Among Goffman's examples are the child's orientation licence (a licence to dissolve in tears or laughter, to burst out with glee etc., to drift in and out of the situation); its licence to effect patently ineffective means to achieve what it wants (hiding behind its hands as protection for the whole body or 'pummelling' – a half serious and wholly ineffectual kind of attack against an adversary one knows to be impervious to it). These are examples of ritualizations in the classic ethological sense and provide an analysis of 'what it is to act childishly' (1979: 4) and indeed we might add, of what it is *to be* childish – at least within our culture, in which there is a defined notion of the child that licenses and, in a sense, elicits and encourages those behaviours.

In addition to the licence granted to the child there are privileges. The child is subject to 'protective intercession' (the dangerous and breakable world is managed for it), to the principle of the 'erasability of the offence' (the child can wipe the slate clean with contrition) and to 'indulgence priorities' (like being the first in a distribution of sweets). As Goffman points out, some of these are generalized so that other adults may operate in this way with respect to the child. There is, though, a price to pay for all this. The child is subjected to various forms of 'non-person' treatment – control by physical fiat; exclusion from informational rights (the requirement to be quizzed upon a range of feelings, ailments etc. that would be impertinent in adulthood); expendable rights to time and territory; the modulation of the harsh things of this world, for which read, also, the censorship of information, and of exclusion from various rights to judgement, such as those relating to its own appearance.

The main purpose of the long digression Goffman undertakes into the forms of behavioural imagery typical of idealized parent/child relations is to effect the introduction of notions of super- and sub-ordination into the discussion of gender. Gender is observed to offer parallels, in the social situations in which it is explicitly played out, to those found between the parent and child. Women, and subordinate males, are equivalent to children and benign, intrusive prerogatives, exercised 'in their best interests', pervade the lives of these 'lessers' in the everyday social situations that are the focus of Goffman's concern. The pervasive character of this modelling of parent/child relations means that perhaps the only gentling of the world that we have – in this private sphere – is itself shot through with such superordinate and subordinate displays. One specific way in which the parent/child complex is applied is particularly telling, and that is in the mitigation of potential distance, coercion and hostility through 'gentle prerogatives', but 'however distasteful and humiliating lessers may find these gentle prerogatives to be, they must give second thought to openly expressing displeasure, for whosoever extends benign concern is free to quickly change his tack and show the other side of his power' (1979: 5). Such a description will of course be familiar to anyone from the way in which many a sexual assault plays out.

Gender displays, then, as 'behavioural styles' – often not very stylish, says Goffman – enact and embed power relations. Although he describes a 'loose gearing' between these displays and social structures, it is clear that whatever meaningful subordination and superordination exists is established here:

> The expression of subordination and domination through this swarm of situational means is more than a mere tracing or symbol or ritualistic affirmation of the social hierarchy. These expressions considerably constitute the hierarchy; they are the shadow *and* the substance. (1979: 6, emphasis in original)

Whilst the multiple meanings of precedence of entry through a door (which is accorded both to the honoured guest, those of an undeniably eminent social position and to those defined as constitutionally weak – with women combining both in a manner which, under the impact of feminism, has almost come to seem ironic) may look like a form of symbolization of something established elsewhere, the slogan 'the personal is political' reminds us that, in a certain sense, there *is* no 'elsewhere'. If one takes the social structural to describe the formal configurations within which we live (legal provisions, organizational positions, economic relations more generally), we know at one level that this is not what subordination and superordination are *really* about. It is in the daily creation and re-creation of relations that subordination is constructed. It might even seem fair to say that what is deemed to be 'the social structural' is an *expression*, consolidation and enshrining of the more fundamental choreographing and enactment of relations. Or, perhaps, more properly, that these things are of a piece. The giving of ontological status to one or other facet of social relations, the formalizations or the *potentially* (but not always) negotiable re-creations, tells us more about different stances taken upon the solidity of the object of sociology – and the construction of disciplinary identities – than it does about what it describes.

Precisely what is interesting about the stylizations enacted in a display is the fact that they too are formalized. Furthermore, in being formalized, they are also treated as indexical. In other words, they acquire their substantiality from the way in which they function semiotically (although that form of conceptualization is absent from Goffman) and from the relative stability supplied by their formalization. They are the 'means of making *assumptions* about life palpable in social situations'; they represent a 'choreography' in the sense that they pre-pattern a series of moves and attitudes (ibid., emphasis added). The use of bodies and faces – pre-eminent in social situations – is very powerful here. Only in face-to-face situations can individuals be physically coerced, for example. Gesture, styling, portraiture: the shadow *and* the substance.

Fishes live in the sea

The interesting thing is the manner in which they function as both shadow *and* substance. Even if Goffman had not intended that it should do so, this description tells us something novel about what one might term 'structuration', in other words the construction of something to appear to be, and to function as, enduring, and this relates particularly to indexicality. The most basic way of thinking about ourselves is to appeal to our natures. The ontological certainty is that we are as we are because it is in our nature so to be. Furthermore, as part of a desire to explore our natures more deeply, a central belief has it that, 'an object produces signs that are informing about it' (1979: 6). Indeed, Goffman says, it is difficult to imagine a society in which something distal is not read into what is perceived. However, it is the configuration of signs (as 'natural, indexical signs') that counts. Thought to have their ultimate source in the object and to be able to be both understood by experts (see, for example, the deployment of medical expertise in Foucault's *Herculine*) and read by the rest of us, signs are treated as 'expressions':

> There is a wide agreement that fishes live in the sea because they cannot breathe on land, and that we live on land because we cannot breathe in the sea. This proximate, everyday account can be spelled out in ever increasing physiological detail, and exceptional cases and circumstances uncovered, but the general answer will ordinarily suffice, namely an appeal to the nature of the beast, to the givens and conditions of his existence, and a guileless use of the term 'because.' Note, in this happy bit of folk wisdom – as sound and scientific surely as it needs to be – the land and sea can be taken as there prior to fishes and men, and not – contrary to genesis – put there so that fishes and men, when they arrived, would find a suitable place awaiting them. (ibid.)

This little parable about the fishes draws attention to the fact that we explain what happens by dint of an appeal to 'the very conditions of our being'. It is not solely a question of the assumption that the origins of gender displays are biological, it is that there is a very deeply held belief in our culture that objects are informing about themselves through the imprints they leave on the surrounding environment, that they structure it or give off unintended signs of what it is that they are: 'they cast a shadow, heat up the surround, strew indications, leave an imprint; they impress a part picture of themselves' (ibid.). Sometimes these 'natural indexical signs' are iconic. Displays are thus ideally suited to play that role, especially as they are structured to be the equivalent of those familiar to us not merely from ethology but from intra-species communication which dates back a long way before the advent of ethology as a discipline. Goffman stresses that this indication is, precisely, not seen as communication as such, nor as instrumental physical action but as epiphenomenal to these things, an accidental by-product of the fact that the creature doing the communicating or performing the action is of a particular kind. Although we are all of us aware of the capacity human beings have to stage these deliberately, they are read as 'given off' unintentionally, with the conscious performance being read as potentially, even inevitably, unconvincing. That lack of conscious intentionality supplies a part of their 'naturalness'. Of course, as phenomenology reminded us, the learning of social skills and repertoires is analogous to learning to ride a bicycle: eventually it all comes 'naturally'. The further conflation of what are in effect highly ritualized codes of behaviour with notions of 'body language', themselves conceived of as expressive of the truth (whether it be of one's intentions or of a situation), embeds this still more deeply in the notion that they pertain to our natures.

The configurations of these allegedly expressive signs are therefore seen as independent of context, rather than situationally specific, and stable, rather than of passing significance. They are seen as essential, in other words, as supplying information 'about those of an object's properties that are felt to be *perduring, overall*, and *structurally basic*' (1979: 7, emphasis in original). The assumption is also that these objects give off natural signs to a greater extent than other objects, as if they cannot help but overflow with meaning; the emotions, Goffman says, and the 'various bodily organs through which emotions most markedly appear, are considered veritable engines of expression':

> As a corollary, we assume that among humans a very wide range of attributes are expressible: intent, feeling, relationship, information state, health, social class etc. Lore and advice concerning these signs, including how to fake them and see behind fakeries, constitute a kind of folk science. All of these beliefs regarding man, can be referred to as the doctrine of natural expression. (ibid.)

The doctrine of natural expression does not allow, in other words, that any of these may constitute conventionalized portrayals, a repertoire which is *learned*. Furthermore, gender is in some sense deemed to be prototypical of essential expression precisely because it is believed to be the most fundamental form of characterization of a human being, a belief which is marked by the fact that the first gesture made in relation to a baby when it is born is what Kessler and McKenna would refer to as gender assignment, the attribution of a gender. This means that, however fleetingly it may be conveyed, and it is, in a sense, capable of being conveyed more fleetingly than other attributes *because* it is deemed to be so fundamental, it is taken to be a deep-seated trait. But of course, as Goffman points out, the complicating factor lies in the fact that the human objects themselves *seek* not merely to express what they are about, but to abide by their own conceptions of expressivity. Iconicity abounds, he says, and people obligingly symbolize things for us, selecting certain features for presentation in situationally specific ways. As Weber would have said, these actions are social insofar as they are *oriented*. In that sense, configurations of 'expressions' are not incidentally related to the social situations in which they occur, but intrinsically so. 'Expressions' are not only learned but learned to the extent that their presentation *can be*, but may not always be, unselfconscious: in learning this, human beings not only learn to be a particular kind of object, but to be 'the kind of object to which the doctrine of natural expression applies, if fallibly; they are learning to be objects that have a character, that express this character, and for whom this characterological expressing is only natural. We are socialized to confirm our own hypotheses about our natures' 1979: 7).

What might the components of this learning be? Goffman does not say, understandably in view of the fact that he is concerned with display, but potential candidates are perhaps to be found in notions of individuality, and the coherence and integrity of the human being, in conceptions of the natural, but also of the animality of the natural as regards human beings, as well as more specific sets of expectations about behaviours – in other words, in a series of discursive configurations of what the human being is about. Insofar as actors intend anything in relation to their displays, they intend them to be read in accordance with the doctrine of natural expression, as natural indications of who they are and what their relationships consist of; in that sense, there is a 'working agreement' amongst human beings to provide each other with 'gestural pictures of the claimed reality of their relationship' and of their human nature (ibid.).

By virtue of being persons

This leads Goffman to a particular account of the human being – a philosophical anthropology if you will – which implies both an interactional and a psychic dynamism and, more importantly perhaps, stresses the lack of any specific content to that *being*. In that sense, contents of one kind or another become the material out of which human beings construct their presentations of themselves and of the relationships they engage in, the grist to the mill of these human engineers of social situations:

> What the human nature of males and females really consists of, then, is a capacity to learn to provide and to read depictions of masculinity and femininity and a willingness to adhere to a schedule for presenting these pictures and this capacity they have *by virtue of being persons*, not females or males. One might just as well say there is no gender identity. There is only a schedule for the portrayal of gender. (1979: 8, emphasis added)

The expressions of gender, its indications and its portrayals, then, do not tell us about the sex to which they allegedly refer. What they tell us about is the act of portraiture itself and the intentions and abilities of individuals to portray themselves as gendered. One might say that study of the signs of gender, treated as expressions of sex, is the stuff of much contemporary writing. Consider the findings of sex difference research or the discussions of evolutionary psychology. The point is not primarily that most sex difference research turns out to be 'sex similarities' research because the distribution of the variables under study overlaps rather than distinguishes between the sexes or that what is found is really an effect of gender rather than sex. For Goffman, such variables are better regarded as signs having no 'natural' and intrinsic relationship to the sex they are taken to express. Whether they overlap or differentiate is beside the point. What overlap or differentiation tells us is not about the character of the sexes but about the prevailing character of portraiture. Shifting findings detect shifts in behavioural displays, shifts in the willingness to portray 'gender' or in the tools used to do so. The contemporary worry over boys' scholastic achievements – often presciently discussed as a worry over boys 'performance' – is surely nothing other than an indication of a shift in the willingness of boys to adhere to gendered portraits that a previous generation had found comfortable and a preference for a rather different version of things, or, at least, of those things that they deem to *matter*.

Through these practices, then, human beings construct, negotiate and co-ordinate joint or collective activity. It might seem reasonable to regard the provision of information about whom one is and what might be deemed to be happening as no more than the framing of that which is more fundamental.

After all, as Goffman points out, whether you are 'let go' from your job with abruptness or kindness, you have still lost your job. But, perhaps in that respect, the terms 'display' and 'portrayal' are misleading because they do not suggest to what extent they constitute the very substance of what goes on. For example, whose point of view gets heard, whose opinion is listened to and voiced most frequently, who is permitted to make the small ongoing decisions by means of which a course of action is structured, and whose passing concerns do more than pass, are all a consequence of this choreographing of relationships. All the *machinery* of superordination and subordination is there. In a sense, this fleshes out what we have already seen in Walkerdine's work, when we looked at the discursively based negotiation of the terms of an encounter, a relationship, or what is conventionally referred to as an identity. What is interesting about this account of Goffman's is that it gives us a means of thinking about the way in which portrayal, negotiation and construction come to give the appearance of substantiality and structure, of a particular portrayal being 'the way the world is'.

The shadow *and* the substance

Goffman finds himself at something of a loss to characterize what he seems to see as the fundamental underpinning of gender: 'There is no relationship between the sexes,' he says, 'that can so far be characterized in any satisfactory fashion. There is only evidence of the practice between the sexes of choreographing behaviorally a portrait of relationship' (1979: 8). For Goffman, however, feminine displays do affirm the place of the 'female sex-class' in the social structure insofar as they hold female persons to this place. They also indicate an attachment to such positions (subordinate ones) and, *in part*, constitute them. But such displays are specific, temporal and local. They are not continuous, although continuity is precisely what they express. The whole is indicated by fleeting moments. The coherence of gender, what professional sociology and everyday life take to be its continuous social relevance, is a product of discrete behavioural displays united under a doctrine of natural expression, and, by that token, gendered displays are deemed to implicate an entire sex.

To the extent that expressions hold people to positions, they constitute stabilizing factors and to the extent that people accept the depictions of activity, minor allocations have substantive consequences. Displays can, however, counterbalance or compensate for other substantive arrangements; in that sense, they may or may not affirm what Goffman defines as social structural features. What these consist of he does not say, but the description of losing one's job would seem to indicate that we are talking about more formal and consequential aspects of social relations. Goffman describes himself as taking a functionalist view of gender, by which he means that the only thing that distinguishes between members of the different sex-classes is the content of the displays. What characterizes persons as members is their competence and willingness to sustain appropriate schedules of displays and it is through these displays that things get done. Social situations *require* such techniques for the conduct of affairs, for both beginnings and endings (to usher people in and out of rooms, to begin and terminate meetings and so on) and to colour the encounter and structure what takes place:

> A principal means men in our society have for initiating or terminating an everyday encounter on a sympathetic note is to employ endearing terms of address and verbal expressions of concern that are (upon examination) parental in character and profoundly asymmetrical. Similarly, an important ritual available for displaying affectionate concern, emphasizing junctures in discourse and marking differential conversational exclusiveness is the laying on of the hand, ordinarily an unreciprocable gesture of male to female or subordinate male. (1979: 8)

Why the conduct of affairs should be organized through gender is not clear. What impresses Goffman is both the sheer ubiquity of gender expression and how deeply the facilitation of these enactments runs into the organization of society. As he puts it: 'Gender expressions are by way of being a mere show; but a considerable amount of the substance of society is enrolled in the staging of it' (ibid.). Indeed the writing sometimes points toward the view that this manufactured staging is all that there is. The idea of expression normally invokes the notion of something that is being expressed, something that lies behind – the referent of the sign. What Goffman is directing our attention to is the way in which the process of signification, if that is what we want to call it, constructs its referent as an intrinsic part of what it signifies: if sex is that referent, what the signs signify are the elements that are deemed to give away its presence. A social-structural or biological 'something' lying behind these signs, then, is not what Goffman intends, although he undoubtedly also presupposes its existence – in *some* form, albeit not in the form of the nature of human persons. If the variety and multiplicity of what he calls 'genderisms' points toward an apparent convergence, this might only be telling us something about how signs operate to support such a belief. Goffman memorably concludes his short essay on gender with these words:

> Nothing dictates that should we dig and poke behind those images we can expect to find anything there – except of course the inducement to entertain this expectation. (1979: 9)

There is some small ambiguity here as to whether or not the expectation we entertain is in fact *à propos* 'sex' or 'gender'. If gender is about the identity of female or male persons, rather than what he terms 'sex-class' or 'the relationship between the sexes', and 'gender' is deemed intrinsically to refer to *sex*, then this can be read as indicating that there is no such thing, beyond a set of portrayals which are assumed to point towards the sex of the person. In short, those things we read as, in some sense *belonging* to sex do not do so. The implication is that the correlates of sex which are deemed to constitute gender (as a consequence of biology) do not exist. But if display is the conventionalized portrayal of the *correlates* of sex, i.e. gender (which might be in consequence of either biology or learning), then we also have to read gender as not existing in the social sense (as a consequence of learning). *Persons*, in that sense, are neither gendered nor sexed – although bodies might be sexed.

Difference and division

Goffman's work on gender may not be widely referenced or read these days but it has an extraordinary contemporary resonance, especially perhaps to those attuned to the re-examination of gender through recent 'deconstructive' writings such as those of Judith Butler. The central idea that gender consists only in the displays, the behavioural styles that make it up, has been very influential and has even become commonplace. The effect of this focus is to sideline interest in the biological and to imply a reduction in its importance. The puzzle that it leaves in its wake is precisely the one that Goffman himself mentions, namely why it is that gender display is used to organize so much of social behaviour and why it constitutes 'a sovereign means of accounting for our own behavior'. In relation to age-grade, he says, 'it lays down more, perhaps, than class and other social divisions an understanding of what our ultimate nature ought to be and how and when this nature ought to be exhibited' (1979: 8).

For Goffman, this is perhaps less of a problem than it is for Butler, for whom even the supposed 'materiality of sex' has been rewritten in terms of performativity. Precisely because of those elements which Goffman deems to lie beyond the performance that is gender (put briefly, sex and sex-class), his work is open to a more conventional structural form of explanation, which, if it doesn't resolve the problem, has the virtue of postponing it. This may be why he suggests that no satisfactory explanation of the relationship between the sexes has been arrived at. And yet, he is also ambivalent about proposing that there is 'something biological or social-structural that lies behind or underneath these signs' on the grounds that 'this is perhaps to accept a lay theory of signs' (1979: 9). This brings the problem right back onto one's doorstep: why does this *particular* form of domination exist and, furthermore, construct itself so as to appear pervasive and ubiquitous? The doctrine of natural expression might be deemed to exist simply to naturalize domination, but *why* domination? Even intimacy, as Goffman notes, 'brings no corrective':

> And this can only remind us that male domination is a very special kind, a domination that can be carried right into the gentlest, most loving moment without causing strain – indeed those moments can hardly be conceived of apart from these asymmetries. (1979: 9)

Of course, this is just what has changed since 1979; it cannot now be carried into intimate moments without strain. Indeed, it cannot be expressed in public spaces without rendering the encounter problematical. This is not to say that male domination has disappeared, but certainly that discrepancies and gaps between portrayals have become greater and the appearance of the whole is more fractured. The 'naturalness' of domination has been exposed for what it is, and this also means that most moments can now be conceived of, and some of them can even exist, without this hierarchical admixture. The same has yet to be so systematically achieved for children, for whom alleged considerations for their welfare are allowed to continue to disguise elements that many of us might read as unwarranted and as expressive of no more than domination. Children's liberation never did get very far. At least Goffman's account allows one to theorize that fact which, arguably, Butler's account of gender, which makes it paradoxically both anti-foundational and fundamental, renders more difficult.[3] In Butler's *Gender Trouble*, gender constitutes a part of a compulsory *order* of sex/gender/desire in which 'gender' represents the orchestration of the power relations that produce 'sex' as prediscursive and natural, 'a politically neutral surface *on which* culture acts' (1990: 7, emphasis in original). Using Goffman's analysis, however, his puzzlement about the apparent ubiquity of gender, which he reads as so intimately bound up with superordination and subordination, need no longer be ours: '*Any* scene, it appears, can be defined as an occasion for the depiction of gender difference, and in any scene a resource can be found for effecting this display' (1979: 9, emphasis in original). For Goffman, this inevitably seems to mean that superordination and subordination are also potentially everywhere. Yet in terms of what we identified earlier as characteristic of display, this is obviously a matter of *possibility*, rather than one of necessity. Furthermore difference is not *per se* division, even if they initially seemed indivisible from one another. We have already seen that there is no necessary *content* to the depictions provided by human beings; what characterizes them as beings is their capacity and willingness to provide depictions – of themselves and the encounters in which they are engaged. Is it not possible, as well, then, to disengage the question of the indexicality of signs from the doctrine that what they signify is 'the natural'? And is that association not highly discursively and historically specific?

The implication of this, of course, that it *is* possible to discriminate between difference and division, which most accounts of gender do not give us the mechanism to do, even if we do so in practical terms every day of our lives. Because gender was constructed as a concept which answered to difference with division, and because, as a concept, it tends to be all encompassing, it does not offer the theoretical means for then making a distinction between those two things as they begin to construct themselves differentially in the world through the discursive interventions of feminism. Goffman's theory, and what amounts to his dismantling of gender (although he holds, at least tangentially to a notion of a structural set of relations in the form of the idea of 'sex-class'), by contrast, offers us some potential to do so insofar as it allows for the examination of specific portrayals.

The idea of a 'display' or 'portrayal', of course, even if some of it has to be regarded as spontaneously 'given off' rather than deliberately 'staged', implies a systematic and *regulated* presentation, whose 'intention' might be describable as that of portraying gender. Whatever level of individual self-consciousness the portrayer evinces in doing so, the *effect*, as Goffman points out in *The Presentation of Self in Everyday Life*, is that of projecting a given definition of the situation and endeavouring to foster the understanding that a given state of affairs obtains (1971: 6). As audiences, we can thus engage with what is being presented to us about both difference and division, and the solidarily presented relation between the two.

Rather than gender appearing as a general category, which is performatively constituted, as it does in Butler, its substance is the product of highly discontinuous behavioural displays, in which we 'fill in the blanks' by means of the doctrine of natural expression. In that sense, Goffman's analysis, because of its focus on 'everyday life' to the neglect of a set of structures to which he pays obeisance but about which one senses him to be unconvinced, is the inverse of Butler's. What she appears to be doing, instead, is seeking to accommodate the 'deconstructive' theoretical transformations wrought by concepts of discourse, Lacanian and post-Lacanian psychoanalysis, Derridean philosophy, and so on, into the architecture of sex/gender, thus transforming the meanings that these concepts have whilst retaining the fundamental framework of a divisioning of the world. Goffman, on the other hand, finds gender a useful occasion for thinking about the presentation of self in a different modality, and doing so gives him the indication that what is alleged to lie behind it is not what we have generally taken it to be, but an *expectation* constructed by the staging.

Some writers have thought that people are *always* doing gender (Messerschmidt, 1993). Goffman knows better. For strips of activities in social situations one has a *schedule* of displays. Gender identity itself is defined as existing only in terms of the schedule for its own portrayal. And the importance of the schedule, indeed the very reason for having a schedule, is *because* gender displays are discontinuous. The schedule is the temporal arrangement of discrete behavioural styles which allows for recognition of the character of a social situation. The perduring, overall, basic – we might also say 'structural' – character of gender looks to be the product of the assembled niceties of display, but because of the way these signs are read, there also seems to be nothing, no matter how incidental, how fleeting, that cannot be taken as informing us as to the assumed continuity and consistency of gender. Situationally specific signs are read as conveying the whole, the essential gender. And gender is the set of configurations of these expressions, configurations which, we saw above, are the intrinsic consequence *of what can be generated.* In that sense, it certainly *seems* as if gender is ubiquitous. However, as we shall see when we come to look at Riley's work, putting this in an historical context (and using a different theoretical framework) allows us to understand how such readings come about. And as to why we feel compelled to fill in the blanks, we have only to look back to Laqueur and Foucault as well.

Language in brackets

The absence in all of this, of course, is of anything pertaining to language – appreciably, since Goffman is drawing attention specifically to those aspects involving action, posture, demeanour. But it is absent in two particular ways. One is that it exists as if in brackets in the description of the portrayals: in all this talk of gender display, of behaviour, of style and action, there is little mention of its accompaniments in speech or writing. Gender advertisements have headlines and slogans but they do not constitute Goffman's primary concern in *Gender Advertisements*. People perform, they act in formal ceremonial occasions, they hold their heads and their hands in particular, distinctive ways but they do not speak 'gender'. One reason for this is that Goffman is concerned primarily with those elements which are 'ritual-like', in which exchanges of words are presumably conventionalized. The problem is that 'behavior and appearance' represent something far broader than the *explicit* and ritualized portrayal, and if these give the occasion for the interpretation of every fleeting moment on the same model, then everyday life and the language deployed within it become of moment as opportunities for both signification and interpretation. Even if we know – from pre-operative transsexuals, for example – that no one does, or needs to be constantly doing, gender – we know that this is precisely because the doctrine of natural expression is at work well into the everyday. In that sense, there is a latent irony in Goffman's *The Presentation of Self in Everyday Life*, when he quotes from and analyses the first appearance of Preedy on the beach in William Samson's novel, *A Contest of Ladies*, because there is an obvious linguistic accompaniment to Preedy's action, not merely in his interior monologue, through which he self-consciously reflects upon his presentation of himself, but in the reference he makes, by means of the careful manipulation of the cover of his book, to his 'classic yet cosmopolitan' selection of a Spanish translation of Homer. However, it is not just that words are the inevitable accompaniment, in some form or other, of actions. Preedy acts out a little schedule of display intended to convey various (apparently non-gendered) characteristics about his person to an audience on the beach who, most likely, are not even attending to the show. The irony lies in the fact that although Preedy is providing various behavioural portraits these are accompanied by an interior description of the portraits and their intended meanings to himself. Preedy is being Goffman. But this means, of course, that what is open to Preedy, and to all of us, is the possibility that our portraits will be painted in words as well as in actions and, more strongly, that they may depend upon words for their successful execution.

What is also absent is a concept which has not really arrived on the scene in its fully fledged post-Foucauldian form when Goffman is writing *The Presentation of Self* and *Gender Advertisements* – at least not in the USA – and that is discourse. Discourse constitutes part of the means by which we reflect upon and analyse the presentations that are being made to us, the means by which we set about transforming them, but also the origins of the portrayals we make and of the spontaneous interpretations we make of those portrayals. The doctrine of *natural* expression is nothing if not a discursive product. All of these activities also have other components. The capacity to 'read' displays is, undoubtedly, in ethological terms, a fundamentally necessary survival skill. The fact that it is interwoven with social knowledges need only surprise us if we wish to keep two domains, social or cultural and 'natural' or biological, hermetically sealed from one another. It is perfectly logical that what we might describe as neurological capabilities are also at the very same time social capabilities. What a concept of discourse would allow us to reflect upon here are the sources for the construction of particular practices in particular forms, such as the interpretation of signs designed to convey gender as the expressive imprint of sex upon the world. Without the construction of a concept of 'sex' of the kind that permeates our world, the interpretation of displays would have been different.

Gender and social structure

Goffman is often thought of as using a theatrical metaphor to capture the character of social life. People are actors putting on a show. It may be show but there is considerable work invested in the staging of that show, although when you look backstage you find nothing there. Indeed the show itself is designed to convince you that there *is* a back stage. His theory of gender, though, is the exact inverse of this metaphor. It is not that there is a show put on by actors who are 'real' and who, when the curtain falls, resume their (real) identities. It is that the show is everything. And part of the show itself is an invitation to believe that behind the show is a back stage with a (more) real puppet master. In the case of gender that real would be 'sex'. But for Goffman the idea of sex as the lodestone of gender is part of gender itself. More precisely it is part of the doctrine of natural expression. So Goffman would not dissent from the arguments of Christine Delphy or Kessler and McKenna or Butler, but there appears to be a tension in the text between this view expressed clearly enough and the repeated references to another reality that does seem to exist in some other relation to the show that is gender. The sense is that there exist, somewhere else, structured relationships (and biological realities). And this unfortunately opens up the possibility of an unprofitable debate as to the nature of the relationship between the two. At one point Goffman refers to this as a 'loose gearing' (1979: 3), which does imply something like a substance which is separate from the shadow. If, as he asserts, 'the relationship between the sexes objectively... taken as a whole' is *'quite another matter*, not yet well analyzed' (1979: 8, emphasis added); if he believes that these portraits and their interpretations 'provide a very poor picture of the overall relationship between the sexes' (ibid.) if displays are a 'symptom' of the social structure's 'fundamental features', which they can 'iconically' reflect (ibid.), then there clearly is something behind displays that requires quite a little digging and poking to unearth. So the puzzle that remains is what precisely does Goffman want to do with the idea of social structure?

His references to Durkheim, ethology and the importance of functional readings should make clear that, even if he is often read as an 'interactionist' writer, he lies outside the phenomenological tradition that rigorously eschews notions of social structure. Having suggested that to accept the idea that expressions of masculinity or femininity 'as indicating something biological or social-structural that lies behind or underneath these signs, something to be glimpsed through them' is to 'accept a lay theory of signs', Goffman invites exactly such a reading of his own work. And the bringing together of the biological and social-structural here is as unfortunate as the unexplicated references to 'sex-class'. It connects two realms which offer each an impression of a particular solidity, a particular reality that is not to be afforded to a mere show, no matter what the effort spent in staging it. Goffman's own attitude to this problem is curious. It does not surface in the essay on gender but, in the opening pages of *Frame Analysis*, he explicitly points out that he will not be 'addressing the structure of social life but the structure of experience'. He goes on to say:

> I personally hold society to be first in every way and any individual's current involvements to be second; this report deals only in matters that are second. This book will have weaknesses enough in the areas it claims to deal with; there is no need to find limitations in what it does not set about to discover. (Goffman, 1986: 13)

It seems perhaps a little odd to affirm explicitly that x is the most important thing in the world so you are going to deal with y. Most writers are of course busy trying to argue exactly the opposite and some urge us to believe that some desperately obscure study that they have embarked upon is of central importance. Whether we should read Goffman's account as refreshing or as ratiocination matters less than the fact that the relationship between 'society' and 'experience' is poorly articulated, and why the latter should not actually *be* the former requires some explanation. He is clearly trying to divert attention from that which he is not purporting to deal with, and which may perhaps hold no interest for him, but, for some reason or another, making a gesture towards its importance, as if to deflect an anticipated criticism of him for dealing with what he *does* deal with.

Some of these difficulties and a number of the problems that worry Goffman could be solved by looking towards Foucault. Goffman invokes the idea of social structure seemingly to deal with the idea of the generally subordinate position of women, which is compared to that of children. He worries about the pervasive gendering of the intimate world, of private life and, given differential distributions of power, about the difficulties of political change. Additionally his schedules for display, his sequences of action which depict gender, are presented as if they have a general and generally gendered character that would be readable in 'social situations'. But the idea of a 'social situation' is far too unspecific a designation and the behaviour of people within it also far too generalized. Furthermore, regarding the purpose of these actions, via ethology, as functional also then poses the problem of why it is that gender should be used to get things done.

Foucault offers a far better way into such problems. Social situations now become the historically and socially precise locations of the clinic, the prison, the asylum or even the bedroom. There are no general ways of disposing of one's body in all these different locations in different times. But there are describable social technologies, repertoires that regulate the conduct of conduct in these settings. They are perfectly concrete and observable. They are not, though, reducible to social divisions like gender though they may be marked by a particular discourse of gender. This world is one where the pervasive character of power is well recognized and the consequences for political action are also faced. It is now much more common to see the requirement to make the long march through the institutions – to relocate the May 1968 revolutionary Daniel Cohen-Bendit's phrase. Change does require attention not just to the seizure of the levers of power but to the social technologies that regulate the fine grain of social life.

Foucault also has something to say about 'structure'. We cannot really be sure of what Goffman thought of it but it might have offered another way of thinking about the loose gearing to experience. For Foucault, whose interest is in the role of thought in the form of life, the idea of knowledges is united to that of the regulation of conduct and to institutional form, as well as to experience. There is certainly a structuring of conduct but it is not on the model given by a notion of social structure. And Foucault's discussion of discourse does not neglect the role of speech and writing nor pose the impossible 'why' question of functionalism.

Agnes the practical methodologist

If Goffman describes the fact that human beings constitute themselves as the kinds of objects to whom the doctrine of natural expression applies, Garfinkel gives us an understanding of the means by which they do so, through the case history of Agnes. Agnes, who presents as an intersexed person, faces a problem that most of us do not, namely that of securing the right to be attributed the sex that she describes herself as being, in social circumstances in which the transition possibilities from one sexual status to another are extremely limited. Not only is this 1950s America,[4] in which transitions are relatively rare and there is less perceived variation and mutability in what we would now see as gendered social categories, but the morality binding Agnes and all other persons 'who regard themselves as normally sexed' (for she does do so) is much more stringent.

Agnes is what Garfinkel describes as a 'practical methodologist'; she has 'an abiding practical preoccupation with competent female sexuality' (1990: 121). As someone who has to secure appropriate attributions and, furthermore, prevent the possibility of 'ruin', she studies 'how the organized features of ordinary settings are used by members as procedures for making appearances-of-sexuality-as-usual decidable as a matter of course' (1990: 180). Agnes, unlike the rest of us, treats normally sexed persons as cultural events – at least in practical terms. What she says about herself, however, is quite another matter. Garfinkel makes it evident that the way in which she describes herself is highly motivated. Her purpose, after all, in meeting with him and others at UCLA is to secure her right to an operation to remove the fully developed penis and scrotum which she possesses in addition to what Garfinkel describes as 'a very female shape' which gives her all the appearance of being 'convincingly female' (1990: 119).

What is interesting about Agnes is that, notwithstanding the practical knowledge she gradually acquires, perfects and demonstrates about how the world of 'natural, normally sexed persons' functions, she is a vehement subscriber to the beliefs that such normally sexed persons hold about the sexual character of their world. 'For such members,' Garfinkel says, 'perceived environments of sexed persons are populated with natural males, natural females, and persons who stand in moral contrast with them, *i.e.* incompetent, criminal, sick and sinful' (1990: 122). Agnes appears to respond to her environment in just the same way, '*treating it, as do they, as a matter of objective institutionalized facts, i.e.* moral facts' (ibid., emphasis in original). Her behaviour reveals the manner in which the facticity of the 'natural world' of two – and only two – sexed categories of person is constructed as a *moral* order, rather than in accordance with any set of facts:

> From the standpoint of an adult member of our society, the population of normal persons is a morally dichotomized population. The question of its existence is decided as a matter of motivated compliance with this population as a legitimate order. It is not decided as a matter of biological, medical, urological, sociological, psychiatric, or psychological fact. The question of its existence is instead decided by consulting both the likelihood that compliance to this legitimate order can be enforced and the conditions that determine this likelihood. (ibid.)

This idea will be familiar to us both from Foucault's *Herculine* and from Kessler's later work on intersex. The restoration of the morally appropriate order of things, whether through surgery or reassignment, indicates the prevalence of a set of beliefs that, as Garfinkel points out, go way beyond lay opinion and into the professions whose very investigations problematize this order. Bona fide members of society do not merely belong to, but are in some sense deemed to respect this order:

> For normals, the presence in the environment of sexed objects has the feature of a 'natural matter of fact.' This naturalness carries along with, as a constituent part of its meaning, the sense of its being right and correct, *i.e.* morally proper that it be that way…Hence the *bona fide* member of the society, within what he subscribes to as well as what he expects others to subscribe to as committed beliefs about 'natural matters of fact' regarding distributions of sexed persons in the society, finds the claims of the sciences like zoology, biology and psychiatry strange. (1990: 123)

Agnes, like normals, counted persons who did not belong to this moral order 'as freaks, unusual or bizarre' and was at pains to distance herself from them. Persons are held to compliance with this order, as Garfinkel says, 'regardless of their desires, *i.e.* "whether they like it or not"' (1990: 125) and Agnes proved herself as capable as the rest of us of insisting on such compliance. She is not a cultural critic. She wants to secure her place in the world of normally sexed persons, a world whose normative and therefore morally legitimate character she wholly accepts. She evinces distaste at the idea of homosexuals and transvestites and whenever Garfinkel moves the conversation in that direction she has 'great difficulty simultaneously managing her fascination for the topic and the great anxiety that the conversation seemed to generate' (1990: 131). Her 'voice would break as she denied all knowledge of this or that' and, far from finding any kinship with homosexuals and transvestites, she finds 'the comparison repulsive' (ibid.). Like normals she expresses herself as at a loss to understand 'why a person would do that' (have homosexual sex), but she delivers such an expression with 'flattened affect and never with indignation' (ibid.). She also, Garfinkel notes, regards her chances of securing treatment 'in terms of deservingness and blame' (1990: 177). Since she is *really* a woman, she is *entitled* to have the vagina that goes with that status, even if her boyfriend Bill persuades her that it is 'second best' because 'man-made'.

Although she acknowledged having been brought up as a boy and it was known that she had been living as a woman for only the last twenty-six months of her life, Agnes defined herself as a 'normal natural woman', whose male genitals constituted some kind of unfortunate trick of fate. She treated them as an abnormal growth, tumour or wart. What she sought to secure for herself were the appropriate insignia for the sex that she ought to have been had nature not, for some unaccountable reason, forced something else upon her. When asked, on many occasions, how she could account for her fierce desire to be a woman – to be what she already described herself as being – she would reply: 'There is no explaining it' (1990: 130). Fractures such as these in her account of herself, however, do not disturb the fabric of her presentation and Garfinkel admits that they are co-conspirators in the representation of her as female. Having said that, his understanding of her is, of course, that she is intersexed and, especially in view of her appearance (and notwithstanding the anomalous evidence of her biography), it would be an eminently reasonable and socially undisruptive conspiracy to share since he needs to secure a measure of trust from her. Garfinkel's objective, after all, is at odds with Agnes's: she wishes to secure the correct attribution from him to obtain the surgery, whilst he is interested in something quite tangential to her case as a medical and psychiatric one, namely what Agnes can tell him about 'the managed achievement of sex status'.

Agnes' account of her circumstances, then, is purposive. There is evidence that she spends a good deal of time trying to give Garfinkel the answers that she believes will contribute to her objective. For example, she idealizes biographical details of her time as a boy, presenting a picture of herself as heavily feminized during this period, and insistently emphasizes Bill's masculinity. This means that her utterances are best read not as true or false but as functional. Of course, Garfinkel knows this. He notices her euphemisms, evasions and point blank refusals to answer key questions. Asking, then, for something like the 'true' sexual identity of Agnes – if indeed it makes sense to ask for such a thing – is beside the point and, furthermore, is impenetrable from the case history.

As a student of the everyday activities that will result in the production of sexuality-as-usual, Agnes engages in a number of practical activities variously called by Garfinkel management devices, passing devices, and 'witnessable displays of talk and conduct' (1990: 180). We should regard them as exactly the same kinds of activities, gestures, dispositions as those for which Goffman borrowed (from ethology) the name 'displays' and Butler may have borrowed (from Austin) the name 'performatives'. In fact Garfinkel speaks both of 'displays' (as above) and 'performances' (1990: 176) and of Agnes' descriptions of this work as having 'an unavoidably "performative" character' (1990: 182, n. 9)[5]. Agnes' concerns for adequate motivation, relevance, evidence, her sensitivity to 'devices of talk' (which is not covered by

Goffman's description of displays), her anticipation of and ability to pass everyday 'sex tests' (what Kessler and McKenna would refer to as processes of attribution) are all a testament to her knowledge of the organized activities of everyday life that constitute the reality of normally sexed persons.

Passing

Given the moral character of normally sexed adulthood, should Agnes fail to carry off the impression of femininity the consequences, she feels, would be disastrous. Because of her anomalous position, she acquires an extraordinary awareness of what to everyone else is a taken-for-granted background to everyday life, constituted by what Garfinkel calls 'the omnirelevance of sexual statuses', and an anxious desire to ensure adequate, even triumphantly successful and, thereby, vindicating performances (1990: 118). This background is generally overlooked because routinized. For Agnes, however, as we noted earlier, it constitutes an abiding preoccupation. However much someone like Agnes seeks to routinize the everyday, the appropriate impression must be constantly sustained. What Garfinkel calls 'passing' thus unavoidably seems to be a present participle. Although as a concept it has now moved from sociology into common culture, in its inaugural definition 'passing' is formally stated to be: '[t]he work of achieving and making secure their rights to live in the elected sex status whilst providing for the possibility of detection and ruin carried out within the socially structured conditions in which this work occurred' (ibid.). In all of this, there is a balance to be struck between pursuing ordinary goals and making that status secure, and, whenever that status seems to be at risk, Agnes chooses security every time. Her main imperative is minimizing the risk of disclosure. Some of the work she does in order to pass may be characterized as happening in a 'game-like' structure, but, for most of it, an attempt to apply such a model produces structural incongruities. Game-like occasions have an episodic quality, are pre-planned and have rules that are known in advance and assumed to be binding on participants such as family members who are in some measure privy to the secret. Other occasions require that the rules be learned – riskily – within the encounter and they have a longer-term, developmental character. Within this developmental process, some individuals, like Bill and his mother, play the explicit role of instructors: Agnes talks of the 'long lectures' she received from Bill when she did something of which he disapproved (1990: 146).

As a result of what she refers to as 'a big gap in my life' in which she did not have a female biography, Agnes lacks a 'historico-prospective context for managing current situations' (1990: 130), and there are a number of elements both pre- and post-operatively which she has to conceal differentially in relation to different people. For example, before the surgery, both Garfinkel and Bill know that Agnes has a penis; the wider world does not. Garfinkel knows that Agnes was reared as a boy; Bill does not. Working to secure her rights to live in her elected sex status whilst providing for the possibility of detection and ruin means different things before these different audiences. Passing always entails a manipulation of the unnoticed background to the 'texture of relevances that comprise the changing actual scenes of everyday life' (1990: 118) and it involves, in a chronic way, 'situations of structured strain' (1990: 137). What these will consist of depends very much upon the nature of the information that has to be managed in each encounter.

The routinization of everyday life

What does this tell us about the world of 'normal' sexed persons? After all, what is described with the concept of 'passing' seems to belong specifically to a situation in which an ascription is being sought which it is assumed might not otherwise be made. For example, if Agnes is using management devices with Garfinkel, it is also fair to say – as he points out – that he is using management devices and is passing with her. Because he allegedly constitutes a member of the psychiatric and medical team dealing with her case, he finds himself needing to pretend to medical or legal expertise, and to obtain information requested by Agnes rapidly, or to rationalize his referring her to someone else for it, in order 'to preserve the friendship, the conspiracy, and the sense that we were in league with each other' (1990: 164). We could say that, in some respects, all this case history does is to put more theoretical detail on the account given to us by Kessler and McKenna, by indicating the manner in which the to-ing and fro-ing of reciprocal performances and attributions are woven into the texture of everyday life. Where Goffman talks of 'displays' that set the tone for social encounters and make it possible to get the work of them done, Garfinkel talks of 'the unnoticed background in the texture of relevances'. Fundamentally, both are describing the supply of appropriate behaviours, dispositions, and information that combine to generate the appropriate impression – or at any rate do not introduce incongruities into it that bring the background into the foreground and make it an issue. Normals, Garfinkel says, are able to advance their claims to be treated in a particular way without a second thought, whereas for Agnes these had to be 'bolstered and managed by shrewdness, deliberateness, skill, learning, rehearsal, reflectiveness, test, review, feedback, and the like' (1990: 165).

  A question we might pose here though, over forty years on, is to what extent this continual process of management would be necessary now, and, perhaps, even then. Were things really as bad as Agnes feared and Garfinkel described? We know, of course, that such concealment might not be necessary now, but what is interesting is the extent to which, even having the information, as we often do now, it is possible to override it in the making of an attribution. How many people, in the UK and elsewhere, faced with watching the transsexual Jackie on the television screen in *Paddington Green* find the idea that she was once a boy even remotely believable? And to what extent was the position of transsexuals and the intersexed, even in 1950s America, not closer to that described by Kessler and McKenna, in which an attribution, once made, is actually difficult to shift, allowing people to be accepted and taken on trust as, for example, 'a woman with a deep voice' or 'a woman who is taller than average'? There certainly would have been more fear of the consequences of being discovered to belong to an anomalous category in the USA of the 1950s.

But, by the very same token, to what extent might the existence of such a category be suspected, even allowing for more sex-stereotypical ways of behaving?

These are matters of cultural history, but, at the same time, what they draw attention to – as does the work of Goffman and Garfinkel[6] in general – is the role played by the routinization of information and behaviours in everyday life and the means by which this is achieved. For Garfinkel, routine is a necessary condition of rational action, as understood in a classically Weberian sense, and in the same way in which Durkheim understood that the validity and intelligibility of the terms of a contract 'depended upon the unstated and *essentially unstatable* terms that the contracting parties took for granted as binding upon their transactions' (1990: 173, emphasis in original):

> But sociological inquiry accepts almost as a truism that the ability of a person to act 'rationally' that is, the ability of a person in *conducting his everyday affairs* to calculate, to act deliberately; to project alternative plans of action; to select before the actual fall of events the conditions under which he will follow one plan or another; to give priority in the selection of means to their technical efficacy; to be much concerned with predictability and desirous of 'surprise in small amounts'; to prefer the analysis of alternatives and consequences prior to action in preference to improvisation; to be much concerned with questions of what is to be done and how it is to be done; to be aware of, to wish to, and to exercise choice; to be insistent upon 'fine' as opposed to 'gross' structure in characterizations in the knowledge of situations that one considers valuable and realistic knowledge; and the rest – that this ability depends upon the person being able to take for granted, to take under trust, a vast array of features of the social order. (1990: 172-3, emphasis in original)

This list would be a familiar one not merely to sociologists concerned with rationality or contracts in the specifically modernist sense in which we have come to understand them, but to any neurologist concerned with the human capacity to act with deliberation and to calculate adequately for the consequences of their decision-making. As such, the list refers to something much broader than any specific list of contents might indicate. The fact that sex currently constitutes one of the pieces of 'background information' that may be deemed relevant to the calculation of behaviours is in that sense no different from 'the background information' that an eighteenth-century slave owner might have needed to invoke in addressing his slaves, or a twenty-first-century motorist in addressing a police officer. It is all a matter of knowing whom one is dealing with. The marked particularity of persons, or the specification of objects in the 'natural world' (dangerous or benign snakes, for example) is there merely to allow one to know how to respond appropriately, safely and in a way which allows for some prediction of the outcome. What is interesting about Garfinkel's account of the world of normal sexed persons, then, is the fact that it has to be constructed and maintained as a *moral* order which contains a definition to which Agnes has to aspire, namely that of 'the real thing' and the manner by means of which it may be recognized (in much the same way as poisonous snakes are recognized by their markings).

This might seem a paradoxical way of reading a theorist who would appear to belong to a sociological tradition in which all of the quintessentially de-naturalizing qualities of sociology are concentrated, because it focuses so centrally upon language and what was referred to in an earlier age as 'the social construction of reality' – even allowing for our reading of him in tandem with Goffman's ethologically based account. To that degree, his work also seemed to enhance the potential imperialism of the object of sociology in elbowing out of the way the kinds of explanations (usually natural-scientific) which were sufficiently empiricist to believe in an unproblematic world of objects. Nevertheless, what we are suggesting here actually implies the possibility of an integration of such a sociological perspective with contemporary neuroscience, such as the work of Antonio Damasio (1995, 2000), Vilayanur S. Ramachandran (and Sandra Blakeslee, 1998) or Susan Greenfield (2000).

If one is seeking historical 'truths', the case history of Agnes is bound to frustrate such an endeavour. Even the postscript, in which Garfinkel reveals that Agnes confessed, eight years after her operation, that she had had a source of exogenous oestrogens which she had been taking since the age of twelve, conceals as much as it reveals. The case leaves a series of enigmas in its wake, about how Agnes represented herself to herself, about the psychical investment of Bill in this somewhat bizarre courtship, and so on. Ethnomethodology is not designed to reveal such information, since what it presents is always a 'situated account', which has the same character as that which it describes, in other words it 'leads the members to see a setting's features, which include a setting's accounts, "as determinate and independent objects"' (1990: 288). We may nevertheless still retain a fond belief that somewhere behind this account is to be found some kind of psychic truth about Agnes' 'identity', which might then also make it clear 'what really happened'. The next chapter, however, will reveal that the search for such a thing poses yet another set of enigmas.

Notes

[1]Roles are in the paradoxical position of being both constitutive and incidental, constitutive because roles like father or daughter and so on are fundamental to what is assumed to be individual identity and incidental insofar as a conventional philosophical humanism lies at the heart of these accounts and makes of roles something of a 'bolt-on', something to be cast on and off as the theatrical metaphor would imply. The idea of 'role conflict' is inconceivable without some notion that it implicates identity. For Goffman, however, there is no such a thing, for instance, as gender identity, a colouring of the person from their appurtenance to a sex.

[2]The differences between these two concepts, 'performativity' and 'performance', relate fundamentally to what it is that 'performativity' borrows from J. L. Austin (1962; 1970), namely the role of language. 'Performativity' is used in a context in which, like Austin's notion of the performative uses of language, discourse brings something into being, in this case gender.

[3] Butler uses the notion of iteration to make possible breaches in gender. Because gender is something which has to be continually reiterated, performatively re-enacted, the possibility arises for its transformation. This might seem very close to what Goffman is arguing here but in Butler it is related to fundamental forms of cultural and bodily intelligibility: 'Bodies cannot be said to have a signifiable existence prior to the mark of

their gender; the question then emerges: To what extent does the body *come into being* in and through the marks of gender?' (1990: 8, emphasis in original) and 'To what extent do *regulatory practices* of gender formation and division constitute identity, the internal coherence of the subject, indeed the self-identical status of the person' (1990: 16, emphasis in original). This is understandable in the context of the influence of post-Lacanian psychoanalysis in her work. What for Goffman provides puzzlement, is for Butler a starting point, whose constitution she explores.

[4] The case history dates from 1967, but the events described in it relate to the 1950s.

[5] Garfinkel makes a very interesting observation here about what it is that gives her descriptions their 'performative' character, which differs somewhat from Butler's account of all gender as performative. For what makes Agnes' account have this character is her possession of a knowledge which she cannot quite share:

> Her anguish and triumphs resided in the observability, which was particular to her and incommunicable, of the steps whereby the society hides from its members its activities of organisation and thus leads them to see its features as determinate and independent objects. For Agnes the observably normally sexed persons *consisted* of inexorable, organizationally located work that provided the way that such objects arise. (1990: 182, emphasis in original)

This is what Garfinkel refers to in terms of Merleau-Ponty's concept of the 'préjugé du monde'.

[6] Part of Garfinkel's discussion involves a criticism of Goffman's account for what the case history of Agnes shows up, namely that the management of impressions cannot be as ubiquitous as he suggests; in other words, exchanges cannot be as chronically problematic as they are for Agnes. Normal members not only take on trust everything that Agnes felt unable to, but expect to be treated in a trusted and trusting manner, and require of each other that evidences of such trust be supplied: 'Agnes would have wanted to act in this trusting fashion *but routine as a condition for the effective, calculated and deliberate management of practical circumstances was, for Agnes, specifically and chronically problematic*' (1990: 174-5, emphasis in original).

10 A Melancholy Gender

Judith Butler's work could be read as representing the integration of the different theoretical approaches we have been exploring in the last three chapters, for it combines, amongst other things, elements of a Foucauldian approach to power and discourse, the idea of gender as something achieved through its performance and a depth psychology derived from Freud and Lacanian and post-Lacanian psychoanalysis. One might therefore be forgiven for thinking that it would constitute the ideal confluence of strands of theorizing which we have – at least in some measure – endorsed. However, as Paul Hirst and Penny Woolley (1982) pointed out in *Social Relations and Human Attributes*, not only can bringing theoretical approaches together be an endeavour fraught with problems, but the precise purpose for which, and manner in which, they are brought together is fundamental to the success or failure of the enterprise.

Butler is best known for her account of gender as performative. In relation to the work of Kessler and McKenna, Goffman and Garfinkel, her initial figuration of gender as a 'corporeal style' a 'dramatic and contingent construction of meaning' (1990: 139), whose inner truth is a fabrication without ontological status, will seem perfectly in keeping. There are nevertheless some important differences. Goffman's work, for example, is humanist in orientation and stresses the performance of gender as a function of an innate human capacity to provide depictions of who people are and of the nature of the encounter they are embarked upon. Garfinkel's work is solidly within the tradition of ethnomethodology and, although there are clearly phenomenological roots in the Lacanian psychoanalysis drawn on by Butler, her overall orientation is a combination of different strands which, as we have argued elsewhere (Hood-Williams and Cealey Harrison, 1998), sit somewhat uneasily together.

In *Gender Trouble*, the book in which she first introduced the idea of gender as performative, Butler searches to express, in a language of both surface and depth, both the produced, fictive character of gender and the development of gender identities. She asks what produces the *effect* of a stable inner core of gender: what is it that produces the perception of a gendered ontology, foundational, fixed, real but actually fictional, produced, chimerical? Her answer is that, performatively, *acts, gestures, and enactments* do this work: 'Such acts, gestures and enactments, generally construed, are *performative* in the sense that the essence of identity that they otherwise purport to express are *fabrications* manufactured and sustained through corporeal signs and other discursive means' (1990: 136).

In an argument reminiscent of that of Goffman, she argues that the fixing of gender is 'an enactment that performatively constitutes the appearance of its own fixity' (1990: 70). The way in which that fixity is arrived at is through repetition and here she deploys a concept of citationality derived from Jacques Derrida's reading of J. L. Austin, from whom the idea of the performative is taken (Austin, 1962; 1970). Gender is to be understood 'as a reiterative or citational practice by which discourse produces the effects that it names' (1990: 2). Following Derrida, she characterizes gender as *undecidable* between surface and depth. However, what one might refer to as the ontological burden of her argument seems to fall most heavily on the substantiality of discourse and the fictive character of interiority. This is especially evident in her use of Foucault, in which she adopts the concept of discourse to argue against the idea of an interior soul in favour of the redescription of intrapsychic processes as bodily inscription, the corporeal stylization of gender. Bodies are compelled to signify by disciplinary processes – by analogy with Foucault's account of the prisoner – the gestures, acts and enactments of gender, and it is this bodily inscription which produces the *effect* of a signifying inner space:

> The figure of the interior soul understood as 'within' the body is signified through its inscription on the body, even though its primary mode of signification is through its very absence, its potent invisibility. The effect of a structuring inner space is produced through the signification of a body as a vital and sacred enclosure. (1990: 135)

Gender therefore ought not to be construed as a stable identity or locus of agency and both *Gender Trouble* and her next book, *Bodies That Matter*, are quite forceful in foregrounding language and discursivity as the basis for the effect and appearance of interiority.

This is quite a curious position for a theorist concerned with psychoanalytic objects, even allowing for any Lacanian inflections. The important thing, however, might not be whether or not these two problematics can be successfully tied together, but whether or not knitting psychoanalysis into an account of gender *identity*, however deconstructed 'gender' may be, does not close down precisely that deconstructive potential of psychoanalysis which might have made it compatible with notions of performativity.

The troubling of identity and the gendered ego

What made Butler's work in *Gender Trouble* revolutionary was that she took apart the notion of 'an existing identity' which was presumed to lie at the heart of feminist endeavours, as she put it, 'understood through the category of women, who not only initiates feminist interests and goals within discourse, but constitutes the subject for whom political representation is pursued' (1990: 1). Subsequently, in *Bodies That Matter*, she did a similar job on the materiality of bodies and described the body's 'materiality' as performatively constituted by the regulatory norms of 'sex'. In the first chapter, for example, she poses the question of how and why 'materiality' has become a sign of irreducibility, of that which only bears constructions, and therefore cannot itself *be* a construction (1993: 28). Here she seeks to connect gender performativity to a process of 'materialization', in which the regulatory norms of 'sex' work 'to materialize the body's sex, in other words to materialize sexual difference in the service of the construction of the heterosexual imperative' (1990: 2).

> In this sense, what constitutes the fixity of the body, its contours, its movements, will be fully material, but materiality will be rethought as the effect of power, as power's most productive effect. And there will be no way to understand 'gender' as a cultural construct which is imposed upon the surface of matter, understood either as 'the body' or its given sex. Rather, once 'sex' itself is understood in its normativity, the materiality of the body will not be thinkable apart from the materialization of that regulatory norm. 'Sex' is thus not simply what one has, or a static description of what one is: it will be one of the norms by which the 'one' becomes viable at all, that which qualifies a body for life within the domain of cultural intelligibility. (ibid.)

'Sex', then, although constituted as a regulatory norm, is also paradoxically foundational since it constitutes the necessary condition for cultural intelligibility of any kind for the human being. In some respects, this paradoxical combination of the anti-foundational and the foundational characterizes Butler's work, not because the foundational is revealed to be the fictive, but because her writing seems to want to engage both types of discourse, and, oddly, it is in her use of psychoanalysis that this becomes most evident, since the account she gives seems to run counter to the provisions of an identity which is only ever performatively constituted.

It is scarcely possible to begin to do justice to all of Butler's complex *œuvre*, so we shall examine only this central issue of gender identity, and the psychoanalytic core that she places at the heart of the idea of gender as performativity. Butler developed this psychoanalytic component more fully in *Bodies That Matter* but, over the period of time since the publication of *Gender Trouble*, some details of the argument have been modified. The skeleton of the most recent version is given in Chapter 5 of *The Psychic Life of Power* (Butler, 1997) and it is this that we focus on here. Butler's use of psychoanalysis is of course in keeping with its original reception within latter-day feminism. When psychoanalysis was first entertained as an explanatory possibility within feminism, it was largely in the hope that it might provide the key to the establishment of sexual difference, to the production of what were then described as 'sexed subjects'. In keeping with this, Butler describes the acquisition of gender in terms of processes of identification, which shape the ego on the model of characteristics of the object, talking of 'internalization' and 'incorporation'.[1]

Her argument derives from the deployment of the logic of particular psychoanalytic theses concerning the ego and the Oedipus complex. Butler's argument is that the ego is gendered and that the gendering of the ego comes about by means of the passage through the Oedipus complex and the loss of debarred attachments to same-sex objects. One psychoanalytic understanding of the concept of the ego refers to the way in which it is formed out of the precipitates of lost love objects. When Freud came to write about the ego in

The Ego and the Id (1923), six years after publication of *Mourning and Melancholia* (Freud, 1917 [1915]), he observed that the process he had seen at work in melancholia, by means of which a lost object is set up inside the ego as an identification, had proved to be more general than he had at first suspected and that it had a great share in determining the form taken by the ego and building up what is called its 'character' (Freud, 1923: 28). This is the idea that Butler uses in an argument that suggests that gender is melancholic, because it is rooted in such loss. She characterizes the initial attachments of the infant (girl) child to its mother as 'homosexual'. Such attachments *must* be lost in the journey to stabilized, 'normal' gender, hence that stability and normality is bought at the price of melancholy. As a function of the Oedipus complex, the child will come to identify with the mother that she cannot have as an object of desire.

Psychoanalysis and 'gender'

What Butler did, which is in keeping with psychoanalysis but *contra* sociology, was to reinstate a connection between what she calls 'gender' and sexuality. For her, gender is consonant with a normalized and normalizing heterosexuality. However, there is no concept of 'gender' in psychoanalysis nor indeed of 'identity'. Freud, by contrast, speaks of masculinity and femininity, which is rather different. 'Normal femininity', for example, is achieved through making heterosexual object choices, having a preference for passive aims and demonstrating feminine forms of attachment to those objects (narcissistic rather than anaclitic). However, 'femininity' is by no means co-terminous with the psyche of a female human being. It would be more appropriate to characterize it as comprising a number of discrete and relatively autonomous features which it is assumed *ought* to coincide with the female person but do not necessarily do so. Freud often speaks of it as if it were an available *configuration*, a way of being, to which a human being might cleave. For example, he describes the Wolf Man being prepared to accept femininity as a consolation for castration, in much the same way as he speaks of the little girl's acceptance of potential maternity as a consolation for the penis that she cannot have.

It is clear from a number of his writings that he was unable to resolve 'the riddle of femininity' partly because he had to tussle with the inherent assumption that femininity was the destiny of women and masculinity the destiny of men, which he found hard to reconcile with what is also very evident in his case histories, namely that masculinity is not the sole preserve of men, nor femininity the sole preserve of women. Equally, when he actually sought to identify the components that might be said to characterize 'masculinity' and 'femininity', the concepts rather fell apart in his hands. In a footnote added to the *Three Essays on the Theory of Sexuality* in 1915, he writes as follows:

> It is essential to understand clearly that the concepts of 'masculine' and 'feminine', whose meaning seems so unambiguous to ordinary people, are among the most confused that occur in science. It is possible to distinguish at

least *three* uses. 'Masculine' and 'feminine' are used sometimes in the sense of *activity* and *passivity*, sometimes in a *biological*, and sometimes, again, in a *sociological* sense. The first of these is the essential one and the most serviceable in psychoanalysis. When, for instance, libido was described in the text above as being 'masculine', the word was being used in this sense, for an instinct is always active even when it has a passive aim in view. The second, or biological, meaning of 'masculine' and 'feminine' is the one whose applicability can be determined most easily. Here 'masculine' and 'feminine' are characterized by the presence of spermatozoa or ova respectively and by the functions proceeding from them. Activity and its concomitant phenomena (more powerful muscular development, aggressiveness, greater intensity of libido) are as a rule linked with biological masculinity; but they are not necessarily so, for there are animal species in which these qualities are on the contrary assigned to the female. The third, or sociological, meaning receives its connotation from the observation of actually existing masculine and feminine individuals. Such observation shows that in human beings pure masculinity or femininity is not to be found in either a psychological or a biological sense. Every individual on the contrary displays a mixture of the character-traits belonging to his own and to the opposite sex; and he shows a combination of activity and passivity whether or not these last character-traits tally with his biological ones. (Freud, 1905b: 219-20)

Freud's designations of 'masculine' and 'feminine' individuals, of course, occur in a world before the advent of the idea of gender, so that they merely represent the adjectival form of 'male' and 'female'. Even so, he identifies the confusion he sets out to disentangle with combinations of biological and sociological meanings, some of which he finds moderately serviceable and others less so. Even the one whose 'applicability can be determined most easily' presents ambiguities insofar as the biological characteristics deemed proper to the presence of spermatozoa or ova respectively, and to the functions proceeding from them, are not *necessarily* distributed in the way that one might expect. 'The third, or sociological, meaning' exacerbates the difficulty since it 'shows that in human beings pure masculinity or femininity is not to be found in either a psychological or a biological sense'.

The deployment of psychoanalysis in the service of a theory of 'gender' therefore already prompts a certain uneasiness. Butler says that she 'went with' the term 'gender' because it was less fixed and more mobile than, for example, certain Lacanian usages of 'sexual difference', in which the installation of sexual difference is co-terminous with the acquisition of language itself (Rubin with Butler, 1994: 68-9). Gender identity – however performatively constituted – nevertheless seems implicitly to be defined as the property of a sexed subject and therefore to presuppose explaining the acquisition of the characteristics that define it. Psychoanalysis, on the other hand, seems *prima facie* to suggest that there is no such thing.

Melancholic gender

Butler begins her account of the production of gender identity by recalling Freud's observation that the initial definition of the ego is as a 'bodily ego' and not merely a surface but, as Freud has it, 'a projection of a surface'. Furthermore, this bodily ego 'assumes a gendered morphology, so that the bodily ego is also a gendered ego' (1997: 132). In a reading of *The Ego and the Id* and *Mourning and Melancholia*, she suggests that the ego is formed out of precipitates of lost love objects which are incorporated into the ego and that these objects are set up inside the ego as identifications. The character of the ego is then made up from 'the sedimentation of objects loved and lost, the archaeological remainder, as it were, of unresolved grief' (1997: 133). Put briefly, then, the ego is gendered because the child identifies with a same sex object which it has to forgo as a possible love object. Attachments to lost objects are never 'let go'; instead they are brought into the ego as identifications and the attachments are thereby 'magically' preserved. These melancholic identifications represent the way in which the subject preserves the lost object and deals with its loss.

Butler refers to Freud's account in *Three Essays on the Theory of Sexuality* of the laborious and difficult journey towards the production of heterosexuality. She depicts this journey as one which demands the loss of certain sexual attachments along the way and where 'those losses must *not* be avowed, and *not* be grieved' (1997: 135, emphasis in original). In *Mourning and Melancholia*, Freud draws a distinction between an acknowledged loss, which results in mourning, and a loss which, for one reason or another, is not available to consciousness. There are two crucial differences between Freud's use and Butler's however. One is that Freud's use of the term 'melancholia', however generalizable the process he identified within it,[2] represents an affliction, the affliction we would nowadays describe as depression. It implies, at the very least, self-berating or a loss of self-regard. The second is that Butler describes the prohibition on the object choice that is tabooed as 'foreclosed'. Foreclosure is a concept particularly associated with Lacanian notions of psychosis, in which the pre-emptive expulsion of a signifier occurs as a complement to the installation of the symbolic, and it is this installation which is constitutive of the very possibility of the human being as a subject.[3] There are two things to note and, perhaps, to query here: one is the way in which the prohibition on homosexuality has a *primordial* character and the other is the way in which this prohibition is implicitly linked to the pathological. Why, we should ask, does Butler want to describe gender as 'melancholic'?[4]

Given the connections between a stabilized heterosexuality and normal masculinity/femininity, and between that and what is here called gender, this means that gender itself is believed to be achieved through the prohibition on an object choice whose existence cannot be symbolized, namely homosexual choice. As Freud puts it, 'the ego rejects the incompatible idea together with its affect and behaves as if the idea had never occurred to the ego at all' (1894: 58). Heterosexuality is bought at the price of the prohibition on homosexuality:

> Consider that gender is acquired at least in part through the repudiation of homosexual attachments; the girl becomes a girl through being subject to a prohibition which bars the mother as an object of desire and installs that barred object as a part of the ego, indeed, as a melancholic identification. Thus the

identification contains within it both the prohibition and the desire and so embodies the ungrieved loss of the homosexual cathexis. (1997: 136)

The connections between heterosexuality and (normal) gender mean that homosexuality always threatens this normality. Gender is panicked and in fear of homosexuality, which may explain some cultural reactions to homosexuality: 'If one is a girl to the extent that one does not want a girl, then wanting a girl will bring being a girl into question' (1997: 136). The choice of a girl as object implies that one might not be a girl. Bearing in mind the argument that loss is dealt with through identification and incorporation into the ego, these foreclosed attachments to homosexuality are always 'there' within heterosexuality and normal gender.

Gender depends on the breaking of attachments to same sex objects in the journey through the Oedipus complex. There is an enforced cultural logic here that prohibits homosexual attachments in the journey to 'normal' femininity and masculinity:

> If the girl is to transfer love from her father to a substitute object, she must according to Freudian logic, first renounce love for her mother, and renounce it in such a way that both the aim and the object are foreclosed. She must not transfer that homosexual love onto a substitute feminine figure, but renounce the possibility of homosexual attachment itself. (1997: 137)

Heterosexuality is melancholic in that it is forbidden to mourn the loss of homosexual attachments, but Butler recognizes that *inter alia* the same applies to homosexuality. The non-grieving of homosexuals, however, is taken up rather differently. What homosexual melancholia has in addition (for, presumably, *social reasons*) is 'anger' (1997: 147). This is where the political dimensions of the argument become relevant. The construction of the ego in this account is counter to the idea of clearly differentiated lesbian and gay identities that stand in a closed relationship to heterosexuality – and vice versa. Heterosexuality is not monolithic precisely because it contains that lost object within it. The denial of any relationship between the two may therefore involve a rejection of heterosexuality that is to some extent an identification with that rejected sexuality (1997: 148-9). Clearly the idea of a coherent, separate identity has been important to gay and lesbian politics but Butler believes that this may be at some cost – the cost of 'abjected spectres' that threaten the closed off domains of subject positions. 'Perhaps', she suggests, 'only by risking the incoherence of identity is connection possible' (1997: 149). As a form of incoherence, however, this is arguably fairly limited, as is evident in the way in which the idea of the ego is taken up.

The ego and a gendered morphology

The question of the place of the ego in psychoanalysis is a very large one and we cannot really explore it in much depth here. As we have seen, Butler's characterization follows Freud's remark that 'the ego is first and foremost a bodily ego' and not merely a surface entity but 'the projection of a surface' and she asserts that 'this bodily ego assumes a gendered morphology, so that the bodily ego is also a gendered ego' (1997: 132). But is it? The logic here appears to be that of the sex/gender problematic: morphological differences (sex) constitute the foundation of the person (gender). In *Bodies That Matter* Butler constructs an argument that seeks to *avoid* a directly mimetic relationship between the biological body and the bodily ego, but which is nevertheless committed to arguing for the construction of masculine and feminine morphologies at the heart of bodily morphogenesis: 'Suffice it to say that the boundaries of the body are the lived experience of differentiation, where that differentiation is never neutral to the question of gender difference or the heterosexual matrix' (1993: 65). The logic here is broadly Lacanian: subjects come into being through the institution of the law and that law is the law of sexual difference. Thus, anatomy is never given outside the terms of 'the signifying chain by which sexual difference is negotiated' (1993: 90).

We should note first of all that Freud is bringing together two ideas here: the idea of the ego as deriving from the surface of the body and the idea of the ego as a *mental projection* of the surface of the body. One suggestive reading of the ego, that by Jean Laplanche (1976) in his *Life and Death in Psychoanalysis*, makes much of the fact that there are two meanings of the ego in psychoanalysis, that of the *Ich*, or I, and that of the agency, and that it is the interplay between these two meanings that constitutes the problematic of the ego. We might follow Laplanche and say that there are two *derivations* of 'ego' – the term that Freud had borrowed from common parlance and aimed to make his own (as was typical of him). The first is essentially banal and in fact non-psychoanalytic: it designates the individual, the whole person differentiated from the other in contact with the real. This is the ego of American ego psychology. Problems abound with this conception. What is differentiated? The biological organism? This is covered by its own skin, so the question then becomes, what is the relation between that psychic differentiation and this skin? What might the relation be between this 'psychical individual' and the 'biological individual'? Freud tried to ground this anatomically – rather dubiously – by observing that the central nervous system is derivative of the ectoderm. One heir to this line of thinking is Didier Anzieu (1989) who conceives of the mental image of the skin as the *primordial* form of the ego and writes of the 'skin ego',[5] seeking to reconcile the biological and the psychical. 'Every psychical activity,' he says, 'is anaclytically dependent upon a biological function' (1989: 40). Is there a certain echo of this in Butler's notion of a gendered morphology, since sex is the absent presence behind the idea of a gendered morphology? If gendering, understood in terms of the heterosexual matrix, en-genders sex, then sexual difference must also be written on the body.

The banal question that also arises is what precisely is meant by a 'gendered morphology'? How can 'difference' be lived? Whilst it is undeniable that phantasies of a 'womanly' or a 'manly' body exist (witness Freud's 1911 [1910] case history of Senatspräsident Schreber), why ought we to assume them to be constitutive? The answer, we would suggest, is because of the allegedly foundational character of 'sex'. This is hardly without its precedents, of course, in Freud himself. One of his later essays is after all entitled 'Some Psychical

Consequences of the Anatomical Distinction Between the Sexes' (1925). The idea that there must be some constitutive relation between morphology – howsoever this is understood – and the nature of the human person, between what we now call 'sex' and what we have come to characterize as 'gender', has become a taken-for-granted feature of our world. But it belongs to the very architecture identified by Laqueur, so we should, at least *prima facie*, be very suspicious of it.

Butler is a theorist who is of course well aware of the potential complexities of the relation of the psychical to the bodily, as is especially evident in her discussion of materiality in *Bodies That Matter* (see especially 'The Lesbian Phallus and the Morphological Imaginary'). But for all the complexities, there seems to be something simpler at stake here, which concerns the way in which the sex/gender problematic constitutes the envelope within which all of these discussions take place. She says, for example, that 'it may also be that gender-instituting prohibitions work through suffusing the body with a pain that culminates in the projection of a surface, that is, a sexed morphology which is at once a compensatory phantasy and a fetishistic mask' (1993: 65). Although gender-instituting prohibitions *produce* sex here, sex is only there because gender is automatically '*about*' sex. 'Sex' is the foundation (however fictitious and constructed) of 'gender'. At the simplest level, then, it seems as if a gendered morphology is a condition of the fact that bodies have to be identified as having a sex.

If the ego derives from the surface of the body, then it looks as if Freud is already thinking of it as specular and anticipating Lacan's Mirror Phase (1977). When the child sees itself in the mirror, which is not of course a literal mirror but an index of psychic development, it sees a whole, a misrecognized unity belied by motor uncoordination. It sees an illusion. This plenitude will later come to be signified as phallic, but at this stage it is, according to Lacan, the prototypical identificatory relation, which produces the sense of the body as a whole through its alienation in the image. But what could this surface be to which Freud refers? Only one thing: the skin. According to Laplanche, in its genesis the ego fills a sack of skin whose chief effect is to establish a boundary of inside and outside (1976: 81). Does the proto-ego thus formed, then, have a visual or a tactile basis? Steven Connor's discussion in a recent issue of *New Formations* makes a distinction between the skin as defining tactile sensation and the skin as defining visible form: 'The skin ego is formed from, and remains powerfully associated with, sensory impressions which are pre-visual or at best weakly visual.' These primal or prenatal ego forms can only be constructed, he says, by Klein's notions of projection/introjection, 'good'/'bad', part/whole (Klein, 1950; Klein et al., 1952) make no sense. And because this must happen so early we can be sure of one thing: *at its inception, even in this sense, the ego is not gendered.* Does it become so later?

It may well be that gendered morphologies *do* come to be constituted later, and we would suggest that, rather than being primordial, they would have to be the fruit of much later phantasies. Connor provides what is in fact a much more nuanced set of possibilities for how one might conceive of a relation between the skin as a defining exterior limit, producing the phantasy of the psychic envelope, and its later inflection with phantasies of a gendered morphology, phantasies which would most probably be articulated around the erotogenicity of particular parts of the body and the phantasied significance of particular bodily conformations. Such developments, however, would belong to the later stages of childhood and, perhaps, adolescence. In psychoanalytic terms, what will be material here will be the fate of the phallic, castration. There can be no gendered morphologies prior to that stage.

There is a puzzling ambiguity here, however, for, in discussing lost objects, Butler is focusing on a later Oedipal stage. This would place the gendered morphologies as effects of the identificatory processes which are alleged to produce gender, in other words not as early as her discussion of the installation of a sexed morphology in *Bodies That Matter* would seem to imply. What she describes is reminiscent of Freud's stipulations in discussing male homosexuality, that when the ego remodels itself on the model of the lost object, it does so comprehensively, and specifically in relation to what he calls 'its sexual character' (1921: 108). This is what we can describe as a regressive form of identification, in which the human being regresses from object-love to identification as a means of preserving the relation to the lost object. Thus, if we follow Freud's model rather than Lacan's, it would seem to suggest *either* that those first identifications to which the subject regressed must have been gendered *or* that they become gendered in the Oedipal moment, when the child begins to make sense of sexual difference.

The ego as individual and the ego as agency

Is it this first sense of ego that most recalls Butler's reading? The ego as *Ich,* the ego as 'an actualized metaphor of totality' (Laplanche, 1976: 136). It is certainly not a sense that should be forgotten for all its delusions, its passing itself off. But it is a sense closer to the banal understanding of the ego as person, as personality, as individual. Central to this meaning is indeed the text that Butler reads, *The Ego and the Id*. Laplanche has said of this work that it is 'a crucial text in the turn toward ego psychology' (1976: 52-3). It would be a strange paradox if a writer such as Butler, so well versed in European philosophy, had made a reading of the ego with a close affinity to that peculiarly American reading of psychoanalysis – what one might indeed call that peculiar distortion – ego psychology, the object of Lacan's ire in his putative return to Freud.

However, it is, as Laplanche says, never for nothing that the same word comes to designate two apparently different things. The second meaning of ego is of the ego, not as whole, not the totality but part of the totality. It is ego as *agency* and, which is the same thing, as entity. One of the key insights of psychoanalysis is that the subject is constituted by internal objects or, to put it more strongly, that the constitution of the subject is on the model of these objects, which is of course precisely the aspect that Butler picks up. One cannot then lose this second sense of ego without losing the extent to which the ego is a psychoanalytic (rather than a sociological) object.

In Freud's second topography, the ego is an agency that mediates between the demands of the id and those of external reality and the super-ego. Essentially it operates defensively; as the *Studies on Hysteria* had put it, it 'takes pleasure in defence' (Laplanche and Pontalis, 1980: 132). In psychic processes the ego restricts the free flow of excitations, links ideas and (tries to) constitute and maintain relatively stable forms. Its task is coherence, forming, binding. The ego is also then said to be formed out of the confrontation of the id and reality. It is a differentiation from the id. In the first topography, the ego operates beyond the conscious/pre-conscious systemm: its defensive work is unconscious. The main effect on the conception of the ego in the second topography, after 1920, is to constitute the ego more fully as an agency, which moderates between other agencies and is itself largely unconscious, and to stress conflict.

If it is true that, as Laplanche claims, the 'entire problematic of the *derivation of the psychoanalytic ego*' (1976: 76, emphasis in original) is the passage from the first to the second sense what would it mean to collapse them? Laplanche regards the idea of the ego as the image of the living being as a delusion, but '*a delusion which is not simply that of the advocates of "ego psychology," but of the ego itself*' (1976: 82, emphasis in original). Does it make sense to regard the ego – in the sense of a psychic agency engaged in conflict within the subject – as gendered? Freud describes the ego of the Wolf Man managing the conflict between those tendencies which would later deserve the name of masculine or feminine by putting into operation the repression of relevant material but does not speak of his ego *itself* as masculine or feminine.[6]

Furthermore, in a long and difficult discussion of the ego in relation to the Oedipus complex, Freud suggests that the first identifications of infants 'are not what we should have expected since they *do not* introduce the abandoned object into the ego' (1923: 32, emphasis added). It seems that the idea of egos formed out of the precipitates of lost love objects is not one that applies to these first, Oedipal identifications and object-cathexes – although this is the central assumption of Butler's theory of gender identity. For Freud such a notion is much more peripheral. He adds only that this outcome 'may also occur'. In fact, the forming of precipitates in the ego from the Oedipus complex is said to retain a special position in relation to something else: to the development of the super-ego – and it is well known that there is assumed to be a distinct difference between women and men in the relative strengths of the super-ego. In her original discussion of melancholic gender in *Gender Trouble*, Butler does in fact tie it to the installation of the ego-ideal (here understood as the super-ego) so that the identification with the object is accompanied by the prohibition of both object and modality of desire:[7]

> In melancholia, the loved object is lost through a variety of means: separation, death, or the breaking of an emotional tie. In the Oedipal situation, however, the loss is dictated by a *prohibition* attended by a set of punishments. The melancholia of gender identification which 'answers' the Oedipal dilemma must be understood, then, as the internalization of an interior moral directive which *gains its structure and energy from an externally enforced taboo*. (1990: 64, emphasis added)

In *Civilization and its Discontents* (1930 [1929]), however, Freud's discussion of the formation of the super-ego does not suggest such a straightforward relationship between external prohibition and the construction of internal punishment. Morality is an internal construction, in which it is the aggression born of the *frustration* of satisfaction by the external authority that is turned against the child. It is predominantly the aggressiveness which the child *would have liked to have exercised* against the authority – rather than the stringency of the prohibitions put in place by that authority – that dictates the strength of the super-ego.

The more general point, however, is that Butler's primary interest is in tracing the development of a *stabilized* gender, of 'normal' (heterosexual) gender and the place of ungrieved and ungrievable loss in this development. She describes this as a 'stark and hyperbolic construction'. But are either 'gender' or heterosexuality *ever* to be regarded as stabilized? If gender is performative it requires the reiterative maintenance of its stability. In that sense, as well, is her 'stark and hyperbolic construction' actually a psychoanalytic construction? To be fair to Butler, she does characterize her writing as offering 'a certain *cultural engagement* with psychoanalysis that belongs neither to the fields of psychology nor to psychoanalysis, but nevertheless seeks to establish an intellectual relationship to those enterprises' (1997: 138, emphasis added). The difficulty that arises, then, is what we are to make of the status of that engagement: a 'certain cultural engagement' seems to imply something rather different than its straightforward use.[8] We could potentially read this engagement in two ways, as an historically informed and critical deployment or, more worryingly, as an *acculturation* of psychoanalysis.

'Homosexual' attachments

Let us examine what that engagement consists of in more detail. Butler has argued that the acquisition of heterosexuality, and hence of gender, is the result of a laborious journey during which a key set of attachments, characterized as homosexual, must be disavowed. In the *Three Essays*, Freud describes the acquisition of heterosexuality in terms of such a journey but he does not describe the attachments that must be given up as 'homosexual'. The development of adult sexuality, whether it turns out 'normally' and ends with genital heterosexuality or in any of the perversities or in homosexuality, begins in the polymorphously perverse pleasure-seeking of the infant. The infant negotiates a difficult journey through the psychosexual stages: oral, anal-sadistic, phallic and genital. The key moments of this journey are the Oedipus and castration complexes. The initial attachments that the infant makes to its mother and father and the switches and substitutions involved in the entry into and resolution of the Oedipus complex all take place before the genital stage is reached. *But it is only at the genital stage that one can speak about hetero- or homosexuality.* Before that, the infant's first attachments are of an anaclitic type, deriving from the instincts for self-preservation – for love, care and nourishment. In other words, the subsequent *sexual* instincts are closely related to and 'lean on' these initial vital functions, which, as Laplanche and Pontalis say, 'furnish them with an organic source, an orientation and an object' (1980: 29). These are attachments to part-objects governed by the force of component instincts whose character shifts as they progress through the stages of infantile sexuality – oral, anal-sadistic and phallic. Although the phallic phase might be deemed to usher in a relation to a whole object, it makes little sense to describe the infant girl's attachment to her mother or to her mother's breast as 'homosexual'.

When she first introduced these ideas about the melancholy character of gender in *Gender Trouble* Butler alighted upon remarks Freud made about 'masculine' and 'feminine' sexual dispositions in *The Ego and the Id*, although she re-read these dispositions as constructions (1990: 63-4). A development of her argument now says that we must suppose 'that masculine and feminine are not dispositions, as Freud sometimes argues, but accomplishments, ones which emerge in tandem with the achievement of heterosexuality' (1997: 135). On the same page of *The Psychic Life of Power* she turns to the argument from the *Three Essays*. But this new position does not perhaps go as far as it might. If she is right now to recognize that the idea of early 'sexual dispositions' assumes what the theory of sexual development sets out to explain then the logic would be also to recognize, as the *Three Essays* argue, that heterosexuality (like homosexuality) may, similarly, only be regarded as an accomplishment at the end of a long journey. And what then follows is the recognition that initial attachments may not be characterized in such terms. Freud writes in his 'Femininity' lecture that, '[w]ith the entry into the phallic phase the differences between the sexes are completely eclipsed by their agreements. We are now obliged to recognize that the little girl is a little man' (1933: 118). How then can her attachment be called homosexual?

We should also note that the logic of dropping the attachment to the idea of masculine and feminine sexual dispositions would have an important consequence for Butler's account. What would happen would be that the argument became partial. It would be an account of femininity and not of masculinity at all. The boy's attachment to the mother is, from the very beginning, 'heterosexual' – at least in Butler's terms. He therefore has no homosexual attachments that he is forced to disavow in order to accede to heterosexuality, since his primary orientation is, in these terms, 'heterosexual'. In the earlier version of the theory what the boy gave up was *his feminine sexual dispositions* and this was the way in which it could be said that he was giving up a *homosexual (feminine)* cathexis to his mother. Once the idea of masculine or feminine sexual dispositions is given up the idea of the boy having an initial homosexual attachment to his mother is lost and this would logically imply that male gender identities could no longer be argued to be melancholic.

However, Butler continues to maintain the relevance of the theory to masculinity by speaking of the necessity of the 'normal' heterosexual man to repudiate femininity:

> Becoming a 'man' within this logic requires repudiating femininity as a precondition for the heterosexualization of sexual desire and its fundamental ambivalence...the desire for the feminine is marked by that repudiation: he wants

the woman he would never be. He wouldn't be caught dead being her: therefore he wants her. She is his repudiated identification. (1997: 137)

Here we need to ask: what is this feminine that is being repudiated? It is not a sexual disposition. For the infant boy, the feminine, no less than the masculine, is something to be acquired (out of disorganized active and passive impulses and so on). It is not something 'there' to be repudiated or identified with. Femininity, to an infant boy (or girl), is an unknown, sociological notion. The theory of gender identity advanced here is one of cross-gender (repudiated) identification. Furthermore, there are in actual fact two *different* and counterbalanced processes of identification in play, which are differentially emphasized for each sex: the girl's *incorporative* (melancholic) identification with her mother *qua* debarred homosexual object choice and the boy's *repudiated* identification with the feminine, which were it not repudiated would result in homosexuality.

There is what looks like something of a sleight of hand here: for the girl, her mother is debarred as an object of desire so she incorporates her into her ego, and in some senses becomes her: she thereby becomes gendered. For the boy, his father is debarred as an object of desire, so he too has to identify with him, incorporating him into his ego and becoming gendered. But the boy's initial object of desire is his mother. How is he to relinquish her? The answer is that, in losing her, he must also identify with her, but that identification cannot be gendering so it must be repudiated. The foreclosing of the inappropriate object of desire, however, is also described as a repudiation. Both boy and girl, then, effectively repudiate the mother as object of desire but, for the boy, that object of desire is only inappropriate by virtue of being incestuous, so that here identification serves to heterosexualize desire rather than to produce gendering. It is almost as if, for the boy the mechanism goes in reverse, repudiation of a gender is there to produce desire for the correct object, whereas for the girl, repudiation of a desire is there to produce gendering. Is the lost object of desire for the boy the mother or the father? Arguably, of course, it is inevitably both, which is what allows both types of identification to hold sway for both sexes where relevant.

Positive and negative complexes notwithstanding, there is still the matter of the asymmetry of the Oedipus complex. The problem here is how to square the asymmetry of these different identificatory processes with the general idea that gender is melancholic, or, alternatively, how to reconcile the general claim about the melancholic character of gender, which suggests an apparent symmetry, with the asymmetry of the Oedipus complex. In other words, attempting to inhabit Butler's account is somewhat like being in a theoretical hall of mirrors. This need only worry us, however, if we take it on trust that the debarring of homosexual attachments *is* the key to us all becoming little boys and little girls.

Allowing, *for the moment*, that the boy repudiates the feminine, we should consider the matter of 'becoming a woman'. This would point to the repudiation of the masculine in order to produce the cross-gender identification that is one of the bases of the theory. Freud, of course, thought no such thing. What the girl repudiates on the way to 'normal' femininity is not the masculine but the feminine. Freud thought that one of the great problems of the world was the repudiation of the feminine *by both men and women*. The girl breaks with her mother at the moment of the castration complex. She hates her mother, and hence is able to separate from her, for failing to provide her with a penis – for giving her a castrated body: the narcissistic wound. If we do accept this account of the heterosexualization of desire for the boy, this is the conundrum that confronts us. Nevertheless, Butler – like Freud – also casts some doubt on the idea that gender identities, particularly the homosexual, should be thought of in terms of cross-gender identifications and repudiated identifications (1997: 146). This would be to suggest a theory of psychic hermaphroditism ('a feminine brain in a masculine body') to which Freud repeatedly gave short shrift.[9]

Finally, there is a further problem, to which we alluded above. Butler regards the acquisition of heterosexuality in terms of the bar against 'homosexual' attachments, pointing out that the ego has been formed by bringing into it the identifications of objects that must be given up in the Oedipal situation. As she notes, Freud says that identification may be the sole condition under which the id can give up its objects (1997: 133). But this means that the boy's (gendered) ego would be feminine. The boy must give up his (let us assume feminine) mother. He can only do that by identifying with her, bringing her into his ego. But if this was what typically *did happen*, then, within this logic, the (feminine) boy's 'normal' object choice would be homosexual and of course it is not. This is a puzzle endemic to Butler's scheme and supported by many of Freud's remarks. How can it be resolved? The short answer is that Butler resolves it by the differential stress on the identification processes of boy and girl: for the boy successfully to repudiate the feminine and become masculine, the stress has to be placed not on the loss of the mother but, implicitly, on that of the father. It is through the *cross-gender* (repudiated) identification of the man that identification with the masculine is able to be sustained.

Hetero- and homosexuality, then, must be considered to be organized genital sexual states, *the result* of the vicissitudinous journey, states that are never securely obtained. This criticism – that Butler has attributed the character of organized genital states to component instincts – is, however, one that Butler levels at psychoanalysis itself, arguing that '[t]he oedipal complex presumes that heterosexual desire has already been *accomplished*' (1997: 135, emphasis in original). Freud's early attraction to ideas of bisexuality and masculine and feminine sexual dispositions does indeed lead to such a presumption – a presumption that Butler seems to repeat. However, the account of the infant as polymorphously perverse runs counter to such a conception. An infant's attachment to the breast is oral and the aim is pleasure from sucking. That the infant may be a girl does not make the attachment 'homosexual'. Freud described the form of the attachment to the mother on the part of *both* infants as 'masculine'. The infant boy and girl share the same 'active' libido characterized, culturally, as masculine. Hence if one were to speak in terms of organized stable sexualities (which is of course impossible at this stage) one would have to describe the infant girl's attachment to her mother as *heterosexual*.

Freud came to recognize the great importance of the pre-Oedipal attachment of the infant girl (and also of the infant boy) to the mother only late in his life (1933: 129). In this context he suggests that the character of the attachment is various and not well known. He speaks of the girl's attachments as both masculine *and* feminine:

> We shall be glad to know the nature of the girl's libidinal relations to her mother. The answer is that they are of very many different kinds. Since they persist through all three stages of infantile sexuality, they also take on the characteristics of the different phases and express themselves by oral, sadistic-anal and phallic wishes. These wishes express active as well as passive impulses; if we relate them to the differentiation of the sexes which is to appear later – *though we should avoid doing so as far as possible* – we may call them masculine and feminine. (1933: 119-20, emphasis added)

The consequence of all of this is to make it difficult indeed to characterize these pre-Oedipal and Oedipal attachments as 'homosexual'.

Melancholic loss

If we assume for a moment that it is proper to characterize the attachments of infant children as 'homosexual', it is still difficult to see why it is said that the key prohibition necessary for the achievement of heterosexuality is the disavowal of homosexuality. The short answer, of course, is that the stress on the prohibition on homosexual attachments and the ungrieved and ungrievable response to that loss comes from the dialectic of the Oedipal schema. In one sense this is uncontroversial since Freud's account of 'normal' femininity does centre on the requirement to make heterosexual object choices. But in the psychic journey to heterosexuality securing heterosexual object choices is not the direct converse of repudiating 'homosexual' ones. The child has to give up many attachments along the way. The story of the development of the child is that of the break-up of the psychic monad. The infant's pleasure is initially closed in on itself: it is auto-erotic, then narcissistic. There is no given path that takes it towards the acquisition of objects, which are *contingent*. As Laplanche and Pontalis put it, '[i]t is in the evolution of human sexuality, and in the way that it is structured by the Oedipus complex, that Freud seeks the *preconditions* of access to what he calls "full object-love"' (1980: 381, emphasis added). At the Oedipal stage, Freud does talk about 'homosexual' and 'heterosexual' object choices and does grant them the full dignity of describing them as forms of love no less deserving of being taken seriously. But the Oedipus complex is also co-terminous with the unification of the component instincts under the dominance of the phallic phase. The problem is that there is a gap between the cultural prohibition on the forms of 'full object-love' defined as homosexual and these pre-genital attachments to objects that from the vantage point of adult genitality could be termed 'homosexual'. The desire to read psychoanalysis as a theory of the installation of a culture makes it tempting to conflate them.

The point is that *there is nothing special about the loss of homosexual attachments* in all this. One might just as well say that normal gender is bought at the price of burying an attachment to faecal matter, of an ungrieved and ungrievable loss for shit. An attachment to its own faeces is precisely what characterizes the child's anal-sadistic phase of psychosexual development. At this phase, the child's object relationship is not to its mother's breast but to the function of defecation and to the symbolic value of its own faeces, with their expulsion/retention; with giving and withholding; with the symbolic equation faeces = gift. But this cathexis has to be broken for 'normal' psychosexual development. One may as well speak of incorporating an attachment to faecal matter as an identification with a part-object that is psychically preserved and haunts the ego as one of the lost objects out of which it is constituted. Of course one can properly characterize the social world as hegemonically heterosexual and with a general prohibition against homosexuality. There is also a prohibition against cathexis to your own (or other people's) shit. This is not intended to be offensive but to suggest that, outside very *particular* forms of explanation (e.g. the genesis of paranoia), psychoanalytic logic offers no special place to the loss of 'homosexual' attachments. The sexual impulses that one is forced to abandon on the journey to genitality cannot be described as having such a clear and cohesive identity. Only from the vantage point of a political concern with heterosexuality do homosexual attachments assume this kind of importance.

The Wolf Man case history is instructive here because it demonstrates just how complex and particularistic are the negotiations of the various attachments. The Wolf Man, because of his experience of the primal scene to which he was exposed,[10] retained an attachment to faecal matter, which expressed itself in extremely recalcitrant disturbances of intestinal function. These disturbances represented, as Freud saw it, the small hysterical underpinning of the obsessional neurosis which he had carried over more or less unchanged since childhood, and Freud persuaded the hysterical organ to 'join in the conversation' during the course of the analysis. In that symptom were wrapped up a dread of death; the repudiated identification with his mother in the primal scene (repudiated because it entailed castration); his sexual excitation at that point; the regression from that knowledge to a cloacal theory of sexuality which avoided the implication of castration; his rivalrous relation to his sister in respect of his father; his jealousy of his mother for having loved a child other than himself; his disparagement of God, and so on. As Freud put it, his intestinal disorder had put itself in the service of his (feminine) homosexual attachment to his father and was both prototypical of and simultaneously refusing of castration, but it was by no means a simple concatenation of ideas:

> In this connection, once again, he behaved in the manner which was so characteristic of him, but which makes it so difficult to give a clear account of his mental processes or to feel one's way into them. First he resisted and then he yielded; but the second reaction did not *do away* with the first. In the end there were to be found in him two contrary currents side by side, of which one abominated the idea of castration, while the other was prepared to accept it and console itself with femininity as a compensation. But beyond any doubt a third current, the oldest and deepest, which did not as yet even raise the question of

the reality of castration, was still capable of coming into activity. (1918[1914]: 85, emphasis in original)

What is striking about this is that, for the Wolf Man, the repressed feminine currents represent a *compensation* for castration, which he learns, through the primal scene, is the price of love from his father. The dilemma, then, is also not about the sex that *he* cannot love, but from whom love comes at a price, a price he both accepts and rejects. We are therefore already at some distance from Butler's 'heterosexual matrix', in which heterosexuality is bought at the price of the loss of homosexuality, if by 'matrix' we understand a set of combinatorial possibilities.[11] The Wolf Man displays an ostensible heterosexuality which represents something like the *preservation* of a passive and homosexual current (also a later development in his life than his heterosexual cathexes), not through melancholic identification, but through the *compromise* that his choice of object represents. The servant girls who constitute his only possible object of desire represent his revenge against his sister for being his father's favourite. Even in his heterosexual choices, then, it is his father's love that he is courting. Although this is a retention of homosexual object choice within heterosexuality, it is not in the form of a correlative melancholic identification, but is right at its heart.

The character of identification

Even if we were to give homosexuality such a pivotal role, there is still the issue of how it engenders gender, the issue of identification. The point is that what is incorporated into the ego when the love object is lost are not necessarily characteristics of the object that derive from its membership of a particular social category. It is not that the love object happens to be male or female or sexless and inanimate that matters. *It is what the love object represented for the subject*, its symbolic or phantasied significance. To speak of the social categories to which the love object belongs, in those cases where the object is human, is to sociologize psychic processes. Remember that an identification may be with a trait or an act of speech or a suffering organ (in hypochondria) or with the whole world (in megalomania). In discussing two examples of identification Freud once observed that, '[i]t must also strike us that in both cases the identification is a partial and extremely limited one and *borrows a single trait* from the person who is its object' (1921: 39, emphasis added). One of the examples of this given by Freud is of the Oedipal rivalry of a girl who develops her mother's painful cough, so that the symptom neatly condenses the wish to substitute for her and the punishment for that wish. What is brought into the ego, then, may not be assumed to be a (generalized) homosexual loss or a heterosexual loss. The question must always be, what property or attribute of the object is being identified with? Hence the fact that the object may be a member of a social group (woman of colour, person with disability, working-class man, or, more simply, male or female) *may* be quite irrelevant. There is simply no general, sociological, rule that may be applied here. The question is, if one *does* become a 'gender', what is the 'gender' that one becomes? What does 'being a girl' or 'being a boy' *mean*?

Laplanche has indicated how relatively problematic the conceptualization of identification is. In spite of repeated attempts by Freud to define and specify different types of identification, 'the notion remains either too simplistic or too vague, as though it were being used to mask under a single rubric phenomena which are quite diverse' (1976: 79). Laplanche therefore sets out to distinguish types of identification in terms of three things: what is being identified with, the process and the result. In relation to the first, he raises one issue over and above what we have mentioned above, which is relevant to the process that Butler is describing: 'If identification, with the whole object, what sense is to be attributed to that "wholeness"? Is it, for example, a perceptual totum?' (ibid.) This seems appropriate, he says, in relation to the genesis of the ego but, at times, the idea of the 'whole object' seems to designate something else. He links this to Melanie Klein's stipulations about the *response* of another human being. More important for our purposes is the issue of the modality of the identification, which he raises in discussing the process:

> An examination of the process in play would lead us to ask if there is a common denominator among phenomena habitually classed under the same rubric: the early perceptual imprint, of which the most striking examples in animal psychology are revealed by ethology; the introjection of an object, an act modeled on a bodily process; or a type of identification, referring explicitly to structure: an identification with the *position* of the other, which consequently presupposes an interpersonal interplay of relations and, as a rule, at least two other positions coinciding with the vertices of a triangle: clearly such would be the case for oedipal identifications. (1976: 80)

Butler seems to have elected to go predominantly with the first two of these, in a way which tends to depart from the earlier feminist stress on positionality in relation to the phallus and from the evidence in a case history like that of the Wolf Man. However, her discussion of Lacan in 'The Lesbian Phallus and the Morphological Imaginary' (Butler: 1993) also suggests otherwise.

The Oedipus complex

Whatever the character of identification, there is a more general question of whether or not the Oedipus complex does, as Butler, and indeed Freud, claim, function to knot together appropriate object choice, identification and the acquisition of the instinctual dispositions that are said to be characteristic of 'femininity' and 'masculinity'. In an extended and complex discussion of identification and the Oedipus complex (1991, 1996), Parveen Adams has drawn attention to what she says are *two* accounts of 'femininity' and 'masculinity' which are to be found in Freud's texts, one of which, she argues, is not derivable from the terms of Freud's psychical system. The first, which is fundamentally that of the positionality we have just described, is one in which a term like 'femininity' can be assumed to have no content other than its difference from the other term, 'masculinity'. This was the one preferred by much post-Lacanian feminism since it tended to suggest the fictitiousness of those images of femininity from which it had sought to distance itself. There is, however, a description of a content to 'femininity' and 'masculinity' in Freud, a content which is alleged to be put in place by the phallic differentiation. In an analysis of two dreams from *The Interpretation of Dreams*, one the hysteric's dream of the smoked salmon and the other a dream of Freud's (the uncle with the yellow beard), and an examination of the case history of Dora, Adams argues that this second account does not work.

As she points out, Freud assumed a certain logic for the relation between identification and object choice. The boy child, for example, 'has not merely an ambivalent attitude towards his father and an affectionate object-choice towards his mother, but at the same time *he also behaves like a girl* and displays an affectionate feminine attitude to his father and a corresponding jealousy and hostility towards his mother' (Freud, 1923: 33, emphasis added). We should note, incidentally, that at the heart of this Oedipal dynamic there is presumed to be a fundamental heterosexuality: an object-cathexis for one's father, if one is a boy, automatically implies femininity. This is how Freud describes the progression of the positive complex for the boy in *The Ego and the Id*:

In its simplified form the case of the male child may be described as follows. At a very early age the little boy develops an object-cathexis for his mother, which originally related to the mother's breast and is the prototype of an object-choice on the anaclitic model: the boy deals with his father by identifying himself with him. For a time these two relationships proceed side by side, until the boy's sexual wishes in regard to his mother become more intense and his father is perceived as an obstacle to them; from this the Oedipus complex originates. His identification with his father then takes on a hostile colouring and changes into a wish to get rid of his father in order to take his place with his mother. Henceforward his relation to his father is ambivalent; it seems as if the ambivalence inherent in identification from the beginning had become manifest. An ambivalent attitude to his father and an object-relation of a solely affectionate kind to his mother make up the content of the simple positive Oedipus complex in a boy.

Along with the demolition of the Oedipus complex, the boy's object-cathexis of his mother must be given up. Its place may be filled by one of two things: either an identification with his mother or an intensification of his identification with his father. We are accustomed to regard the latter outcome as the more normal; it permits the affectionate relation to the mother to be in a measure retained. In this way the dissolution of the Oedipus complex would consolidate the masculinity in a boy's character. (1923: 31-2)

Freud makes it clear in this passage that there is an early identification with the figure of the father, which results in 'masculinity'. This is the way in which Butler can consistently maintain both a pre-Oedipal, primordial identification which is gendered, and gendering which is the result of the melancholic Oedipal identification, since the latter could constitute a regression to the former. Freud maintains, after all, that identification is the first form of the relation to the object. However, the question, for both Butler and Freud, is how we reconcile the idea that children only give meaning to the difference between the sexes at the height of the phallic phase, which is the stage of the Oedipus complex, and then only within the terms phallic/castrated. Here it looks as if the pre-Oedipal child clearly knows what's what. Furthermore, how do we relate Freud's account here to that of the character of pre-Oedipal attachments and the nature of the instinctual dispositions as both active *and* passive, 'masculine' *and* 'feminine'? What is the 'masculinity' that is consolidated here?

In relation to the case history of Dora, Adams asks whether identification with a man, a masculine identification, necessarily implies choice of a woman as object, or identification with a woman, a feminine identification, choice of a man as an object. The implication in an Oedipal scenario is that if you can establish who is being identified with, you can establish whom it is that someone loves, in other words that identification and object choice are correlative. Dora was caught up in the midst of a love affair between her father and a married woman called Frau K., and an attempted seduction by Herr K., whose advances she had repelled. Freud read this as an Oedipal scenario (which concealed a repressed love for Herr K.) in which Frau K. was Dora's rival for her father's affections. Freud had identified a symptom of Dora's, a cough, with a phantasy in which, as he put it: ' she pictured to herself a scene of sexual gratification *per os* between the two people whose love affair occupied her mind so incessantly' (1905a: 48). But this sentence, as Neil Hertz has pointed out, does not make it clear 'who is gratifying whom, *per* whose *os* the pleasure is being procured, or with whom Dora is identifying' (cited in Adams, 1996: 21). As Adams notes, there has been much crowing over the idea that Freud failed to notice that the principal object of desire in Dora's case was Frau K. rather than Herr K., female rather than male. In other words, the suggestion is that Freud came up with the wrong phantasy: he was phallocentrically blind to the importance of Dora's love for Frau K. and he therefore assumed, wrongly, that she was identifying with Frau K. in the phantasied scenario. But the question of which phantasy is the 'correct' one, Adams argues, is rather beside the point. In identifying the underlying phantasy in Dora's case, both Freud and his commentators forget one crucial element and that is that a phantasy, as a scenario, allows for interchangeability of positions, a point which is made in *Instincts and Their Vicissitudes* (1915). This implies that where there is masochism, there is also sadism; where there is passivity, activity; where there is scopophilia, there is also exhibitionism. It is not only that Dora's own identification, as an hysteric, is bisexual, or oscillatory, it is that the drive *itself* is oscillatory:

> Hysterical identification is characterised, it turns out, by oscillation. Of course I know that Freud recognized the bisexual identifications of the hysteric. But it is one thing to say that the hysteric identifies with both men and women and quite another to say that where there is identification with one there is also identification with the other. (Adams, 1996: 14)

What this means is that in Dora's phantasy there are not in fact two positions for her to identify with but four: 'Dora must suck and be sucked regardless' (1996: 21). This has a further consequence if we conceive of some of these alternatives, say activity and passivity, as components of 'masculinity' or 'femininity' and that is that these pairs cannot meaningfully be split. 'Activity' cannot be assigned to the one and 'passivity' to the other. Furthermore, as Adams argues in the first version of her chapter (1991), the components of these pairs of opposites, although they are meant to coincide under the headings of 'masculinity' or 'femininity', often appear to have rather tangential relations to one another: 'Reading modern accounts of masochism it seems not only that the passivity is at best secondary, but more importantly has nothing to do with femininity' (1991: 84). The puzzle that continues to play itself out, and in fact to deepen, is: *if* we are identifying with a 'gender', what does that 'gender' comprise?

Adams' discussion implies that we cannot conceive of psychoanalysis as providing us with an account of 'femininity' or 'masculinity' as an identificatory position that arrests and fixes this oscillation of the drive, nor one in which identification and object choice go together. It suggests, in other words, that the logic that binds identification, object choice and instinctual dispositions collapses. She argues that 'where there is identification with the woman, there is also identification with the man' (1996: 13). What this means is that we cannot look to the Oedipus complex as a formula that prescribes the installation of a content for masculinity and femininity through a logic that links identification and object choice. To this we could place a further question mark over how what are described as 'instinctual dispositions', such as passivity or activity for example, the alleged content of 'femininity' and 'masculinity', could be *guaranteed* by identification with a sexed figure, a woman or a man. There are a number of problems, then, in construing gender as the product of a heterosexual matrix.

Gender as hyperbole

The questions to be addressed to Judith Butler's highly creative argument are not those that concern Talmudic truths of psychoanalysis. One can only contest the claims made by means of an exegesis of a psychoanalytic logic in psychoanalytic terms, as we do here. The problem still remains of the precise use that Judith Butler is intending to make of psychoanalysis and of its status in her account. If Butler's account of gender *is* a hyperbolic construction, then why is it so? Why should one *need* to render the account hyperbolic?

Perhaps that is the key to the issues we have explored here. To what extent will Butler's use of psychoanalysis, because it obeys a cultural and political agenda, produce a very particular reading of psychoanalysis? What we have suggested is that it does and that it runs counter to what we take to be some of the fundamental characteristics of psychoanalysis as a form of explanation of human behaviour. The *Ego and the Id* is a text which allows for a much more sociological reading of psychoanalysis than do other texts. For example, it allows for an interpretation of objects which is much closer to that of whole persons. Beginning from an end point, which is the political concern with the consolidation of 'gender', may tend to read this back into a past for which it is inappropriate, in other words to sociologize the psyche at the Oedipal and pre-Oedipal stages. In a recent interview Butler speaks enthusiastically about the application of this theory of gender melancholy to 'race' (Bell, 1999). One has to wonder at this, however, for we seem now to be heading firmly into the territory of the 'et cetera clause' in which designations and identities accumulate in the pursuit of empirical specificity (see Cealey Harrison and Hood-Williams, 1998). To give all of these a construction is to attempt to provide a more consolidated basis for what Denise Riley has described as the pressing problem 'for any emancipating movement which launches itself on the appeal to solidarity, to the common cause of a new group being, or an ignored group identity', in other words the impermanence of collective identities (1988: 16).

  This is not to suggest that it is improper to consider the social in relation to the psyche; one could in point of fact describe the psyche as the meeting point of the social and the instinctual. By contrast, how one is to identify the 'sociality' in a case history in which psyche, social situation, culture and interpersonal dynamics are all of a piece is a complex question and not one to be resolved through granting an implied ontological dominance to the social and the cultural and reading the construction of the psyche in terms of a general account of the institution of a cultural prohibition on a particular form of sexuality. If there is a cultural prohibition at stake here, it is not the one against homosexuality but the one against incest. Homosexuality, coprophilia, voyeurism, and any number of other perversions – deviations from the 'path' of heterosexuality – are a 'part of the deal', since polymorphous sexuality has to be turned into adult genitality, but not the crucial pivot around which the institution of culture turns.

  Butler's account is certainly licensed by some aspects of the Freudian account, and, in particular, by the basic structure of the Oedipal dialectic as it was described by Freud. The fact that there are problems with this dialectic is, we feel, related to the fact that it fails in some measure to obey the portrayal of the human being that one finds in many of the case studies, and in some of the more detailed conceptualizations and specific stipulations, such as the one about the nature of the instinct. The picture of the human being emergent there, the polymorphously perverse infant, for whom heterosexual genitality is only achieved by means of the 'soldering together' of a diversity of components, the creature whose orientation to the object is achieved through contingency, and for whom 'masculinity' and 'femininity' constitute culturally constructed complexes to which it feels that it must solder its desire, seems to us to be a very compelling one. There is much more mobility and flexibility in this picture and, indeed, much more psychic, social and historical specificity than in a concept of 'gender'.

  Are we, then, in *any* way warranted in describing the ego as gendered? In a starkly hyperbolic, what we might call a sociological sense, one might just about be able to say, *perhaps*. However, when we remember that the ego is also an agency such an idea becomes much more troublesome. If it is a sedimentation of objects loved and lost, what does that sedimentation consists of? And insofar as this first sociological sense is common parlance it might not be telling us very much. We do know that people go around thinking of themselves as 'gendered'. But what that means, what contents are invoked, how radically incoherent such conceptions are, how tightly and how consistently they cleave to such notions are difficult and interesting questions. And it is in Freud's case histories that we find the most dramatic demonstrations of these various difficulties.

Once we take on Freud's insight that the development of 'masculinity' or 'femininity' is consonant with the development of sexual object choices, we face opportunities and puzzles. What is an object choice, or better, what do we choose when we make an object choice? Freud once said that all choices were typically narcissistic. More precisely, if not all libidinal relations then all love relations might be regarded as narcissistic (Laplanche, 1976: 77). Does that make us all, typically, homosexual? According to Freud, in his 1915 footnote to the *Three Essays*, psychoanalysis 'has found that all human beings are capable of making a homosexual object choice and have in fact made one in their unconscious' (1905b in *SE*, 1956: 145). And if we have all made one we cannot be melancholic for having had such a choice foreclosed. There is also the problem of what it is that one chooses in making what is deemed to be a 'heterosexual' or a 'homosexual' object choice. If, in psychoanalytic terms, a man chooses a woman with a developed 'mental masculinity' and a fierce clitoral attachment, in what sense is that choice 'the same' as another man chosen by a passive, feminine, vaginal, woman (since, as Freud notes, even 'passive' aims can involve enormous amounts of activity)? In genital sexuality does one choose an *organ*? And is the maleness of the man sufficient to make these encounters the same?

In his 1920 footnote to the *Three Essays*, Freud, quoting Ferenczi, noted that 'a large number of conditions, which are very different from one another and which are of unequal importance both in organic and psychical respects, have been thrown together under the name of "homosexuality"' (1905b in *SE*, 1956: 146-7). Everything he wrote on the subject tells us that he knew that this applied equally well to heterosexuality. But *if* a heterosexual object choice is the linch-pin of 'normal' femininity or masculinity, what happens when we recognize its disaggregated character? And if we want to cleave to a concept of 'gender', does it mean that gender only makes sense as a statistical abstraction that never exists anywhere? Consider the choices made by the Wolf Man (Freud, 1918 [1914]) or the young girl in 'The Psychogenesis of a Case of Homosexuality in a Woman' (Freud, 1920). These are choices of the greatest particularity. Can they be illuminated by stark hyperbole?

In a discussion with Rosi Braidotti, in which Braidotti describes the sex/gender framework as re-essentializing sex, Butler echoes this with a refusal of the sexual difference framework as a linguistically essentialist approach. Braidotti's reply is that she does not recognize this reading of sexual difference other than as a caricature, describing it as a classical anti-sexual difference line first formulated by Monique Plaza and then repeated by Monique Wittig, Christine Delphy and the whole editorial board of *Questions féministes*, according to whom sexual difference is psychically essentialist, ahistorical and apolitical. She reads it, she says, as entirely the *opposite* of this (ibid.). This criticism is an interesting one, because it seems to us that Butler's choice to read a psychoanalytic account of difference through the lens of 'gender', in spite of its aim of avoiding fixity and inflexibility – its politicizing and historicizing intentions – tends to produce just such an effect of psychical essentialism and ahistoricity. Although her account is suggestive, because it represents a particular *kind* of reading, it seems to lose much of the flexibility and particularity – which is potentially a *social and historical* particularity – of the Freudian account. Psychoanalysis is often at its weakest when it seeks to generalize about women and men and forgets its roots in the laboratory of the consulting room and the complexities of a case history. Using it to explain 'gender' unfortunately does the same thing. How human beings negotiate and situate themselves vis-à-vis the cultural designations of, and the meanings they ascribe to, being 'a woman' or 'a man' is always highly specific.

Notes

[1] 'Incorporation' is regarded in psychoanalysis as one of the prototypical forms of identification, whereas 'internalization' is seen to refer to intersubjective relations (see Laplanche and Pontalis, 1980: 297-8).

[2] Freud does compare the process here to the process observed in melancholia (of an alteration in the ego consequent upon the setting up of an object *inside* it), but he states that the exact nature of the substitution is unknown.

[3] The text on which Lacan relies quite substantially for his elaboration of this concept is that of the case history of the Wolf Man, a text we shall use for different purposes later on.

[4] There are also other puzzles here: 'foreclosure' relates to the very early stages of the acquisition of the symbolic, in other words, for Lacan, to the acquisition of language. Even allowing for the links that Lacan makes between the acquisition of the law of the symbolic and the installation of sexual difference, Freud's conception of the Oedipus complex and his account of melancholia both relate to somewhat later stages in the life of the human being. Although Lacan's use of the French term 'forclusion' is licensed by Freud's 'Verwerfung', there are differences between the ways in which each of them uses the respective terms.

[5] In fact, as Steven Connor noted, the title of Anzieu's 1985 book *Le Moi-Peau* might well have been translated as *The Ego-Skin*, rather than as *The Skin Ego*.

[6] He does, however, talks of the Wolf Man experiencing an affront to his masculinity and whilst this clearly refers to his image of himself, what he takes himself to be (his ego-ideal?), it does not necessarily mean that his *ego* has 'masculine' or 'feminine' characteristics.

[7] The ego-ideal was originally not distinguished from the super-ego by Freud, but later came to constitute a *function* of it.

[8] But that is rather the point: what happens to the insights of psychoanalysis when one seeks to deploy it to other purposes? See Cealey Harrison, 1995.

[9] For a more extended discussion of this, see Hood-Williams and Cealey Harrison, 2000).

[10] The primal scene to which the Wolf Man was exposed, at the age of around eighteen months, was allegedly one of coitus *a tergo*, in which the sight of the female genital, interpreted retroactively, confirmed for him the reality of castration as the cost of being loved by his father, for whose love he had been in competition with his older sister.

[11] Freud does nevertheless present the Wolf Man's choices in terms of passive femininity (his mother's position) versus active masculinity (his father's position) but this is given by the child's assumptions about what is happening in the primal scene. Freud undoubtedly also reads this in terms of the classical Oedipal schema with which it so helpfully coincides.

11 The Vagaries of Language

Denise Riley's elegant essay of 1987 'Does a Sex Have a History?', and its later version in her book *Am I That Name?* (published the following year), take us full circle back to the beginning of our exploration. Like Ann Oakley, she describes what she calls the historical 'loops' by means of which women cycle between a refusal to inhabit the femininities that are thrust upon them and an assertion of an alternative, but no less compelling, account of a female nature, which, as she says, an older feminism had always sought to shred to bits. But, unlike Oakley, she doesn't seek to settle the argument, but to avoid re-treading these loops entirely, recognizing that 'factions flourish in the shade cast by this powerful naturalism about "women"' (Riley, 1988: 36). Instead, she suggests the making of a grander gesture, that of stepping back and announcing that 'women' *are not*. In other words, not only should we dodge the very suspect 'Woman', whose capital letter, as she puts it, alerts us to her dangers, or, indeed, the more modest, lower-case 'woman', which is overshadowed by her, but we should also extend our suspicions to the innocent-sounding 'women', that ordinary, commonsensical collectivity:

> And here someone might retort that there *are* real, 'concrete' women and there always have been. There were women long before the nineteenth century unfolded its tedious course. What Foucault did for 'the homosexual' cannot be done for women, and historical constructionism has run mad if it's thought otherwise. Nor can it be overlooked that women's distinctive needs and sufferings are all too real. And then how is it possible to have a politics of women – feminism – if that's accompanied by an apparent disdain for real women? (1987: 36)

That last point, that one cannot have a politics of women if one does not sustain a conceptual category of 'women', embodies a number of problems. First, it confuses the political gestures one might make with the analytical categories which it is necessary to use in order successfully to make sense of what is happening. This is not to say, necessarily, that one might cynically employ a category for rhetorical purposes in which one did not believe, but it is to suggest, as Barry Hindess and Paul Hirst (1977) pointed out, that a distinction needs to be made between theoretical analysis and the conditions of political calculation. Secondly, it tends to imply that, if we can identify distinctive needs and sufferings for women, they must self-evidently exist as a category *sui generis*. Or, alternatively, it seems to suggest, quite unacceptably as far as we are concerned, that political imperatives should drive the nature of the theory that one produces. Marx's nostrum about philosophers seeking only to understand the world is here given rather too wide an interpretation, an interpretation at which, given his painstaking struggles in *Capital* to understand such things as the mysterious character of the commodity, we believe he might have been alarmed.

Since, as Riley points out, women's sufferings are a function of the way in which women are conceived of and 'positioned, often harshly or stupidly, as "women", a positioning in languages and in practices', it makes little sense to counterpose 'women' as an entity to what gets said about them, which is what a notion of the natural collectivity of women does (1987: 36). Neither do the progressive or reactionary implications flow naturally from the nature of the words or the ideas used. As Hilary Allen (1990) has pointed out, sometimes an apparently helpful 'naming', like that of the 'recognition' of pre-menstrual tension and its use as the basis for a defence in a criminal trial, could be deemed to have potentially deleterious effects. Whether such a practice would or would not have such effects is, of course, a matter for calculation; for Allen, in this instance, the potential consequences are quite specific. Based upon a calculation of the numbers of women who might, on such a legal precedent, claim special treatment (25 per cent for 25 per cent of the time) and relating it to the rather smaller numbers of individuals who could claim psychological disorders that they might wish to have taken into account (e.g. one in thirty for depression, one in a hundred for schizophrenia) one could expect such a basis for defence to have major legal consequences:

> First, one would expect a major increase in the absolute number of cases in which mental abnormality would be deemed relevant to legal decision-making, and thus an absolute increase in the involvement of the medical profession in the criminal law. Second, since this absolute increase would be entirely restricted to women, it would result in a massive increase in the (already existing) sexual *disparity* in the deployment of medical and psychiatric evidence in legal actions. Third, and as a corollary, it would result in an overall change in the sentencing patterns for female offenders, with a significant reduction in the imposition of severe and custodial sentences and an increase in the number of women receiving compulsory medical treatment. (1990: 210)

Each of the variable invocations of 'women', then, has to be explored; it will not be a matter of lining them up on one or other side as pro- or anti-women with a reference point that we can take for granted. As Riley says, who will be addressed or defined as 'women', how they will be addressed or defined and under what circumstances 'often needs some effort of translation to follow. For becoming, or indeed desisting from being named as, a sexed creature is a restless business' (1987: 37).

A restless business

It is interesting to note that the category she invokes here at the core of the process of 'naming' is that of the 'sexed creature'. In short, in the parlance of sex/gender, what is at stake in a gendering process is the *sexing* of a group. 'Women' as individuals, or indeed as clusters of individuals, are sometimes sexed and sometimes not: there is no gap between this and 'gender'. In a very precise sense, then, 'gender' is about being, at given moments and for given periods of time and for particular reasons and with a given content, sexed. In other words, in terms of the disposition of concepts within the sex/gender problematic, sex and gender are here given a different relationship. In the classic version of the sex/gender problematic, women are, *of necessity*, sexed – they are, after all women – and it is in this sense that 'women' are deemed naturalistically to *exist*. 'Gendering' is then about the giving of meaning and social consequences to that 'reality'. Within this alternative optic of Riley's, women are sometimes invoked as 'women' and sometimes not, with particular contents to that invocation, but what that invocation represents *is* the reproductive differentiation (which would nowadays invoke the category of sex) of a human being for social purposes. If we extend that idea, and think back to the work of Kessler and McKenna, we could talk about the sexing of the child at birth as the first and foundational social ascription of the label, which will then make possible all of the others. But these will not be consistent, in either content or duration. Taking for granted the concept of 'sex' as naturalistically defining of 'women' is, in a sense, homogenizing that which is not homogeneous. It means both forgetting that that early social ascription *is* an ascription and doing the job more thoroughly than the opponents of women have traditionally done.

This might seem to be a politically necessary gesture but for the fact that feminism itself has often been about refusing identifications of one kind or another. Twentieth-century European feminism, according to Riley, has been '*constitutionally* torn between fighting against over-feminization and against under-feminization, especially where social policies are concerned':

> For there are always too many invocations of 'women', too much visibility, too many appellations which were better dissolved again – or at best are in need of some accurate, delimiting handling. So that the precise specification of 'women' in the name of feminism might well occasionally mean forgetting 'women' or rather, *remembering them more helpfully by not naming them*. (1987: 37, emphasis added)

Even where feminism finds itself needing to take on or further delimit or specify an appellation or invocation, it is a tussle over the *content* of that appellation or invocation which is at stake.

Riley gives these invocations of women different temporalities, some long-term and relatively slow to alter, and some, as she puts it, descending like lightning from almost anywhere in the political firmament. Obviously, it is those with a longer temporality which allow the stability of the category of women to be assumed and taken for granted.. This means that there is no necessity, she says, for feminism to be caught between two equally inappropriate alternatives, between 'a political realism which will brook no nonsense about the uncertainties of "women" as a collectivity, and deconstructionist gestures without allegiances' (1987: 35). A belief in the solid existence of 'women' is neither necessary nor historically accurate; indeed it is the instability itself that has 'an historical foundation' (1987: 37-8).

She describes this historicity both within the longer chronologies by which 'collectivities and characterizations of "women" are established in a myriad historical-discursive formations' (1987: 38) and within what she describes as the odd phenomenology for each individual of possessing a sex. And here she makes a telling point in describing the ways in which a particular characterization can descend upon an individual, pulling her back into "being a woman" out of a reverie in which she was perhaps scarcely conscious of 'self' never mind of any kind of 'identity' as others might perceive it. It is a point reminiscent of the contention we saw in Goffman that all such 'identities' are portrayals of which the human being *qua* human being is capable, but which, as we have argued earlier, one only inhabits by 'believing in' – having an investment in – one's own portrayal(s) and accepting, correcting or modifying the portrayals foisted upon one:

> And the question of how far anyone can take on the identity of being a woman in a thoroughgoing manner recalls aspects of the 'fictive' status of sexual identities. Can anyone fully inhabit a gender without a degree of horror? How could someone 'be a woman' through and through, make a final home in that category without suffering claustrophobia – or hysteria? To lead a life soaked in the passionate consciousness of one's gender at every moment, to will to be a sex with a vengeance – impossibilities, and far from the aims of feminism. (1987: 38)

Indeed, for that way madness lies. And, whatever protestations people make, it would be hard to believe that any human being *could* live like that. Instead we are all of us in the business of negotiating how we feel about, and will respond to, the characterizations that are made of us. And sometimes one *cares* and sometimes one does not. As she says, citing Hanif Kureishi's character in *My Beautiful Laundrette*, who insists that he is a professional businessman not a professional Pakistani, 'more commonly, you will skate across the several identities which will take your weight, relying on the most useful for your purposes of the moment' (1988: 16). In that sense, identities as such do not exist, although there is undoubtedly the intermittent discursive negotiation of such characterizations as impinge.

Above whose bodies changing aerial descriptions dance

The point about the use of a concept of discourse to describe this is one that we have drawn attention to before. In other words, this is not a matter of a set of ideas *about* a pre-given reality termed 'women'; on the contrary, these characterizations and negotiations are the very stuff of social life. As Riley so delightfully puts it, 'nothing is assumed about an underlying continuity of real women above whose bodies changing aerial descriptions dance' (1987: 39).[1] To make such an assumption is to lose the full historicity – and, even, although Riley does not say it, the full psychical complexity – of what is at stake. That image, of a set of bodies with aerial descriptions above them, metaphorizes well the topology of the sex/gender distinction and makes it evident why it is that we have sought to displace it.

To miss the historicity of the categories is to miss the fact that 'women' is counterposed to other conceptions, which are themselves changing, which means that what the category 'women' entails, and the ways in which people will live it, will be historically specific. The apparently eternal polarity is, she says, an *air*, one whose achievement we have suggested that we need to seek to analyse. In this context, she mentions something we have noted before via the work of both Laqueur and Oudshoorn, which is the increasing sexualization of 'women', 'a process whereby female persons become held to be saturated with their sex, which invades their reasoning and spiritual faculties – this reaches a pitch of intensification in eighteenth-century Europe' (1987: 39-40). To the degree that the sexual polarity is taken to be eternal, it may largely be as a result of this most recent of sexualizations. It is no accident that what we might define as a recognizably contemporary feminism is born at around the same time.

Riley is careful to point out that what is to be found before that time by way of protestations by women against their characterization and treatment does not have the same character. Certainly, she says, there *appear* to be grounds for a kind of 'pre-feminism' in 'those fourteenth- and fifteenth-century treatises which began to work out a formal alignment of sex against sex' (1988: 10). But not only are these undoubtedly different from 'the earlier complicated typologies of the sexes of the works of the women mystics' (1988: 11), but they are also, whatever their furious lyricism or their stoical protest against the injustices visited upon them by men, made of different stuff. This is principally because they are not written against the background of an increasing sexualization which is progressively consolidating and imprisoning women behind what is defined as their sexual particularity, debarring them from access to a full humanity. It is the difference, she says, between an assertion in which women are 'glowingly moral and unjustly accused' and 'a sexual species fully apart' (1988: 13).

Thus, she seeks to tread between both the timeless polarities of 'women' and 'men' and a history of 'femininity' and 'masculinity' as *ideas*, avoiding both. The way in which she describes this is in terms of a history of 'massifications' or 'consolidations'. She is clear, therefore, that feminism's concern with the lack of homogeneity of the social category, the desire to allow for, as an example 'elderly Cantonese women living in Soho', is not the same concern as her own. It may be more *helpful* to refine the category 'women', but these are refinements built upon an existing ontological consistency. It is important to say, at this point, that not all invocations of 'women' will appeal to any kind of ontological consistency. If women constitute a category which is defined in relation to other categories which themselves change, this implies that the means by which 'women' will be explained, the entities that define the ontologies in relation to which they are constituted, will themselves change.

The slow loss of the democratic soul

This is most vividly demonstrated if we go back just a few centuries in European history to a point before the current sexualized regime came into being, in which 'it is femininity which comes to colour existence to the point of suffusion' (1988: 18). What was there beforehand can, however, be difficult to hear, muffled as it is behind that regime, now that the ideas that defined it have 'fallen away from our thought' (1988: 19). These ideas define a panorama which will be unfamiliar to us now, in which a triumvirate of mind, body and soul delineate the human person, and the soul is gender-indifferent:

> In the broad traditions of Christian theology, even though women's being may be dangerously close to the body, carnality is *not restricted* to the feminine, and the soul is relatively unscathed by its sex. But a newer and relatively secularised understanding of that person – in particular the woman, who became an ambulant Nature – represents a differently constructed ensemble altogether. The gradual processes of secularisation and theological revision were accompanied by an increasing sexualisation which crowded out the autonomous soul –while at the same time a particularly feminised conception of Nature began to develop. (1988: 18, emphasis added)

This 'slow loss of the democratic soul' (ibid.) displaced a field of philosophical and theological disputation going back into Antiquity in which the neutrality of the soul may be endangered by its proximity to the body but is not fundamentally in question. In Platonic philosophy, for example, 'the soul does not itself possess a gender and the formal equality of the souls of men and women is not raised as a question' (1988: 20). Similarly, in the early Christian church, the risk of contamination of mind and soul by carnality is ever-present, but neither its origins nor the imperative to master it are gender-specific. Over and above that may be elaborated typologies of men and women, in which varying carnalities exist, based, for example, on the four humours. Riley gives as an example the writings of Hildegard of Bingen, on theology, physiognomy and medicine, in which there is never any espousal of what would later be seen as a female nature. Nowhere, for instance, is there a simple equation of 'women' *tout court* with a dangerous carnality. Tellingly, Riley contrasts the theological struggles of both female and male mystics over sensuality with its later interpretation:

> Between the twelfth and the fourteenth centuries, mystical writers, men and women, laboured over and refought the requirements of their faith for asceticism. It is not that 'women' were fully consigned to the body, or that a unique hysteria characterised the female mystic. A continuum of sensual and spiritual ecstasy was at the least a possibility for both sexes, while struggles between flesh and spirit, where these were felt to be at war with each other, were not the prerogative of men alone. The religiosity of a swooning female passivity, the eroticised icon most familiar to us in Bernini's rendering of St. Theresa, is a later interpretation, which reviews the mystic writers with a sardonically sexualising eighteenth-century gaze. (1988: 23)

This is not to say, however, that there was equality between women and men; it is a matter, she says, 'of the changing dominions and territorial annexations which presented themselves for, in shorthand, sexualisation' (ibid.). In short, the ways and places in which one might belong to a 'sexed' category (*pace*, therefore, what Laqueur is telling us about 'sex' before the Enlightenment) will shift and rearrange themselves historically.

The myriad namings of 'women'

There is a certain ambiguity here over the degree to which the categories we are talking about are in fact *social* categories and the degree to which they are categories in the philosophical and conceptual sense, and perhaps this is intentional, for the impression one gets from Riley's discussion is that the discursive, i.e. the conceptual, categories are the condition of existence of the social categories, and that it is to the extent that the social categories borrow their variable ontological statuses from their discursive constructions that they acquire the capacity to *produce* 'massifications', which can then be recognized as self-evident social categories. Thus, for example, the thoroughgoing sexualization of the female body from the eighteenth century onward, the way in which it was constituted as being defined by the having of a sex, in which it was marked and male bodies remained unmarked, could be argued to be responsible for that particular obduracy of gendering, because the social category was deemed to be given by the nature of things.

The question does arise, however, of the potential gap between a discourse (understood as a regulated way of referring to particular sorts of objects) and the other practices associated with, and informed or validated by it. Riley is clearly aware of such a gap, if for no other reason than that she is aware that the 'women' so designated may refuse their assignation to the other categories to which they are being bound:

> It is true that the trade-off for the myriad namings of 'women' by politics, sociologies, policies and psychologies is that at this cost 'women' do, sometimes, become a force to be reckoned with. But the caveat remains: the risky elements to the processes of alignment in sexed ranks are never far away, and the very collectivity which distinguishes you may also be wielded, even unintentionally, against you. Not just against you as an individual, that is, but against you as a social being with needs and attributions. The dangerous intimacy between subjectification and subjection needs careful calibration. There is, as we have repeatedly learned, no fluent trajectory from feminism to a truly sexually democratic humanism; there is no easy passage from 'women' to 'humanity'. The study of the historical development and precipitations of these sexed abstractions will help make sense of why not. That is how Desdemona's anguished question, 'Am I that name?', may be transposed into a more hopeful light. (1988: 17)

This is, of course, a warning to feminism that allegiance to a category of 'women' is a double-edged sword, but what is interesting for our purposes is that it reads 'discourse' in terms of the 'dangerous intimacy between subjectification and subjection', in other words in relation to the idea that those forms of language that speak *about* us constitute transpersonal forms of domination to which we are subjected and within which we need to be wary of identifying ourselves. Furthermore, the term 'subjectification' carries the tacit implication that the objects that are formed by such processes are 'subjects'. This combination of 'subjecthood' and 'subjection' did at one point look as if it might supply an account of social determinacy which also allowed for the fact that human beings might conceive of themselves and be describable as 'subjects', with a measure, and characteristic forms – a particular quality – of agency. We have to remember that Riley was writing this in 1988, and that hers constitutes one of the first forays into endeavouring to deploy a concept of discourse within English-speaking feminist politics. Inevitably, since what she is writing is by way of an historical sketch of the ebb and flow of forms of characterizations, she is also led to focus primarily on concepts and the relations they entertain with other concepts, and the question of the relation between these concepts and what it is they are alleged to bring into being does not arise. But what it does quite usefully is to raise the issue of precisely what it is that we are talking about when we invoke a concept of 'discourse', and specifically, how that is related to language and conceptuality. The lack of clarity over what is delineated by the concept of 'discourse' is one of the things that has made it difficult to get away from the association of discourse with thought and language alone, divorced from practice and human activity.

Of course, it is impossible to escape the fact that discursivity entails language, nor the fact that it is its association with the idea of language that has given it much of its force. It is the perception of the way in which our apprehension of the world is, at in least in part, shaped by the language that we use that constituted the revolutionary impetus behind the use of it as a concept, and specifically, of the idea of construction it entailed. As both Colin MacCabe (1979) and Sara Mills (1997) stressed, eighteen years apart, the etymology of the term describes 'language *in motion*'. It is this sense that is responsible for the idea that, as Mills says, 'a discourse is something that produces something else (an utterance, a concept, an effect), rather than something which exists in and of itself and which can be analysed in isolation' (1997: 17). It is, if we might put it like that, a generative systematicity, and one which is overwhelmingly associated with human thought. However, much of the impetus for the development of the concept came from what one might describe as a paradoxical quarter, namely the transformation wrought in the human sciences by the advent of the Saussurean account of linguistics, and its subsequent deployment within structuralism and post-structuralism. Central to this account of language was the sense that meaning and representation was generated neither by the intentions of a speaker nor by the structure of the world but within the systemic relations between signifiers within a language. What was often assumed was that it was language that provided the shaping of thought and, by extension, the 'worlding of the world' (Kirby, 1997: 17). It was paradoxical insofar as it made meaning and representation intra-linguistic products. It is already evident, then, that this may pose a problem for an account in which language and thought are described as intrinsically bound up with what is often deemed (erroneously in one sense) to be extra-linguistic human activity and objects, and thereby to invoke what we can, *pro tempore,* describe in terms of a notion of reference. We have argued earlier that it is this residual association with a problematic of representation and signification, derived in the first instance from the Saussurean account of language, that presents problems for the conceptualization of discursivity.[2] Riley herself describes 'namings', 'invocations', 'characterizations', 'descriptions' and 'self-descriptions', which means that her account is bound up, not merely with language, but with the constitution of something which was traditionally described by means of the concept of 'identity'. In fact, in the second version of her discussion, she seems to eschew a concept of discourse in favour of these apparently looser but also more specifically linguistic terms. How, then, might we conceptualize 'discourse' and the relation of discourse to language?

The train leaves Paris for Geneva

In certain respects, Foucault, with whom the concept of 'discourse' is most strongly associated, is no great help in this regard. Even in *The Archaeology of Knowledge*, in which he sought a systematicity which was perhaps not the most successful aspect of his work,[3] he said of 'discourse' that he had multiplied its meanings:

> Instead of gradually reducing the rather fluctuating meaning of the word 'discourse',
> I believe I have in fact added to its meanings; treating it sometimes as the general
> domain of all statements, sometimes as an individualizable group of statements, and
> sometimes as a regulated practice that accounts for a number of statements. (1972:
> 80)

Even if the provisions of the *Archaeology* were later to be abandoned, it is worth looking at it in some detail because it allows us to raise some more general issues.

The first very noticeable thing about the quotation above is the insistent centrality of the concept of the 'statement' (*énoncé*). In 'The Linguistic Fault', Beverley Brown and Mark Cousins (1980) take issue with the way in which Foucault conceptualizes the statement and specifically with the fact that, as is the case with some other uses of the concept of discourse, the relation it has to language, and more precisely to linguistic concepts, is essentially fudged. They argue that, although the concept of a discursive formation provides the means to criticize conventional treatments of discourse (specifically historical, linguistic and epistemological forms of investigation), Foucault fails to displace linguistic categories sufficiently. In fact, when he comes close to having to specify precisely what the relations are between 'discourse' and 'language', he seems to skirt around the problem by asserting that discourses 'do more than use signs to designate things' (1972: 49), which Brown and Cousins refer to as 'a somewhat cavalier treatment of signs' (1980: 278, n. 13):

> We have sought to demonstrate that in Foucault's text the concept of the statement is
> dependent upon the use of 'signs' and that the concentration of analysis upon the
> sentence and the proposition is both a diversion from and a concealment of this. If
> this is so it places the text in an embarrassment, the unwanted return of the 'sign'
> and the theoretical problems it brings in its train, which in fact leaves Paris for
> Geneva. Our argument is simply that this be confronted, and its implication is it
> would then have what would undoubtedly be regarded as the uncongenial task of
> dealing with, rather than dismissing, the arguments of Derrida. (ibid.)

Through a sophisticated analysis of the text of the *Archaeology*, Brown and Cousins make the case that, because Foucault proves unable to define the statement in such a way as to differentiate it adequately from linguistic categories, he is forced back towards a distinction between discourse and its conditions of existence analogous to a distinction between discourse and its institutional context of the kind from which he was seeking to get away. The concept of a 'discursive formation', which was an attempt to bridge that general form of differentiation through a particular form of regularity, acts, they say, to stitch together statements and institutions but does not resolve the problem. Because of Foucault's attempts to distance himself from a series of forms of conceptualization proper to conventional conceptions of discourse, he attempts to construct a concept of 'discursive formation' which overcomes them. Where discourses might conventionally be unified in relation to the fact that what they comprised referred to the same object; shared the same style; had a common set of concepts, or dealt in a common theme, Foucault rejects each of these possibilities:

> Objects of discourse are not singular; the 'style' or mode of statements slides away from any definition; in respect to 'themes' what was discovered was that a discourse could permit the strategic possibilities of different themes, and that different discourses could support the same theme. Where a principle of unity had been sought only the fact of dispersion had been found. (Brown and Cousins, 1980: 256)

Although Foucault resolutely refuses all of the standard mechanisms by means of which what he defines as a set of statements might be unified into a group, he nevertheless seeks to conceive of a discursive formation as a *system* of dispersion. What Brown and Cousins argue is that this conceptualization of it as a system is both deeply problematical and unnecessary – even, strictly speaking, impossible. They deny that discursive formations constitute 'a general form of positivity possessing a total regularity and definite limits' (1980: 252).

That system of dispersion which Foucault seeks to identify does not take the form of a set of elements interior to discourse, which are unified and contrasted to a general realm of the 'non-discursive'. As Brown and Cousins point out, what falls outside a discourse simply falls outside it, 'external events' may themselves include other discourses and 'there will be no general degree, form or mechanism at work' to connect the two things (1980: 254). A discursive formation is used to define a system of dispersion for a number of statements, amongst which a series of regularities obtain within and between the levels at which statements can exist: 'each of the levels entails definite social agents, practices, sites and statuses as their conditions of emergence, existence and transformation. Nor are these conditions of existence merely enabling conditions, accidental supports of the discourse' (ibid.).

Nevertheless, there is an ambiguity in the way in which Foucault describes the discursive formation, because, although the whole point of using a concept of discourse is to avoid treating it – as might be done in the history of ideas – as a sign of something else that dictates, predefines or causes it to come into being (a set of social forces, say), he does talk of a system that 'makes possible and governs' the formation of what comprises it. In short, there is a regularity of practice which appears, at least potentially, to be indicative of a 'governing' system, even if he rigorously eschews any form of structuralist combinatory that would generate all possible statements or any notion of the ideal archive of the historian which might contain the totality of statements made. There are no deep structures or empirical forms of closure. Furthermore, discursive formations have to allow for 'contradictions'.

There is a struggle here, then, between the attempt to define a system of regularity, with rules for the generation of possible statements, and making sure that that system of regularity respects the dispersion and differentiation it finds. This problem continues to be evident in the way in which the common acceptations of 'discourse' can cover anything from the supposedly recognizable set of unities of an academic discipline to a loosely affiliated set of ideas of the kind that would traditionally have been identified as an 'ideology'. Foucault uses the metaphor of a tree to describe a series of derivations 'which constitute the effective field of appearance of statements' (1980: 267), but, as Brown and Cousins say, 'the tree of Jesse has more conditions than arboreal science dreams of' and the concept of a 'rule' comes to be loaded with so many disqualifications that it becomes difficult to know what it might mean.

The statement

Brown and Cousins explore this ambiguity over the individuation and governance of a discursive formation through analysing the concept of 'the statement', which, in Foucault's terms, was 'designed to provide the means of specifying the elements of a discursive formation in a way which decisively breaks from the normal means of characterizing discourse' (1980: 257). The group of statements represents those things which are governed by a discursive formation. Yet statements do not constitute 'elementary particles' of a discursive formation, for they can only be individualized by reference to the discursive formation in which they appear.

But what is the statement? The potential difficulty is already indicated by the fact that the term 'statement' (*énoncé*) traditionally belongs to a linguistic domain, and, at the most general level, Foucault does define it as an 'enunciative function'. Again, an enunciative function maps a group of signs in the production of statements so that 'discursive formations, enunciative functions and statements are not ontologically distinct classes of being. To analyse the discursive formation is at the same time to specify the operation of the enunciative function and to describe the statement' (1980: 261). But, in spite of the reference to signs, Foucault insists that a statement is not to be defined as a sentence or a speech act, nor in terms of supra-sentential units of the kind that might be identified in linguistics or of propositions of the kind that might be identified by logic or epistemology. 'The same sentence,' say Brown and Cousins, 'can be the support of different statements' and 'there are statements that cannot be isolated as sentences. Conventional series, say a book balance, a graph or a genealogical table can all support a statement but cannot be isolated as sentences' (1980: 261). This is not to say, however, that statements may not accidentally coincide with each of these forms.

There remains an ambiguity about the linguistic and logical status of statements, however, insofar as Foucault merely says that these things –

statements, sentences and propositions – exist at different levels of analysis. As Brown and Cousins argue, this is a somewhat haphazard way of dealing with the way in which logic and linguistics individuate the units of which they speak without reference to their discursive conditions of existence. There is, to say the least, an incompatibility here: as long as those units (the sentence and the proposition) have a phenomenal existence within statements (with which they may coincide and even exemplify) statements are inevitably going to be dragged back to specification in terms of the properties of a language as defined by linguistics or of a proposition as defined by logic or epistemology. If statements and discursive formations are mutually defining, then the appearance of such things as sentences and propositions works against that. Furthermore the use of a series of signs is simply assumed by Foucault as the positive condition of the appearance of the statement. Because the disengagement from both sentences and propositions has not been made systematically but only arbitrarily and they retain a privileged position as bearing a possible relation to statements, Foucault avoids dealing with the fact that, ultimately, he also makes statements bear upon signs. Sentences and propositions act as intermediate stages between signs and statements as possible forms of statements, thus deflecting attention from signs *per se*, which are able to operate as an unexplicated and unexplored resource. But signs, of course, invoke the notion of semiological systems. Furthermore, sentences or propositions represent an *arbitrary* choice in relation to a semiological framework, in which signs might logically be able to take the form of traffic lights, gestures or advertising images:

> The qualifications that Foucault does make in respect to the relation between sentences, propositions and statements is insufficiently radical and this insufficiency is what protects Foucault from directing a necessary attention to semiological systems in general. This insufficiency also protects Foucault from dealing with the production of sense by semiological systems. For while of course he is indifferent to problems of meaning in general, he simply assumes that 'signs' have meaning, and indeed his use of 'signs' seems to suggest that there is some meaning of signs independent of their discursive employment, even while a discourse invests them with 'something more'. This is not as it were to accuse Foucault from the point of view of an insistence upon the pertinence of semiology. Rather it is that his sleight of hand protects him from the criticisms which can be directed against the concept of semiological systems. In the absence of this attention to problems of the sign, the categories of sentence and proposition are accorded, in respect to the analysis of discursive formations, an arbitrary privilege, at the very moment when Foucault denies that this is the case. (1980: 264)

The point, say Brown and Cousins, is that privileging the sentence and the proposition in this way constitutes a putative 'separation of the statement from "language" that remains curiously parasitic upon it' (ibid.).

This has a series of knock-on effects in the form of the reappearance of forms of conceptualization which have been declared inadmissible. For example, in spite of the fact that elements of institutions are made *internal* to discursive formations as a part of the enunciative function, because of the privilege accorded to the sentence and the proposition, institutions also effectively become external to discourses and turn into the conditions for their appearance. So the very attempt to refuse the notion of a general realm of the discursive, which meets another general realm of the non-discursive, finds this distinction sneaking back in, unintended and unwelcome. Also, in spite of Foucault's attempts to work away from both humanist and anti-humanist versions of the subject, residual effects of the subject-form reappear, put in place by the fact that, conceptually, it acts to bind together the cleavages that have been allowed into the conceptualization of the statement and of institutions. Through the category of speaking, the subject-form provides a link between an authorized status, an institutional location and objects that may be spoken about, because it is 'something which can have status, be in a place and "know"'(1980: 271), even though statements are not conceptualized as communicative but are said to support a practice. This Brown and Cousins describe as 'a magnificent perversion by Foucault of the relation famously known as subject and object, by which he seeks to escape from posing a philosophical question' (1980: 270). As they point out, '[t]he subject of philosophy has been expelled only to admit the subject of sociology and the subject of language' (1980: 271).

Running against the grain of the text, then, a number of forms of conceptualization re-emerge which are explicitly argued against. It is difficult indeed to know how to speak of 'enunciation' without automatically invoking one who enunciates. Nevertheless, Foucault does make a distinction between subject position and first-person grammatical form in that, amongst other things, a statement may not contain any such forms but still have a subject position; having a particular grammatical form does not thereby entail having the same relation to the subject of a statement, and identical sentences are to be found within different statements with different subjects. In short, he is seeking to separate the subject of the enunciation from the enunciation itself, even though the linguistic framework within which this conception is normally deployed makes them solidary with one another: 'Put baldly, Foucault never considers what a non-linguistic enunciation would be' (1980: 272). And, although Foucault produces a disjuncture between the subject of enunciation and the person, he nevertheless does move to define conditions of individuation for subject positions, 'determining,' as he puts it, 'what position can and must be occupied by an individual if he is to be the subject of it' (1972: 96). Brown and Cousins' point is that the questions of both status and institutional sites *and* linguistic positionality are drawn towards the specification of individuals: 'The subject of language and the subject of sociology have been expelled only to admit the individual subject of philosophy' (1980: 273).

Foucault's failure to confront the question of the relation of discourse to the idea of natural language as conceptualized by linguistics considerably undermines his attempts to conceptualize discourse in novel ways that depart from the forms of conceptualization supplied, not merely by linguistics, but by the history of ideas or epistemology. Discourse will thus have a tendency to keep collapsing back onto precisely those forms of conceptualization it has sought to get away from because it is allowed to continue to exist as a supra-linguistic organization of signs, thus tending to 'consolidate the institutional and conditionality with the non-discursive [which] would be to return to the most banal of sociologies' (1980: 274). As Brown and Cousins make clear, this is not a problem to be 'repaired by adding botanical tables and laundry lists as groups of signs capable of supporting statements' (ibid.).

Foucault's attempt to define a means of individuating and distinguishing between discursive formations is an attempt to displace what we might refer to as general philosophical questions. The reason why Brown and Cousins suggest tackling the problem of the sign is not, they say, to suggest a return to such questions, but 'a purgative required by the inadequacy of the displacement' (ibid.). There is a broader problem, however, brought about by the endeavour itself, which is that the attempt to identify the 'regularity of a practice' tends to run together its different types of conditions – 'regularity, regulation, possibility, government, derivation, enabling conditions, mutuality of effect' – into the general category of 'conditions of existence':

> This suggests that such unity (or unification of levels) is neither possible nor desirable in the analysis of discourses. The objects, subjects, concepts and strategies simply need not display that definitive cohesion-in-dispersion that Foucault would require. And it is not an accident that where such unity is sought for, the otherwise rejected forms of unification return. (1980: 275)

This does not mean giving up on the process of identifying forms of discursive organization, merely on expecting them to constitute some form of unity, which, in itself, entails a kind of rationalism that the concept of discourse should have made inappropriate.[4]

Reconceptualizing language

Foucault's is not the only attempt to specify the nature of the discursive and its relation to language. In many respects, though, the *Archaeology* is the text that comes closest to a systematic and satisfactory attempt to do so, because it is the one that most clearly attempts to eschew any associations between the concept of discourse and the provisions of linguistics or epistemology, which, as we have seen throughout this book, are so deeply problematical. So how are we to think of language within the context of discourse?

The answer is not a simple one and not one to be elaborated overnight. It will require a lengthy disquisition and investigation into language, thought and a great deal more besides, which we cannot undertake here. Some theorists, like Stephen Gaukroger (1983), have attempted to look towards alternative conceptions of language, such as that of Frege, in a bid, for example, to resolve the problem of reference, but this does not necessarily satisfactorily deal with the issues at stake. Rather than simply seeking to *replace* the Saussurean account – especially given both the importance that it has had and its deeper roots in a much older problematic of representation – it is worth starting with the problematization of the concepts associated with it in order to get some sense of the measure of the difficulty and the character of the problem. One might look to Foucault's historicization of the relation between words and things in *Les Mots et les choses* (translated as *The Order of Things*), but that

Foucauldian historicization, although it provides a welcome counterpart to the assumption that the representational model is a description of the structure intrinsic to human cognition and language use, provides no means of beginning to elaborate an alternative means of conceptualizing language. And it is this that we feel is necessary in order to obviate some of the problems we described earlier. Another philosophical starting point lies in the reflections on Saussure by Jacques Derrida and the related account of Vicki Kirby.

As a first stage, then, it seems appropriate, as Brown and Cousins indicate, to examine Derrida's arguments and, specifically, what he makes of Saussure. Derrida also seems ironically appropriate as a commentator on language given his association with the notorious and much misunderstood apodictic statement: 'There is nothing outside the text' – although, as Geoffrey Bennington points out, Derrida's is not a philosophy of language (Bennington and Derrida, 1993: 27). Getting to grips with the thought of Jacques Derrida, however, is no mean feat and few have managed it successfully. One of those who stands out in this regard is Bennington, author of a collaborative book with Derrida, entitled simply *Jacques Derrida*, in which is to be found one of the most lucid accounts of Derrida's reflections on Saussure. A crucial advantage it has over other accounts is that it does not constitute a synthesizing gloss, a gesture which Derridean theory itself makes it impossible to undertake without beginning to travesty the very thing of which it seeks to give an account. Bennington's account is very much evidence-, that is to say text-based, and, furthermore, if one is to accord anything to the intentionality of the author, it has Derrida's imprimatur. What follows here, however, will probably (and according to Derrida perhaps necessarily) violate those conditions in producing a gloss of something, Bennington's 'Derridabase', which tries to be a systematization without closure.

Derridabase

Geoffrey Bennington describes the book, of which 'Derridabase' constitutes almost precisely half, as presupposing a contract in which he undertook to describe, if not the totality of Jacques Derrida's thought, 'then the general system of that thought' (Bennington and Derrida, 1993: 1). The ideal for that exposition would have been 'an interactive program which, in spite of its difficulty, would in principle be accessible to any user' (ibid.). The nature of the contract, however, was based upon the fact that any such system remains open and the systematization thus undertaken is doomed to failure, its interest lying in the demonstration of that failure. In the light of this, Derrida undertook to use the second half of the work to write something escaping that systematization. In reading it as we are here, then, we are imposing on it a double closure, that which is the normal result of any re-presentation that seeks to re-produce within a work an order which is arguably both its own and not its own, and a violation of the principles enunciated by the contract. Nevertheless, since our interest is in Saussure, rather than Derrida, we have to start somewhere, even if it is with a productive reading at third hand.

There are two expository gestures in 'Derridabase', one of which obeys the orthodox principles of description and the other of which, in a certain sense, enacts Derridean thought in its manner of exposition, not by mimicking it, but by demonstrating at each turn how the very gesture of exposition comes up against that thought. Significantly, perhaps, in more than one way, Bennington starts the former, more conventional expository task with Derrida's reflections on the sign, which, as he points out, was also the place at which Derrida himself started with 'The *Ideality* of the Literary Object' (Bennington, 1993: 23), not the normal beginning for a philosopher. What Derrida does, in essence, is to take apart what one might call in un-Derridean fashion the metaphorical architecture of the sign. Rather than drawing attention initially to the tripartite nature of the sign with which we are all familiar (signifier/signified/referent), Bennington draws attention to the sign's intrinsic secondariness, which has a number of dimensions and could be said to summarize the general theme of Derrida's deliberations.

At the initial level, the sign is the representative of the thing in its absence, both detached from the thing insofar as it is its delegate and attached insofar as it is supposed to refer to it alone, and to evanesce in its presence. The 'thing' that the sign represents, which is itself a sign, also refers to two things, the 'referent' and the 'sense', the signified. This sense is the level of ideas or concepts, which, in its turn, refers to the world. Signifier and signified are indissociable in the sign, so that the thing that is absent is the referent. The sign is said to be arbitrary, unmotivated or conventional, hence this paradoxical attachment/detachment between sign (or signifier) and referent and the particular limitations that one must place on the use of the term 'representation'. This tripartite division, which, as Bennington points out, is in this form not peculiar to Saussure, sits philosophically in the midst of an ideal/material distinction, constituting, to use a very different metaphor from the one used by Bennington, a kind of sandwich of an ideality between two materialities. To put it crudely, the idea is caught between the word and the world, whichever end of these oppositions is valorized, be it that of the materiality of things and, as was the case with Lacanian-Marxist interpretations of Saussure, 'via a perilous extension, of the signifier' or 'of thinking things as creations on the prior model of the idea or *eidos*' (1993: 27).

These oppositions will be familiar to us from the positions we have encountered and, in some cases, examined over the course of this book, from the dilemmas faced by such as Laqueur and the indictments made of discursive analyses by others. This opposition is intrinsically given in the structure of the sign itself, which is one reason why we have argued that the nature and role of language in discourse has to be rethought: 'We can distribute as we wish the values of truth and illusion in these two realms *without escaping the basic schema*: the sign has always been thought of on the basis of this distinction between the sensible and the intelligible, and *cannot be thought of otherwise* (1993: 27, emphases added). The sign must, of necessity, compromise between the two realms.

The problem that arises is how the sign can retain its identity, through its re-iterations, since one cannot appeal to the referent, which is only identifiable as such through the sign that refers to it, nor to the signifier as the materiality of the sign. It may identify the sign but it cannot sensibly be spoken of as material. As Bennington puts it, after an apparently paradoxical discussion of the non-existence of the signifier, the idea of the materiality of the signifier, and that of the sign in general, runs aground on the famous issue of 'differences without positive terms' (1993: 32). If one relied upon the materiality of the signifier, it would be problematical to recognize it amidst its non-identical repetitions, in which accent, tone and different written forms would interfere with our identification of it. It is in that sense an ideal-ity (ibid.). This means that the differences we established earlier between the character of different parts of the sign as ideal or material become blurred: it is neither entirely sensible nor entirely intelligible. This is further complicated if we think not just of the differences between repetitions but of the differences within the system of signs, the means by which it is said to acquire value.

Given that the whole system is said to be constituted by differences, it becomes hard to see how the signifier can remain material and sensible: 'the matter or stuff from which it seemed that the signifiers were cut out, as it were, disappears from the essential definition of the sign, even on its signifier side' (1993: 33).[5] Yet the signifier is still granted the privilege of being that which, in referring to other signifiers, constitutes the system of differences, which means that the signified, or meaning, as Lacan would say, 'never arrives'; one only ever meets with another signifier and it is this that produces meaning as an 'effect'. At the same time, if we go down the road of privileging the signifier in this way, which indeed Lacan did, we lose the logical implication of signifier and signified, which, as Saussure insisted, were like recto and verso of a piece of paper. We fall, as Bennington says, like Humpty Dumpty, into a conventionalist view of language ('When *I* use a word...it means just what I choose it to mean').

So, just as we suggested earlier, we need, Bennington says, to find a new language:

> But this runs the risk of being a scarcely less naïve fantasy than the one that wants to continue to use the old terms, changing their use all at once by simple decree. Let us imagine that we replace 'signifier' with a new symbol, say '#.' We should have changed nothing at all insofar as this symbol would take the same place in the network of differences as that occupied by 'signifier,' while giving our description a purely mystificatory look of scientificity or algorithmicity. And if this symbol managed to take the place of 'signifier' and made us lose all memory of the reasoning we have just sketched out, then we could bet that the new symbol would function, amnesically, just as metaphysically as the old. The point is to shake up the system, not just to replace a few terms. Of course we must invent new terms, but we cannot create them ex nihilo by divine performative: rather take up the terms which are already a problem for metaphysical thought (writing, trace) and accentuate their power of diversion – while knowing a priori that we shall never find anything but nicknames, fronts (LI, 37), pseudonyms (LOB, 114). (1993: 36)[6]

One might have thought that since the material/ideal divide was at the *heart* of the problematicity of the representational model of language, the status of the sign as neither material nor ideal would be a solution. However, the problem is that the concept of the sign functions as if these distinctions *were* in place. We shall have to make more profound discursive changes to our understanding of language than a simple replacement of terms. However, Derrida it seems, has more confidence (if confidence is the right word) in the persistence of metaphysics. Without the concept of the sign, for example, we do away with the means of understanding translation, says Bennington, so that it is not possible triumphantly to say, for instance, that there is no signifier. But the reasons for this confidence go deeper and affect the very mechanics of the way in which we might go about constructing an alternative, for, according to Derrida, the incoherence identified within the sign affects a whole series of other concepts, including 'concept' itself, 'which complicates irremediably all the traditional notions of critique, progress (but we shall see this progressively) and even of truth and history. The deconstruction of the sign thus affects *all* these other cornerstones of the conceptual edifice of metaphysics, up to and including the values of construction and edifice' (1993: 37).

  Where does this leave us? According to Derrida, in Bennington's account, this incoherence lies at the heart of metaphysics but it is also that which 'gives us our measure of coherence' (1993: 38). In short, it is constitutive, and it is thereby impossible to avoid complicity with that metaphysics. The concept of the sign is defined here as a *resource* (just as Foucault deemed it to be), of which we should not deprive ourselves, and yet its use also constitutes the trap from which we have sought to extricate the thinking described in this book:

> The metaphysical concept of the sign poses the distinction signifier/signified on the foundation given by the sensible/intelligible distinction, but works toward the reduction of that distinction in favour of the intelligible: it thus reduces or effaces the sign by posing it as secondary from the start. Any attempt to reduce the distinction in the other direction works within the same logic, and, wanting to make the sensible intelligible, only manages to make the sensible intelligible according to a structure we shall explain later under the name of *transcendental contraband*. Deconstruction also reduces the sign in a sense (according to the demonstration we have summarized) precisely by *maintaining* it *against* this metaphysical reduction (SP, 51; WD, 281): this *maintenance* is achieved by insisting, in an obviously untenable way, on the priority of the sign with respect to the referent (which implies that there is no thing in itself outside the network of referrals in which the sign functions [GR 48-50]), and, in the sign, on the priority of the signifier with respect to the signified (which implies that there is no signified and therefore no signifier) – in general, *on the originarity of the secondary*: it is obvious that this formulation is a non-sense in the very simple sense of going against the very sense of sense. A secondary origin can be neither originary nor secondary, and there is therefore no origin. As we announced above, we find that there is no thing, no sign, and no beginning. (1993: 39-41)

It is obvious from this why it is that critics anxious to dismiss Derrida use this to indict him with some sort of nihilism, yet, we would argue, both those who use the concept of the sign and those who wish to replace it need to come to terms with such argument, which, after all, derives only from the logic of the concept itself. There are a number of avenues that one can take to move things forward, which cannot be followed here, but the important thing is that it demonstrates just how vexed and potentially entrenched are the difficulties within the problematic of signification and representation. These are, if anything, made more explicit, but perhaps better able to be grappled with, by Vicki Kirby's attempts to think through the oddity of the matter of the sign, in her book *Telling Flesh*.

Telling Flesh

In a brilliant chapter on Saussure, 'Corporeal Complexity – The Matter of the Sign', Vicki Kirby takes apart what has come down to us as Saussure's thought – via the complexities of posthumously compiled student notes put together by two of his colleagues, who had themselves never attended his lectures. Be that as it may, the result 'is both fascinating and frustrating in its ambiguity, a paradox of disparate propositions expressed in confusing and often contradictory terminology' (1997: 8). She felt the need, she says, to address Saussure 'in order to explain how the question of language can render substance and corporeality entirely problematic' (1997: 4).

The overall intentions of the book *Telling Flesh*, in which this chapter is situated, are to attempt a new account of corporeality that treads between a 'naïve materialism' and the claim that 'there is no outside of the text' as it is often understood within critical and cultural studies, seeking not to leave the categories of nature and culture intact but to place them in tension with one another (1997: 2-4). As an example of the kind of phenomenon that inspired this enquiry, Kirby gives the example of the Hindu ritual festival of *thaipusam*, in which devotees undergo extraordinary piercings with long metal spokes that, from a distance, give the appearance of an 'elaborate metal scaffolding' impaling their bodies. As Kirby says, '[t]o be skewered by any one of these metal prongs would prove at least painful for most of us, and conceivably lethal. Bleeding, scarring and internal injury would be the inevitable results of what, in a different context, could be read as abuse' (1997: 3). None of this appears to happen, however:

> Indeed, whatever the *weltanschauung*, structural frame – call it what you will – through which this man's body is ciphered and located as 'being in the world,' one can only presume that this information also informs the very matter of his body's material constitution. This is data whose language and text is the very tissue of his body. Its interior and exterior surfaces, the skin and membranes that divide as they connect the complexity of its parts, have not functioned as borders that separate one body part from another. This confounding of the inside/outside division, although *within* the individual, suggests that perhaps even the relationship *between* individuals is also one of profound implication. (ibid.)

As Kirby points out, these capabilities are extended neither to tourists, nor to members of the same community who witness the ritual, but because of the conception of the body held by both social scientists and others as 'that universal, biological stuff of human matter' (ibid.), there tends not to be a problematization of what the body is and 'researchers stop short of asking how it is that the cultural context that surrounds a body can also come to inhabit it' (1997: 4).

These questions are very important ones, although not ones to which we can return within the compass of this book. In her introduction, Kirby poses such questions baldly, asking, for example, whether it is a 'dumb reading' of Michel Foucault to consider the possibility that if discourse forms its object, matter might not be being 'constantly rewritten and transformed' (ibid.). Or whether or not it is absurd to assume 'that if there is no outside textuality, then the differential of language is articulate in/as blood, cells, breathing, and so on' (ibid.). In a certain sense, then, she brings what she talks of in terms of 'materiality' and the 'insubstantial' differential structures of language together, intending to rethink, as her subtitle would have it, the 'substance of the corporeal'.

Corporeal complexity

Kirby finds Saussure forced into a restless series of repetitions in which he begins and begins again, trying to displace a problematic of language as nomenclature. She quotes him as describing a necessary absence of any starting point and as intending to place the same idea before the reader three or four times (1997: 8). This is partly because, according to his own account, all aspects of language are interconnected and no property of it can be regarded as primordial. However, he also describes it as a consequence of the difficulty of exposition, hence the fact that he says that he finds himself tempted five or six times between beginning and ending a sentence to rewrite (ibid.).

Part of Saussure's difficulty concerns the problem of reference, which, although not given explicit conceptualization, smuggles itself intermittently into the conception of the signified, so that there is a slippage between thing and idea, concept and reality. Inevitably, this allows Saussure to be read in one of two ways, although, most typically he is accused of eschewing the 'real', of 'an abrogation of ethical and social responsibility' (1997: 12). One of the most interesting of these commentaries – from the point of view of what can be done with it conceptually – comes from Vincent Descombes who, in *Objects of All Sorts*, discusses the *Course*'s image of 'arbor' and 'equos' in terms of what he calls the 'mystery of the left-hand box' (thereby imposing a grid-like structure on the image):

> The mystery refers to what he regards as a semiological sleight of hand whereby these boxes that represent parts of the sign are surreptitiously filled. Although this composite representation would appear to describe an ostensive notion of language that Saussure disputes, Descombes queries how the image nevertheless "works" as a sign. For Descombes, the figurative illustration presumes precisely what needs to be explained. Descombes also suggests that Saussure's use of Latin cleverly deflects some important questions. 'We know that Saussurean linguistics excludes semantic problems from its field of study. The "referent," to use an expression that came later, would be bracketed off'. (Kirby, 1997: 12-13)

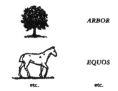

ARBOR

EQUOS

etc.   etc.

As Kirby points out, a number of processes are going on in the reading of this image, not least of which is that, in defiance of convention, we seek to read the 'left-hand box' as the signified and, perhaps because of this, we blur the distinction between 'concept' and 'reality'. Do we do this, she asks, because we assume that a word is an arbitrary and *cultural* object, where we identify the graphic image – which, after all, like the contents of the 'right-hand box', is itself a sign – with nature? Descombes remains, she says, surprisingly unaware of the many ambiguities in his question.

This blurring is something that Benveniste attempts to solve at a stroke by both assuming and bracketing off an extra-linguistic world, deemed to be the province of others who are specialists in such things. But, as Kirby points out, 'if the thing and the concept of the thing are entirely dissimilar, then how are they made synonyms for each other?' (1997: 19). It is not a matter of whether or not Saussure contradicted himself, it is a matter of how one is to resolve the paradox. Roy Harris, for example, struggles to differentiate between the linguistic re-presentation of the tree and the '"external" botanical facts' of that tree, which, of course, simply expands the mentalist space through which he struggles to reach the material. It moves the paradox further across towards a 'real' which recedes still further.[7] Benveniste also grapples with the relation of thought to language, a problem which, we have to say, is not resolvable within this disciplinary framework, but one which, depending upon the resolution one gives it (is it language that 'worlds the world'?) engages the ontological status of those objects to which, variably, Saussure, Benveniste, Harris, Ryan and so on want to appeal. As Kirby says, '[t]he uncanny result of this economy is that the only proper account of the sign, the one that can finally decide its identity or limit, is ultimately purchased from a perspective *within* the sign's own labyrinthine structure – an outside that is also strangely at home with/in itself' (1997: 24). Hermeneutic undecidability, however, is the least of our worries, for what Kirby also raises is the fact that 'the complexity of the sign is inseparable from the riddle of the copula' (1997: 25). 'Being' as 'the transcategorical condition of any category' (ibid.) both lives within and exceeds language:

> However, we have been down this path before. Perhaps we are even becoming a little more comfortable with its tortuous circuit, for the topography of the landscape remains, to some degree, always familiar – even when we sense ourselves to have 'gone astray.' If there is more to language than we acknowledge, an elusive 'something' that confounds its representation, then the 'outside' of language, thought, and representation, may be caught within the folds of its own expression,

inhabiting 'the being-language-of-language' that entirely exceeds the word/concept, 'Being' or 'to be.' The confusions of Saussure's text map the contours of a landscape to which we will relentlessly return. This is not to say that a certain leave-taking is impossible whenever we begin again. Indeed, we will discover that, however faithfully we retrace our steps, we will always be 'elsewhere' or 'other' than the place where we think ourselves to be. (ibid.)

Apart from what Kirby describes as the 'waywardness of the sign', Saussure faces a further set of problems once he tries to circumscribe the identity of the sign through the notion of value. There are essentially two accounts of that identity and, in Kirby's words, 'various attempts to correct the confusion inevitably repeat it' (1997: 26). The notion of value, she says, is the corollary of the system and establishes the identity of the sign through its differential position within that system, but Saussure distinguishes this from signification which represents the denotational unity between signifier and signified. The classic example of this is to be found in translation, in which, for example, French has only 'mouton' and 'agneau' to denote what English would cover with three terms, 'sheep', 'mutton' and 'lamb'. Thus terms may have the same signification from language to language, but will not have the same value. The metaphor of the dictionary can – inevitably – be used to demonstrate both of these properties. But if language is a system without positive terms how can a sign have signification which is not the product of value? Alternatively, how can translation be possible *without* signification, that is, if the sign's closure upon itself cannot be sustained and 'signification is also pregnable to the infinite vagaries of semiosis' (1997: 27)?

In an increasingly complex and sophisticated argument, then, in which she turns Saussure in upon himself again and again through readings of a range of theorists, Kirby progressively establishes the impossibility of the identity of the bi-partite sign.[8] There is a difficulty of conceptualizing even those ideas that Saussure makes fundamental, such as the notion of arbitrariness, and these problems progressively disassemble the Saussurean edifice from the inside. However, the fact that they do so does not demonstrate that Saussure was wrong but the difficulty of thinking language with the conceptual tools that we have. As Saussure himself says, 'it is often easier to discover a truth than to assign it its proper place' (Kirby, 1997: 18). As Kirby points out, 'Saussure discovers a system that is regulated by the exigencies of its own internal necessity, but a system whose frontiers cannot be defended against an exteriority that involves something more than the science of linguistics is prepared to embrace' (1997: 48).

Reading Saussure against himself, we find that one of the enduring signatures of his work is legible in the perverse way that he subverts the unity of identity – perhaps even his own. We have seen how the assumption that an entity can be determined in any final way as the proper unit of analysis has been displaced by the force field of 'value.' Consequently, the smallest atomic particle of the language system, its larger analytical agglomerations, and even the sense-certainty of the speaking subject, have now all been put into question. But where does this leave us regarding what can only be a theoretical *non sequitur*, namely, a persistent belief in the unity of the language system itself? Further to this, how is the autonomy of the language system dissected out from the operations of other social systems? And finally, how does the unity of 'the social,' or 'the cultural,' secure its particular identity against 'an outside,' namely, the natural order? (1997: 48-9)

What Kirby describes is the way in which the attempt to think language – by which we understand the nature of language itself – deregulates many of our most fundamental assumptions – both small and large. In this respect, her thesis bears a certain similarity to that of Mikkel Borch-Jacobsen in *The Freudian Subject*, in which he identified the way in which the very thing that Freud struggles to think – what Borch-Jacobsen calls 'the scandal of the unconscious' – derails the very means he uses to think about it, a problematic of the subject which, in spite of being rendered impossible, is somehow simultaneously indispensable. As François Roustang says, the Freudian edifice 'coheres in its very inconsistencies' (Borch-Jacobsen, 1988: viii). At stake is a similar problem of identity – in this case the identity of the subject in the context of psychoanalysis. As Roustang points out, Freud is the inheritor of a concept of the human subject 'that led him towards a series of brilliant solutions to false problems' (ibid.). Although the solutions may not always be as brilliant as those of Freud, the fact that this is what we have encountered again and again in a diversity of settings, and with an increasingly familiar cluster of what are fundamental features of our conceptual landscape, suggests that the thinking we need to do has only just begun. 'Sex' and 'gender' – and the attempt to think beyond them in a more coherent and productive way – calls all of these aporias into being. How we finally resolve them is obviously beyond the scope of this book.

Notes

[1] Brown and Cousins describe the correlative presupposition to this belief, which lies behind the 'History of Ideas' as a discipline, and that is that 'ideas' form 'an order of motivated representations whose distribution (appearance, persistence, mutation) in time forms a coherent object of investigation. Calabashes, microscopes, wafers, falling apples, displaced bathwater can all be made to yield their tithe of ideahood' (1980: 275).
[2] Moreover, we know that the problematic of representation has a much deeper and longer history than Saussure's *Course in General Linguistics*.
[3] Although Foucault vehemently denied being a structuralist, the ideal architecture of the *Archaeology* would seem to reflect at least its rationalism. Be that as it may, however, Foucault always remained enough of a philosopher to be captivated by the grand theoretical and rhetorical gesture rather than the messiness of the empirical, and this, in some measure extended to the way in which he approached discourse and the role he gave it. *Discipline and Punish*, for example, is marked by his concern with the programmatic intentions of those devising institutions such as the prison or the schoolroom, rather than with the rather more chequered history of the institutions themselves. It is therefore not surprising that the emblematic figure of *Discipline and Punish* is Bentham's Panopticon, which was effectively never really built (although there are numerous buildings that show the mark of the model). It is also this *desire* which, in some measure, has led his critics both to bemoan his historiography and to talk (erroneously in respect of other texts such as the 'Afterword' in Dreyfus and Rabinow's 1982 book) of the fact that resistance seems absent from the picture. Of course, we nevertheless have to do justice to the particularities of *Discipline and Punish* as a text, to

the fact that, not only is it subtitled *The* Birth *of the Prison*, but to what we have to remember is its pedagogic and philosophical intent, and the way in which Foucault saw the role of the intellectual. Arguably, it was this philosophical drive that led him towards that tendency to do what Pierre Bourdieu describes as slipping 'from the model of the reality to the reality of the model' (1977: 29).

[4] Brown and Cousins also argue that the fact that the problems within the *Archaeology* are unresolved is the reason for what they describe as the notorious problems in Foucault's later works around the category of the body, the questions of historical reference and the concept of strategy.

[5] Bennington points out that it is this that 'ruins the tendency of linguistics to privilege one "substance of expression" (voice) over another (writing) and begins the deconstruction of phonocentrism, a prelude to the deconstruction of logocentrism' (1993: 33).

[6] The brackets '(LI, 37) and '(LOB, 114)' in Bennington's text are references to passages in Derrida's writings in which discussions of specific concepts are to be found. However, rather than this referencing serving a merely expository purpose, it constitutes a form of inter-textuality between Bennington's and Derrida's texts, which is why we have left these brackets in this quotation and equivalent brackets in the quotation to follow.

[7] Such a move is not unenlightening, however, for it indicates the way in which the dictionary as an artefact of the construction of the unity of language – the object of linguistics – is already penetrated by discursivity. Any dictionary worth its salt will indicate, through the etymological origins of a term as well as its definitional contents, its appurtenance to one or more discursive frameworks. What an ordinary dictionary is not is discourse- or discipline-specific.

[8] We have scarcely done more than sketched some of the points that Kirby makes in her chapter and, clearly, exploration of the issues that she raises will have to await a future book.

References

Adams, Parveen (1991), 'Per Os(cillation)' in James Donald (ed), *Thresholds: Psychoanalysis and Cultural Theory*, London, Macmillan, pp. 68-88

Adams, Parveen (1996), *The Emptiness of the Image: Psychoanalysis and Sexual Differences*, London and New York, Routledge

Adams, Parveen and Cowie, Elizabeth (eds) (1990), *The Woman in Question – m/f*, London and New York, Verso

Allen, Hilary (1990), 'At the Mercy of Her Hormones: Premenstrual Tension and the Law', *The Woman in Question – m/f*, Parveen Adams and Elizabeth Cowie (eds), London and New York, Verso

Anzieu Didier (1989), *The Skin Ego: A Psychoanalytic Approach to the Self*, Chris Turner (trans.), New Haven and London, Yale University Press

Ashe, Geoffrey (1974 [1957]), *King Arthur's Avalon: The Story of Glastonbury*, London and Glasgow, Fontana Books

Austin, John Langshaw (1962), *How to Do Things with Words*, Oxford, Clarendon Press

Austin, John Langshaw (1970), *Philosophical Papers*, Oxford, Clarendon Press

Bagemihl, Bruce (1999), *Biological Exuberance: Animal Homosexuality and Natural Diversity*, London, Profile Books

Barthes, Roland (1983), 'The World of Wrestling', Susan Sontag (ed), *Barthes: Selected Readings*, London, Fontana, pp. 18-30

Bauman, Zygmunt (1973), 'On the Philosophical Status of Ethnomethodology', *Sociological Review*, 21, 1: 3-23

Bauman, Zygmunt (1991), *Modernity and the Holocaust*, Cambridge and Oxford, Polity Press with Basil Blackwell

Bell, Vicki (1999), 'On Speech, Race and Melancholia: An Interview with Judith Butler', *Theory, Culture and Society*, 16, 2, April: 163-74

Bennington, Geoffrey and Derrida, Jacques (1993), *Jacques Derrida*, Geoffrey Bennington (trans.), Chicago, University of Chicago Press

Bleier, Ruth (1984), *Science and Gender: A Critique of Biology and its Theories on Women*, New York, Pergamon Press

Borch-Jacobsen, Mikkel (1988), *The Freudian Subject*, Catherine Porter (trans.), Stanford CA, Stanford University Press

Bourdieu, Pierre (1977), *Outline of a Theory of Practice*, Richard Nice (trans.), Cambridge, Cambridge University Press

Braidotti, Rosi with Judith Butler (1994), 'Feminism By Any Other Name', *Differences*, 6, 2+3. Summer-Fall: 27-61

Brown, Beverley and Cousins, Mark (1980), 'The Linguistic Fault: the Case of Foucault's Archaeology', *Economy and Society*, 9, 3, August: 251-78

Butler, Judith (1990), *Gender Trouble: Feminism and the Subversion of Identity*, London, Routledge

Butler, Judith (1993), *Bodies That Matter: On the Discursive Limits of 'Sex'*, London, Routledge

Butler, Judith (1997), *The Psychic Life of Power: Theories in Subjection*, Stanford, CA, Stanford University Press

Califia, Pat (1983), *Sapphistry: The Book of Lesbian Sexuality*, 2nd edn, USA, Naiad Press

Cannon, Walter Bradford (1942), '"Voodoo" Death', *American Anthropologist*, 154 (44)

Carlson, Neil R. (1991), *Physiology of Behaviour*, 4th edn, Boston, Mass., Allyn and Bacon

Cealey Harrison, Wendy (1995),'The Socialization of the Body's Pleasures', *New Formations*, 26, Autumn: 163-71

Cealey Harrison, Wendy and Hood-Williams, John (1997), 'Gender, Bodies and Discursivity: A Comment on Hughes & Witz', *Body & Society*, 3, 2: 103-18

Cealey Harrison, Wendy and Hood-Williams, John (1998), 'More Varieties than Heinz: Social Categories and Sociality in Humphries, Hammersley and Beyond', *Sociological Research Online*, 3, 1, <http://www.socresonline.org/socresonline/3/1/8.html>)

Chown, Marcus (2000), 'Random Reality', *New Scientist*, 2227, 26 February: 24-8

Connell, Robert W. (1987), *Gender and Power: Society, the Person and Sexual Politics*, Cambridge, Polity Press

Connor, Steven (1999-2000), 'Integuments: the Scar, the Sheen, the Screen, *New Formations*, 39, Winter: 32-54

Damasio, Antonio R. (1995), *Descartes' Error: Emotion, Reason and the Human Brain*, London, Macmillan Press

Damasio, Antonio R. (2000), *The Feeling of What Happens*, London, Vintage Press

Davis, L. and Delano, L. (1992), 'Fixing the Boundaries of Physical Gender: Side Effects of Anti-Drug Campaigns', *Sociology of Sport Journal*, 9: 1-9

de Beauvoir, Simone (1972 [1949]), *The Second Sex*, Harmondsworth, Penguin

Delphy, Christine (1984), *Close to Home: A Materialist Analysis of Women's Oppression*, Diana Leonard (trans.), London, Hutchinson

Delphy, Christine (1993), 'Rethinking Sex and Gender', *Women's Studies International Forum*, 16, 1: 1-9

Delphy, Christine and Leonard, Diana (1992), *Familiar Exploitation*, Cambridge, Polity Press

Douglas, Mary (1995 [1966]), *Purity and Danger: An Analysis of the Concepts of Pollution and Taboo*, London and New York, Routledge

Dreyfus, Hubert and Rabinow, Paul (eds) (1982), *Between Structuralism and Hermeneutics*, Brighton, Harvester Press

Dyer, K. F. (1982), *Catching up the Men: Women in Sport*, London, Junction Books

Elias, Norbert (1994), *The Civilising Process: The History of Manners and State Formation and Civilization*, Edmund Jephcott (trans.), Oxford UK and Cambridge Mass., Basil Blackwell

Evans-Pritchard, E. E. (1937), *Witchcraft, Oracles and Magic among the Azande*, Oxford, Clarendon Press

Farnsworth, Marjorie Whyte (1988), *Genetics*, 2nd edn, New York and Cambridge, Harper and Row

Fausto-Sterling, Anne (1989), 'Life in the XY Corral', *Women's Studies International Forum*, 12, 3: 319-31

Fausto-Sterling, Anne (1993) 'The Five Sexes: Why Male and Female Are Not Enough', *The Sciences*, March-April: 20-25

Firestone, Shulamith (1971), *The Dialectic of Sex: The Case for Feminist Revolution*, London, Cape

Foucault, Michel (1972), *The Archaeology of Knowledge*, A. M. Sheridan Smith (trans.), London, Tavistock Publications

Foucault, Michel (1974), *The Order of Things: An Archaeology of the Human Sciences*, (trans. not listed) London, Tavistock Publications

Foucault, Michel (1979a), *Discipline and Punish: The Birth of the Prison*, Alan Sheridan (trans.), Harmondsworth, Penguin

Foucault, Michel (1979b), Truth and Power: an Interview with Alessandro Fontano and Pasquale Pasquino', Meaghan Morris and Paul Patton (eds), *Michel Foucault: Power/Truth/Strategy*, Sydney, Feral Publications, pp. 29-48

Foucault, Michel (1980), *Herculine Barbin, Being the Recently Discovered Memoirs of a Nineteenth-Century Hermaphrodite*, Richard McDougall (trans.), Brighton, Harvester Press

Foucault, Michel (1981), 'The Order of Discourse', Robert Young (ed.), *Untying the Text: A Poststructuralist Reader*, London, Routledge and Kegan Paul

Freud, Sigmund (1894), 'The Neuro-Psychoses of Defence', *The Standard Edition of the Complete Psychological Works of Sigmund Freud*, James Strachey (trans.), Vol. III, Hogarth Press, London, 1962

Freud, Sigmund (1905a), 'Fragment of an Analysis of a Case of Hysteria', *The Standard Edition of the Complete Psychological Works of Sigmund Freud*, James Strachey (trans.), Vol. VII, Hogarth Press, London, 1956

Freud, Sigmund (1905b), *Three Essays on the Theory of Sexuality, The Standard Edition of the Complete Psychological Works of Sigmund Freud*, James Strachey (trans.), Vol. VII, Hogarth Press, London, 1956

Freud, Sigmund (1911 [1910]), 'Psychoanalytical Notes on an Autobiographical Account of a Case of Paranoia (Dementia Paranoia)', *The Standard Edition of the Complete Psychological Works of Sigmund Freud*, James Strachey (trans.), Vol. XII, Hogarth Press, London, 1958

Freud, Sigmund (1915), 'Instincts and their Vicissitudes', *The Standard Edition of the Complete Psychological Works of Sigmund Freud*, James Strachey (trans.), Vol. XIV, Hogarth Press, London, 1957

Freud, Sigmund (1917 [1915]),'Mourning and Melancholia', *The Standard Edition of the Complete Psychological Works of Sigmund Freud*, James Strachey (trans.), Vol. XIV, Hogarth Press, London, 1957

Freud, Sigmund (1918 [1914]), 'From the History of an Infantile Neurosis' ('The Wolf Man), *The Standard Edition of the Complete Psychological Works of Sigmund Freud*, James Strachey (trans.), Vol. XVII, Hogarth Press, London, 1955

Freud, Sigmund (1919), 'A Child is Being Beaten', *The Standard Edition of the Complete Psychological Works of Sigmund Freud*, James Strachey (trans.), Vol. XVII, Hogarth Press, London, 1955

Freud, Sigmund (1920), 'The Psychogenesis of a Case of Homosexuality in a Woman', *The Standard Edition of the Complete Psychological Works of Sigmund Freud*, James Strachey (trans.), Vol. XVIII, Hogarth Press, London, 1955

Freud, Sigmund (1921), *Group Psychology and the Analysis of the Ego, The Standard Edition of the Complete Psychological Works of Sigmund Freud*, James Strachey (trans.), Vol. XVIII, Hogarth Press, London, 1955.

Freud, Sigmund (1923), *The Ego and the Id, The Standard Edition of the Complete Psychological Works of Sigmund Freud*, James Strachey (trans.), Vol. XIX, Hogarth Press, London, 1961

Freud, Sigmund (1930 [1929]), *Civilization and its Discontents, The Standard Edition of the Complete Psychological Works of Sigmund Freud*, James Strachey (trans.) based on Joan Riviere (1930), Vol. XXI, Hogarth Press, London, 1961

Freud, Sigmund (1933), 'Lecture XXXIII: Femininity', *The Standard Edition of the Complete Psychological Works of Sigmund Freud*, James Strachey (trans.), Vol. XXII, Hogarth Press, London, 1964

Garfinkel, Harold (1990 [1967]), *Studies in Ethnomethodology*, Cambridge and Oxford, Polity Press with Basil Blackwell

Gatens, Moira (1983), 'A Critique of the Sex/Gender Distinction', J. Allen and P. Patton, *Beyond Marxism?* Sydney, Intervention Publications

Gatens, Moira (1996), *Imaginary Bodies: Ethics, Power and Corporeality*, London and New York, Routledge

Gaukroger, Stephen (1978), *Explanatory Structures: Concepts of Explanation in the Early Physics and Philosophy*, Hassocks, Harvester Press

Gaukroger, Stephen (1983), 'Logic, Language, and Literature: the Relevance of Frege', *The Oxford Literary Review*, 6, 1: 68-96

Goffman, Erving (1971), *The Presentation of Self in Everyday Life*, Harmondsworth, Penguin

Goffman, Erving (1979), *Gender Advertisements*, London, Macmillan

Goffman, Erving (1986), *Frame Analysis: An Essay on the Organization of Experience*, Boston, Northeastern University Press

Gould, Laura (1996), *Cats Are Not Peas: A Calico History of Genetics*, New York, Springer-Verlag

Greenfield, Susan (2000), *The Private Life of the Brain*, London, Allen Lane/Penguin Press

Hacking, Ian (1989), *Representing and Intervening: Introductory Topics in the Philosophy of Natural Science*, Cambridge, Cambridge University Press

Hampson, J. L. and Hampson, J. G. (1961), 'The Ontogenesis of Sexual Behaviour in Man', W. C. Young (ed.), *Sex and Internal Secretions*, London, Bailliere, Tindall and Cox

Heap, James and Roth, Phillip (1973), 'On Phenomenological Sociology', *American Sociological Review*, 38 (June): 354-67

Hindess, Barry (1987), *Politics and Class Analysis*, Oxford, Basil Blackwell

Hindess, Barry and Hirst, Paul (1977), *Mode of Production and Social Formation: An Auto-Critique of Pre-Capitalist Modes of Production*, London and Basingstoke, Macmillan Press

Hirst, Paul and Woolley, Penny (1982), *Social Relations and Human Attributes*, London, Tavistock Publications

Hood-Williams, John (1995a), 'Is the Genetic Sexing of Humans Tautological?', *Social Biology and Human Affairs*, 60, 2: 3-9

Hood-Williams, John (1995b), 'Sexing the Athletes', *Sociology of Sport Journal*, 12, 3: 290-305

Hood-Williams, John (1996), 'Goodbye to Sex and Gender', *Sociological Review*, 44, 1, February: 1-16

Hood-Williams, John (1997), 'Stories for Sexual Difference', *British Journal of Sociology of Education*, 18, 1: 81-99

Hood-Williams, John and Cealey Harrison, Wendy (1998), 'Trouble with Gender', *Sociological Review*, 46, 1: 73-94

Hood-Williams, John and Cealey Harrison, Wendy (2000), 'Gendered Melancholy or General Melancholy? Homosexual Attachments in the Formation of Gender', *New Formations*, 41, Autumn: 109-26

Hubbard, Alan (n.d.), 'Doctors Demand Changes in Sport's Sex-Test Code', *The Observer*

Hughes, Alex and Witz, Anne (1997), 'Feminism and the Matter of Bodies: From de Beauvoir to Butler', *Body & Society*, 3,1, March: 47-60

Irvine, John, Miles, Ian and Evans, Jeff (eds) (1979), *Demystifying Social Statistics*, London, Pluto Press

Jefferson, Tony (1998), 'Muscle, "Hard Men" and "Iron" Mike Tyson: Reflections on Desire, Anxiety and the Embodiment of Masculinity', *Body and Society*, 4, 1: 77-98

Kessler, Suzanne J. (1993), 'Letter to Anne Fausto-Sterling on the Five Sexes, *The Sciences*, July/August: 3

Kessler, Suzanne (1998), *Lessons from the Intersexed,* New Brunswick, New Jersey and London, Rutgers University Press

Kessler, Suzanne and McKenna, Wendy (1978), *Gender: An Ethnomethodological Approach*, Chicago and London, University of Chicago Press

Kirby, Vicki (1997), *Telling Flesh: The Substance of the Corporeal*, New York and London, Routledge

Klein, Melanie (1950), *Contributions to Psycho-Analysis*, London, Hogarth Press

Klein, Melanie, Heiman, P., Isaacs, S. and Rivière, J. (1952), *Developments in Psycho-Analysis*, London, Hogarth Press

Kuhn, Thomas (1970), *The Structure of Scientific Revolutions*, Chicago, University of Chicago Press

Lacan, Jacques (1977), 'The Mirror Stage as Formative of the Function of the I', *Ecrits*, Alan Sheridan (trans.), London, Routledge, pp. 1-7

Laplanche, Jean (1976), *Life and Death in Psychoanalysis*, Jeffrey Mehlman (trans.), Baltimore, Johns Hopkins University Press

Laplanche, Jean and Pontalis, Jean-Bertrand (1980), *The Language of Psycho-analysis*, Donald Nicholson-Smith (trans.), London, The Hogarth Press with the Institute of Psycho-Analysis

Laqueur, Thomas (1990), *Making Sex: Body and Gender from the Greeks to Freud*, Cambridge, Mass. and London, Harvard University Press

Lévi-Strauss, Claude (1977), *Structural Anthropology*, Claire Jacobson and Brooke Grundfest Schoepf (trans.), Harmondsworth, Penguin

Mac An Ghaill, Máirtín (1994), *The Making of Men: Masculinities, Sexuality and Schooling*, Buckingham, Open University Press

MacCabe, Colin (1979), 'On Discourse', *Economy and Society*, 8, 3, August: 279-307

Maccoby, E. E. and Jacklin, C. N. (1975), *The Psychology of Sex Differences*, London, Tavistock Publications

Martin, Emily (1991), 'The Egg and the Sperm: How Science Has Constructed a Romance Based on Stereotypical Male-Female Roles', *Signs*, 16, 3: 485-501

Messerschmidt, J. (1993), *Masculinities & Crime: Critique and Reconceptualization of Theory.* Lanham, Maryland, Rowman and Littlefield

Mills, Sara (1997), *Discourse*, London and New York, Routledge

Mitchell, Juliet (1982), 'Introduction I', in Jacques Lacan and the école freudienne, *Feminine Sexuality*, Juliet Mitchell and Jacqueline Rose (eds), Jacqueline Rose (trans.), London and Basingstoke, Macmillan, pp. 1-26

Modares, Mina (1981), 'Women and Shi'ism in Iran, *m/f*, 5 & 6: 61-81

Money, John (1965), 'Psychosexual Differentiation', John Money (ed.), *Sex Research: New Developments*, New York, Holt, Rinehart and Winston

Oakley, Ann (1972), *Sex, Gender and Society*, London, Temple Smith

Oakley, Ann (1981), *Subject Women*, Oxford, Martin Robertson

Oakley, Ann (1985), *Sex, Gender and Society*, Hampshire, Arena Gower Publishing

Oakley, Ann (1997), 'A Brief History of Gender', Ann Oakley and Juliet Mitchell (eds), *Who's Afraid of Feminism? Seeing through the Backlash*, London, Hamish Hamilton, pp. 29-55

Ortner, Sherry and Whitehead, Harriet (eds) (1981), *Sexual Meanings: The Cultural Construction of Gender and Sexuality*, Cambridge, Cambridge University Press

Oudshoorn, Nelly (1994), *Beyond the Natural Body: An Archaeology of Sex Hormones*, London and New York, Routledge

Page, David; Mosher, Rebecca; Simpson, Elizabeth M.; Fisher, Elizabeth M. C.; Mardon, Graeme; Pollack, Jonathan; McGillivray, Barbara; de la Chapelle, Albert and Brown, Laura G. (1987), 'The Sex-Determining Region of the Human Y Chromosome Encodes a Finger Protein', *Cell*, December 24: 1091-1104

Parsons, Talcott (1949), *Essays in Sociological Theory: Pure and Applied*, New York, Free Press

Ramachandran, Vilayanur S. and Blakeslee, Sandra (1998), *Phantoms in the Brain: Probing the Mysteries of the Human Mind*, New York, William Morrow

Riley, Denise (1987), 'Does a Sex Have a History? "Women" and Feminism', *New Formations*, 1, Spring: 35-45

Riley, Denise (1988), *'Am I That Name?' Feminism and the Category of 'Women' in History*, Basingstoke and London, Macmillan Press

Ritvo, Harriet (2000), 'Defining Moments', *New Scientist*, 2220, 8 January: 38-9

Rose, Jacqueline (1983), 'Femininity and its Discontents', *Feminist Review*, 14: 5-21

Rubin, Gayle (1975), 'The Traffic in Women: Notes on the "Political Economy" of Sex', Rayna Rapp Reiter (ed.), *Towards an Anthropology of Women*, New York, Monthly Review Press, pp. 157-210.

Rubin, Gayle with Judith Butler (1994), 'Sexual Traffic', *Differences*, 6, 2+3, Summer-Fall: 62-99

Savage, Mike and Witz, Anne (eds) (1992), *Gender and Bureaucracy*, Oxford, Basil Blackwell

Scott, Joan (1986), 'Gender: A Useful Category of Historical Analysis', *American Historical Review*, 91, 5: 1053-75

Scott, Sue and Morgan, David (1993), *Body Matters: Essays on the Sociology of the Body*, London and Washington DC, Falmer Press

Smith, Richard W. (1979), 'What Kind of Sex is Natural?' in Vera Bullough (ed.), *The Frontiers of Sex Research*, Buffalo, Prometheus

Stoller, Robert (1968), *Sex and Gender*, New York, Science House

Ussher, Jane M. (ed.) (1997), *Body Talk: The Material and Discursive Regulation of Sexuality, Madness and Reproduction*, London and New York, Routledge

Walker Bynum, Caroline (1989), 'The Female Body and Religious Practice in the Later Middle Ages', Michael Feher et al. (eds), *Fragments for a History of the Human Body*, New York, Zone, pp. 161-219

Walkerdine, Valerie (1984), 'Some Day my Prince Will Come: Young Girls and the Preparation for Adolescent Sexuality', Angela McRobbie and Mica Nava (eds), *Gender and Generation*, Basingstoke. Macmillan Educational

Walkerdine, Valerie (1990), *Schoolgirl Fictions*, London and New York, Verso

Walkerdine, Valerie and the Girls and Mathematics Unit, Institute of Education (1989), *Counting Girls Out*, London, Virago Press

Wilkie, Tom (1991), 'At the Flick of a Genetic Switch', *The Independent*, 13 May: 18

Wittig, Monique (1992), *The Straight Mind and Other Essays*, Hemel Hempstead, Harvester Wheatsheaf

Wynn, Margaret and Wynn, Arthur (1991), *The Case for Preconception Care of Men and Women*, Oxford, AB Academic Publishers

Index